General Economic History

MAX WEBER

With a New Introduction by
Ira J. Cohen

D0022085

Transaction Books
New Brunswick (U.S.A.) and London (U.K.)

New material this edition copyright© 1981 by Transaction, Inc., New Brunswick, New Jersey 08903. Original edition copyright 1927, Greenberg, Publisher, Inc.

Library of Congress Catalog Number: 79-64859
ISBN: 0-87855-317-7 (cloth), 0-87855-690-7 (paper)
Printed in the United States of America

Library of Congress Cataloging in Publication Data

Weber, Max, 1864-1920.
General economic history.

(Social science classics series)
Translation of Wirtschaftsgeschichte.
Reprint of the 1927 ed., published by Greenberg, New York, which was issued in Adelphi economic series.
Includes bibliographical references and indexes.
1. Economic history. I. Title. II. Series.
HC21.W46 1979   330.9   79-64859
ISBN 0-87855-317-7
ISBN 0-87855-690-7 pbk.

CONTENTS

PART ONE

HOUSEHOLD, CLAN, VILLAGE AND MANOR

v

6064

PART TWO

INDUSTRY AND MINING DOWN TO THE BEGINNING OF THE CAPITALISTIC DEVELOPMENT

CONTENTS

PART THREE

COMMERCE AND EXCHANGE IN THE
PRE-CAPITALISTIC AGE

CONTENTS

PART FOUR

THE ORIGIN OF MODERN CAPITALISM

CONTENTS

Introduction to the Transaction Edition*

Max Weber on Modern Western Capitalism

Ira J. Cohen

Recent generations of students and scholars have come to the clear recognition that we live in an historical epoch both conditioned by and oriented toward the operations of the capitalist economic order. This fact more than any other has impelled a return to the classical interest in the nature and growth of Western capitalism. Recent generations have returned also to the methodological commitment to historical analysis, which so clearly informed the classical tradition. These young social scientists seek not only to disclose the structural configuration of capitalist society, but also to determine the powerful economic, social, political, cultural, and technological forces by which this configuration has been produced.

The convergence of these two interests, focused on the nature and historical development of modern Western capitalism, marks this republication of Max Weber's *General Economic History* as a most important contribution to contemporary social scientific analysis. *General Economic History* is unique in that it represents the only full-scale historical analysis of the development of modern capitalism to have been produced by any of the generally recognized classical progenitors of the social sciences. This is not to diminish the significance of other works, such as those commentaries on the line of development from feudalism

*I would like to thank Tony Giddens, Edith Kurzwell, and Reggie Feiner Cohen for their criticism and support in the development of this work, and acknowledge the assistance of Sally Winkle of the Department of German, University of Wisconsin-Madison, for her translation of a prolegomenal passage from the German edition of *General Economic History*.

to capitalism which are scattered throughout the writings of Marx (e.g., 1973: 471–514; 1967: 323–37; 593–613; 782–813). But these remarks inevitably must suffer from an overall lack of expository continuity. On the other hand, while related works by Durkheim, Veblen, and Tönnies do not lack for thematic integration, such works manifest an overall level of abstraction that makes historically specific analyses difficult to envision. When seen against this backdrop, *General Economic History* appears as a singularly valuable classical benchmark against which both present and future generations will be able to measure their own theoretical interests and research results involving the nature and development of the capitalist era.

The great significance of *General Economic History* for the generations of social scientists who meet it here for the first time can be indicated briefly with reference to some of its potential applications. The first centers on the possibilities it holds for understanding Weber's comprehensive views on the nature of modern Western capitalism and the lines of historical development which converged to make it an historically unprecedented economic order. In particular it permits the reconciliation of Weber's more general conceptualization of the institutional aspects of modern capitalism with his well-known account of the spirit of capitalism. A central portion of this introductory essay will be devoted to this topic.

Once the social scientific community has recognized the nature of Weber's thematic intentions, a second application of *General Economic History* comes into view. This republication opens up the possibility for the direct confrontation of Weber's view of modern capitalism and its historical development with alternative models derived from the works of Marx and others. Hence those students who wish to follow the lead of Norman Birnbaum (1953) and Anthony Giddens (1970) find here an indispensable resource.

Perhaps the single most important application of the present work centers on more contemporary projects. Recent scholar-

ship has retrieved and reconfigured the threads of earlier arguments concerning the transition from feudalism to capitalism
which initially were developed in the 1940s and 1950s by Karl
Polanyi (1944) on the one hand, and Marxist historians including most notably Maurice Dobb (1963; see Hilton, 1978) on the
other. Those who follow leaders of diverse strands in the current
movement such as Immanuel Wallerstein (1976, 1979, 1980) or
Ferdinand Braudel (1973), undoubtedly will be among the first
to find *General Economic History* a most formidable resource for
both constructive and contrastive purposes. Others who take a
theoretically more eclectic approach to the questions of the
nature and historical emergence of Western capitalism may
very well prefer to extend Weber's analysis to incorporate the
manifest changes which have occurred over the sixty years since
it originally was produced. This republication coincides with the
presentation of a programmatic commentary along these lines
by Randall Collins (1980).

Before any of the latter projects can be undertaken it is necessary to have in view the overall thematic purposes which lay
behind Weber's development of *General Economic History*. Social scientists have sought to conceptualize the fundamental
nature of Western capitalism since before it became a predominant force in the modern world. The most broadly influential
classical attempts in this regard were developed by Adam Smith
and Karl Marx. *General Economic History* does not present a
conception of modern Western capitalism specifically derived
from either of these two sources. Yet fully sixty years after
Weber first presented this work the social scientific community
has yet to arrive at a full appreciation of what Weber conceived
to be the nature of modern capitalism, and why he conceived of it
in this manner.

A great deal of the difficulty in this regard can no doubt be
attributed to Weber's complex style of exposition, which persistently shuttles back and forth between various lines of analysis,
comparative contrasts, and conceptual definitions. On stylistic

grounds alone *General Economic History* is not the easiest work
to understand. Without an appreciation of the thematic intent
that led Weber to conceive of modern capitalism in the way he
did, the reader is more likely to be intrigued by the relevance of
certain passages in the context of a Marxian perspective, the
relevance of others in the context of a Smithian perspective, etc.
What is lost along the way is the sense of Weber's thought as it
stands on its own. In section I of this essay I shall attempt to
reconstruct Weber's overall view of capitalism and to indicate
why this conception is significant in the context of his overarching thematic interests. Weber's overall conception of capitalism devolves into two components: profitability-oriented industrial enterprises that provide for everyday wants, and the
spirit of capitalism that impels those entrepreneurs who set
these capitalist business organizations in motion. The former
appear most prominently in *General Economic History* as well
as in certain portions of *Economy and Society,* while the latter
figures most prominently in *The Protestant Ethic and the Spirit
of Capitalism.* I shall deal separately with each of these components before integrating them into an overall account. The
general point to make is that the character of each component is
most significant when seen in the context of the rationality
theme, which provides the focal point for all of Weber's sociohistorical interests. It is the specific task of this section to
indicate how the rationality theme provides a foundation for the
proper appreciation of Weber's conception of modern Western
capitalism.

Section II deals with the lines of historical exposition to be
found in *General Economic History*. The present work can be
conceived as a series of analytically distinct historical arguments that trace the development of particular factors included
by Weber in his conception of the capitalist industrial enterprise. The problem is to establish a sense of the significance of
these arguments. One solution to this problem is to abstract a
genetic model incorporating certain of the major factors em-

phasized by Weber. The development of an approach along these lines may be found in the aforementioned work by Randall Collins (1980). In the present essay I shall forego abstraction in order to remain with the arguments in the form the reader finds them. I shall attempt to identify the thematic significance of each argument based upon the discussion of Weber's view of the institutional aspect of modern capitalism presented in section I.

Section III deals with the construction of *General Economic History*. It may not be apparent in its present form that this volume was originally prepared as a series of lectures delivered by Weber just months before his death. These lectures were conscientiously reconstructed from very accurate notes, some of which most likely were taken by means of a form of legal stenography commonly employed in Germany at the time Weber delivered his lectures. *General Economic History* thus may be accepted as a reliable account of Weber's argument in the same way that contemporary scholars accept George Herbert Mead's *Mind, Self, and Society*.

Before embarking upon this course of discussion there are two topics that must be briefly discussed. The first deals with the nature of Weber's approach to sociohistorical analysis and sociological concept formation. Contemporary scientific social theorists often overlook the fact that method, i.e., the philosophically informed logic of analysis, necessarily is implicated in the thematic substance of the concepts and explanations they present (see I.J. Cohen, 1980a: sections I and III). This oversight has led to more than five decades of misinterpretations of Weber's work. There now exist a number of accounts that provide a sound introduction to Weber's methodology as a whole (see Giddens, 1971: 133–44; Wrong, 1970:8–17). The practicing scholar who requires more detail in this regard may wish to consult the excellent commentary produced by Thomas Burger (1976). I shall not attempt a complete exposition of Weber's method in the present context. However, several remarks are necessary at this point to provide a proper background for the analysis to follow.

In the first place, it is fundamental to Weber's method that the individual social actor is the sole locus for the empirical production of all historical events. Social action conceived by Weber from this standpoint always involves the subjective meaning conferred by the actor on her/his own behavior, taking account of the actor's sense of the meaningful nature of both the behavior of others as well as the nonhuman elements implicated in the social action. All causal explanations of particular constellations of events, in the last analysis, must be reduced to this level of historical *praxis*. It should be noted that Weber did conceive of patterns of regularity among social actors on the empirical level of analysis (see 1977:98–143). However, he also argued that while such regularities do occur, there potentially exist an extraordinary variety of ways in which any particular historical sequence may not conform to these patterns.

In the second place, because all causal sequences are conceived by Weber on the level of historically specific actions among individuals, there is never any suggestion in his work of an empirically existent or deterministically conceived group dynamic, nomological regularity, or historical *telos*. Weber's conceptualization of structured patterns of social action as well as the structural factors implicated in general developmental trends take place on the level of ideal-typical analysis. An ideal type ultimately is intended as a guide to the empirical analysis of specific historical events. But it is apparent that Weber spent a great deal of his career developing works that move on the ideal-typical level of analysis. Ideal-types are conceptual constructs that exaggerate particular features of historical reality into a logically perfected, and hence, artificial form. Recent scholarship suggests that Weber employed several different levels of abstraction among the ideal-types to be found in various portions of his works (see Roth, 1971a, 1979; Burger, 1976: 130–35). Guenther Roth, in particular, has argued that there exist two different levels of ideal-typical analysis of the genesis

and consequences of general sequences of events. Roth's criterion is based upon the scope of thematic comprehension which is
involved. The more general of these, which Roth terms the level
of sociohistorical concepts, pertains to sequences making no
specific reference to time or place. The more specific, which Roth
terms the level of secular theories, pertains to sequences that
incorporate references to a number of instances bounded by
spatial and temporal dimensions (Roth, 1979:125). There have
been some interesting arguments that in his sociohistorical
writings Weber transgressed his own methodological pro-
scription on the structural explanation of historical events (see
Fullbrook, 1978). If Roth's account is accepted, such difficulties
may be cleared up. Seen from Roth's standpoint the arguments
in *General Economic History* would appear for the most part to
move on the level of secular theories, although empirical
analyses of causation by individuals also come into play at
several points.

In the third place, it is important to understand that for
Weber the facts do not speak for themselves. The hypothetical
historian or social scientist *ab initio* confronts reality only to
find a logically infinite number of potential constellations of
historical events to be explained, and, similarly, a logically
infinite number of configurations of historical factors which
may be invoked for explanatory purposes. Anyone who has ever
entered an archive or a library without a firm grasp of a topic to
be investigated has faced the same problem. The constellation of
circumstances and events to be taken as the theme for analysis
in terms of causes and consequences Weber calls an "historical
individual." What leads the researcher to choose a specific "historical individual" are her/his "value-relevant" interests. It is
Weber's view that each of us adopts from a heterogeneity of
possible value positions a series of related values that generate
our interest in the significance of a specific constellation of
historical facts. The "historical individual" of *General Economic
History* to be discussed in the following sections is the modern
capitalist industrial enterprise. It will emerge in this discussion

that Weber's "value-relevant" interest in the penetration of a peculiar type of rationality in the Western world is what led him to conceive as he did of this "historical individual."

There have been a number of attempts to criticize and reconfigure Weber's methodological views. Anthony Giddens' (1976, 1977, 1979) works are the most comprehensive attempts to incorporate the virtues of Weber's logic of analysis into a much more broadly informed new approach to sociological method. Giddens provides a new methodological foundation for those who pursue the study of the nature and development of capitalism.

A second topic deserving some mention is the renaissance of Weberian scholarship presently underway. The peculiarities of Weber's manner of exposition have been major obstacles to those scholars who have sought to develop a coherent thematic account of his works. But Friedrich Tenbruck (1980), Guenther Roth and Wolfgang Schluchter (1979), and Stephan Kalberg (1979, 1980) have employed a variety of strategies and arguments that now permit the development of a comprehensive conception of Weber's view of contemporary Western civilization and its historical development. There are many points in their arguments still under debate and other topics remain to be addressed, but the basic parameters of what has come to be called the rationality theme in Weber's already are in view. There seems to be general agreement that three works are of particular importance for an understanding of this overarching theme: (1) the introductory essay to the *Protestant Ethic and the Spirit of Capitalism* (1958a:13–31), which was actually developed much later than the remainder of the volume as an overall introduction to Weber's studies of religion, economy, and society (including: 1951, 1952, 1958b) published in Germany as *Collected Studies in the Sociology of Religion* (see Nelson, 1974); (2) "The Social Psychology of World Religions" (1946a); and (3) "Religious Rejections of the World and Their Direction" (1946b). These works provide an excellent foundation for an

appreciation of the thematic implications of the arguments in
General Economic History.

The overall thrust of the arguments advanced by those involved in the present renaissance in Weberian scholarship
stands behind much of the commentary to follow. While Kalberg's work figures most prominently in this context, I would
like to express my indebtedness to these scholars for providing a
most important foundation for the analysis that appears in part
I.

The task of preparing this introduction was originally assigned to the noted European-American scholar Paul
Kecskemeti. It is to be deeply regretted that Professor
Kecskemeti died on September 25, 1980. Professor Kecskemeti
was a personal acquaintance of Max Weber. While *General
Economic History* stands on its own as a scholarly work, by all
reports Weber delivered the lectures from which it was prepared
in a most forceful and dramatic manner. Beyond what undoubtedly would have been a most valuable intellectual introduction
to the present work, Professor Kecskemeti was uniquely qualified to restore for us the personal sense of emphasis Weber
invested in his arguments. This is a task that must now remain
unfulfilled. Those who would like to gain a fuller appreciation of
Kecskemeti's own work may be interested to read his *Meaning,
Communication, and Value* (University of Chicago Press, 1952)
as well as his introductory essays in Karl Mannheim's *Essays on
the Sociology of Knowledge* (Oxford University Press, 1952), and
Essays on Sociology and Social Psychology (Oxford University
Press, 1953).

I. Modern Western Capitalism and the Rationality
Theme in the Works of Max Weber

It has been remarked that "Weber concurred in many essential respects with Marx's characterization of capitalism"
(Zeitlin, 1981:129). It also has been suggested in this regard that

Weber was the "bourgeois Marx." Such broad comparisons usually contain both a certain amount of truth as well as a certain amount of distortion. On the one hand there can be little doubt that Weber was aware of the dark side of capitalism that so distressed Marx and his successors. On the other hand it must be pointed out that Weber's overall view of modern Western capitalism bears little detailed resemblance to that presented in Marx's works. To say that Weber concurred in many respects with Marx's characterization of modern capitalism implies, in particular, that Weber accepted the central importance of the surplus theory of value that allowed Marx to meld the economic relationships in the capitalist mode of production with the social exploitation of the proletariat by the capitalist class. While Weber does emphasize the relationship between wage labor and capital, the surplus theory of value plays no central role in his conception of modern capitalism. To suggest that Weber is the "bourgeois Marx" might be taken to imply that the most basic premise of his view of capitalism involves the play of free market competition. While free markets do play a substantial role in Weber's view, he does not make the play of these markets the fulcrum of his account of modern capitalism, as did Adam Smith and his successors.

Weber's writings clearly indicate that he was influenced both positively and negatively by the conceptions of capitalism developed by Smith and Marx. A more proximate source of influence was Werner Sombart, whose works Weber critically acknowledged throughout his career. Nevertheless, Weber retained sharp differences of opinion with Sombart (Roth, 1971b:239). It therefore seems quite unlikely that he directly borrowed his own conception of Western capitalism from Sombart's *Modern Capitalism,* despite the acclaim which the latter work received during Weber's lifetime in German academic circles. Here then is an intellectual problem fraught with implications both for an understanding of Weber's analysis in the *General Economic History* as well as for the more general use of

Weber's works as a classical benchmark against which contemporary students of capitalism can measure their own efforts. What is Weber's view of modern capitalism, and why did he conceive of it as he did?

The Rationality Theme in Weber's Work

The answer to these questions requires that we first recognize that Weber's overall view of modern capitalism was conditioned by thematic interests which in a particular sense reach far beyond the capitalist economic order to embrace the whole of Western civilization. These thematic, or "value-relevant" interests encompass the cultural as well as the economic character of the Western world. This is not surprising since for Weber neither economy nor culture nor any other factor provides a monolithic moving force for history. Rather, it is fundamental to Weber's methodology that:

> specifically economic motives . . . (have) everywhere conditioned and transformed not only the mode in which cultural wants and preferences are satisfied, but their content as well, even in their most subjective aspects. The indirect influence of social relations, institutions, and groups governed by "material interests" extends (often unconsciously) into all spheres of culture without exception . . . . On the other hand, all the activities and situations constituting an historically given culture affect the formation of material wants, the mode of their satisfaction, the integration of interest-groups and the types of power which they exercise. They thereby affect the course of "economic development" (1949:65-66).

The most general characterization of Weber's comprehensive thematic interests involves the historically unprecedented penetration into the context of all institutional orders and cultural ways of life in modern Western civilization of a peculiar type of rationality. When seen from the perspective of the Weberian *oeuvre* as a whole what appears to have moved him most profoundly were the enduring consequences of the penetration of this type of rationality with regard to the cultural ways of life undertaken by members of Western civilization. The overall character of these ways of life is summarized by Weber when he remarks:

> The fate of our times is characterized by rationalization and intellectualization and above all by the "disenchantment of the world." Precisely the ultimate and most sublime values have retreated from public life either into the transcendental realm of mystic life or into the brotherliness of direct and personal human relations (1946c:155).

What does Weber mean when he suggests that the modern Western world is characterized by rationality and intellectuality? The heart of the matter is that technical means involving precise calculations and abstract principles are employed in the pursuit of similarly formulated ends. This form of rationality is seen by Weber to have usurped the motivating cultural force of all substantive ethical values. The penetration of this rationality based upon intellectual calculation rather than spiritual or moral beliefs has reached such unprecedented levels that suffering no longer can be alleviated through the investment of spiritually inspired hope in the deliverance of the virtuous to a world where goodness and justice prevail. Rather, humanity is left to recognize the fact that the social world is a product of its own voluntary *praxis*. The Western world is thus disenchanted.

As a consequence of the intellectuality, rationality, and disenchantment of the modern Western world, Weber argues that humanity has been emancipated from the organic cycle of natural life, which formerly was prescribed by the great religions of the world. Today abstract calculations of means and ends usurp all considerations of passion and pain. Moreover, the manifold of pursuable ends and the means to their attainment are themselves often self-contradictory and mutually antagonistic. Hence:

> Culture becomes ever more senseless as a locus of imperfection, of injustice, of suffering, of sin, of futility. . . . Viewed from a purely ethical point of view, the world has to appear ever more fragmentary and devalued in all those instances when judged in the light of the religious postulate of a divine "meaning" of existence (1946b:357).

This conclusion puts Weber in diametrical opposition to the predominant trend of both classical and contemporary social thought. Early thinkers such as Comte, Marx, Spencer, and Durkheim and their modern successors such as Parsons, Wallerstein, and Habermas all join in the Enlightenment faith insofar as history promises to deliver virtue and meaningful ways of life to Western civilization, or the world. Weber despairs of the likelihood of this turn of events. The fundamental tragedy in the Weberian vision is that we must conduct our lives within circumstances laid down by an historically unprecedented type of rationality that has penetrated the diverse institutional and cultural contexts of our civilization to create a "housing hard as steel" from which no escape seems imminent. The spiritually inspired ethical assurance of earlier historical periods is gone. The blush of optimism generated by the Enlightenment has faded. All that is left, as Weber observes, is the darkness inside an iron cage.

Capitalistic Institutions: The Economic Formal Rationality of Industrial Enterprise

General Economic History is not a work where Weber principally focuses upon the nature or development of modern culture. It is in the nature of Weber's overarching perspective that the peculiar and unprecedented rationality indigenous to the modern Western world has penetrated not only cultural ways of life, but also the patterns of action involved in the operation of virtually every institutional order. The institutional order at issue in the present work is modern Western capitalism. What must be clearly understood then, is that just as Marx was led to presuppose the surplus theory of value as a means to analyze the exploitative nature of the capitalist economy, and just as Adam Smith was led to presuppose the play of free markets as a means to emphasize the maximization of public welfare through the exercise of private avarice, so Weber was led to conceive of the presuppositions he implicates in the modern capitalist institutional order as a means to further develop the significance of the unprecedented penetration into the Western world of a peculiar kind of rationality. It is the explication of Weber's conception of modern Western capitalism in the context of Weber's rationality theme to which the following discussion is devoted.

Most commentaries on Weber's view of modern capitalism begin, and sometimes end, with his account of the nature and emergence of the spirit of capitalism. What is made clear in *General Economic History,* however, is that for Weber modern capitalism consists not only of the profitability-oriented ways of life of bourgeois entrepreneurs, but also of the economic institutions that provide the context within which such entrepreneurs single-mindedly pursue their goal. This is not to suggest that the view Weber presents of either the spirit of capitalism or the capitalist economic institutions takes analytic priority or empirical precedence over its counterpart. A thorough reading of *The Protestant Ethic and the Spirit of Capitalism* or *General Economic History* will reveal arguments that turn with differing degrees of emphasis in both directions. But since the institutions constitutive of the capitalist economic order figure more prominently in the present work, it is this aspect of Weber's conceptualization of modern capitalism that will be treated first in the present discussion.

It is fundamental to Weber's method to conceive of subjective orientations as involved in virtually all nonhabitual social action. This postulate has led many commentators dealing with the rationality theme to stress Weber's typification of the uniquely modern form of rationality involved in the orientation to social action pursued by individuals. This is the *zweck-rational,* or instrumental-rational orientation (see 1968:24). But it is evident in *General Economic History,* as elsewhere, that most of Weber's historical-sociological analyses do not focus on the dessicated short-term strands of social action undertaken by discrete individuals. Rather he devotes the largest part of his analyses to patterns of action within and between large-scale institutions, modes of domination, and cultural ways of life. Modern Western capitalism is one of the most prominent of the institutional orders in this regard.

The often implicit problem posed to Weberian commentators has been how to come to grips with Weber's rationality theme in the context of patterns of action that move on the level of large-scale social groups. Stephan Kalberg appears to have provided a key to the solution of this problem by establishing a four-fold typology of rational orientation pertaining to patterns of action on the level of social groups and institutions. Although this typology is reconstructed rather than explicitly found in Weber's work, a thorough reading of Weber reveals continuous references that testify to the validity of Kalberg's conclusions.

Kalberg notes (1980:1148) that we must realize that for Weber rationality as a generic term is not involved solely in the patterns of action indigenous to Western civilization from the Enlightenment onward. There are, from Weber's standpoint, diverse types of rationality that pertain to action in almost every civilization. Hence Weber's wide-ranging comparative analyses of non-Western civilizations identify a variety of rational orientations. All of these are in some respects distinct from the type of rationality that reaches an unprecedented degree of penetration only in the modern Western world.

Moving from this point of origin, Kalberg explicates four typical patterns of rational action on the level of social groups and institutions. I shall not discuss the practical and theoretical types of rationality in the present context (see Kalberg, 1980:1151–55). Practical rationality refers to pragmatic self-interests, which are not unique to Western civilization. While theoretical rationality does not directly introduce patterns of action, the two types of rationality useful in the present context are substantive rationality and formal rationality. Substantive rationality directly orders patterns of action in relation to constellations of past, present, or future "value postulates." The scope of these patterns of action is indeterminate. But in any event the substantive-rational orientation does not order patterns of actions on the basis of a purely means-end calculus. Substantive rationality always exists in reference to ultimate points of view. From the standpoint of substantive rationality the calculations of the capitalist or the bureaucrat are conceived of as "irrational" (cf. Kalberg, 1980:1155–57). Formal rationality, on the other hand, legitimates a calculation of both ends and means to their attainment with reference to universal-ly-applied abstract regulations, laws, rules, etc. To the degree that such calculations penetrate the patterns of action in an institutional order the decisions are made without regard to personal qualities of individuals or any other arbitrarily applied standard of reference (cf. Kalberg 1980:1158–59).

An appreciation of Weber's sense of the overall character of the patterns of action indigenous to an unprecedented degree in modern Western civilization begins when it is understood that as opposed to all other civilizations studied by Weber where substantive rationality was found to be implicated in critical institutions and institutional orders, only in Western civilization is found a broad spectrum of institutions that manifest patterns of action involving the formal rational orientation. Hence Western institutions are unique in the extent to which ends and means are calculated in the most precise manner possible according to abstract principles universally applied.

A widely gauged focus on the formal rational characteristic of

patterned regularities of action in the Western world does not
take us very far with regard to the nature of specific kinds of
institutions or institutional orders which operate therein.
Weber is extremely careful to indicate that specific kinds of
institutions and social groups bear specific modes of the formal
rational action throughout the Western world. While bureau-
cause it has been argued at times that there exists in Weber's
work an emphasis on the bureaucratic mode of domination as
the singular locus for the penetration of modern patterns of
rational action throughout the Western World. While bureaucracy indeed appears in Weber's works as a most formidable
locus of formal rationality, to suggest that it is by itself the
comprehensive locus of formal rationality is to overlook the fact
that Weber identifies formal rationality in specific contexts
where the influence of bureaucratic modes of domination is only
marginally at issue. For instance, Weber finds a specific mode of
formal rationality among groups of musicians. The abstract
calculations involved here refer to modern Western theories of
music, and in particular to the rules governing chordal harmony
(see 1958c). Again, Weber suggests that the formal rationality
of scientific technologies involves means-ends calculations in
terms of the rules of mechanics. This he identifies at one point as
the technical rational orientation (1968:65–67).

Music and technology, however, are not the dominating institutional loci of patterns of formal rationality in the Western
world as they appear in Weber's work. The bureaucratic mode of
domination and the institutions constituitive of the modern
capitalist economic order are much more central in this regard.
What is suggested then is that each of these two large-scale
institutional configurations bears a specific mode of formal rationality.

The bureaucratic mode of domination appears in Weber's
work in an extraordinary variety of institutional contexts. Most
social scientists are familiar with his ideal-type of modern bu-

reaucracy (1968:217-26, 956–1005). Hence the constituent elements involved will not be presented at length. What is important to note is that the conceptual lynch-pin for all ideal-typical elements of the modern bureaucracy other than the sphere of policy-making reserved for top-level administrators is a formal rational orientation of patterns of action with reference to an administrative code of regulations. Thus, modern bureaucratic office jurisdiction, office hierarchy, office management, and the duties of office-holders are all calculated in terms of both ends and means of the organization at large through an orientation to universally applied abstract regulative principles. It can be said that below the decisions on policy taken by top-level officials, the patterns of action in a modern bureaucracy are deeply penetrated by the legal mode of formal rationality, i.e., what Weber terms at one point legal formal rationality (1968: 656–57).

Weber does not present a comprehensive conceptualization of the generic nature of capitalism in *General Economic History* or elsewhere. Capitalism, in Weber's view, is present wherever industrial provision for the needs of a human group is carried out by the continuous rational activity of entrepeneurial organizations (below p. 275; cf. 1958a:17). It is clear to Weber that capitalism conceived with an emphasis on the operation of entrepreneurial organizations has been present to some degree in virtually every civilization. What is unique to the Western world, especially since the middle of the nineteenth century (below p. 276), is not the mere presence of capitalism, but the degree to which it has penetrated the provision of everyday wants.

Moving from this point of origin, in *General Economic History* Weber presents the general presuppositions of the modern capitalist enterprise that conjoin in this institutional form to facilitate the industrial provision of the vast majority of everyday wants.

The general presuppositions of modern capitalism may be found on pp. 275-78 of the present volume. The single most general presupposition of modern Western capitalism as Weber conceives it is that of rational capital accounting as the norm for all large industrial enterprises concerned with the provision of everyday wants. This most general presupposition can be seen as the formal analogue of the administrative code in Weber's account of modern bureaucracy. Just as the administrative code is implicated by Weber in all constitutive aspects of the bureaucratic mode of domination below the level of top-level policy formation, so too does Weber implicate rational capital accounting in a variety of factors below the level of entrepreneurial control of the industrial organization. These factors are: (1) the appropriation by private enterprise of all physical means of production; (2) the freedom of the market from all irrational limitations on trade or labor such as those imposed by restrictions based upon class-monopoly, religiously inspired ways of life, etc.; (3) rational technology, i.e., one reduced to calculation to the largest possible degree, this implies mechanization; (4) calculable law, which is necessary for industrial enterprise as a dependable source of adjudication and administration; (5) free labor, involving persons who are legally free and economically compelled to sell their labor on the market without restriction; (6) the commercialization of economic life, i.e., the use of instruments to represent share rights in enterprise and property ownership.

While the conjunction of these six factors must constantly be borne in mind, what is most critical at this point is that rational capital accounting provides the lynch-pin that unites them all as presuppositional foundations for the modern capitalist industrial enterprise. Therefore it is of great importance to understand what is involved in the definition of this phenomenon. According to Weber:

> There is a form of monetary accounting which is peculiar to
> rational economic profit-making; namely, "capital accounting."
> Capital accounting is the valuation and verification of op-
> portunities for profit and of the success of profit-making activity
> by means of a valuation of the total assets (goods and money) of
> the enterprise at the beginning of a profit-making venture, and
> the comparison of this with a similar valuation of the assets still
> present and newly acquired at the end of the process. . . . [This
> occurs when] a balance is drawn between the initial and final
> states of the assets. "Capital" is the money value of the means of
> profit-making available to the enterprise at the balancing of the
> books; "profit" and correspondingly "loss," the difference between
> the initial balance and that drawn at the conclusion of the period.
> . . . An economic "enterprise" is autonomous action capable of an
> orientation to capital accounting. This orientation takes place by
> means of "calculation": *ex ante* calculation of the probable risks
> and chances of profit, *ex-post* calculation for the verification of the
> actual profit or loss resulting. "Profitability" means in the ra-
> tional case, one of two things: (1) the profit estimated as possible
> by *ex ante* calculation or (2) that which the *ex-post* calculation
> shows actually to have been earned in a given period. . . . In both
> cases it is usually expressed . . . today in percentages—in relation
> to the capital of the initial balance (1968:91).

This definition requires some further explication in order to
properly identify the role of capital accounting in the industrial
enterprise. First, it should be noticed that the norm of profitability is the decisive criterion or point of reference applied in all
decisions made with regard to every operation undertaken by
the enterprise (1968:92–93). These decisions are calculated by
means of capital accounting procedures oriented to this norm.
Hence in the ideal-typical case the patterns of action of the
industrial enterprise are conditioned in every respect through
this orientation to the norm of profitability.

A point of great significance is that the institutional locus of
the patterns of action oriented to profitability by means of capital accounting procedures is the industrial enterprise and not
the play of free markets. There can be no question that Weber

ascribes an important role to the operation of free market exchange in the actual conduct of profit-making activity (1968:90–91). But the determination of the goods to be produced, the means of production to be employed, and so forth are calculated *on an ex ante basis* within the enterprise itself. Profitability-oriented patterns of action are thus characteristic of the enterprise. Of course the potential marketability of the goods produced by the enterprise constitutes a major consideration in the *ex ante* procedures of capital accounting which are employed. But in arriving at decisions concerning potentially profitable patterns of action the enterprise must balance this potential against other projected costs including: the cost of labor, which has its own market; the cost of raw materials, which may be controlled by the enterprise or purchased on the market; the cost of technological means of production, which may be designed and constructed from within the enterprise or purchased externally; and the cost of transportation and storage, which again may be either controlled by the enterprise or purchased externally, etc.

By emphasizing the overarching significance of profitability-oriented procedures of rational capital accounting in industrial enterprises as the most general presupposition of the institutional aspect of modern capitalism, Weber thus permits a view that extends far beyond the marginal-utility theory which is central to most market-oriented conceptions of the capitalist economic order (1968:92). Where the latter selects as its most general presupposition the decisive significance of patterns of action among *consumers,* Weber emphasizes the fundamental importance of the patterns of action among producing organizations, as determined by *ex ante* calculations of the profitability of each step taken by the organization through the procedures of rational capital accounting (1968:92). It should be noted that in modern times these procedures generally involve the method of double-entry bookkeeping.

Because Weber conceives of every step in the operation of an enterprise as determined with reference to profitability-oriented procedures of capital accounting, the six factors listed above are not presented as coequal with rational capital accounting as presuppositions of the institutional aspect of modern capitalism. Rather, Weber implicates these factors as analytically subordinate to the calculation of profitability by means of these accounting procedures When seen in this light the patterns of action ideal—typically determined with reference to the norm of profitability as calculated by rational accounting—are presuppositional to Weber's institutional view of modern capitalism in the same formal sense that the surplus theory of value is presuppositional to Marx's view, and the play of free markets is presuppositional for Adam Smith.

Weber points out that the analytically subordinate presuppositional factors involve patterns of action that extend far beyond the realm of economic activity *per se*. Hence he includes the legal system and the administrative functioning of the state, as well as rational technology among the six factors listed in *General Economic History*. It is most important to bear in mind that regardless of whether or not the factor in question pertains to economic action *per se*, its significance in terms of Weber's conception of the modern capitalistic enterprise turns on the role each factor plays in facilitating patterns of action calculated against the abstract norm of profitability with reference to the procedures of rational capital accounting. Modern scientific technology, for example, manifests its own mode of formal rationality. This involves distinctive abstract principles referring to mechanical efficiency. But, as Weber points out, quite often a most rational technological procedure in the context of a capitalistic industrial enterprise is compromised by considerations of an economic nature (1968:65–67). Hence, in the modern capitalistic enterprise the determination of the appropriate technological procedure is calculated on the basis of an orientation to the abstract norm of profitability by means of rational capital accounting, rather than on the basis of the abstract norm of mechanical efficiency. This can be visualized with reference to the decision of a hypothetical enterprise to forego the most technically efficient form of automated production equipment due to its lack of potential for profitable operation as measured against the capital investment required, the current output of the enterprise, or other considerations as these are calculated through rational accounting procedures. The same reasoning applies to operations involving other subordinate presuppositional factors implicated by Weber in the presence of the capitalistic industrial enterprise.

But why does Weber select the profitability-oriented accounting procedures of modern industrial enterprises as the most general presupposition of the institutional aspect of modern Western capitalism? We know that Marx's presuppositional emphasis upon the surplus theory of value was founded on his interest in discovering the nature of the exploitation of the proletariat by the bourgeoisie. We also know that Adam Smith's presuppositional emphasis on the play of free market competition was founded, in the ironic manner of Mandeville's Fable of the Bees (see below p. 369), on his interest in discovering how private avarice may be transmuted into the maximization of conditions for economic welfare. Certainly a scholar of the magnitude of Max Weber also must have had a "value-relevant" interest that led him to his most general presupposition of modern capitalism rather than any other.

The key to understanding why Weber chose to emphasize rational capital accounting as the most general presupposition of the institutional aspect of modern capitalism presented in *General Economic History* is to be found in a discreet section of *Economy and Society* dealing with the principles for the maximization of formal rationality of capital accounting in production enterprises. This passage is noteworthy for the remarkable way in which it parallels and extends the account of the secondary presuppositions of modern capitalistic industrial organizations in *General Economic History*. The parallels between this passage and the account of the secondary presuppositional factors appearing in the present work have been inserted into the quotation at appropriate points.

> The following are the principal conditions necessary for obtaining a maximum of formal rationality of capital accounting in production enterprises: 1) complete appropriation of all material means of production by owners and the complete absence of all formal appropriation of opportunities for profit in the market; that is market freedom (cf. numbers 1 and 2 above); 2) complete autonomy in the selection of management by the owners, thus complete absence of formal appropriation of rights to managerial functions; 3) complete absence of appropriation of jobs and of opportunities for earning by workers and, conversely, the absence of appropriation of workers by owners. This implies free labor, freedom of the labor market, and freedom in the selection of workers (cf. number 5 above); 4) complete absence of substantive regulation, regulation of consumption, production, and prices, or of other forms of regulation which limit freedom of contract or specify conditions of exchange. This may be called substantive freedom of contract (cf. number 2 above); 5) complete calculability of the functioning of the technical conditions of the production process, that is a mechanically rational technology (cf. number 3 above); 6) complete calculability of the functioning of public administration and the legal order and a purely formal guarantee of all contracts by the political authority. This is a formally rational administration and law (cf. number 4 above); 7) the most complete separation possible of the enterprise and its conditions of success and failure from the household or private budgetary unit and its property interests. It is particularly important that the capital at the disposal of the enterprise should be clearly distinguished from the private wealth of the owners and should not be subject to divisions or dispersion through inheritance. For large-scale enterprises, this condition tends to approach optimum force from a formal point of view: in the fields of transport; manufacture, and mining if they are organized in corporate form with freely transferable shares and limited liability, and in the field of agriculture, if there are relatively longterm leases for large scale production units (cf. number 6 above); 8) a monetary system with the highest possible degree of formal rationality (1968:161–2).

Leaving aside the role of the entrepeneur to be considered shortly, it is not surprising that a high degree of correspondence exists between this passage and the account of the factors implicated in rational capital accounting in the present work once it is realized that Weber was at work on this portion of *Economy and Society* at approximately the same time as he delivered the lectures republished here as *General Economic History* (see section III). What is most significant in the present context is that we are now at the heart of Weber's concern with profitability-oriented rational capital accounting implicating a constellation of six factors as the most general presupposition for the form of enterprise that is typical of modern capitalism. As previously suggested, all of Weber's historical-sociological analyses are shaped by his comprehensive "value-relevant" interest in the penetration to an unprecedented extent of a peculiar type of rationality into diverse contexts of Western civilization. It is now evident that this great thematic interest is what lies behind Weber's selection of rational capital accounting as the most general presupposition of the institutional aspect of modern capitalism. While some omissions can be found, in general it can be said that the constellation of secondary presuppositional factors appearing in *General Economic History* represent the largest number of what Weber designates in *Economy and Society* as the principal conditions for obtaining a maximum of formal rationality of capital accounting in production enterprises. It can be concluded that Weber chose to present the account of the general presuppositions for the existence of the capitalistic industrial enterprise as they appear in *General Economic History* in order to explicate the penetration of the maximal conditions for formal rationality into a most important institutional order, i.e., modern capitalism.

Rational capital ccounting under conditions approaching maximization of formal rationality conforms to Kalberg's discussion of the formal rational type of orientation involved in institutional patterns of action. In Kalberg's account all formal rational patterns of action involve the most precise possible calculations of means and ends according to abstract principles. While Kalberg stipulates that these abstract principles may be rules, regulations, or laws, it is apparent that the norm of profitability to which all rational capital accounting procedures refer legitimately can be included as an abstract principle of the kind involved in his reconstructed conception of Weber's formal type of rationality. This is so, insofar as it is understood that the term "norm" as it is used in the present context bears no immediate relationship to any form of value-postulate of a substantive nature. Rather, it is an abstract principle maintaining the same status as the administrative code in a modern bureaucracy.

When seen from this point of view the modern capitalistic industrial enterprise exhibits patterns of action of a formal rational nature to the degree that all ends of the organization as well as the means by which they are pursued are calculated against the abstract principle of profitability by means of the procedures of rational capital accounting. In this way all factors involved in the operation of the enterprise, including not only the marketability of the goods produced, but also the cost to the enterprise of labor, fixed capital, technological expertise, transportation, storage, etc., are determined with reference to their projected potential for the production of profit as measured by the procedures of capital accounting. Ultimately a balance is struck on these accounts between income and costs. This provides the actual calculation of the profit of the enterprise. And again, it is the precisely calculated orientation to the abstract norm of profitability that provides the most prominent mark of the formal rationality of modern capitalistic enterprise.

The thematic interest that led Weber to his conception of the institutional aspects of modern capitalism involves his comprehensive concern with the penetration of formal rational pat-

terns of action into the Western economic order. The bureaucratic organization of institutionalized domination has been
shown to embody a high degree of the legal mode of formal
rationality. However, while both the modern form of bureaucracy and the modern capitalist enterprise represent outstanding institutional loci of formal rationality in the modern Western world, it seems unlikely that Weber would argue that they
would exhibit patterns of action involving exactly the same
mode of formal rational orientation. This is not to suggest that
Weber dismissed the significance of bureaucratic domination
for the conduct of capitalistic industrial production. He is careful to point out that the modern form of bureaucratic domination
is an indispensable tool in this regard (1968:224). Indeed, as
many commentators have suggested, there is no difference in
administrative terms between Weber's conception of the capitalistic expropriation of the means of production from the workers, and the expropriation of the means of administration from
bureaucratic office-holders. But the presuppositional lynch-pin
of the modern bureaucracy involves the administrative code of
regulations. While the presuppositional lynch-pin of the modern capitalistic industrial enterprise involves the abstract norm
of profitability as calculated through application of rational
capital accounting procedures.

The nature of the specific mode of formal rationality involved
in the modern capitalistic industrial enterprise can be found in
Weber's definition of "the formal rationality of economic activity" in Economy and Society. I shall hereafter refer to this as
economic formal rationality.

> The term "formal rationality of economic action" will be used to
> designate the extent of quantitative calculation or accounting
> which is technically possible and which is actually applied . . .
>
> A system of economic activity will be called "formally" rational
> according to the degree in which the provision for need . . . is
> capable of being expressed in numerical calculable terms, and is
> so expressed . . . (1968:85).

In order to see how this definition of economic formal rationality is involved in Weber's account of the modern capitalist industrial enterprise it is necessary to return once again to the nature of capital accounting. These procedures involve the calculation of profitability for each and every action taken by the enterprise. When it is considered that the secondary presuppositional factors implicated by Weber in the account below approach the conditions for the maximization of this profit-oriented rationality, *ipso facto* it can be concluded that these calculations have been taken as far as technically possible. Hence, such calculations fall under the preceding definition of the economic mode of formal rationality. Thus, although modern bureaucracies and modern capitalistic enterprises both are deeply penetrated by formal rational patterns of action, each manifests a different mode of such rationality. The bureaucratic patterns of action are referred to the administrative codebook in a legal formal mode of rationality. The capitalistic enterprise, on the other hand, manifests patterns of action referred to profitability-oriented procedures of capital accounting in an economic formal mode of rationality.

In summary, the comprehensive interest that informs all of Weber's historical sociology is the penetration into all contexts of Western civilization of a peculiar type of rationality. On the level of patterns of action pertaining to social groups or institutions, the Western world has been penetrated by the formal type of rationality involving means-ends calculations oriented to abstract principles which are universally applied. The bureaucratic form of domination provides one locus for Weber's analysis of the institutionalization of formal rationality in its legal mode. But Weber conceived of a second institutional locus of formal rationality, this time in its economic mode. This locus is the modern capitalistic industrial enterprise. Weber chose to designate profitability-oriented rational capital accounting as the most general presupposition of modern capitalist economic institutions because, above and beyond all else, he was interested in demonstrating the penetration of economic formal rationality into the Western capitalist institutional order. This interest conditions Weber's conceptualization in a manner analagous to the way in which Marx's interest in the exploitation inherent in the capitalist mode of production conditioned his presupposition of the surplus theory of value, and as Adam Smith's interest in the maximization of economic welfare conditioned his presupposition of the free play of the market.

Capitalist Entrepeneurs: The Economic Formal Rationality of the Spirit of Capitalism

The nature of capitalist institutions has been the focus of the discussion thus far. However, to stop here would be to leave the impression that Weber conceived of capitalism as a whole in terms of structural institutions which, while they manifest profitability-oriented patterns of action, nevertheless appear to have no dynamic impulse setting them in motion. In this light, Weber justifiably could be charged with having presented an overall conception of Western capitalism in a most architectonic manner. This is sometimes thought to be the case with Weber's conception of the modern form of bureaucracy, but it must be remembered that in its ideal-typical form a place is set aside at the top of a bureaucratic structure for the policy decisions made by a small group of top-level officials. While such officials do have a sphere of responsibility delimited by the administrative code, only these officials possess the autonomous authority to set the bureaucratic structure in motion (1968:988). Since the modern bureaucratic organization of domination is applicable in such a wide variety of institutional contexts, Weber is most careful not to indicate what goals or purposes the top-level bureaucratic administrators may have in mind when directing their organizations. However, he showed no such reluctance with regard to his discussion of bourgeois entrepeneurs.

Weber was very much aware of the structural analogy between top-level bureaucratic officials and the leaders of modern capitalistic enterprises. He comments in this regard: "It is the peculiarity of the modern entrepeneur that he conducts himself as the 'first official' of his enterprise, in the very same way in which the ruler of a specifically modern bureaucratic state . . . spoke of himself as the 'first servant' of the state" (1968:957). Of most importance in the present context is that Weber made clear throughout his work that only the capitalistic entrepeneur can set the modern industrial capitalistic enterprise in motion as a means to pursue particular ends.

The discussion of the ends pursued by capitalist entrepeneurs, and the motivating force involved in this pursuit, moves beyond the analysis of the institutional aspects of the capitalistic industrial enterprise. This issue does not refer to the entrepeneurial means employed by capitalists in pursuit of their goals. Rather, attention turns to the cultural way of life maintained by those capitalists who control the direction of such enterprises. We thus have arrived at one of Weber's most familiar historical constructs, the spirit of capitalism.

The question to be posed at this point is: what are the goals pursued by the modern capitalists through the direction of their industrial enterprises? Weber's answer in this regard is that among modern entrepreneurs: "Man is dominated by the making of money, by acquisition as the ultimate purpose of his life" (1958a:53).

The sheer existence of these economic interests among modern entrepreneurs is hardly surprising from Weber's point of view. In fact such interests constitute an almost universal feature of all civilizations (below, p. 354). However, in Weber's detailed analyses of Chinese, Indian, and ancient Judaic civilizations the motivating impulse for the pursuit of economic interests was found to be persistently compromised by patterns of action involving what Kalberg terms substantive rational considerations. That is, the sheer desire to make money was always and everywhere outside of the modern Western world subordinated at crucial points with reference to patterns of action involving one or another constellation of "value-postulates."

The cultural way of life of the modern Western capitalist entrepreneur differs from that of any deeply influential group in any other civilization in that the bearers of an economic interest in making money are motivated by an impulse no way compromised by religious, spiritual, or any other form of substantive rational orientation. The focus on this unfettered impulse lies at the very center of Weber's account of the unique cultural significance of modern Western capitalism. Only in the West does one find entrepreneurs who treat making money as the singular impulse in the conduct of their way of life. Only in the West do there exist entrepreneurs who bear an impulse that subordinates any and all enjoyment of wealth to the motivation involved in actions in pursuit of monetary gain. Only in the West has the spirit of capitalism penetrated the orientation of those who direct the economic order.

Weber characterizes the motivating impulse behind the spirit of capitalism as an economic ethic in the following passage:

> The *summum bonum* of this ethic, the earning of more and more money, combined with the strict avoidance of all spontaneous enjoyment of life, is above all devoid of any eudemonistic . . . (involved in the pursuit of happiness-IJC) . . . , not to say hedonistic admixture. It is thought of so purely as an end in itself, that from the point of view of happiness, or of utility to, the single individual it appears entirely transcendental and absolutely irrational (1958a:53).

Weber observes that at the heart of the spirit of capitalism lies an impulse that can be conceived in terms of Kalberg's typology as the substantive irrationality of the spirit of capitalism. However, from the standpoint of Weber's previously quoted definition of the formal rationality of economic action, the patterns of

action generated among modern capitalist entrepeneurs appear
to exhibit economic formal rationality to the highest possible
degree. This point can be established through a close look at that
portion of the later introduction to *The Protestant Ethic and the
Spirit of Capitalism,* where Weber discusses the nature of "capitalistic economic action."

> We will define a capitalistic economic action as one which rests on
> the expectation of profit by utilization of opportunities for ex-
> change, that is on (formally) peaceful chances of profit. . . . *Where
> capitalistic acquisition is rationally pursued* (my emphasis), the
> corresponding action is adjusted to calculations in terms of capi-
> tal. This means that the action is adapted to a systematic utiliza-
> tion of goods or personal services as a means of acquisition in such
> a way that at the close of a business period the balance of the
> enterprise in money assets . . . exceeds the capital, i.e. the esti-
> mated value of the material means of production used for acquisi-
> tion in exchange. . . . The important fact . . . (in modern times) . . .
> is always that a calculation in terms of money is made . . . by
> modern bookkeeping methods (1958a:17–18).

It is not difficult to understand at this point that, while the
impelling force of the spirit of capitalism from a certain standpoint apart from modern capitalism may appear to manifest a
substantive irrationality, the patterns of action typical of the
way of life among modern capitalist entrepreneurs bears the
character of economic formal rationality. For here again we find
the central orientation to the norm of profitability as calculated
in terms of the technically most perfect bookkeeping procedures, i.e., rational capital accounting.

On the basis of the preceding discussion it should be evident
why Weber chose to emphasize the significance of the spirit of
capitalism. For, as with modern capitalist entrepeneural institutions, in conceiving the cultural way of life among modern
capitalist industrial leaders Weber clearly focuses on the penetration into the Western world of the economic mode of formal
rationality. To balance the orientation of the capitalistic in-

stitutions in this regard, Weber presents an account of the orientation involved in the culturally inspired way of life among those who control their direction. Hence both the enterprise and its leaders share the same mode of economic formal rationality.

Weber's Overall View of Modern Capitalism

The preceding lines of analysis can be conjoined to develop an overall conception of Weber's view of modern capitalism. The fulcrum of Weber's conception of modern capitalism is the orientation to the norm of profitability as calculated by means of the technically most perfect procedures of rational capital accounting. The penetration of this economic mode of formal rationality into the institutional patterns of action of modern capitalist industrial enterprises has been discussed at length. It was noted, however, that a singular emphasis on this institutional aspect of capitalism leaves Weber open to the charge of presenting an architectonic picture of the modern capitalist economy. However, it should be apparent that Weber indeed does provide a dynamic impulse that sets the modern capitalist institutional machinery in motion. This impulse is identified by Weber with reference to the economic ethic which generates the motivation of patterns of action among those who control the operations of the enterprise. It can be no accident then that Weber conceives of the rational orientation of both the modern capitalist industrial enterprise and its controlling entrepreneurs in exactly the same way. In Weber's overall view of modern Western capitalism, both conjoin in an orientation to the abstract norm of profitability as calculated by means of rational capital accounting procedures.

The fulcrum provided by this conjoint institutional and entrepreneural orientation to economic formal rationality permits Weber to integrate a broad variety of diverse factors into his more detailed analyses of modern capitalism. First, modern capitalist institutions, while they must always keep the balance on the capital accounts before them, nevertheless are conceived by Weber to provide for the satisfaction of most everyday wants in Western civilization. Hence the whole sphere of life, which includes material patterns of consumption and cultural life-styles, is most profoundly influenced by the output of production by these profitability-oriented enterprises.

Secondly, included among subordinate presuppositional factors that Weber implicates in rational capital accounting as the foundation for the modern enterprise are: the play of free markets, formally free labor; the separation of workers from the means of production; rational technology; rational commerce; and the existence in the state of both rational administration and a dependable legal system. The relationships that ebb and flow between both capitalist entrepreneurs and the enterprises they control on the one hand and the patterns of action in each of these other spheres of social life appear with great complexity throughout Weber's observations on modern Western civilization. No attempt can be made here to adumbrate even the most basic of these relationships. The point to be made in the present context is that Weber's interpolation of all of the subordinate factors in the context of the profitability-oriented rational capital accounting procedures of the industrial enterprise permits him to conceive of the nature and consequences of modern Western capitalism in terms of the broadest possible scope of comprehension.

Finally, in the spirit of capitalism Weber provides us with one, but not the only, dynamic force which appears from the Weberian standpoint to be necessarily involved in whatever events may come to pass as the history of Western civilization proceeds. Alongside the dynamic force introduced by the top-level bureaucratic administrators in the state and elsewhere, there exists a distinctive impelling dynamic that single-mindedly continues to direct capitalist industrial enterprise

INTRODUCTION XLIX

toward the never-ending goal of acquisition of profit in the most
formally rational way.

II. Lines of Exposition in *General Economic History*

It should be clear by now that Weber did not approach the
conceptualization of modern Western capitalism in a desultory
or derivative manner. Rather, he originated a most precise
vision of the constellation of phenomena involved, and he did so
in a manner firmly rooted in his "value-relevant" interests.
General Economic History appears in this light as Weber's attempt to trace the origins of the institutional aspects of modern
capitalism.

The Manner of Exposition

Despite the great value of this work, there is no denying that
it can be a trying task to determine the significance of the
particular lines of historical exposition presented. Weber rarely
adopted a straight-forward chronological narrative as a means
to organize his historical arguments. Rather, many of his
analyses trace the development of a specific configuration of
structural and/or cultural circumstances that are significant to
the final emergence of the "historical individual" under investigation, only to shuttle backward in time to trace the development of a second configuration, and so forth. For this reason
works such as *General Economic History* often appear as if they
were constructed on an historian's loom where thematic threads
of varying hues are woven together through a process of advance
and regress. In such circumstances it would have been helpful if,
at the beginning of the present work, Weber had provided an
overall sense of the final thematic pattern he intended to produce. This is generally the function of the theoretical remarks
contemporary historical sociologists include at the head of their
presentations. Unfortunately, Weber provides no similar guidance of this kind. It is quite likely that this characteristic of

Weber's style of exposition constitutes the greatest stumbling block to those who approach *General Economic History*. I shall attempt to provide some guidance in this regard below.

Before proceeding on this course, however, there are certain additional features of Weber's manner of exposition that should be mentioned. First of all, here and elsewhere Weber's historical arguments make it plain that beyond all else he maintained an exquisite sensitivity to the complexity and ironic consequences contained in the weave of various social, economic, technological, political, and cultural forces as they are involved in the production of a given set of circumstances. Hence his account of the emergence of any single factor in *General Economic History* is likely to implicate a variety of historically specific dynamics that are enmeshed in ever-changing configurations. Such dynamics merge, separate, and dissolve to produce consequences ranging from the commonplace to the totally unprecedented. For example, the consequences of the Protestant Ethic appear in the present work in terms of the effects of the cultural ways of life among sixteenth through eighteenth-century British and Dutch entrepreneurs. Future analyses no doubt will be able to use *General Economic History* as a principal resource in ferreting out the historically specific interrelationships that Weber identifies between the Protestant Ethic and the various institutional factors conjoined in the development of modern Western capitalism.

Because the strands of various historical forces are so tightly interwoven in Weber's analyses, each line of exposition must be read with great care before any conclusion is reached concerning specific dynamics to which Weber ascribes decisive importance in any particular context. It is particularly important to avoid any conclusion that Weber saw empirically recurrent group-dynamics or nomological regularities. Such conclusions are totally antithetical to Weber's methodological foundations.

Secondly, a reading of the entire Weberian *oeuvre* reveals him to have mastered, in broad scope and fine detail, the history of a wide variety of major ancient and modern civilizations. In the particular case of Western civilization Weber researched and published a tremendous range of studies moving from ancient Judaic civilization through Graeco-Roman antiquity to analyses of structural configurations and cultural ways of life in many corners of the Western world from medieval feudalism to the first part of the twentieth century.

Weber's application of the comparative technique of historical sociological analysis is particularly striking in *General Economic History*. There exists in the various lines of exposition a persistent and unremarked interplay between the emergence of the particular factor under consideration and the presentation of comparative instances from diverse civilizations, nations, and cultures where the factor in question either did not emerge in the same form, or did not emerge at all. These comparative instances have an overall thematic justification that should be borne in mind throughout the present work. As discussed in the preceding section of this essay, the emergence of Western capitalism penetrated by economic formally rational patterns of action was seen by Weber as a unique event in the history of all civilizations. All other civilizations manifested substantively rational traditional ways of life that interacted with correspondent regularities of a structural nature to preclude the emergence of at least some of the factors Weber implicates in formal rational modern capitalism. Weber employs contrastive cases drawn from these contexts in order to draw attention to unprecedented features of particular historical events that uniquely permitted the emergence of modern capitalism in Western civilization. These comparative cases, at times, can be most intriguing in their own right. But it is best to bear in mind that Weber had a particular purpose for employing each of them.

The Lines of Exposition

The preceding characteristics of Weber's manner of exposition should provide some guidance to the reader who is about to embark on the present work. However, as previously mentioned, the most serious difficulty is likely to be in developing a sense of thematic significance for the various lines of exposition. The problem is to find a substitute for the outline of thematic development which Weber omitted. One solution to this problem, which has been adopted by Randall Collins (1980), is to abstract a genetic model from central portions of the work. While this strategy may prove to be quite useful for purposes of the extension of Weber's arguments, the logical reconfiguration of the textual discussion which necessarily is involved in this procedure diminishes its significance as a guide to the work itself.

There is another means to provide this guidance. Although Weber failed to develop an extensive thematic plan for his lines of exposition in *General Economic History,* it seems safe to assume that in planning the lecture series, which constituted the original mode of presentation, he in some way had in mind the development of the constellation of factors implicated together with profitability-oriented rational capital accounting as the presuppositional foundation for the institutional aspect of modern Western capitalism. Some justification for this assumption can be identified if it is borne in mind that in developing this conceptualization Weber was guided by his interest in investigating the penetration of economic formal rationality into the context of modern capitalism. When seen from this perspective the following passage from the prolegomenal chapter of the German edition of the present work takes on a particular significance:

> The current economic system is . . . rationalized to a high degree, owing to the penetration of bookkeeping, and in a certain sense,

and within certain limits the entire economic history is the history of economic rationalism, which is based on accounting and today has attained a triumph (1958d:16).

Since Weber acknowledges that economic history can be conceived as the development of economic rationalism based on capital accounting, it would appear legitimate to understand *General Economic History* as an attempt to trace the development of the factors implicated in this profitability-oriented procedure as practiced by the modern industrial enterprise. I shall adopt this conception in providing the synoptic overview of Weber's lines of exposition.

There are a few points of clarification to be made. In the first place, it will be recalled that Weber presents two lists of factors implicated in rational capital accounting, one of which may be found below (pp. 276–78), and the other in *Economy and Society* (1968:161–62). While I have relied on the latter to establish the formal rational character of his conception of the presuppositional aspects of capitalism, in the present context it seems wise to use the six factors listed in *General Economic History* as a key to interpret the thematic significance of the arguments presented here. Rearranging this list in an order suitable for the purposes at hand they are:

1. formally free labor
2. free trade on the market
3. the appropriation by entrepreneurs of all physical means of production
4. the commercialization of economic life
5. rational machine technologies for production
6. calculable adjudication and administration of the law

Secondly, *General Economic History* is chronologically divided into two periods. Parts One through Three develop a series of expository lines that carry the development up to the era

immediately preceding the dawn of capitalism. In all, four of
the six factors are extensively discussed in this portion of the
work. Part Four carries these factors forward into the capitalist
era and develops new lines of exposition concerning the two that
remain. While different lines of exposition appear to have a
major thematic focus on one factor or another, it must be recognized that Weber did not completely separate the development
of any one factor from the development of others. Hence all lines
of exposition must be read before the full picture of the
emergence of each factor is complete.

Part One of *General Economic History* traces the development
of familial and political economic relations moving from primitive agrarian communism to the dissolution of the manorial
system at the close of the feudal era. The discussion is crucial to
Weber's overall thematic concerns on two counts. First, this
survey of precapitalist economic relations permits Weber to
establish a foundational view of the early impediments to the
emergence of formal rationality with regard to many of the six
factors. Secondly, it is in this line of exposition that Weber
traces the initial precapitalist emergence of a formally free
labor force (factor 1), and the early unshackling of retail markets for industrial goods (factor 2). The pivotal discussion in this
regard occurs in the chapters devoted to the feudal system of
politico-economic relations, especially chapter VI, which out-
lines the movement of the manorial system in the direction of
modern capitalism.

The manorial system involved a form of hereditary political
and economic domination of the feudal lords over the peasants.
There were many different forms of this relationship, almost all
of which involved the obligation of the peasants to the lord in
terms of either labor, dues in kind, or rent. As the system
developed, these relationships became complicated by the policy
of farming out tax privileges to the nobility of the court. These
princes proferred military protection to the unarmed peasantry

in return for the payment of tax. Hence an interconnected system of mutual dependence was established and a complex set of judicial-economic relationships emerged.

The critical period for the emergence of free labor came with the dissolution of the manors. This came about in England as the result of the development of market operations involving the lords' own agricultural production. The subsequent policies of the Enclosure Acts were established to enhance the income of the English aristocracy at the expense of the peasants. Ultimately these policies forced a large number of English peasants from the land, and thus established the conditions necessary for the emergence of a labor force free from feudal domination.

The rise of agricultural markets alone was not sufficient to dissolve the manorial system in other countries. An additional factor in these cases was the struggle against the feudal lords, undertaken by the newly emergent town bourgeosie. The new bourgeoisie had two reasons for desiring the dissolution of the manorial system, both of which were connected to their economic interests in a free peasantry. First, by virtue of their manorial obligations the peasants were unable to devote their efforts entirely to production for the agricultural market. Hence, the manorial system limited the purchasing power for the entrepreneurs' goods. Secondly, because of the restrictive policies of the guilds, the new entrepreneurs were thrown back on the exploitation of rural labor power. This could only come about by the sundering of the bonds between lord and peasant.

The dissolution of the feudal politico-economic relationships manifested different consequences in different countries. In many cases other than England a free landed peasantry continued as an important force in the economy far beyond this period. While this obviously did allow for the development of retail markets for goods produced by capitalist industries, it was not always the case that a large pool of landless peasants immediately became available for capitalist exploitation. Nevertheless, at the close of Part One Weber has observed the dissolution of the bonds imposed on economic relationships by the feudal system that permitted the initial growth of free labor and the retail markets.

While Part Two includes some mention of the further development of both labor and markets, the central focus now shifts to the initial emergence of precapitalist forms of industrial organization (factor 3). At the start Weber shuttles back to antiquity. However, the bulk of this line of exposition traces the movement from the medieval craft guilds to the development of the first factories, which involved the appropriation of all physical means of production by private entrepreneurs. In the course of this discussion Weber also takes note of the premodern development of industrial technique and labor discipline (factor 5).

The medieval craft guild maintained a broad array of formally irrational policies, as seen from the standpoint of the capitalistic organization of industry. The basis of these policies was the attempt to ensure a traditional standard of living for all members. This could only be done if all aspects of the organization of production were oriented, as far as possible, to the prevention of accumulation of differential amounts of capital in the hands of individual guild members. The fear was that the growth of capitalistic power in the hands of one member might reduce the others to the status and economic position of wage workers. As a result, the guilds established traditional and often inefficient regulations covering virtually every aspect of the production process—from the use of tools and raw materials, through the division of labor, to the standard of quality for the products ultimately produced. Additional measures were taken externally to protect the monopoly of production maintained by each guild with regard to specific products.

Ultimately the guild policies began to collapse as asymmetrical relationships developed both within and between the guilds, and with the external merchants. At the same time, however, a transitional stage toward the development of modern forms of industrial organization emerged in the domestic system, i.e., "putting-out." While England was an exception in this regard, for the most part the domestic system did not grow out of the guilds but rather alongside them. Its principal significance was that ultimately both the regulation of the production process and the provision of tools came under the control of an entrepreneurs who strove to monopolize disposal of the final product. Here for the first time the worker was entirely separated from control of the means of production.

The domestic system was an intermediate step toward the ultimate emergence of the modern capitalist industrial organization. This was because of the decentralized nature of the relatively small amount of fixed capital involved. The final step in the modern direction, which Weber traces in Part Two, is the emergence of a separation of household and industry involved in shop production and the factory. Weber finds industrial shop production, in various forms, to be a common phenomenon in economic history. Unique to the West was the emergence of the factory, which Weber conceives as a shop industry involving free labor and fixed capital, both controlled by an entrepreneur oriented to capital accounting. (For contemporary accounts of the rise of capitalist forms of industrial organization see: Pollard, 1965; Marglin, 1974.)

Weber takes note of several prerequisites for the emergence of the factory. This permits him to comment on the development of factors other than the control of the means of production per se. In order to ensure the success of the factory it was necessary for the entrepreneurs to have a sufficient supply of formally free workers. Weber rejoins the discussion on this topic in Part One to point out that the early eviction of the peasantry from the land placed England in a particularly favorable position from whence it emerged as "the classical land of the later factory capitalism" (below, p. 164). The provision of labor to the factories in the continental nations, however, generally involved efforts of the state to provide work for those left destitute by the decline of guilds.

Another prerequisite of the factory involved the development of a large and stable mass-market demand for the goods produced. Weber extends the analysis in Part One to trace the growth of retail markets in the postfeudal era. The initial markets for factory-produced goods centered on the need for military supplies and luxury goods. Neither of these constituted a steady source of mass demand. Weber briefly traces the emergence of somewhat larger markets through the development of imitation luxury goods, which were within the reach of sizeable groups within the society.

A final prerequisite for the initial emergence of the modern factory was the development of relatively inexpensive technical processes of production. Weber observes that at this early date these techniques involved labor discipline (cf. Thompson, 1968), as well as power provided by animals, wind, and water rather than the more sophisticated forms of machinery employed later on. The decisive movement in the direction of modern machinery first occurred in the mining industry, to which a separate chapter is therefore devoted.

Summarizing the overall course of development of the factory in the precapitalist era, Weber notes that this form of entrepreneurially-controlled industrial organization grew side by side with both the craft guilds and the domestic system. With regard to the former, Weber notes that the factories initially produced goods that depended upon new sources of raw material or production techniques, and thus were not in competition with craft work. In the eighteenth century in England, and the nineteenth century elsewhere, the factories overtook the craftworkers on their own grounds. The domestic system similarly survived whenever the volume of fixed capital required for production was relatively small. Where new forms of production required larger amounts of fixed capital, the factory emerged. In general the entrepreneur took over a site of a shop industry formerly operated by feudal rulers.

A sense of thematic closure for Part Two can be gained through a comparison of the guild system and the factory as Weber portrays them. Where the former involved a plethora of formally irrational regulatory policies as a means to protect the traditional standard of living for its members, the emergence of the factory signified a separation of the workers from control of the means of production, which thus permitted the capitalist entrepreneur to begin the rationalization of industrial production. This line of exposition is extended into the capitalist period in Part Four, chapter XXVII, which will be discussed below.

Part Three of *General Economic History* principally focuses on the early development of commerce (factor 4) and further expands Weber's commentary of the growth of market trade (factor 2), which has been previously discussed from noncommercial points of view in Parts One and Two. As opposed to earlier portions of the work, the account here does not advance in a straight line from primitive circumstances to the precapitalist era. Rather, Weber shuttles back and forth several times with an emphasis upon different aspects of commercial trade.

The largest portion of Part Three is devoted to the development of mercantile commerce. After briefly surveying early circumstances in both trade and transportation, Weber launches an extended account of the movement from the alien trader to the medieval fairs. A critical development in this line of exposition is the emergence in several places during the medieval period of the *commenda*. This was an association involving two types of members: one remained in the home port, while the other conducted the sale of goods overseas. Initially the *commenda* was a joint risk venture among all members which often involved sponsorship by the state. However, it gradually became an arrangement for the investment of capital. It is important to note that the *commenda* was not yet a permanent commercial enterprise, but rather an individual venture that was dissolved at the close of its mission.

Medieval mercantile trade was a risky business both on land and sea. This was due to the primitive form of caravan system employed, which was subject to robbery or, in the case of overseas expeditions, natural catastrophes. As a consequence of the risk involved in foreign expeditions, there arose the need for the protection of the merchant on both a physical and legal basis. The latter was quite difficult to obtain at the start, since the merchant was a foreigner in the land where trade was conducted.

A step forward on both of these counts was taken when the merchants organized a guild licensed by rulers of the local city in which trade was conducted. The last step in the development of foreign trade was the emergence of a fixed time for trading, and hence the rise of the fixed market. A principal development at this point was the sale of market concessions by the local political authorities, concomitant with the political regulation of transport and the establishment of a market court. These conditions of foreign trade ultimately were not yet completely rational, due to the dependence of the merchant on the good will of the local political officials.

The preceding types of trade were indigenous not only to medieval Europe, but were common throughout the world. Weber notes that a significant further development in the West occurred in the late Middle Ages with the advent of resident traders. Trade on this basis was generally of a retail nature. A significant factor conditioning the rise of these trading settlements was the emergence of factories. At this point traders possessed sufficient capital to maintain independent settlements in distant lands. Weber points out that the conduct of trade by resident merchants was far from smooth. There were various struggles between resident and nonresident merchants, as well as among the merchants themselves. A general result of these struggles was the further implication of the local political authorities into the regulation of commercial activities.

To this point Weber has been discussing retail trade. However, the Middle Ages also saw the emergence of the first steps toward wholesale exchange. This occurred with the rise of trade at the fairs. At this early stage such fairs involved trade between merchants of the goods on hand. The development of more modern forms of wholesale exchange remained for a much later period. Weber addresses this topic in Part Four, chapter XXV to be discussed below.

The most critical line of exposition in Part Three concerns the development of commercial enterprise based upon rational accounting. In early times the conduct of commerce involved a small turnover that produced large profits. Hence no sophisticated means of technical calculation were required. A prerequisite to more modern forms of commercial enterprise was the emergence of Arabic positional notation in the West. On this basis the Western world, among all civilizations, became the home of money computation. This computation developed on the basis of the trading company.

As previously noted, the first form of trading company was the *commenda*. These organizations were not permanent in nature. However, out of them developed the permanent enterprise. This was especially the case in Italy during the fifteenth and sixteenth centuries. Initially the *commenda* were undertaken as a family venture. Here the books of the household and the capital transactions were combined indiscriminately. But ultimately there arose the need for long-term credit. When this occurred the institution of joint family responsibility became necessary as a safeguard for the creditor. Concomitant with this emerged a body of civil law to regulate these commercial relationships. As a result the conduct of trade became a part of economic life independent from the family budget.

Following a brief account of the mercantile guilds, Weber proceeds to trace the early development of money. It may be of interest to note that the existence of a formally rational monetary system is considered as a separate factor in rational capital accounting in the list presented by Weber in *Economy and Society*. Weber shuttles back to the primitive era. An important point in the development of modern money was the stability introduced into coinage policy by the increased inflow of precious metal in the Middle Ages. The rationalization of coinage throughout most of Europe was inhibited, however, by the variety of coins issued from various political sources as well as by imperfections in the techniques of coinage. As a result most commercial dealings were conducted in bullion. The emancipation of monetary policy from fiscal considerations occurred first in England during the early eighteenth century. Thus occurred the initial development of money as a stable basis for rational capital calculations.

Having dealt with the rationalization of monetary policy, Weber next turns to a parallel discussion of the history of banking and other trade involving bills of exchange. Once again the discussion begins in antiquity. In the early Middle Ages there appears the first instance of bank financing of large enterprises. This was involved in certain *commenda* undertaken for military as well as commercial purposes. These banking operations were very unstable on financial grounds. The next step in the development was the concession by the state of banking monopolies that were able to issue bills of exchange. This instrument increased the liquidity of the banks, and hence stabilized their operations. The final step traced by Weber in this discussion is the introduction of the discount on bills of exchange by the Bank of England.

To close Part Three, Weber briefly surveys the emergence of the practice of taking interest on loans. This is one topic where religion most clearly enters the line of exposition. In general the taking of interest was proscribed by the church, although a variety of means for the evasion of this policy did emerge. In northern Europe the prohibition on interest was finally broken up with developments following the advent of Calvinism. Readers who desire to pursue this topic further may wish to consult the Weberian inspired treatment of the topic by Benjamin Nelson (1969).

Although Part Three traces a variety of discreet lines of exposition, all of them close on the emergence of relatively rational commercial practices. In the course of these discussions Weber has traced the precapitalist foundations that were formed in retail and wholesale trade, in the commercial enterprise employing rational calculation, and in the related fields of money, banking, and interest.

At the close of Part Three, four of the six factors implicated in rational capital accounting in the modern production enterprise have been traced from their initially tradition-bound points of origin to the point where they have assumed a form more closely approximating the prerequisites for modern capitalist institutions. These factors are formally free labor, free market trade, the expropriation of the workers from the control of the means of production, and the conduct and organization of commerce. The early chapters of Part Four carry these four factors into the modern era.

Parts One through Three also include various observations on the development of precapitalist techniques of production and the emerging role of the adjudication and administration of the law by various political bodies in various forms of commerce. The middle chapters of Part Four carry these factors up to the capitalist era.

The closing chapter of Part Four moves away from the discussion of institutional aspects of modern capitalism to implicate the significance of the spirit of capitalism in the preceding account. This chapter should not be considered an adequate summary of the argument contained in *The Protestant Ethic*.

Rather, its most important purpose in the present work appears to be Weber's attempt to stress that the material developments previously discussed could never have emerged from their tradition-bound origins were it not for the complementary influence of cultural developments in the area of religious and economic ethics. As crucial as this argument is to Weber's overall historical account, the fact that it is so widely known in its more extended form suggests that there is little need to provide a synopsis at this point.

Part Four opens with what has been taken in the present context as the key to interpreting the lines of exposition in the entire work. This is the discussion of the six factors implicated in rational capital accounting in the industrial enterprise as the presuppositional foundation for modern Western capitalism.

Following this discussion, chapters XXIII-XXVI draw the history of both commerce and free market trade up to the present era. Commercialization in the capitalist era involves the appearance of paper representing shares in enterprise and rights to income. This is a feature unique to the modern Western world.

In modern economic life the issuance of these credit instruments is a means for the rational assembly of capital, especially in the form of the joint stock company. Weber traces the modern development of the stock company along two lines. One involves the sale or lease by the political authorities to stock companies of various forms of revenue which are owed. This occurred both in Italy and Germany during the Middle Ages. The significance of this system was that for the first time credit obligations were floated that appealed to the voluntary economic interests of investors.

The second line of development toward the joint stock company, and the more significant from Weber's point of view, involves the medieval enterprises for the purposes of interregional trade. While, in part, the political authorities of the

ORMAT

FIX

cities financed these enterprises themselves, the more significant cases occurred where the public was invited to participate. For a variety of reasons involved in city regulation of both of these investments and the conduct of commerce *per se,* such enterprises represented only embryonic forms of the joint stock company. However, ultimately, all that was necessary for this final result was the removal of official control. Along this line Weber traces the development of the great colonial companies such as the Dutch and English East India companies as well as other forms of state financing that similarly involved commercial enterprise.

A second element of modern commerce traced by Weber is the financial operations of the state itself. Weber traces the rise of state bonds as a form of commercial paper, as well as the development of the budgetary practices of the state. Finally, Weber observes the practice by the state in the sixteenth and seventeenth century of conceding their monopoly over certain enterprises in return for large payments by industrial entrepreneurs. But, as was especially the case in England, most of these monopolies quickly broke down. Weber thus concludes that it is mistaken to argue that Western capitalism was the outgrowth of the monopolistic policies of the medieval rulers.

Chapter XXIV refers to the first great crises of commercial speculation. Speculation is conceived by Weber as a semi-autonomous presuppositional factor implicated in rational capital accounting, following the advent of commercial paper (below, p. 278). The historical significance of the first great crises of commercial speculation, which occurred in France and Britain during the first part of the eighteenth century, was the final popularization of freely transferable stock certificates. However, it is also important to note the profoundly negative consequences that ensued from the cycle of crises of commercial speculation and financial collapse that occurred at short-term intervals throughout the nineteenth century. Weber takes cognizance of the emphasis Marx placed on these crises with regard to the downfall of capitalism (below, p. 290). While he does not appear to concur with Marx in this regard, Weber does stress the plight of those who suffer from the effects of these bouts of speculative irrationality. From Weber's perspective this suffering is particularly acute for those who are rendered unemployed and destitute since, unlike other civilizations where economic crises also have occurred, in the modern Western world religion can provide no solace. Rather, those who suffer the consequences of these crises are left to draw the conclusion that it is the society itself that is to be faulted and changed. This, in Weber's view, provides a necessary condition for the emergence of modern socialism (below, p. 291).

Before any further implications are drawn from this passage it is wise to consult Weber's more extended discussion contained in a political speech entitled "Socialism" (1980), which he delivered in 1918. Among other points made in that context (1980:208), Weber clearly states his opinion that the danger of economic crises has been greatly diminished by virtue of the concentration of control of entrepreneurial organization and, with specific reference to early twentieth-century Germany, the regulation of credit practices by the state-owned banks.

Chapter XXV returns to the modern development of wholesale trade, which in Part Three had been advanced only to the point of the medieval fairs. It was in the eighteenth century that the wholesaler finally became separated from the retailer. This gave rise to new forms of trading practices. Previously merchants were required to personally meet at the fairs to exchange goods on hand. With the emergence of the wholesale class of merchants there developed the procedure of sale at auction.This means importers could turn over their goods and secure payment from abroad at a much more rapid rate.

Consignment trading developed concomitantly with the establishment at auction of regular exchange quotations. On this basis there emerged a role for middlemen, and, in the eighteenth and nineteenth century, sale by sample. Ultimately both of these procedures were displaced by the development of the standardization and specification of grades for various goods. The final step in the emergence of wholesale trade occurred with the advent of rational speculation for a rise based upon the exchange of commerical paper, i.e., dealing in futures.

In Part Three Weber stressed the importance for the development of commerce of the technical processes of transportation necessary for the sale and exchange of goods. The closing portion of chapter XXV brings this line of exposition up to the present era. The development of public news services came about at an extremely late date. While the first newspapers such as *The Times* of London had been established in the eighteenth century, the transmission of commercial information by private arrangements and the organized exchange of letters were still the established means of commercial communication. Originally all commercial exchanges were private clubs. Hence no public distribution of information was needed. It remained until the nineteenth century for generally circulated price bulletins to emerge. As far as the transportation of goods was concerned little changed up to the modern era, with the exception of the development of improved roads and turnpikes. In the modern era the railroad finally came on the scene with profound consequences for commerce and economic life in general.

There has been much recent debate on the significance of colonialism and slavery on the development of modern capitalism. (For a summary in this regard see Patterson, 1979:249–58; see also Wallerstein, 1979:ch. 13.) The issue obviously must turn, in part, on how the particular analyst conceives of the nature of modern capitalism. In chapter XXVI Weber devotes a brief comment to the relationship between colonialism and slavery on the one hand and the rise of modern capitalism *as he conceives it* (see section I of this essay). From his

Outline of the "Conceptual Preface" to
General Economic History

Heading	*Location in Economy and Society*
I. Basic Concepts	
A. Economic Acts	Part One, Chapter II, number 1:(1968:63-68)
B. Economic Trade	Part One, Chapter II, number 4:(1968:71-74)
C. Means of Exchange	Part One, Chapter II, number 6:(see also 7, 10, 12) (1968:75-80)
D. Types of Economy: Household and Profits	Part One, Chapter II, numbers 10, 11:(1968:86-100)
II. Types of Economic Division of Labor	Part One, Chapter II, numbers 15-23. (1968:115-144).

The final part of the "Conceptual Preface" raises three questions that Weber conceives to be the duty of economic history to investigate. First, how were the given tasks in a given epoch distributed, specialized, and combined on a technical and economic basis as well as in relation to the property system? This introduces the problem of classes and social structure in general. Secondly, is this division of labor a matter of household or commercial revenue of the appropriate production and prospects? Finally, Weber raises the question of the relation of rationality and irrationality in economic life.

It is at this point that Weber injects the passage cited above (section II), suggesting that the entire economic history is the history of economic rationalism based on capital accounting. He goes on to indicate that in order to study this phenomenon the transcendence of traditional boundaries of a religious and status-bound nature are necessary. Thereafter he comments on the mathematical calculability of the modern economy. But he notes that there also exist strong material irrationalities, espe-

engine in the late eighteenth century as being critical to the modern production of these materials. Weber identifies three major consequences of the advent of coal, iron, and steam engines. First, coal and iron released technology and productive possibilities from limitations formerly imposed by the use of organic materials and animal power. Secondly, the steam engine released production from many of the limitations imposed by human labor power. Finally, the development of production in conjunction with iron, coal, and steam power permitted the union of industry and science.

At this point Weber rejoins the line of exposition at the close of Part One to trace the recruitment of labor into the newly mechanized factories. Weber had left the English labor force as it was released from the bonds of feudal relationships by means of the Enclosure Acts. He traces the movement of the dispossessed peasants into the factories, which initially occurred through indirect compulsions imposed by the monarchy. Weber also notes the difficulty with which the new workers adapted to the factories, and the support of the judicial authorities in controlling the labor force. Finally, he surveys the development in England from the eighteenth century onward of the state regulation of the relations between entrepreneurs and laborers.

In Part Three Weber discussed the initial development of mass market demand involving military supplies, as well as genuine and imitation luxury goods. In the present context Weber traces this line more extensively and advances it to the point where mass markets developed in conjunction with newly mechanized industries. A powerful stimulant to the cheapening of production and the lowering of prices resulted from the inflow of precious metals in the sixteenth and seventeenth centuries. This development had the effect of raising prices for agricultural goods, thus opening new production for market. At the same time prices for industrial goods remained steady as the emergence of factories, discussed by Weber in Part Two, began to cheapen the production process. Thus, as Weber notes, the decline of prices on the market set in before capitalism arose.

The movement toward rationalized technology and economic relations in general generated an extraordinary pursuit of invention in connection with the cheapening of production during the seventeenth century. Outside of mining, however, much of this work was more trial-and-error rather than scientific in nature. A critical step toward modern technology was the development of rational patent law, which first occurred in England in the seventeenth century. These laws led to the development of the inventions necessary for the emergence of the pivotal English cotton industry.

The final paragraphs of chapter XXV reveal that Weber has now concluded his discussion of the emergence of the economic factors implicated in his conception of modern Western capitalism. The commentary indicates the manner in which Weber conceives these factors to have uniquely surmounted traditional barriers that stood in the way of the emergence of similar circumstances in non-Western civilizations.

At this point Weber details the cultural side of the development of capitalism. Reference is made to the critical significance of the spirit of capitalism, as well as modern science. But the new factor Weber introduces as a topic for analysis is the emergence, unique to the West, of the modern state. His particular emphasis is that only in the West has there emerged a body of law, based on the concept of citizenship, that is made by jurists and rationally interpreted and applied (factor 6).

Chapters XXVIII and XXIX are devoted to the development of citizenship and the state. These chapters have proven to be of great value to Weberian scholars since they constitute one of the few places where Weber develops the discussion of historical developments in this regard. This project had been planned for inclusion in *Economy and Society* (see Roth, 1968:LX) but unfortunately Weber died before completing this work. The significance of these remarks is indicated by the fact that Johannes Winckelmann, editor of the fourth German edition of *Economy and Society*, used them as a primary source for the reconstruction of Weber's sociology of the state (see Roth, 1968:XCVIII, n. 121).

The juridical and political influence of the precapitalist state appears at many points in diverse lines of exposition prior to the emergence of modern Western capitalism. With regard to labor, it was the English Enclosure Acts that drove the peasants from the land, and later through the Poor Laws assisted the entrepreneur in pressing the workers into the factories. In the capitalist era the state enforces labor contracts and regulates other relationships between entrepreneur and capitalist. Where the state worked more strongly against the landed aristocracy, as was commonly the case on the continent, it helped to create the circumstances for free market trade by the newly liberated peasantry. Further assistance by the state was provided by the demand for military goods and luxury items that created new markets in the seventeenth and eighteenth centuries. These markets in turn were necessary prerequisites for the development of entrepreneurally-controlled factories, involving the final expropriation of the means of production. In the capitalist era, the state enforces the contracts of exchange on the market, as well as the property rights of those who control the means of production. In the field of commerce the state was involved in the financing of commercial ventures from the time of the *commenda* onward. Among the consequences of these operations was the formation of commercial enterprise involving the separation of the budgetary interests of the household and the entrepreneur. From an early period the state was also involved in the areas of banking and the operation of the monetary system where its influence continues into the capitalist era. Finally, by providing legal protection through the issuance of patents from the seventeenth century onward the state provided a vital foundation for the development of modern industrial technology. Seen in this light, it is possible to agree with Randall Collins (1980:932) that for Weber the state provides the historical key to all of the institutional factors involved in rational capitalism. (For a consideration of the historical development of nationalized industries see I.J. Cohen, 1980b.)

The development of citizenship in the medieval cities, as presented by Weber in chapter XXIII, involves a series of historical analyses and comparative cases too complex to be summarized in the present context. The critical period in this line of exposition with regard to the emergence of modern capitalism in the West occurred after the cities lost their freedom. Weber points out that the development of Western capitalism was conditioned in a most important way by the emergence of absolute nation-states engaged in a perpetual struggle amongst themselves. By virtue of this fact, each state was forced to compete for mobile capital. As a result a new national citizen class ultimately emerged beside the aristocracy of the state—the modern bourgeoisie.

In chapter XXIX Weber traces the development of selected aspects of the state as they are germaine to the rise of capitalism. The first of these involves the emergence of a rational, calculable legal system (factor 6). Weber does not present a detailed account in this regard (see 1968:641–938). His general observation is that rational modern jurisprudence emerged from the sixteenth century onward as the result of an alliance formed by the states with the jurists for the purpose of legitimizing the states' claim to power.

Weber traces the emergence of a recognizably modern economic policy on the part of the state, i.e., one which is continuous and consistent, to the mercantile system, which originated in fourteenth-century England. In connection with colonialism, however, Weber points out that capitalism did not directly emerge from mercantilist origins. Rather, in England a stratum of entrepreneurs who emerged side by side with the political administration were most instrumental in this regard. In the eighteenth century the private capitalist business interests came head to head with the business interests of the state, following one of the initial speculative crises referred to earlier. This, in Weber's view, represented the last confrontation between the rational capitalism represented by the bourgeois industrialists and the irrational capitalist policies of the state.

Finally, in chapter XXX, Weber injects into the analysis the development of the spirit of capitalism. As mentioned previously, while this discussion is most valuable in its own right, it should be supplemented by reading *The Protestant Ethic* in order to arrive at a more comprehensive view.

III. The Production of *General Economic History*

Weber's central contributions to the development of concepts and methods in contemporary social science tend to obscure the fact that throughout his career he was regarded as an economic historian. It is of interest to note that *General Economic History* was the first of his works to receive an English translation, which appeared in 1927. (A Spanish edition was published in 1942: see bibliography.) The most significant fact about this work is that were it not for the diligent effort of Weber's students and colleagues it is extremely unlikely that *General Economic History* would have been developed by Weber or made available to the scholarly community.

For the greatest part of his career Max Weber did not engage in the delivery of formally structured lecture courses. However, between 1917 and 1919, at the height of his reputation in German academic circles, Weber accepted a teaching position to fill a chair left vacant at the University of Munich by a friend of long standing, the economic historian Lujo Brentano. It is significant to note that notwithstanding their friendship, Brentano was also a serious critic of Weber's thesis in *The Protestant Ethic and the Spirit of Capitalism* (cf. Samuelsson, 1961:12–14; Seligman, 1962:31ff).

There undoubtedly must have been some pressure from the University to teach political economy as Brentano had. But Weber's interests lay elsewhere. In 1919 he was attempting to complete what has become the first part of *Economy and Society*. This project was directed to the conceptual side of his sociological endeavors. He was also at work on what has now become the introduction to *The Protestant Ethic and the Spirit of Capitalism,* which was intended as a general introduction to his *Collected Essays in the Sociology of Religion* rather than the start of a new project in economic history. Indeed, as recently as 1914 Weber rejected the idea of including a general economic history in his plans for *Economy and Society* (see Roth, 1968: LVII–LVIII). In this context it is not surprising that Weber agreed to accept the post at Munich only after it was stipulated that he might confine the bulk of his lectures to the field of sociology (Marianne Weber, 1975:646).

Weber's effect on his students was registered immediately upon his arrival. While his wife may not be the most detached observer, her words provide some insight in this regard: " . . . students flocked to see him during his office hours; he counseled them and gave them assignments. They regarded him with awe" (Marianne Weber, 1975:662).

Prior to the beginning of the winter term of 1919–20, Weber's students initiated persistent requests that he deliver a lecture series devoted to economic history. Marianne Weber (1975:671) reports that the principal motivation involved the difficulty in following Weber's earlier lectures devoted to abstract sociological categories. However, it is possible to speculate that another motive may have rested behind the student's requests. Weber's students in Munich were separated from him by a great intellectual distance (Marianne Weber, 1975:664). Given the tenor of the times it seems likely that some of them may have maintained historical interests grounded in Marxist or socialist theories. Others may have been influenced by the recently departed Brentano as well as Werner Sombart. Given these circumstances, it may be suggested that at least some of Weber's students desired to hear his views on economic history as a means to have a Weberian benchmark against which to measure various other accounts. The lecture series was given in the winter term under the title "Outline of Universal Social and Economic History."

The critical role of Weber's students does not rest solely on the inspiration they provided. According to the editors of the original German edition of *General Economic History,* Weber by no means intended his lectures for a wider audience, although it is important to note Marianne Weber's report (1975:671) that he possessed most of the knowledge necessary for its presentation. As fate would have it, the decision to develop these lectures for public distribution was not in Weber's hands. Only months after he completed the Munich lecture series, Max Weber died on June 14, 1920.

Weber's death immediately recast the significance of these lectures. In effect this course now represented his most mature publically available thoughts on the development of modern capitalism. Hence, despite the recognition of all concerned that Weber regarded these lectures as provisional in nature, his wife selected two scholars, Siegmund Hellman and Melchior Palyi, to produce a manuscript from these lectures, which has resulted in *General Economic History.*

Hellman and Palyi appeared at the time to be highly qualified to undertake the task. Hellman had served as the editor of a collection to which Weber had submitted several political pieces. Palyi, along with Marianne Weber, was responsible for the task of editing the original edition of *Economy and Society.* This task was most arduous in that a substantial portion of the manuscript took the form of literary remains written in a scarcely legible handwriting (Roth, 1968:CII).

The process by which Hellman and Palyi proceeded has been indicated by Johannes Winckelmann in his foreword to the German republication of *General Economic History* (1958d:XII–XVIII). It should be noted that Winckelmann is himself one of the foremost contemporary Weberian scholars. His efforts produced the substantially revised fourth German edition of *Economy and Society* in 1956. According to Winckelmann the present manuscript was developed from notebooks of several students who attended the lectures. It is not certain how many of these were actually used by Hellman and Palyi. Winckelmann suggests there were probably from six to eight of them.

The sole surviving copy of notes from Weber's lectures, which cannot definitely be established as a source used by the German editors, are transcribed in part, in a form of stenography which all Bavarian law students of that era were required to use. On this basis Winckelmann suggests that there may have been an extreme correspondence between the various sources employed in Hellman and Palyi's reconstruction.

The main German text, which is available below as translated by economist Frank Knight, was principally developed by Hellman. Winckelmann has checked portions of this text against the surviving notes and on the basis of these comparisons he vouches for the overall correspondence between the text and the actual lectures (1958d:XIV). It is his opinion that the editors exercised great care in fulfilling their responsibilities.

The history of classical literature in social science intermittently has included the posthumous publication of several works originally presented in lecture form. Durkheim's *Socialism* and George Herbert Mead's *Mind, Self, and Society* are notable examples. In some ways this procedure is to be trusted more than the reconstruction of works from literary remains, such as is the case not only for large portions of *Economy and Society* but also for the second and third volumes of Marx's *Capital*. While the transcription of lectures still leaves the possibility that the author may have wished to make corrections, the reconstruction of fragments necessarily involves the editor as an active participant in the lines of exposition. The only additions to the present text made by the editors are the separation by paragraphs and the subheadings within the chapters. The table of contents, the bibliography, and the index are also due to their efforts rather than Weber's. It thus appears that the text of *General Economic History* can be relied upon, in a manner similar to other posthumous publications of lectures of this type, as a reliable source of Weber's thought at the time he delivered his remarks.

Before closing it should be mentioned that there is one lecture delivered by Weber that does not appear in the English edition of *General Economic History*. This discrete passage entitled "Conceptual Preface," appears at the head of the main text. Frank Knight chose to exclude this material on the grounds that it appeared to be the result of the editors' efforts rather than a transcription of Weber's comments. However, on the basis of the available notes, Winckelmann has concluded that Knight's judgment was in error. In all likelihood the material presented represents the product of Weber's own thought.

The bulk of this "Conceptual Preface," as it appears with several limited reconstructions by Winckelmann in the 1958 edition, is devoted to the presentation of ideal types. It may be useful at this point to indicate the general outline with reference to corresponding sections of *Economy and Society*. It should be noted that, while ideal-types in the "Conceptual Preface" closely resemble those in the latter source, the order of the presentation of the sentences within each ideal-type differs, and the ideal-types in *Economy and Society* are more extensive.

perspective on modern capitalism it is Weber's view that neither colonialism nor slavery were of decisive importance toward bringing about the capitalistic organization of industry and of economic life (cf. below 300–01).

Prior to Part Four Weber has already presented the initial development of free labor, retail markets, and the appropriation of the means of production by capitalist entrepreneurs. But before industrial production can be said to have finally entered the capitalist era it is necessary to implicate the development of all these factors with the emergence of machine technology. This is Weber's topic in chapter XXVII.

Weber is careful to point out that modern technology *per se* is not the definitive characteristic of the factory. What distinguishes the modern factory, in Weber's view, is the concentration of means of production at a site outside the household in the hands of an entrepreneur. Weber rejoins the line of exposition at the close of Part Two to indicate the final emergence of this phenomenon. The historical movement that determined the development in this regard occurred during the eighteenth century in England. It should be noted, however, that Weber acknowledges that English development followed the example of other countries such as Italy. (For a critical treatment of Weber in this regard see Jere Cohen, 1980.)

Despite his distinction between the factory and industrial technology, Weber ascribes great importance to the advent of the latter. Prior to the mechanization of the production process the apparatus worked as the servant of man. But now the relationship is reversed, and the man becomes the servant of the machine (below, p. 302). The decisive locus for the mechanization of industry and the attendant rationalization of work was the English cotton manufacturing industry.

Mechanization might have stopped at this point were it not for the development of coal and iron. Weber points to a series of technical innovations leading up to the invention of the steam

cially in the distribution of income and goods. These he observes
to be generated by household and speculative interests (see
section II). An analogy is drawn between the struggle of formal
and material rationality in the economy and in the legal system
(see 1968:880–94).

Finally, Weber emphasizes that economic history is not identical with the history of culture in general, as is suggested by
materialist conceptions of history. Economic history represents
merely a foundation for the investigations in other areas of
culture, but a foundation without which the study of these other
areas is inconceivable.

References

An excellent, briefly annotated, bibliography of the works by Weber
and his commentators may be found at the close of the collection edited
by W.G. Runciman, *Weber: Selections in Translation* (Cambridge:
Cambridge University Press, 1978), pp. 391–94.

Birnbaum, Norman. 1953. "Conflicting Interpretations of the Rise of
Capitalism: Marx and Weber." *British Journal of Sociology*
4:127–41.

Braudel, Ferdinand. 1973. *Capitalism and Material Life 1400–1800.*
New York: Harper.

Burger, Thomas. 1976. *Max Weber's Theory of Concept Formation.*
Durham, North Carolina: Duke University Press.

Cohen, Ira J. 1980a. *"Science, Social Theory, and Everyday Life in the
Works of Auguste Comte: A Study in the Constitution of Scientific
Sociology."* Unpublished doctoral dissertation, University of
Wisconsin-Madison.

————. 1980b. "Toward a Theory of State Intervention: The Na-
tionalization of the British Telegraphs." *Social Science History*
4:155–205.

Cohen, Jere. 1980. "Rational Capitalism in Renaissance Italy." *American Journal of Sociology* 85:1340–55.

Collins, Randall. 1980. "Weber's Last Theory of Capitalism: A Sys-
temization." *American Sociological Review* 45:925–42.

Dobbs, Maurice. 1963. *Studies in the Development of Capitalism.* New
York: International.

Fullbrook, Mary. 1978. "Max Weber's 'Interpretative Sociology': A Comparison of Conception and Practice." *British Journal of Sociology* 29:71–82.

Giddens, Anthony. 1970. "Marx, Weber and the Development of Capitalism." *Sociology* 4:298–310.

———. 1971. *Capitalism and Modern Social Theory: An Analysis of the Writings of Marx, Durkheim, and Max Weber.* Cambridge: Cambridge University Press.

———. 1976. *New Rules of Sociological Method: A Positive Critique of Interpretative Sociologies.* London: Hutchinson.

———. 1977. *Studies in Social and Political Theory.* London: Hutchinson.

———. 1979. *Central Problems in Social Theory: Action, Structure and Contradiction in Social Analysis.* London: Macmillan.

Hilton, Rodney. 1978. *The Transition from Feudalism to Capitalism.* London: New Left Books.

Kalberg, Stephan. 1979. "The Search for Thematic Orientations in a Fragmented *Oeuvre:* The Discussion of Max Weber in Recent German Sociological Literature." *Sociology* 13:127–39.

———. 1980. "Max Weber's Types of Rationality: Cornerstones for the Analysis of Rationalization Processes in History." *American Journal of Sociology* 85:1145–79.

Marglin, Stephan A. 1974. "What do Bosses Do?-the origins and functions of hierarchy in capitalist production." *Review of Radical Political Economics* 6:60–112.

Marx, Karl. 1967. *Capital. Volume 3. The Process of Capitalist Production as a Whole.* Edited by Frederick Engels. New York: International. (Originally published in 1894.)

———. 1973. *Grundresse: Foundations of the Critique of Political Economy.* Translated by Martin Nicolaus. New York: Vintage. (Originally written in 1857–1859).

Nelson, Benjamin. 1969. *The Idea of Usury: From Tribal Brotherhood to Universal Otherhood.* Second Edition. Chicago: University of Chicago Press.

———. 1979. "Max Weber's 'Author's Introduction' (1920): A Master Clue to His Main Aims." *Sociological Inquiry* 44:267–78.

Patterson, Orlando. 1979. "The Black Community: Is There a Future?" in Seymour Martin Lipset (editor), *The Third Century: America as a Post-Industrial Society.* Chicago: University of Chicago Press.

INTRODUCTION LXXXI

Polanyi, Karl. 1944. *The Great Transformation: The Political and Economic Origins of Our Time.* New York: Rinehart.

Pollard, S. 1965. *The Genesis of Modern Management.* London: Edward Arnold.

Roth, Guenther. 1968. "Introduction," in Max Weber, *Economy and Society: An Outline of Interpretative Sociology.* Totowa, New Jersey: Bedminster, Pp. XXVII-CVIII.

———. 1971a. "Sociological Typology and Historical Explanation," in Reinhard Bendix and Guenther Roth, *Scholarship and Partisanship: Essays on Max Weber.* Berkeley: University of California Press. Pp. 109–28.

———. 1971b. "The Historical Relationship to Marxism," in Reinhard Bendix and Guenther Roth, *Scholarship and Partisanship: Essays on Max Weber.* Berkeley: University of California Press. Pp. 227-252.

———. 1979. "Charisma and the Counterculture," in Guenther Roth and Wolfgang Schluchter, *Max Weber's Vision of History: Ethics and Method.* Berkeley: University of California Press. Pp. 119–43.

Roth, Guenther and Wolfgang Schluchter. 1979. *Max Weber's Vision of History: Ethics and Method.* Berkeley: University of California Press.

Samuelsson, Kurt. 1961. *Religion and Economic Action.* Translated by D.C. Coleman. New York: Basic Books. (Originally published in 1957.)

Seligman, Ben B. 1962. *Main Currents in Economic Thought. Volume One: The Revolt Against Formalism.* Chicago: Quadrangle.

Tenbruck, Friedrich. 1980. "The Problem of Thematic Unity in the Works of Max Weber." Translated by M.S. Whimster. *British Journal of Sociology* 31:316–51. (Originally published in 1975.)

Thompson, E.P. 1968. *The Making of the English Working Class.* Harmondsworth: Penguin.

Wallerstein, Immanuel. 1976. *The Modern World System: Capitalist Agriculture and the Origins of the European World-Economy in the Sixteenth Century.* New York: Academic.

———. 1979. *The Capitalist World-Economy.* Cambridge: Cambridge University Press.

———. 1980. *The Modern World System III: Mercantilism and the Consolidation of the European World-Economy 1600–1750.* New York: Academic.

Weber, Marianne. 1975. *Max Weber: A Biography*. Translated and edited by Harry Zohn. New York: Wiley. (Originally published in 1926.)

Weber, Max. 1942. *Historia Economica General*. Translated by Manuel Sanchez Sarto. Mexico.

———. 1946a. "The Social Psychology of World Religions," in *From Max Weber: Essays in Sociology*. Translated and edited by Hans Gerth and C. Wright Mills. New York: Oxford. Pp. 267-301. (Originally published in 1915.)

———. 1946b. "Religious Rejections of the World and Their Direction," in *From Max Weber: Essays in Sociology*. Translated and edited by Hans Gerth and C. Wright Mills. New York: Oxford. Pp. 323–59. (Originally published in 1915.)

———. 1946c. "Science as a Vocation," in *From Max Weber: Essays in Sociology*. Translated and edited by Hans Gerth and C. Wright Mills. New York: Oxford. Pp. 129–56. (Originally published in 1919.)

———. 1949. " 'Objectivity' in Social Science and Social Policy," in *The Methodology of the Social Sciences*. Translated and edited by Edward A. Shils and Henry A. Finch. New York: Free Press. Pp. 50–112. (Originally published in 1904.)

———. 1951. *The Religion of China: Confucianism and Taoism*. Translated by Hans Gerth. Glencoe, Illinois: Free Press. (Originally published in 1916.)

———. 1952. *Ancient Judaism*. Translated and edited by Hans Gerth and Don Martindale. Glencoe, Illinois: Free Press. (Originally published in 1917-1919.)

———. 1958a. *The Protestant Ethic and the Spirit of Capitalism*. Translated by Talcott Parsons. New York: Scribners. (Originally published in 1904-1905.)

———. 1958b. *The Religion of India*. Translated by Hans Gerth and Don Martindale. New York: Free Press. (Originally published in 1916-17.)

———. 1958c. *The Rational and Social Foundations of Music*. Edited by Don Martindale and Johannes Riedel. Translated by Don Martindale, Johannes Riedel, and Gertrude Neuwirth. Carbondale, Illinois: Southern Illinois University Press. (Originally published in 1921.)

———. 1958d. *Wirtschaftsgeschichte*. Edited by Johannes Winckelmann. Berlin: Duncker and Humboldt. (Originally published in 1923.)

————. 1968. *Economy and Society: An Outline of Interpretative Sociology*. Edited by Guenther Roth and Claus Wittich. New York: Bedminster Press. (Based on the 1956 German edition. Originally published in 1921–1922.)

————. 1977. *Critique of Stammler*. Translated by Guy Oakes. New York: Free Press. (Originally published in 1907).

————. 1980. "Socialism," in J.E.T. Eldridge (editor), *Max Weber: The Interpretation of Social Reality*. Translated by D. Hytch. Pp. 191-219.

Wrong, Dennis. 1970. "Max Weber," in *Max Weber*. Edited by Dennis Wrong. Englewood Cliffs, New Jersey: Prentice Hall.

Zeitlin, Irving. 1981. *The Social Condition of Humanity: An Introduction to Sociology*. New York: Oxford University Press.

PART ONE

HOUSEHOLD, CLAN, VILLAGE AND MANOR [1]

(The Agrarian Organization)

[1] See notes at the end of the volume.

CHAPTER I

THE AGRICULTURAL ORGANIZATION AND THE PROBLEM
OF AGRARIAN COMMUNISM [1]

The idea of a primitive agrarian communism at the beginning of all economic evolution was first suggested by investigations into the ancient German economic organization, especially by Hanssen and von Maurer.[2] These men originated the theory of the ancient German agrarian communism, which became the common property of scholarship. Analogies from other lands to the ancient German rural organization led finally to the theory of an agrarian communism as the uniform beginning of all economic development, the theory developed especially by E. de Laveleye. Such analogies came from Russia and from Asia, especially India. Recently, however, a strong tendency has set in to assume private property in land and a manorial type of development for the most ancient periods accessible to us, whether in Germany or in other economic systems.

If we consider first the German national agricultural organization as it presents itself to us in the eighteenth century, and go back from it to older conditions poorly and scantily illuminated by the sources, we must begin by restricting ourselves to regions originally settled by the Teutons. Thus we exclude, first, the previously Slavic region east of the Elbe and Saal; second, the region formerly Roman, that is, the Rhine region, Hessia, and South Germany generally south of a line drawn roughly from the

3

Hessian boundary to the vicinity of Regensburg; and finally, the region originally settled by Celts, to the left of the Weser.

The land settlement in this originally German region had the village form, not that of the isolated farmstead.

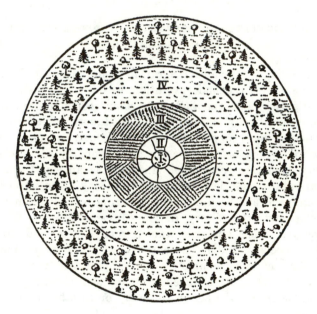

Connecting roads between the villages were originally quite absent as each village was economically independent and had no need of connections with its neighbors. Even later the roads were not laid out systematically but were broken by traffic according to need and disappeared from one year to the next until gradually in the course of centuries an obligation to maintain them was established, resting upon the individual holding of land. Thus the General Staff maps of this region today give the impression of an irregular network whose knots are the villages.

In the sketch, the first or innermost zone contains the dwelling lots, placed quite irregularly. Zone Two contains the fenced garden land (*Wurt*), in as many parts as there were originally dwelling lots in the village. Zone Three is the arable (see below), and Zone Four pasture (*"Almende"*). Each household has the right to herd an equal number of livestock on the pasture area, which, however, is not communal but appropriated in fixed shares. The same is true of the wood (Zone Five) which incidentally does not uniformly belong to the village; here also the rights to wood cutting, to bedding, mast, etc., are divided equally among the inhabitants of the village. House, dwelling lot, and the share of the individual in the garden land, arable (see below), pasture and forest, together constitute the hide (German *Hufe*, cognate with "have.")

The arable is divided into a number of parts called fields (*Gewanne*); these again are laid off in strips which are not always uniform in breadth and are often extremely narrow. Each peasant of the village possesses one such strip in each field, so that the shares in the arable are originally equal in extent. The basis of this division into fields is found in the effort to have the members of the community share equally in the various qualities of the land in different locations. The intermixed holdings which thus arose brought the further advantage that all the villagers were equally affected by catastrophes such as hailstorms, and the risks of the individual were reduced.

The division into strips, in contrast with the Roman custom, where squares predominate, is connected with the peculiarities of the German plow. The plow is universally, to begin with, a hoe-like instrument wielded by the hands or drawn by animals, which merely scratches the soil and makes grooves in the surface. All peoples which did not get beyond this hoe-plow were compelled to plow the fields back and forth in order to loosen up the soil. The most suitable division of the surface for this purpose was the square, as we find it in Italy from Cæsar's time on, and as the general staff maps of the Campagna and the outer boundary marks between the individual land holdings still show it. In contrast, the German plow consisted, as far as we can tell, of a knife which cut the earth vertically, a share which cut it horizontally, and finally, at the right, a moldboard which turned it over. This plow made the criss-cross plowing unnecessary, and for its use the division into long strips was most appropriate. The size of the separate strips was usually determined in this connection, by the amount which an ox could plow in a day without giving out—hence the German names *"Morgen"* (English, "morning" but equivalent to acre) or *"Tagwerk"* (English, day's work). In the course of time these divisions underwent much confusion, since the plow, with its moldboard on the right, had a tendency to work over to the left. Hence the furrows became uneven, and since there were no balks, originally at least, between the separate strips, only boundary furrows being drawn, strips of land belonging to another were often plowed up. The original arrangement would be restored by "field juries" with the rod or later the so-called spring circle.

As there are no roads between the single allotments, tillage operations can only be carried on according to a common plan and at the same time for all. This was normally done according to the *three field system,* which is the most general though by no means the oldest type of husbandry in Germany. Its introduction must be set back at least to the eighth century, since it is assumed as

a matter of course in a document of the Rhenish monastery
of Lorsch of about the year 770.

The three-field husbandry means that in the first place
the whole arable area is divided into three tracts, of which
at any one time the first is sown to a winter grain and the
second to a summer grain, while the third is left fallow and,
at least in historical time, is manured.   Each year the fields
are changed in rotation, so that the one sown with winter grain is the next year put to summer grain and in the
year following left fallow, and the others correspondingly.
There is stall feeding of livestock in the winter, while in
summer they run on the pasture.   Under such a system of
husbandry it was impossible for any individual to use
methods different in any way from those of the rest of the
community; he was bound to the group in all his acts.
The reeve of the village determined when sowing and
reaping were to be done, and ordered the parts of the arable
which were sown with grain fenced off from the fallow
land.   As soon as harvest was over, the fences were torn
down; anyone who had not harvested on the common harvest day must expect the cattle, which would be driven on
to the stubble, to trample his grain.

The hide belonged to the individual and was hereditary.[3]
It could be of varying size and was different in nearly every
village.   Frequently, as a sort of norm, an extent of 40
acres was taken as the amount of land necessary to support
a typical family.   The part of the holding consisting of
dwelling lot and garden land was subject to free individual
use.   The house sheltered a family in the narrow sense of
parents and children, often including grown sons.   The
share in the arable was also individually appropriated,
while the rest of the cleared land belonged to the community of hide-men or peasant holders (*Hüfner*), that is,
of the members in full standing or freemen of the village.

These included only those who held title to some share in each of the three fields of arable. One who had no land or did not have a share in every field did not count as a hide-man.

To a still larger group than the village belonged the common "mark" which included wood and waste land and is to be distinguished from the almend or pasture. This larger group was made up of several villages. The beginnings and original form of the mark association (*Markgenossenschaft*) are lost in obscurity. In any case it goes back before the political division of the land into districts by the Carolingians, and yet it is not identical with the hundred. Within the common mark there existed, joined in inheritance with a certain farm, a "head official" of the mark (*Obermärkeramt*), an office which had usually been pre-empted by the king or feudal lord, and in addition a "wood court," and an assembly of deputies of the hide-men of the villages belonging to the mark.

Originally there was in theory strict equality among the members in this economic organization. But such an equality broke down in consequence of differences in the number of children among whom the inheritance was divided and there arose alongside the hide-men half and quarter hide-men. Moreover, the hide-men were not the only inhabitants of the village. There were in addition other sections of the population. First, younger sons who did not succeed to holdings. These were allowed to go and settle on the outskirts of the holdings on still uncleared land and received the right of pasture, for a payment in both cases (*Hufengeld, Weidegeld*). The father could also give them, out of his garden allotment, land on which to build a house. From the outside came hand workers and other neighbors who stood without the organization of associated hide-men. Thus there arose a division between the peasants and another class of village dwellers, called in South Germany hirelings or cottagers (*Seldner, Häusler*), and in the north *"Brinksitzer"* or *"Kossäten."* These latter belonged to the village only on the strength of their ownership of a house but had no share in the arable. However, they could acquire such a share if some peasant, with the consent of the village reeve or of the overlord (originally the clan) sold them a part of his share or if the village leased them a piece of the almend. Such parcels were called "rolling holdings" (*walzende Äcker*); they were not subject to the special obligations of the hide holding or to the jurisdiction of the manorial court, and were freely transferable. On the other hand their holders had no share in the rights of the hide-man. The number of these people of reduced legal status was not small; it happened that villages transformed up to half of their arable into such rolling holdings.

As a result the peasant population became divided into two strata as regards land ownership, the hide-men with their different subclasses on the one hand, and on the other those who stood outside the hide organization. But there was also formed *above* the hide-men a special economic stratum who with their land holdings also stood outside the main village organization. In the beginning of the German agricultural system, as long as there was unclaimed land available, an individual could clear land and fence it; so long as he tilled it, this so-called *"Bifang"* was reserved to him; otherwise it reverted to the common mark. Acquisition of such "bifangs" presupposed considerable possessions in cattle and slaves and in consequence was ordinarily possible only for the king, princes, and overlords. In addition to this procedure, the king would grant land out of the possessions of marks, the supreme authority over which he had assumed for himself. But this granting took place under other conditions than the allotment of hide land. In this case the allotment affected forest area with definite boundaries, which had first to be rendered tillable, and was subject to more favorable legal relations by being free from the open field obligations. In measuring off these grants a definite area came into use called the royal hide, a rectangle of 40 or 50 hectares (1 hectare $=2\frac{1}{2}$ acres, nearly).

The old German settlement form with the hide system spread out beyond the region between the Elbe and the Weser. Countries into which it made its way include, first, Scandinavia—Norway as far as Bergen, Sweden up to the river Dalelf, the Danish Islands and Jutland; second, England, after the invasions of the Anglo-Saxons and Danes (the open field system); third, almost all northern France, and a large part of Belgium, as far as Brabant, while North-Belgium, Flanders and a part of Holland belonged to the realm of the Salic Franks with a different settlement form; fourth, in south Germany, the region between the Danube and Iller and Lech, including parts of Baden and Wurtemberg, as well as upper Bavaria or the region around Munich, especially the vicinity of Aibling. With German colonization, the old German form of settlement also spread over the Elbe eastward, though in a somewhat rationalized form, since the aim of making the country take up the largest number of settlers led to the establishment of "street villages" with favorable property institutions and with the greatest possible freedom of economic life. The house lots lay not in irregular groups but to the right and left along the village street, each one on its own allotment or hide, which allotments lay adjoining each other in long strips: but here also the divisions into fields and the compulsory common tillage were retained.

With the expansion of the German land settlement system beyond its original home, notable distinctions arose. This was especially true in Westphalia, which is divided by the river Weser into regions sharply distinct as regards the mode of settlement. At the river the Germanic settlement form stops suddenly and on the left begins the region of settlement in isolated farmsteads. There is no village or common (*Almend*), and mixed holdings occur only to a limited extent. The separate farms are cut out of the common mark which is originally uncultivated land. By clearing, new field areas are made which are allotted to the members of the community, called "*Erbexen.*" Moreover, by the process of division other settlers were admitted to the mark, corresponding more or less to the "*Kossäten*" farther east—craftsmen, small peasants and laborers who stand in the relation of renters to the erbexen, or are dependent upon them as wage workers. The Westphalian erbex or farmer is in possession of land to the extent on the average of 200 acres, a result of the mode of settlement, and is in a much more independent position than a peasant with intermixed holdings. The individual farmstead system dominates from the Weser to the Dutch coast and thus embraces the main territory of the Salic Franks.

In the southeast the German settlement region abuts on that of Alpine husbandry and on the territory of the South Slavs. The Alpine husbandry is based entirely on cattle raising and grazing, and the common pasture or almend is of predominant importance. All economic regulations are therefore derived from the necessity of "stooling" (*Schatzung, Seyung*), that is, the control of opportunity for sharing the utilization of the pasture by those entitled to it. Stooling involves division of the pasture into a number of "strikes" (*Stösze*), a strike being the amount of pasture necessary to support one head of stock through the year.

The economic unit of the South Slavs in Servia, in the

Banat and also in Croatia, is in historical times not the village but the house community or *zadruga,* the age of which is a disputed point. The zadruga is an expanded family living under the leadership of a male head of the house and including all his descendants, often with married couples numbering up to forty or eighty persons, and carrying on economic life on a communistic basis. They do not indeed ordinarily live under a single roof, but in production and consumption they act as a single household using the "common kettle."

In the southwest the Germanic rural organization came in contact with the remains of the Roman method of distributing the land, in which we have the seigniorial estate in the midst of small dependent establishments of colons. In lower Bavaria, Baden, and Wurtemberg there came to be a considerable mixture of these two systems, and especially in the upland and hilly districts the Germanic system tends to disappear. There are mixed holdings but on the other hand it also happens that the cleared land of the village falls into unified sections in which the possessions of the individual lie in divisions without there being any effort at equality in sharing or any discoverable principle of division. The origin of this "hamlet distribution," as Meitzen calls it, is uncertain; it may have originated through the granting of land to unfree persons.

The origin of the specifically Germanic agricultural system is obscure. In the time of the Carolingians it is already present, but the division of the open field into equal strips is too systematic to be primitive. Meitzen has shown that it was preceded by another system, a division into so-called *Lagemorgen* ("locus acres"). The *Lagemorgen* designates that quantity of land, varying widely according to the quality of the soil, the "lie" of the field, distance from the dwelling lot, etc., around which a peasant could plow with a yoke of oxen in a forenoon. The Lagemorgen thus forms the basis of the open field or Gewann, which always shows this irregular form wherever the old division has survived, in contrast with the geometrical form given to it by later division into strips of equal size.

This view rejects the recent attempt of Rietschel to prove a military origin for the German land and tillage system. According to this theory, the system developed out of the organization into "hundreds." It holds that the hundred was at the same time a tactical unit and a political grouping of about a hundred hide-men, whose holdings must have been at least four times as large as the later community hide. The central figure of the organization would be available for military service, since they lived on an income derived from the labor of their serfs and could be spared from the community. Thus the hide (*Hufe*), like the later Anglo-Saxon *hyde,* was an ideal unit, suitable for carrying the burden of supporting a full-armed mounted warrior. Out of a hide organization of this sort, it is argued, grew the community hide by a process of rationalization, through the division of the holdings of the great hidemen into four, eight or ten parts. It is decidedly against this theory that the field divisions of the German hide organization did not originate by any rational process, but grew out of the Lagemorgen. On the other hand, there remains the difficulty that in northern France the hide organization arose only in the territory over which the Salic Franks extended their conquests, and not in the territory which belonged to them originally.

The original German settlement form no longer survives. Its disintegration began rather early, and not as a result of steps taken by the peasants, who were not in a position to make such changes, but through interference from above. The peasant very early fell into a position of dependence

upon a political superior or feudal overlord; as a community hide-man (*Volkshufner*) he was weaker in an economic and military sense than the royal hide-man. After
the establishment of permanent peace, the nobility took an
increasing interest in economic affairs. It was the managerial activity of a portion of the nobility which destroyed
the rural organization, especially in south Germany. The
imperial abbey of Kempten, for example, began in the 16th
century the so-called "enclosures" (*"Vereinödungen"*)
which were continued into the 18th century. The cleared
land was re-distributed and the peasant placed upon his
compacted and enclosed farm (the so-called *Einödhof*)
and as nearly as practicable in the center of it. In north
Germany the state set aside the old distribution of land in
the 19th century, in Prussia by the ruthless use of force.
The "Gemeinheitsteilungsordnung" or Decree for the Division of Communities, of 1821, which was intended to
force the transition to an exchange economy, was issued
under the influence of liberal ideas opposed to mixed
holdings, and the common mark, and pasture. The community with mixed holdings was set aside by compulsory
unification and the common pasture or almend distributed.
Thus the peasant was forced into an individualistic economic life. In south Germany the authorities were content
with the so-called "purification" of the common field system. To begin with, a network of roads was laid out between the different field divisions. As a result there were
many exchanges among individual holdings looking toward
consolidation. The almend remained, but as winter feeding of stock was introduced, it was extensively transformed
into arable, which served as a source of supplementary income for individual villagers or as provision for old age. In
Baden especially, this development was characteristic.
Here the aim towards secure provision for the population

was persistently dominant and led to an especially dense settlement. Bounties on emigration even had to be granted, and finally in places the situation gave rise to attempts to separate old settlers and place those later admitted to rights of common in special almend communities within the village community.

Many students have seen in the German rural organization the echo of an original agrarian communism uniformly valid for all peoples, and have sought elsewhere for examples which would permit them as far as possible to reason back beyond the German system to stages no longer historically accessible. In this effort they have thought to find in the Scotch agricultural system down to the time of the battle òf Culloden (1746)—the "runridge system"— a resemblance to the German system which would permit of inferences as to primitive stages. It is true that in Scotland the arable was divided into strips, and holdings intermingled; there was also the common pasture; thus far there is real resemblance to Germany. But these strips were re-distributed by lot annually or at definite times, so that a diluted village communism arose. All this was excluded in the German *Lagemorgen*, which lies at the basis of the oldest German field division accessible to us. Along with this arrangement, and frequently as a part of it, there arose in the Gaelic and Scotch regions the *"cyvvar,"* the custom of communal plowing. Land which had been in grass for a considerable time was broken up with a heavy plow drawn by eight oxen. For this purpose the owner of the oxen and the owner of a heavy plow, generally the village smith, came together and plowed as a unit, with one to guide the plow and one to drive the oxen. The division of the crop took place either before the harvest or after a joint harvest.

The Scotch system of husbandry was distinguished from

the German by the further fact that the zone of arable was divided into two sub-zones. Of these the inner was manured and tilled according to a three-field rotation, while the outer was divided into from five to seven parts, only one of which was put under the plow in any one year, while the remaining ones were in grass and served as pasture. The character of this "wild field grass" husbandry explains the development at the time, of plow associations, while inside the inner zone the individual Scotchman farmed on his own account like the German peasant.

The Scotch agricultural system is very recent and indicates a high development of tillage; for the original Celtic system, we must go to Ireland. Here agriculture was originally based entirely on cattle raising, due to the fact that, thanks to the climatic conditions, cattle could remain in the open throughout the year. The pasture land is allotted to the house community (*"tate"*) the head of which ordinarily owns from 300 upward head of stock. About the year 600, agriculture declined in Ireland and the economic organization underwent a change. As before, however, the land was not permanently assigned, but for a lifetime at the longest. Redistributions were made by the chieftain (tanaist) down as late as the 11th century.

Since the oldest form of Celtic economy of which we know anything is exclusively connected with cattle raising, little conclusion can be drawn from it, or from the Scotch cyvvars, in regard to the primitive stages of Germanic husbandry. The typical German agricultural system, as known to us, must have originated in a period when the need for tillage and for stock raising were approximately equal. Perhaps it was just coming into being at Cæsar's time, and apparently at Tacitus' time wild field grass husbandry predominated. However, it is difficult to work with the statements of either of these Roman writers, of whom Tacitus especially arouses suspicions by his rhetorical embellishment.

In sharp contrast with the German land system is that of the Russian mir (opschtschina). This dominated in Great Russia, but only in the inner political districts, while it was absent in the Ukraine and in White Russia. The village of the Russian mir is a street village, often of remarkable extent, including up to three or five thousand inhabitants. Garden and field lie behind the dwelling lot. Newly founded families settle at the end of the row of allotments. Besides the arable there is utilization of a common pasture. The arable is divided into fields and these again into strips. In contrast with the German land system these are not in Russia rigidly assigned to the single dwelling, but the allotment takes into account how many mouths or how much labor force a dwelling musters. According to the number of these, strips in proportion are assigned, and hence the assignment cannot be final but only temporary. The law contemplated a twelve year interval of redivision but in fact it usually took place oftener, every one, three, or six years. The right to the land (*nadyel*) pertained to the individual soul and related not to the house community but to the village. It was perpetual; even the factory worker whose forefathers had emigrated from the mir generations before might come back and assert the right. Conversely, no one could leave the community without its consent. The nadyel found expression in the right to a periodical redivision. However, the equality of all members of the village usually existed on paper only, as the majority required for a redistribution was almost never obtainable. In favor of redivision was every family which had increased in a large ratio; but there were other interests arrayed against them. The decision of the mir was only nominally democratic; in reality it was often capitalistically determined. In consequence of the need for provisions the single households were usually to a varying extent in debt to the village bourgeoisie or "kulaks," who held the mass of the propertyless in their power through money lending. According to whether they were interested in keeping their debtors poor or allowing them to acquire more land, they controlled the decision of the village when redivision was in question.

Concerning the economic workings of the mir there were two opinions down to the dissolution of the system in Russia. One view saw in it, as contrasted with an individualistic rural organization, the salvation of economic life. It regarded the right of each emigrant worker to return to the village and demand his portion as the solution of the social question. Holders of this view admitted that obstacles were opposed to progress in agricultural methods, and otherwise, but asserted that the right of the nadyel compelled the inclusion of everyone in an advance. Their opponents regarded the mir as a hindrance to progress unconditionally, and the strongest support of reactionary czaristic policies.

The threatening growth in power of the social revolutionaries at the beginning of the 20th century led to the destruction of the mir. In his agrarian reform legislation of 1906–07, Stolypin gave the peasants the right to withdraw from the mir under specified conditions and to demand that their portion be granted them free from liability to later re-apportionment. The share of a withdrawing member had to be in unified form, a single piece of land, so that, similar in principle to the enclosures of Allgau, the farmers were scattered, each individual being placed in the midst of his holding to carry on individually. Thus came to pass the result which Count Witte as minister had demanded, namely, the destruction of the mir. The liberal parties had never dared to go so far, or, like the Cadets, had believed in the possibility of reforming it. The immediate result of Stolypin's agrarian reform was to make the more well-to-do peasants, those in possession of considerable capital, and those who had relatively much land in proportion to the members of the family, withdraw from the mir, and the Russian peasantry was split into two halves. One half, a class of wealthy large farmers, withdrew and went over to a system of individual farms; the other, much more numerous, which was left behind, already possessed too little land and found itself robbed of the right of redistribution and hopelessly given over to the status of a rural proletariat. The second class hated the first as violators of the divine law of the mir; the latter was driven over to unconditional support of the existing regime, and if the World War had not intervened would have furnished a new support and "cudgel guard" for czarism.

Russian scholarship is divided in regard to the origin of the mir. According to the most generally accepted view, however, it was not a primitive institution but a product of the taxation system and of serfdom. Until 1907 the individual member of the mir not only held against the village his nadyel right, but the village reciprocally held an unquestionable claim to his labor power. Even when he had gone away with the permission of the headman of the village, and taken up an entirely different calling, the village could call him back at any time to impose upon him his share of the common burdens. These burdens arose especially in connection with the amortization of the indemnity for the release from serfdom and the purchase price of freedom from taxation. On good land the peasant would obtain a surplus above the share of these burdens falling to him; consequently the town laborer not infrequently found it to his interest to return unsolicited to the village, and the mir often paid, in such cases, an indemnity for relinquishment of the nadyel. But where taxes were too high and indicated a possibility of higher earnings elsewhere, the tax burden was increased for those who remained behind, since it was a joint obligation. In this case the mir would force its members to return and take up their life as peasants. Consequently, the solidarity limited the individual member's freedom of movement and amounted merely to a continuation through the mir of the serfdom which had been abolished; the peasant was no longer a serf of the lord but a serf of the mir.

Russian serfdom was unusually harsh. The peasants were subject to torture; an inspector every year joined pairs of marriageable age together and outfitted them with land. In relation to the overlord there were only traditional rights, no enforceable law; he could undo the arrangement at any time. In the period of serfdom the redivision was carried out, either, in the case of poor land, according to the number of workers in the individual peasant's household, or in the case of good land, according to the number of mouths. The obligation to the land dominated over the right to the land, while in the one case as in the other the community was held jointly for the payments to the overlord. At the same time the Russian manor exploited the peasants down to the present day to the extent that the overlords furnished almost nothing, but tilled the land with the capital and horses of the peasant. The land was either leased to the peasants or tilled under the direction of the lord's bailiff with forced labor by the peasants and their teams.

Joint liability to the overlord, and serfdom, have existed only since the 16th and 17th centuries. Out of them developed the custom of redividing the land. The custom of redivision did not arise in the Ukraine and those parts of

Russia, especially in the west, which were not brought under Muscovite domination in the 16th and 17th centuries. Here the land was permanently assigned to the separate dwellings.

On the same principle of joint liability was based the economic system followed by the Dutch East India Company in their possessions. The company made the *Desa* or community jointly responsible for the dues of rice and tobacco. This joint liability led to the result that the community would finally compel the individual to remain in the village to help pay the taxes. With the abandonment of joint liability in the 19th century, the community with compulsory membership was also allowed to decline.

The economic system included two methods of rice culture, the dry culture (*tegal*) which was relatively unproductive, and wet culture (*sawah*) under which the field was surrounded with dykes and sub-divided within to control the running off of the water collected for the purpose. One who had established a sawah held an hereditary inalienable property right to it. The tegal land was subject to a nomadic husbandry similar to the wild field grass economy of the outer zone in the Scotch village community. The village cleared in common while the individual tilled and harvested singly. The cleared land was cropped from three to four years and then had to be put to grass while the village moved and broke up new land. The older conditions make it clear that only the ruthless and exploitative system of the Dutch East India Company brought about the system of redistribution.

The system introduced by the company gave place in the thirties of the last century to that of *Kultur-stelsel.* Under this system the individual had to cultivate one-fifth of his land for the benefit of the state, in which connection also the crop to be grown was prescribed. This system in turn disappeared in the course of the 19th century, giving place to a more rational mode of husbandry.

A similar system once obtained for a time in China,[4] according to the reports of the Chinese classical writers. The arable land was divided into tracts of nine squares each, of which the outer squares were assigned to individual families, the inner ones being reserved for the emperor. The family received the land only for use; at the death of the head of the house, redivision was carried out. This system was of only passing significance and dominated only in the neighborhood of large rivers where rice culture by flooding was possible. In this case also, the communistic organization of agriculture was dictated by fiscal considerations and did not arise out of primitive conditions. The original Chinese economic organization is found instead in the clan economy still common in the Chinese villages, where the clan has its little ancestral temple and its school and carries on tillage and economic life in common.

The last example of a supposed communistic agricultural system is that of India. Two different forms of village organizations are met with. Common to the two is the common pasture and a garden area corresponding to the tract of arable on which in the German system wage laborers and cottagers lived. Here are settled craftsmen, temple priests, (which in contrast with the Brahmins play only a subordinate role), barbers, laundrymen, and all kinds of laborers belonging to the village—the village "establishment." They hold on a "demiurgic" basis; that is, they are not paid for their work in detail but stand at the service of the community in return for a share in the land or in the harvest.[5] The villages differ in regard to land ownership. In the *ryotvari* village the land ownership is individual and the tax burden likewise. At the head of the village is a reeve. The peasants have no share in the common mark, which belongs to the king (rajah). One who wishes to clear land must pay for the privilege.

Another type is represented by the village placed under a "joint body," a community of a number of privileged nobles, a village aristocracy of full free-holders or hidemen without an individual head. These farmers (*"Erbexen"*) grant out the land and to them belongs the common mark; thus they stand between the true cultivators and the rajah. Within this category two classes of villages may be further distinguished: One is the *pattidari* village, where the land is definitively divided out and appropriated. On the death of the occupant his share goes to his descendants by blood and is redivided when it again passes by inheritance. The other is the *bhayachara* village. Here the land is distributed in accordance with the labor force or the rank of the individual holders. Finally, there are also villages in which an individual is in complete control as tax farmer and overlord. These are *zamindari* villages, and the *pattidari* villages also developed through the partition of feudal holdings. The special feature of Indian conditions is that a large number of rent collectors have intervened between the sovereign and the peasantry through the farming out and re-farming of the taxes. Frequently a chain of four or five rent receivers will have originated in this way. Within this group of rent receivers and large farmers a nominal communism has been evolved. Where several peasants carry on a communistic husbandry they divide the harvest, not the land, and the rent is apportioned among the owners entitled to share. Thus, this case of agrarian communism also traces its origin to fiscal considerations.

In Germany, again, students thought to find in the holdings called *"Gehöferschaften"* of the Moselle the remains of a primitive agrarian communism, until Lamprecht recognized their true character. Down to the present these holdings have consisted chiefly of woodland, but they formerly contained also meadow and arable which were divided out after the manner of common fields, periodically and by lot. This arrangement is not primitive, but arose out of seigniorial policies. Originally the *Gehöferschaft* was a manorial farm or estate which was tilled by the labor of small peasants, members of the mark community. But when the overlords became knights and were no longer in a position to direct operations personally, they found it more advantageous to enlist the self-interest of the peasants, and granted them the land on the terms of a fixed rent. Here again we meet with the principle of joint obligation. The mark organization either undertook a definitive division of the interests, or redistributed periodically by lot.

Not all of these examples serve to prove the thesis of Laveleye that at the beginning of the evolution agrarian communism existed in the sense of communistic husbandry, and not merely that of joint ownership of the soil—two things which must be carefully distinguished. This is not the case since, in fact, husbandry was not originally communal. Here there is a sharp conflict in viewpoint. While the socialistic authors view property as a fall from grace into sin, the liberals carry it back wherever possible to the time of the putative ancestors of the population. In reality, nothing definite can be said in general terms about the economic life of primitive man. If we seek an answer in the relations of populations untouched by European influences, we find no unanimity but ever the sharpest contrasts.

In primitive agricultural life, the so-called hoe-culture predominates. Neither plow nor beasts of burden are used;[6] the implement of tillage is a pointed stick, with which the man goes about over the land and makes holes in which the woman drops the seed. With this method, however, quite different forms of organization may be associated. Among the Guatoes in the interior of Brazil, individual economy is found with no reason for assuming the previous existence of any other organization. Every household is self-sufficient, without specialized division of labor among them, and with limited specialization among the members of the household, and also with limited exchange relations between tribes. The opposite extreme is the assembly of work in a large central dwelling, as in the long-house of the Iroquois. Here the women are herded together under the leadership of a head woman who apportions the work, and likewise the product, among the separate families. The man is warrior and hunter, and undertakes in addition the heavy tasks, clearing the land, building the house, and finally herding the cattle. The latter counted originally as an exalted occupation because the taming required strength and skill. Later, the esteem in which it is held is traditional and conventional. We find similar conditions in all parts of the earth, especially among negro tribes; everywhere among these the field work falls to the women.

CHAPTER II

(A) FORMS OF APPROPRIATION

The forms of appropriation are quite as diverse as the forms of husbandry. The proprietorship everywhere vests originally in the house community; but this may be either the individual family, the zadruga of the South Slavs, or a still larger association, as for example that of the Iroquois long-house. Appropriation may be carried out on two different bases. Either the physical means of labor, especially the soil, are treated as implements, in which case they frequently appertain to the woman and her kindred; or, the land is treated as "spear land," territory which has been conquered and is protected by the man; in this case it belongs to an agnatic clan or some other masculine group. In any case purely economic considerations do not uniquely determine the form of primitive appropriation and division of labor, but military, religious, and magical motives also enter.

In the past the individual had to adjust himself to a plurality of organizations to which he belonged. The following are the types:

1. *The Household.* Its structure is diverse but it was always a consumption group. The physical means of production, especially movable goods, might also pertain to the house group. In that case appropriation might be carried farther within the group, the weapons and masculine accoutrements for example belonging to the man, with a

26

special mode of inheritance, the articles of adornment and feminine accoutrements to the woman.

2. *The Clan.* This also may hold goods in varying degrees of proprietòrship. It may own the land; in any case, the members of the clan regularly keep as a remnant of originally widely extended property rights certain claims against the possessions of the house community, such as the requirement for its consent in case of sale, or a prior option to purchase. Further, the clan is responsible for the security of the individual. To it pertains the duty of avenging, and of enforcing the law of vengeance. It also has a right to share in head money, and a joint proprietorship over the women belonging to the clan, hence, a share in bride purchase money. The clan may be masculine or feminine in constitution. If property and other rights pertain to a masculine clan we speak of paternal succession or agnation, otherwise of maternal or cognation.

3. *Magic Groupings.* The most important group is the totem clan which arose at a time when certain beliefs in animism and spiritual entities were dominant.

4. *The Village and Mark Association,* essentially economic in significance.

5. *The Political Group.* This organization protects the territory occupied by the village and consequently possesses extensive authority in connection with the settlement of the land. In addition it requires of the individual military and court services, giving him corresponding rights;[1] it also enforces the feudal services and taxes.

The individual must also take into account under different conditions the following: 6. *Overlordship of land,* when the soil which he tills is not his own. 7. *Personal overlordship* when the individual is not free but is in bondage to another.

Every individual German peasant stood in the past in relation to an overlord of land and person, and to a political sovereign, one or more of whom had some claim to his services. Agricultural development took various forms according as these different persons were distinct or identical; in the former case, the rivalry of the different overlords favored the freedom of the peasant, while in the latter the trend was toward servility.

(B) THE HOUSE COMMUNITY AND THE CLAN

Today the house community or family household is commonly a small-family, that is, a community of parents and children. It is based on legitimate marriage presumed to be permanent. The economic life of this small family is unitary in regard to consumption, and at least nominally distinct from the productive organization. Within the household all property right vests in the master of the house as an individual, but is limited in various ways in regard to the special belongings of the wife and children. Kinship is reckoned alike on the paternal and maternal sides, its significance being practically limited to the matter of inheritance. The concept of the clan in the old sense no longer survives; only rudiments of it can be recognized in the right of collateral inheritance, and even here there is a question as to the age and the history of these relations.[2]

The socialistic theory proceeds from the assumption of various evolutionary stages in the marriage institution. According to this view the original condition was one of spontaneous sex promiscuity within the horde (endogamy), corresponding to the complete absence of private property. Proof of this assumption is found in various alleged survivals of the original conditions: in religious institutions of an orgiastic character among primitive peoples, meat, alcohol, and narcotic orgies, in which the restraints upon sexual relations disappear; in freedom of sexual relations before marriage, for women as well as men, such as is found among various peoples; in the sexual promiscuity of the hieroduli of the ancient east who gave themselves indiscriminately to any man; finally, in the institution of the levirate found among the Israelites and in various places and involving the privilege and duty of the clan brother to marry the widow of a deceased man and provide him with heirs. In this arrangement is seen a remnant of primitive endogamy which is supposed to have become gradually narrowed down to a claim upon a particular individual.

The second evolutionary stage according to this socialistic theory is group marriage. Definite groups (clan or tribe) form a marriage unit in relation to other groups, any man of the one being regarded as the husband of any woman of the other. The argument rests on inference from the absence of terms for any kinship except that of father and mother among Indian peoples; at a certain age these terms are applied indiscriminately. Further evidence is drawn from isolated cases of marriage groups in the South Pacific Islands where a number of men possess simultaneous or successive sexual rights over a particular woman, or conversely a number of women over a particular man.

Socialistic theory considers the "mother right," (*Mutterrecht*) as a fundamental transition stage. According to the theory, at a time when the causal connection between the sexual act and birth was unknown, the house community consisted not of families but of mother-groups; only the maternal kinship had ritualistic or legal standing. This stage is inferred from the widespread institution of the "avunculate" in which her mother's brother is the woman's protector and her children inherit from him. The matriarchate was also regarded as a developmental stage. Under this arrangement, met with in various communities, the distinction of chieftainship was fixed exclusively in the woman, and she was the leader in economic affairs, especially those of the household community. From this condition it was supposed that the transition to father-right took place through the institution of marriage by capture. Beyond a certain stage, the ritualistic basis of promiscuity was condemned and exogamy displaced endogamy as a general principle, that is, sexual relations became restricted to persons in other groups, involving commonly the obtaining of the woman from these groups by violence. Out of this practice should have developed marriage by purchase. An argument for this course of development is found in the fact that even among many civilized peoples who have long since gone over to contractual marriage the marriage ceremonies still symbolize forcible abduction. Finally, the transition to patriarchal-law (*Vaterrecht,* father-right) and legitimate monogamy is in socialistic thinking connected with the origin of private property and the endeavor of the man to secure legitimate heirs. Herein takes place the great lapse into sin; from here on monogamous marriage and prostitution go hand in hand.

So much for the theory of mother-right and the socialistic doctrine based upon it. Although it is untenable in detail it forms, taken as a whole, a valuable contribution to the solution of the problem. Here again is the old truth exemplified that an ingenious error is more fruitful for science than stupid accuracy. A, criticism of the theory leads to consideration first of the evolution of prostitution, in which connection, it goes without saying, no ethical evaluation is involved.

We understand by prostitution submission to sexual relations for a price, in order to secure a money income, and as a regular profession. In this sense prostitution is not a product of monogamy and private property, but is of immemorial age. There is no historical period and no stage of evolution in which it is not to be found. It is unusual in Mohammedan civilization and is absent among a few primitive peoples, but the institution itself and punishment for both homosexual and heterosexual prostitution are found among the very peoples pointed out by the socialistic theorists for the absence of private property. Always and everywhere the profession is segregated as a social class and generally given an outcast position, with exceptions in the case of sacerdotal prostitution. Between professional prostitution and the various forms of marriage may intervene all possible intermediate arrangements of permanent or occasional sexual relations, which are not necessarily condemned ethically or legally. While today a contract providing for sexual pleasure outside of marriage is void, *turpi causa*, in the Egypt of the Ptolemies there was sexual freedom of contract with enforceable exchange by the woman of sex gratification for sustenance, rights in estates, or other considerations.

Prostitution, however, not only appears in the form of an unregulated sexual submission but is also met with in the sacramentally regulated form of ritualistic prostitution, as for example, the hieroduli in India and the ancient east. These were female slaves who had to function in the temple in connection with the religious services, of which a part consists in their sex orgies. The hieroduli are also found submitting themselves to the public for pay. The institution of the hieroduli goes back to sacerdotal sources, to animistic magic of a sexual character, which has a way of running into sexual promiscuity in view of the progressive self-excitement of an ecstatic situation.

Copulation as a form of magic for stimulating fertility is widespread among agricultural peoples. The sexual orgy was even carried out on the ground itself with the expectation of increasing its productivity. Out of participation in this sacramental process arose in India the calling of the bayaderes which play an important role in the cultural life of India as free hetaerae, similar to the Greek women so designated. But in spite of the favorable conditions of their lives they ranked as outcasts, and as is shown by the Indian bayadere dramas, regarded it as the highest peak of good fortune to be elevated through a miracle to the class of married women living under very degraded conditions.

Besides the hieroduli there are found in Babylon and Jerusalem the temple prostitutes proper, whose principal clients were the traveling merchants. These kept to their occupation after its loss of sacramental and orgiastic character, under the protection of the material interests of the temple. The struggle against officially legitimatized prostitution, and its source the orgy, was carried on by the prophets and priests of the great religions of salvation, Zarathustra, the Brahmans, and the Prophets of the Old Testament. They carried on the fight partly on ethical and rational grounds; it was the battle of those who wished to deepen the inner life of man and saw in subjection to eroticism the greatest obstacle to the triumph of the religious motive. In addition, the rivalry of cults played a part. The God of ancient Israel was a hill God, not a chthonian deity like Baal, and the police power stood beside the priests in this struggle, as the state feared the rise of revolutionary movements of the lower classes out of the emotional excitement connected with orgiastic phenomena. Nevertheless, prostitution as such survived after the discontinuance of the orgy, which was under suspicion of the state; but it was outlawed and illicit. In the middle ages, in spite of the church doctrine, it had official recognition and was organized as a guild. In Japan also the occasional use of the tea-house girls as prostitutes continued down to the present and not merely has not caused them to lose caste, but has made them especially desired in marriage.

The reversal in the status of prostitution did not begin till the end of the 15th century, when it followed the serious outbreak of sexual diseases during the campaign of Charles VIII of France against Naples. From that time began its strict segregation while up to then it had been allowed to lead a mild ghetto existence. The outbursts of ascetic tendencies in Protestantism, especially in Calvinism, worked against prostitution, as did subsequently, but more mildly and cautiously, the rules of the Catholic church. The results were here similar to those of Mohammed and the makers of the Talmud who had likewise taken up the struggle against orgiastic practices.

An analysis of sex relations outside of marriage must distinguish between prostitution and the sexual freedom of woman. Sexual freedom for the man was always taken for granted, being first condemned by the three great monotheistic religions, and in fact not by Judaism until the Talmud. The originally equal sexual freedom of woman finds expression in the fact that among the Arabs at the time of Mohammed temporary marriage in exchange for support, and trial marriage, existed side by side, although permanent marriage was already recognized. Trial marriages are also found in Egypt and elsewhere. Girls of upper class families were especially reluctant to submit to the harsh domestic confinement of the patriarchal marriage, but clung to their sexual liberty, remaining in their parental homes and entering into contracts with men to whatever extent they pleased.

Beside this example of personal sexual freedom must be placed the possibility of the woman being exploited for gain by the clan and hired out in exchange for provisions. Sex hospitality, so-called, must also be recognized, that is, the obligatory giving of wife and daughters to honored guests. Finally, there developed concubinage, which is distinguished from marriage by the fact that it does not give complete legitimacy to the children. It is always conditioned by difference in social class and involves cohabitation across class barriers, after class endogamy has been established. In the period of the Roman Empire it had held full legal recognition, especially for soldiers, to whom marriage was forbidden, and for senators, whose marriage opportunities were limited by social class considerations. It was maintained during the middle ages and first absolutely forbidden by the Fifth General Lateran Council of 1515. But it was condemned by the Reformation churches from the beginning, and since that time has disappeared from the western world as a legally recognized institution.

Further investigation of the socialistic theory of mother-right shows that none of the stages of sexual life which it asserts can be shown to exist as steps in a general evolutionary sequence. Where they are met with, it is always under quite special circumstances. Promiscuity, where it exists at all, is either an especial phenomenon of an orgiastic character or a degenerative product of an older strict regulation of the sexual life. On the side of the mother-right theory, it must be admitted that the history of animistic religious belief shows that the connection between the act of generation and birth was not originally understood. In consequence, the blood bond between father and children was not recognized, just as today illegitimate children live under mother-right. However, purely maternal organizations under which children live with the mother alone, without the father, are not at all general, but occur only under quite specific conditions.

Endogamy within the house or brother and sister marriage is found as an aristocratic institution for maintaining the purity of the royal blood, as among the Ptolemies.

Priority of the clan, under which the girl must be offered to members of her clan before marrying outside of it, or their claim must be bought off, is explained by differentiation in wealth and is a defense against the dissipation of property. The levirate also does not correspond to primitive conditions, but arises from the fact that extinction of a male line was to be avoided on military and religious grounds; the family without a warrior must not be left barren and abandoned to die out.

After social stratification has appeared, class endogamy arises in the further sense that the daughters must be reserved for the members of a particular political or economic group. This was carried out within wide limits by the Greek democracy, in order to keep the property within the citizenship of the city and to monopolize political opportunities for the citizen class by restricting its multiplication.

Endogamy also takes the form of hypergamy, in the case where very intense class differentiation develops, as in the Indian caste system. While the man of a higher caste can enter into sex relations or marry below his level at will, this is forbidden to the woman. As a result the woman of a lower caste may be sold for money while on behalf of the girl of the higher caste, offers may be made to secure a man in exchange for money. The arrangements are made in childhood, and the man may be married to a number of women and be supported by their parents, travelling from one household to another. In India, the English government put an end to this condition, enforcing the support of the women on the part of the nominal husband. Wherever endogamy is found, it is to be assumed that it is a phenomenon of retrogression, not a stage of progress.

Exogamy with regard to the household has obtained everywhere and always, with few exceptions. It arises from the effort to forestall jealousy of the men within the household, and out of the recognition that growing up together does not permit a strong development of the sexual impulse. Exogamy of the clan is generally connected with animistic ideas belonging to the institution of totemism. That this ever spread over the world is, however, unproven, although it is met with in such separated regions as America and the Indian Archipelago. Marriage by capture is always regarded as illegal by the kindred affected, justifying blood revenge or exaction of head money, but at the same time is also treated as a knightly adventure.

The distinguishing mark of legitimate marriage according to patriarchal law, is the fact that from the standpoint of a certain social group only the children of a certain wife of the man in question have full legal standing. This social group may be of several kinds: 1. The house community; only children by marriage have the right of inheritance, not those of secondary wives and concubines. 2. The clan; only the children by marriage share in the institutions of blood vengeance, head money, and inheritance. 3. A military group; only children by marriage have the right to bear arms, share in booty or conquered territory, or in the distribution of land generally. 4. A class group; only children by marriage are full members of the class. 5. A religious group; only legitimate descendants are regarded as fit to carry on the ancestral ritual, and the gods will accept sacrifice only at their hands.

The possible arrangements other than legitimate marriage according to patriarchal law are the following: (1) The pure matriarchate. The father, recognized as legitimate head of the group, is absent; kinship is recognized only between the children and the mother or the kindred of the latter. Pure maternal groupings are found especially in connection with men's societies. (See below.) (2) Pure paternal (agnatic) groupings. All the children of a father have equal standing, including those of secondary wives, concubines, and female slaves, and also adopted children. Both children and women are subject to his unrestrained authority. Out of this condition developed legitimate marriage according to patriarchal law. (3) Succession in the maternal line in spite of a house community including both parents. The children belong to the mother's clan, not that of the father. This condition is found in connection with totemism and is a survival of the organization of the men's-house organization. (See below.)

(C) THE EVOLUTION OF THE FAMILY AS CONDITIONED BY ECONOMIC AND NON-ECONOMIC FACTORS

Treatment of this question calls first for a general survey of primitive economic life. The scheme of three uniformly distinct stages of hunting economy, pastoral economy, and agriculture, current in scientific discussion, is untenable. Neither purely hunting nor purely nomadic peoples are primitive, if they are met with at all, free from dependence upon exchange among themselves and with agricultural tribes. The primitive condition on the contrary is one of nomadic agriculture on the level of hoe-culture, and generally associated with hunting. Hoe-culture is husbandry without domestic animals and especially without beasts of burden; the plow represents the transition to agriculture in our sense. The domestication of cattle required a long period of time. It probably began with work animals, milk animals coming later, while still today there are regions in the East in which milking is unknown. Use of animals for meat followed both. As an occasional phenomenon, slaughtering is certainly older; it took place in a ritualistic connection for the purpose of the meat orgy. Last of all we find the taming of animals for military purposes. Beginning with the 16th century before Christ we meet with the horse which is used on the plains for riding, everywhere else as a draft animal; and the epoch of knightly chariot fighting, common to all peoples from China and India to Ireland, begins.

Hoe-culture could be carried on individually by the small family or with group labor, through the coming together of households even to hundreds of persons. The latter mode of husbandry is the product of a considerable development of technique. Hunting must originally have been carried on in common, though its socialization was the result of circumstances. The keeping of cattle could be carried on individually and must have been; in any case, the social groups engaged in it could not have been very large on account of the scattering of large herds over extensive areas. Finally, extensive agriculture could be carried on by all methods, but the clearing of land called for community action.

Cutting across these distinctions in the mode of husbandry is the form of the division of labor between the sexes. Originally, the tilling of the soil and the harvesting fell mainly to the woman. Only when heavy labor, with the plow instead of the hoe, was required, the man had to participate. In the house work proper, in which textiles take the leading place, the woman alone was involved. Man's work included also hunting, tending domestic animals as far as cattle were concerned—while the small animals were again the woman's province—wood and metal working, and finally and before all, war. The woman was a continuous worker, the man an occasional one; only very gradually, with the increasing difficulty and intensity of work, was he led on to continuous labor.

Out of the interaction of these conditions arise two types of communalization, on the one hand that of house and field work, and on the other that of hunting and fighting. The first centers around the woman and on the basis of it she often occupies a dominant social position; not infrequently she was in complete control. The women's house was originally the workhouse, while the socialization of hunting and fighting gave rise to the men's society. But whether the head of the household was a man or, as among the Indians, a woman, there was always a traditional bondage and a corresponding patriarchal position within the house. In contrast, the socialization of hunting and fighting was carried out under the leadership based on merit or charism of a chieftain chosen for this purpose. Not his kinship connections but his warlike and other personal qualities are decisive; he is the freely chosen leader with a freely chosen following.

Corresponding to the house community in which the economic activity of the women is carried on, is found the men's house. During a precisely limited period of life, embracing from 25 to 30 years, the men live together in a club-house apart from their families. From this as a center are carried on hunting, war, magic, and the making of weapons and other important iron implements. The young men frequently obtain wives by capture, carried out

in groups, so that the marriage has a polyandrous character, or they buy them. Women are forbidden to enter
the men's house, in order to guard its character of secrecy.
It is kept sacred by fear-inspiring surroundings, such as
the *duc-duc* of the South Pacific Islanders. The avunculate is regularly connected with the institution of the men's
house and often though not always with maternal kinship,
while exogamy of the clan regularly obtains. As a rule
also the group of men is divided into age classes. After a
certain age they withdraw from the men's house and repair
to the village and their wives. Generally the men's house
also recognizes a novitiate. At a certain age the boys are
taken out of the families, carried through magic procedures (circumcision being commonly included), receive
the consecration of young manhood, and take up their life
in the men's house. The place is a sort of barracks, a military institution giving rise on its disintegration to various
lines of development, as for example, a magical association
or a political secret society on the pattern of the Italian
Camorra. The Spartan ἀνδρειον, the Greek phratry, and
the Roman *curia* (*coviria*) are examples of the institution.

This primitive military organization did not everywhere
come into being and where it arose it disappeared quickly,
either through a course of demilitarization or through the
development of a military technique favorable to single
combat with the requirement of heavy weapons and a
special course of training for the warrior. Chariot and
horseback fighting worked especially in this direction. The
consequence was regularly that the men joined their
families, living with their wives, and military protection
was secured not through the communism of the men's house
but through an arrangement which gave the individual
warrior special rights in the land, enabling him to equip
himself. At this time the blood tie becomes of especial

significance, while accompanying it is the primitive theology of animism or belief in spirits, which everywhere in the world puts in its appearance in some form.

In the institution of the men's house is apparently to be sought the origin of totemism,[3] resting on animistic grounds, although later it becomes independent of the latter. The totem is an animal, a stone, an artefact, any object whatever, which is viewed as possessed by a spirit, the members of the totem group standing in animistic kinship with this spirit. When the totem is an animal, it must not be killed, for it is of the same blood as the community; and out of this prohibition grow various ritualistic food prohibitions. Those belonging to a totem form a culture union, a peace group, whose members must not fight among themselves. They practise exogamy, marriage between members of the totem being considered incestuous and expiated by terrible punishment. Thus one totem stands over against others as a marriage group. In this regard the totemic group is a ritualistic conception which often cuts through household and political groupings. Although the individual father lives in domestic communion with his wife and children, maternal succession is rather generally the rule, the children belonging to the mother's clan and being ceremonially alien to the father. This is the factual basis of the so-called matriarchate which is thus, along with totemism, a survival from the period of the men's house. Where totemism is absent we find a patriarchate, or paternal dominance with paternal inheritance.

The struggle of the growing tendency toward the patriarchate with an older maternal system might be decided according to the established land tenure. Either the soil was allotted in line with economic principles, that is, it was regarded as the work place of the woman, or in line with military principles, in which case it was viewed as the fruit of conquest and a subject for military protection. If the main burden of tillage fell on the woman, the land was inherited by the maternal uncle as guardian of the children. If on the contrary it was viewed as "spear land" the title rested in the military organization; the children were counted as belonging to the father, and a further consequence was the exclusion of the women from rights in the land. The military group sought to maintain the economic basis of military service on the part of its members by keeping the allotment of land as a function of the paternal clan. Out of this endeavor sprang the levirate as well as the law regarding female heirs, to the effect that the nearest of kin had the right and duty of marrying a female descendant who was the last of a line. This institution is met with especially in Greece.

The other possibility was that individual property relations decided between the patriarchate and a maternal organization. Between economic equals the older form of marriage was apparently exchange of wives;[4] especially as between households, youths exchanged their sisters. With differentiation in economic status, the woman is regarded as labor power and is bought as an object of value, as a work animal. The men who cannot buy a wife serve for her or live permanently in her house. Marriage by purchase and marriage through service, the one with patriarchal law and the other with maternal, may exist side by side and even in the same household; hence, neither is a universal institution. The woman always remains under the authority of a man, either in her own house community or in that of the man who has bought her. The marriage by purchase, like marriage through service, may be either polyandrous or polygamous. While the well-to-do buy wives at will, the propertyless, especially brothers, often club together for the purchase of a common wife.

Back of these relations is the "group marriage" which probably developed out of marriage barriers of a magical significance, as between totem groups or house communities. The man takes a group of sisters either one after the other or at the same time, or a number of women have to be taken over from the other house community, when they also become the property of the group thus "marrying" them. Group marriage occurs only sporadically and is apparently not a general stage in the evolution of marriage.

The wife obtained by purchase is regularly subject to the absolute patriarchal authority of the man. This supreme power is a primitive fact. It was always present in principle, as a characteristic of primitive peoples.

(D)   The Evolution of the Clan

The evolution of the clan will now be described. The Gaelic word clan means "blood kindred," and like the corresponding German word *Sippe* is identical with the Latin *proles*. Different sorts of clans are first to be distinguished.

(1) The clan in the sense of a magical kinship of the members with each other, with food prohibitions, rules for specific ritualistic behavior toward each other, etc. These are totemic clans.

(2) Military clans (phratries) are associations such as originally occupied a men's house. The control over descendants which they exercised has very extensive significance. An individual who does not go through the novitiate of the men's house and submit to the exacting practices and tests of strength connected with it, or who is not received into the cult, is in the terminology of primitive peoples a "woman" and does not enjoy the political privileges of men or the economic privileges which go

with them. The military clan maintains its earlier significance long after the disappearance of the men's house;
in Athens, for example, it is the group through which the
individual holds his citizenship.

(3) The clan as a blood kinship group of a certain scope.
Here the agnatic clan is most important and the present
discussion will relate solely to it. Its functions are, first
to perform the duty of blood vengeance against outsiders;
second, the division of fines within the group; third, it is
the unit for land allotment in the case of "spear land,"
and in Chinese, Israelitish, and old German law the agnates
possess down to historic times a claim which must be
satisfied before land can be sold outside the clan. The
agnatic clan is in this connection a select group; only the
man who is physically and economically competent to equip
himself for fighting is recognized as a clansman. One who
cannot do that must "commend" himself to an overlord
or protector, in whose power he also places himself. Thus
the agnatic clan practically becomes a privilege of property owners.

A clan may be organized or unorganized, the original
condition being rather intermediate. The clan had regularly an elder, although this is often no longer true in historical times. In principle he was only a *primus inter
pares*. He acted as arbiter in disputes between members
of the clan, and divided the land among them, proceeding,
to be sure, according to tradition rather than arbitrarily,
as the clan members either had equal rights or were subject
at least to a definitely regulated inequality. The type of
clan elder is the Arabian sheik, who controls his people
only by exhortation and good example, as the *principes*
of Tacitus' Germans rule more by example than by command.

The clan met very different sorts of fate. In the Occident it has completely disappeared, and in the Orient been just as completely maintained. In the period of antiquity the φυλαί and *gentes* played a large role. Every ancient city was composed originally of clans and not of individuals. The individual belonged to the city only as a member of a clan, a military organization (phratry) and an organization for the distribution of burdens (phylum). In India also, a membership in a clan is obligatory among the upper castes, especially the knightly caste, while the members of the lower and later established castes belong to a *devak,* that is, a totemic group. Here the significance of the clan rests on the fact that the land system is based on enfeoffment through the head of the clan. Thus we find here also a hereditary distinction or charism as the principle of land distribution. One is not noble because one possesses land, but conversely one has an inherited right to a share in the land because one belongs to a noble clan. In the feudal system of the Occident, on the other hand, the land is divided by the feudal lord, in independence of clan and kinship, and the fealty of the vassal is a personal bond. In China today the economic system is still semi-communistic and based on the clans. The clan possesses schools and storehouses within its separate village, maintains the tillage of the fields, takes a hand in matters of inheritance, and is responsible for the misdemeanors of its members. The whole economic existence of the individual rests on his membership in the clan, and the credit of the individual is normally the credit of his clan.

The disintegration of the clan took place as a result of two forces. One is the religious force of prophecy; the prophet seeks to build up his community without regard to clan membership. The words of Christ,—"I came not to send peace, but a sword. For I am come to set a man at variance against his father, and the daughter against her mother'' (Matthew 10:34–35); and "If any man come to me and hate not his father, and mother, and wife, and children, and brethren and sisters—he cannot be my disciple" (Luke 14:26) express the program of every prophet in regard to the clan as an institution. In the middle ages the church strove to abolish the rights of the clan in inheritance so that it might retain land willed to it, but it was not alone in this regard. Among the Jews, certain forces have worked quite similarly. The clan retained its vitality down to the exile. After the exile it is true that the plebeians were enrolled in the clan registers which had earlier been kept for the upper class families. But this division into clans disappeared later, probably because the clan, being originally military in character, had no roots in the demilitarized Jewish state and there remained only membership in a confessional group based on descent or on personal adhesion.

The second force which aided in the disintegration of the clan is the political bureaucracy. In antiquity, we find the greatest development of the latter in Egypt, under the New Empire. There no trace of the clan organization is left because the state does not tolerate it. In consequence, there is equality between man and woman and sexual freedom of contract; children receive as a rule the name of their mother. The royal power feared the clan and encouraged the development of the bureaucracy; the result of the process contrasts with that in China, where the state was not strong enough to break the power of the clan.

(E) EVOLUTION OF THE HOUSE COMMUNITY

The primitive house community is not necessarily a pure communism. There is frequently a considerable development of proprietorship, even over the children, and further especially over iron tools, and textile products. There is also a special right of inheritance of the woman from the woman and of the man from the man. Again we may find the absolute *patria potestas* as the normal condition, or it may be weakened by other organizations as for example the totemic group or the maternal clan. In one respect the house community is almost always a pure communism, namely in regard to consumption, though not in regard to property. From it as a basis proceed various courses of development, to various results.

The small family may evolve into an expanded household and this either in the form of a free community or in that of a manorial household, as the *oikos* of a landed baron or a prince. The first resulted generally where the centralization of work developed on economic grounds, while the manorial development resulted from political conditions.

Out of the house community developed among the South Slavs the zadruga, in the Alps the commune. In both cases the head of the household is generally elected and generally subject to deposition. The primary condition is pure communism in production. One who withdraws from the group forfeits all rights to share in its common possessions. Occasionally in other places, as in Sicily and in the Orient, a different course of development took place, the community being organized not communistically but on the basis of shares, so that the individual could always demand a division and take his portion wherever he cared to go.

The typical form of the seigniorial development is the patriarchate. Its distinguishing characteristics are the vesting of property rights exclusively in an individual, the head of the household, from whom no one has a right to demand an accounting, and further the despotic position inherited and held for life by the patriarch. This despotism extends over wife, children, slaves, stock, and implements, the *familia pecuniaque* of the Roman Law, which shows this type in its classical perfection. This *dominium* is absolute and it is a deviation from principle to speak in connection with the woman of *manus* or in connection with the children of *potestas*. The power of the house father extends with only ritualistic limitations to the execution, or sale of the wife, and to the sale of the children or to leasing them out to labor. According to Babylonian, Roman, and ancient German law, the father can adopt other children in addition to his own and into full equality with them. There is no distinction between female slave and wife or between wife and concubine, or between acknowledged children and slaves. The former are called *liberi* only because of the one distinction between them and slaves that they have a chance sometime to become heads of families themselves. In short, the system is that of a pure agnatic clan. It is found in connection with pastoral economy, also in cases where a knighthood fighting as individuals forms the military class, or finally, in connection with ancestor worship. Ancestor worship must, however, not be confused with worship of the dead; the latter may exist without the former, as for example in Egypt. Ancestor worship involves rather a union of worship of the dead with clan membership; on this union rested in China and Rome, for example, the invulnerable position of the paternal *dominium*.

The patriarchal house community no longer exists in its original condition, unmodified. Its breakdown resulted from the introduction of class endogamy, according to which the upper-class clans married their daughters only to equals and demanded that they receive a status superior to that of female slaves. As soon, moreover, as the wife ceased to represent primarily labor power—which also happened first in the upper classes—the man ceased to buy her as labor power. Then a clan which wished to marry off a daughter had to provide her with a dowry sufficient to maintain the standards of her class. The operation of the class principle gave rise to the distinction between legitimate, monogamous marriage, and the patriarchal *potestas*. Marriage with dowry became the normal marriage, the woman's clan stipulating that she was to be the head wife and that only her children could succeed as heirs. It is not true, as the socialistic theory has assumed, that the interests of the man in legitimate heirs for his property opened the way to the development of marriage. The man's desire for heirs could have been secured in numerous ways. It was the interest of the woman in having assured to her children the property of the man that was decisive. This development, however, by no means involved by absolute necessity, monogamous marriage. In general, partial polygamy persisted; in addition to a head wife secondary wives were kept, whose children possessed limited rights of inheritance or none at all.

Monogamy as the exclusive form of marriage first arose, so far as we know, in Rome, being ritualistically prescribed by the form of Roman ancestor worship. In contrast with the Greeks, among whom monogamy was known but remained very flexible, the Romans maintained it rigorously. To its support came later the religious power of the Christian commandments, and the Jews also, following the Christian example, established monogamy, but not until the time of the Carolingians. Legitimate marriage involved a distinction between concubines and the regular wife, but the female clan went farther in protecting the interests of the woman. In Rome it first carried through complete economic and personal emancipation of the woman from the man, in establishing the so-called free marriage, which

could be terminated at will by either party, and which
gave the woman complete control over her own property,
although she lost all right over the children if the marriage
was dissolved.   Even Justinian was not able to abolish this
institution.   The evolution of legitimate marriage from
the marriage with dowry is manifest for a long time in the
distinction found in many legal systems between marriage
with dowry and marriage without dowry.   Examples are
the Egyptians, and the Jews of the middle ages.

CHAPTER III

The small family may be the starting point of the development of a communistic household, but it may also evolve into the large-scale manorial household. Viewed in its economic relations, the latter is primarily the medium of development of agricultural proprietorship and hence of *Grundherrschaft*, the manor and feudalism.

The differentiation in wealth which lies at the base of this development has different sources. One is chieftainship, whether in the chieftain of a clan or of a military group. The division of the land among the members of the clan was in the hands of the clan chieftain. This traditional right often developed into a seigniorial power which became hereditary. The respect which a clan owed to such hereditary distinction was expressed in gifts and aids in connection with tillage and house building, request services to begin with, but developing into obligations. The leader in war might win the title to land through internal differentiation or through conquest outside the clan. Everywhere he has a privileged claim in the distribution of booty and in the division of conquered land. His followers also demanded privileged treatment in the allotment of land. This seigniorial land did not ordinarily share in the burdens of the normal field divisions—as, for example, in the ancient German economic system—but on the contrary was cultivated with the aid of the occupiers of the ordinary holdings.

Internal differentiation developed through the appearance of a professional military class, which resulted from the progress of military technique and improvement in the quality of military equipment. Neither the training nor the equipment were available for men in a dependent economic position. Thus arose a distinction between those classes which by virtue of their possessions were in a position to render military service and to equip themselves for the same, and those who could not do this and consequently were not able to maintain the full status of free men. The development of agricultural technique worked in the same direction as military progress. The result was that the ordinary peasant was increasingly bound to his economic functions. Further differentiation came about through the fact that the upper classes, skilled in fighting, and providing their own equipment, accumulated booty in varying degrees through their military activity, while the non-military men who could not do this became more and more subject to various services and taxes. These were either imposed by direct force or resulted from the purchase of exemptions.

The other course of internal differentiation is through the conquest and subjugation of some enemy people. Originally, conquered enemies are slaughtered, under some circumstances with cannibalistic orgies. Only as a secondary matter develops the practice of exploiting their labor power and transforming them into a servile class of burden bearers. Thus arises a class of overlords who by their possession of human beings are placed in a position to clear and till land, a thing impossible to the common freeman. The slave or servile population might be exploited communally, remaining in the possession of the group as a whole, and used for collective tillage of the soil, as was partly the case with the helots in Sparta; or, they might be utilized individually, being allotted to individual overlords for the tillage of their personal land holdings. This latter development establishes a nobility of conquest.

In addition to conquest and to internal differentiation must be recognized voluntary submission of the defenseless man to the overlordship of a military leader. Because the former needed protection he recognized a lord as *patronus* (in Rome) or as *senior,* among the Merovingian Franks. Thus he established a claim to representation before the court, as in the Frankish empire, to a champion in the trial by battle, or to the testimony of the lord instead of the compurgation of the clansmen. In return he furnished services or payments, the significance of which is not, however, the economic exploitation of the dependent. He can be called upon only for service worthy of a free man, especially for military service. In the last days of the Roman Republic, for example, various senatorial families in this way called out hundreds of their clients and colons against Cæsar.

The fourth mode of origin of seigniorial proprietorship is through land settlement under feudal terms. The chieftain with large possessions in human beings and work animals is in a position to reclaim land on a quite different scale from the ordinary peasant. But cleared land belonged in principle to him who brought it under tillage, as long as he was able to cultivate it. Thus the differential command over human labor power, where it appeared, worked indirectly as well as directly in the field of winning land for a seigniorial class. An example of such exploitation of a superior economic position is the patricians' exercise of the right of occupancy on the Roman *ager publicus.*

The seigniorial land, after it was broken up, was regularly utilized by the method of leasing. Leases were granted to foreigners,—for example to craftsmen, who then stood under the protection of the king or chieftain—or to impoverished persons. Where the latter are concerned we find, especially among nomadic peoples, the leasing of cattle also; otherwise in general the placing of settlers upon baronial land under obligation to make payments and render services. This is the so-called colonate, met with all over the East, in Italy, in Gaul, and also among the Germans. Money fiefs and grain fiefs, essentially loans, are also frequently a means to the accumulation of serfs and of land. Alongside the colons and slaves, the peons or *nexi* play a large role, especially in the economic life of antiquity.

Frequently there was an intermixing of those forms of dependency which grew out of clan relations with those deriving from seigniorial power. For landless men in the protection of an overlord, or for foreigners, membership in a clan was no longer in question and the distinctions between clan members, mark members, and members of the tribes disappear in the single category of feudal dependents. A further source in the development of seignorial claims is the profession of magic. In many cases the chieftain developed, not out of a military leader, but out of a rainmaker. The medicine man could lay a curse on certain objects, which then became protected by "taboo" against all molestation. The aristocracy of magic thus acquired priestly property, and where the prince allied himself with the priest he employed the taboo to secure his personal possessions; this is especially common in the South Sea Islands.

A sixth possibility for the development of seigniorial property is afforded by trade. Regulation of trade with other communities originally lies entirely in the hands of the chieftain, who at first is required to use it in the interests of the tribe. He makes it a source of income for himself by levying duties which, to begin with, are only

a payment for the protection he grants to foreign merchants, since he grants market concessions and protects
market dealings—for a consideration always, as need not be
said. Later the chieftain often goes on to trade on his
own account, establishing a monopoly by excluding the
membership of the community—village, tribe, or clan.
Thus he obtains the means of making loans, which are the
means of reducing his own tribesmen to peonage, and of
accumulating land.

Trade may be carried on by such chieftains according
to two methods: either the regulation of trade, and hence
its monopolization, remains in the hands of the individual
chieftain, or a group of chieftains unite to form a trading settlement. This case gives rise to a town, with a
patriciate of traders, that is, a privileged stratum whose
position rests upon the accumulation of property through
trading profits. The first is the rule among many negro
tribes, as on the coast of Kamerun. In Ancient Egypt,
monopolization of trade was typically in the hands of an
individual, the imperial power of the Pharaohs resting in
large part on their personal trade monopolies. We find
similar conditions among the kings of Cyrenaica, and later,
in part, in medieval feudalism.

The second form of chieftain trade, the development of a
town nobility, is typical for antiquity and the early middle ages. In Genoa, and in Venice on the Rialto, the noble
families settled together are the only full citizens. They
finance the merchants, without themselves taking part in
trade, through various forms of credit. The result is indebtedness of the other population groups, especially the
peasants, to the municipal patriciate. In this way arose
the patrician landed proprietorship of antiquity, alongside
that of military princes. Thus the ancient nations are
characterized as an assemblage of coast-wise towns with a

nobility of large land owners interested in trade. The culture of antiquity retained a coastal character down into the Greek period. No town of this older period lies farther than a day's journey inland. In the country, by contrast, were the seats of the baronial chieftains with their tenants.

Seigniorial property may also have fiscal roots, in the organization of taxation and the officialdom of the state, and under this caption there are two possibilities. Either there arose a centralized personal enterprise of the prince with separation of the administrative officials from the resources with which they worked, so that political power belonged to no one except to the prince, or else there was a class organization of the administration with the enterprises of vassals, tax farmers and officials, functioning in a subsidiary role alongside that of the prince. In the latter case, the prince granted the land to the subordinates who paid all the costs of administration out of their own pockets. According to the dominance of one or the other of these systems, the political and social constitution of the state would be entirely different. Economic considerations largely determine which form would win out. The east and the west show in this regard the usual contrast. For oriental economy—China, Asia Minor, Egypt,—irrigation husbandry became dominant, while in the west where settlements resulted from the clearing of land, forestry sets the type.

The irrigation culture of the Orient developed directly out of primitive hoe-culture, without the use of animals. Alongside it developed a garden culture with irrigation from the large rivers, the Tigris and Euphrates in Mesopotamia, and the Nile in Egypt. Irrigation and its regulation presupposed a systematic and organized husbandry out of which the large scale royal enterprise of the near east developed, as is shown most characteristically in the

New Empire of Thebes.   The military campaigns of the Assyrian and Babylonian kings, which they undertook with their masses of retainers going back to the men's house system, were primarily man hunts for the purpose of securing the human material for building canals and bringing stretches of the desert under tillage.[1]

The king retained control of water regulations, but required for its exercise an organized bureaucracy.   The agricultural and irrigation bureaucracies of Egypt and Mesopotamia, the foundation of which is thus economic, are the oldest officialdom in the world; it remains throughout its history an adjunct of the king's personal economic enterprise.   The individual officials were slaves, or dependents of the king, or even soldiers, and were often branded to prevent escape.   The tax administration of the king was based on payments in kind, which in Egypt were stored up in warehouses from which the king supported his officials and laborers.   Such a provision is the oldest form of official salary.

The result of the system as a whole was to place the population in a servile relation to the prince.   This relation found expression in the obligatory services of all the dependents and the joint liability of the village for the burdens imposed, and finally in the principle designated under the Ptolemies as ἰδία.   Under it the individual peasant was not only bound to the soil but to his village as well, and was in fact an outlaw if he could not prove his ἰδία.   The system obtains not only in Egypt but in Mesopotamia as well and also in Japan, where from the seventh to the tenth centuries we find the *ku-bun-den* system.   In the one case as in the other, the position of the peasant corresponds throughout to that of the member of the Russian mir.

Out of the obligatory services of the subject population

arose gradually the money economy centering in the prince. This development also might take various courses. One was through an individual economy with production and trade carried on by the prince; or, the prince made use of the labor power politically subject to him to produce goods not only for his own use but also for the market, as was the case in Egypt and Babylonia. Trade and production for the market would be carried on auxiliary to a large household, with no separation between household and industrial establishment. This is the type of economic organization which Rodbertus has designated as "oikos-economy."

This oikos-economy would again be the initial stage in various lines of development. One of these is the Egyptian system of grain banks. The Pharaoh possessed grain warehouses scattered over the land, to which the peasant delivered up not only his obligatory payments in kind but his whole production; against these the king could draw checks which he could put into use as money. Another possibility was the development of royal taxation in money, which however, presupposes a considerable permeation of the use of money into private economic relations, as well as a considerable development of production and a general market within the country; all these conditions were fulfilled in Ptolemaic Egypt. The system encountered difficulties, in view of the then state of development of administrative technique, in the preparation of a budget. Consequently, the ruler generally shifted the risk of the computation on to other shoulders, by one of three methods. Either he farmed out the collection of taxes to adventurers or officials, or he delegated it directly to soldiers, who paid themselves out of the receipts, or finally, he gave over the task to landed proprietors. The placing of the tax collection in private hands was a consequence of the lack of a dependable administrative machine, which again goes back to moral unreliability in the official personnel.

The practise of farming out taxes to adventurers also developed on the largest scale in India.[2] Every such *zamindar* has a tendency to develop into a landed proprietor. The recruiting of soldiers is also given over to contractors called *jagirdar*, who have to provide a certain quota irrespective of the elements of which it is composed; these also strive to become large landholders. Such proprietors are akin to the feudal baron living in full independence upward and downward, in a position analogous to that of Wallenstein, who also had to furnish recruits. When the ruler turns taxation over to officials, he fixes by agreement a definite sum; any surplus belongs to the official, who also has to pay the administrative staff. This is the system of the earlier mandarin administration in China, as well as of the satrap organization of the ancient east. With the transition to modern taxation policies, the Chinese statistics showed a sudden surprising increase in the population, which the mandarins had purposely understated. The third possibility under the head of a money economy centered in the prince, is the delegation of taxation to soldiers. This is a recourse of state bankruptcy and is done when the prince is unable to pay the soldiers. Resort to this device accounts for the transformation in the affairs of the Caliphate under the dominance of Turkish soldiers from the tenth century on. The soldiers develop into a military nobility because the central government no longer has, in fact, control over taxation, and extricates itself by turning the function over to the army.

These three forms of individualization of the originally political functions of securing money and recruits—centering them in private contractors, officials, or soldiers—became the basis of the oriental feudalism which developed

upon the disintegration of the money economy in consequence of the technical incompetence of the state to ad-
minister taxation through its own officials. The result is a
secondary, rationalized agrarian communism, with joint
responsibility of the peasant communities to the tax farmer,
official, or army, and with common tillage and attachment
to the soil. The contrast with the western system comes
out clearly in the fact that in the east no demesne economy
(*Fronhofwirtschaft*) arose, the exaction of forced payments dominating. A further feature is the liability
of collapse into a barter economy on the appearance of
the least difficulty in transforming the payments in kind
of the peasants into money. In such an event an oriental
political system falls back with extraordinary facility from
the condition of an apparently highly developed culture
into one of primitive barter economy.

As a fourth and last method of realizing a royal income,
we find the delegation of functions to chieftains or landed
proprietors. Thus the prince avoids the problem of an
administrative organization. He shifts the raising of the
taxes, and on occasion also that of recruits, upon already
existent agencies of a private character. This is what
happened in Rome when in the imperial period the civilization extended inland from the sea-coast and the country
became transformed from a union of primarily maritime
towns into a territorial empire. The inland knew only
manorial economy without the use of money. The functions of raising taxes and recruits were now imposed upon
it, whereupon the large landed proprietors, the *posses-
sores,* become the dominant class down to the time of
Justinian. The dependent population over which they
rule enables them to furnish the taxes, while the imperial
administrative system has not expanded in keeping with
the growth of the empire itself. On the side of administra-

tive technique, this situation is distinguished by the fact that alongside the *municipia* appear the *territoria,* at the head of which stand the landed barons, responsible to the state for taxes and recruits. Out of this condition developed the colonate in the west, while in the east the latter is as old as the *ιδία.* Under Diocletian this fundamental principle was extended to the empire as a whole. Every person was included in a territorial taxation unit which he was not permitted to leave. The head of such a district is generally a territorial lord, as the center of gravity of the economic and political life has shifted from the sea-coast to the land.

A special case of this development is the appearance of colonial proprietorship. Originally the interest in the winning of colonies is purely fiscal in character,—colonial capitalism. The objective, pecuniary exploitation, was achieved through the conquerer making the subject natives responsible for taxes in the form of money or the delivery of products, especially food stuffs and spices. The state generally transferred the exploitation of the colonies to a commercial company,—for example, the British and Dutch East India companies. Since the native chieftains are made the intermediaries of the joint liability they are transformed into territorial lords, and the originally free peasantry into their serfs or dependents bound to the land. Attachment to the soil with feudal obligations and communal tillage, with the right and duty of redistributing the land, all appear. Another form of the development of colonial proprietorship is the individual allotment of land by an overlord. The type of this is the *encomienda* [3] in Spanish South America. The encomienda was a feudal grant with the right of imposing on the Indians compulsory services, payments, or labor dues, and in this form it persisted to the beginning of the 19th century.

In contrast with the oriental system of individualizing political prerogatives on fiscal grounds and in relation to a money economy, stands the product economy of the western feudal system and that of Japan, with the development of feudal proprietorship through enfeoffment.[4] The ordinary purpose of the feudal system is the provision of a mounted soldiery through the granting of land and seigniorial rights to persons who are in a position to take over the services of vassals. It is met with in two forms, according as the proprietory power is granted as a fief or as a benefice.

For enfeoffment with benefice the organization of Turkish feudalism is characteristic. There was no recognition of a permanent individual proprietorship but only grants for life and in consideration of service in war. The grant was evaluated according to its yield, and proportioned to the rank of the family and to the military service of the recipient. As it was not hereditary, the son of the grantee succeeded only in case he could show specific military services. The Sublime Porte regulated all details as a sort of supreme feudal bureau, after the manner of the Frankish major domo.

This system is akin to that which originally obtained in Japan. After the 10th century Japan went over from the *ku-bun-den* system to one based on the benefice principle. The Shogun, a vassal and commander-in-chief of the emperor, with the aid of his bureau (*ba-ku-fu*) evaluated the land according to its yield in rice and granted it in benefices to his vassals the *daimios,* who in turn re-granted it to their ministerials, the *samurai.* Later, the inheritance of fiefs became established. However, the original dependence upon the Shogun persisted in the form of the latter's control over the administration of the *daimios,* who in turn supervised the operations of their vassals.

The Russian feudal system is nearer to the European. In Russia, fiefs (*pomjestje*) were granted on consideration of certain obligatory services to the czar and the assumption of tax obligations. The recipients of grants had to assume the position of military officers and civil officials, a specification which was first set aside by Catherine II. The transformation of the tax administration from the land to the poll basis under Peter the Great led to the result that the land holder became answerable for taxes in proportion to the number of souls on his holding, determined through periodical surveys. The results of this system for the agricultural organization as a whole have already been described (pp. 17 ff.).

Next to Japan, the medieval occident [5] is the region which developed feudalism in the highest purity. Conditions in the later Roman empire operated as a preparation, especially as to land tenure, which already had a half feudal character. The land rights of the Germanic chieftains fused into the Roman situation. The extent and significance of land holding was extraordinarily increased through the clearing and conquest of land—the victorious armies had to be fitted out with land—and finally through "commendation" on a large scale. The peasant who found himself without property, or who was no longer in a position to equip himself for military service, was compelled by the advance of military technique to place himself in the *obsequium* of an economically more powerful person. A further influence was the extensive transfers of land to the church. The decisive condition, however, was the invasion of the Arabs and the necessity of opposing an army of Frankish horsemen to that of Islam. Charles Martel undertook an extensive secularization of church property with a view to establishing, with the benefices created out of the seized tracts, a tremendous army of vassal knights, the members of which had to equip themselves as heavily armed horsemen. Finally, besides the land, it became the custom to grant as fiefs political offices and privileges.

CHAPTER IV

THE MANOR

The inner development of seignorial proprietorship, especially of the occidental manor,[1] was conditioned, in the first place, by political and social class relations. The power of the lord was composed of three elements, first, land holding (territorial power) second, possession of men (slavery) and third, appropriation of political rights, through usurpation or through enfeoffment; the last applies especially to judicial authority, which became far the most important single force in connection with the development in the west.

Everywhere the lords strove to secure "immunity" (*immunitas*) as against the political power above them. They forbade the officials of the prince to come upon their territory, or if they permitted it the official had to come directly to the lord himself for the performance of his mission on behalf of the political authority, such as collection of feudal dues or serving of military summons. With this negative aspect of immunity is connected a positive aspect. At least a part of the immediate exercise of rights taken away from the officials of the state became the prerogative of the holder of the immunity. In this form immunity exists not merely in the Frankish empire but before it in those of Babylonia, ancient Egypt and Rome.

Decisive is the question of appropriation of judicial authority. The holder of land and of men everywhere struggled for this prerogative. In the Moslem Caliphate he did not succeed; the judicial authority of the general government was maintained unimpaired. In contrast, the land holders of the west usually succeeded in their endeavors. In this part of the world the lord originally had unlimited judicial power over his slaves, while free persons were subject only to the jurisdiction of a popular court. For unfree persons the criminal process of the official court was final, though it was early true that participation by the lord could not be avoided. This distinction between free and unfree became effaced in the course of time, the power of the lord over slaves being weakened and that over free men being strengthened. From the 10th to the 13th century, the public courts increasingly interfered in the determination of cases affecting slaves; their criminal cases were often tried before the popular court. Especially from the 8th to the 12th century, the position of the slaves steadily improved. With the cessation of the great movements of conquest the slave trade declined and it became difficult to supply the slave markets. At the same time the need for slaves increased greatly, in consequence of the clearing of forests. To secure and retain slaves, the lord had progressively to improve their conditions of life. In contrast with the Latin *possessor,* he was primarily a warrior and not a farmer, and found himself hardly in a position to supervise his unfree dependents, so that on that ground also their situation improved. On the other hand (cf. page 63) his power over the free population was strengthened by changes in military technique, and resulted in the extension of the household authority of the lord, originally confined to the *familia,* over the whole extent of his territorial dominion.

There is a correspondence between free and unfree conditions of tenure and free and unfree persons. In this connection we must consider the *precaria* and the *beneficium.*

The *precaria* is a lease relation based on a documentary application, and entered into by free persons of every class. Originally it was terminable at will, but soon evolved into a contract renewable every five years but in fact for life and usually hereditary. The *beneficium* is an enfeoffment in exchange for services, originally of any form whatever, or under some conditions in exchange for payments. Later the *beneficium* differentiates into that of the free vassal, who bound himself to feudal services, and that of the free man who bound himself to service on the lord's demesne. In addition to these forms of lease there was a third, the land settlement lease, by means of which the overlord was in the habit of granting land for clearing against a fixed tax and into the hereditary possession of the grantee. This was the so-called quit-rent (*Erbzins*), which later made its way into the towns also.

Over against these three forms, all of which related to land situated outside the village community (*Gutsverband*), is the manorial estate (*Fronhof*) with the land dependent upon it, of which the *Capitulare de villis* of Charlemagne gives a clear picture.[2] Within the manor was first the seigniorial land, or demesne, including the *terra salica*, which was managed directly by the lord's officials and the *terra indominicata*, seigniorial holdings in free peasant villages; and second the holdings or hide land of the peasants. The latter fell into *mansi serviles* with unlimited services and *mansi ingenuiles* with limited services, according as hand labor or team work had to be rendered throughout the year or only in connection with tillage and harvest. The payments in kind and the whole product of the demesne—(called *fiscus* in the case of royal holdings) were laid up in a storehouse and used for the needs of the army and the seigniorial household, any surplus being sold.

A decided shift in the relations between free and unfree persons resulted from the establishment of territorially bounded limits of jurisdiction of the landlord and judge (socage districts or sokes—*Bannbezirke*). An obstacle to this at first was the scattered condition of the holdings; for example, the monastery of Fulda held some thousand scattered farms. From the early middle ages on, the holders of judicial and proprietory rights strove to consolidate their holdings. This was accomplished in part through the development of "real-dependency," the lord refusing to grant a particular piece of land unless the grantee submitted at the same time to personal suzerainty. On the other hand, there developed the manorial law, in consequence of the fact that within the jurisdiction and seigniorial farm free and unfree persons were thrown together. Manorial law reached its highest development in the 13th century. While originally the lord possessed judicial authority only over the unfree members of his *familia* and outside of this exercised authority over the territory of his "immunity" only on the basis of a royal grant, on his own holdings he had to deal with persons of various classes who were under obligation to render exactly the same services. Under these circumstances the free persons were able to compel the lord to join with all his dependents in forming a manorial court in which the dependent persons functioned as magistrates. Thus the lord lost the power of arbitrary control over the obligations of his dependents and these became traditionalized (similarly to the way in which the soldier councils tried to set themselves up on behalf of soldiers against officers in the German revolution). On the other hand, from the 10th to the 12th century was being evolved the principle that by the mere fact of a land grant the recipient became *ipso jure* subject to the judicial authority of the lord of the land.

The consequence of this development was the modification of the freedom on the one hand and servility on the other, of the dependent population. Modification of free status was politically conditioned by the judicial authority of the lord in connection with the unarmed state of the free men, which was due to economic causes, while the modification of unfree status resulted from the greatly increased demand for peasants for clearing the forests and in Germany for the colonization eastward. Both these circumstances enabled the unfree to escape the authority of the lords and put the latter in competition among themselves in granting favorable conditions of life to their dependents. In addition, the slave trade, and hence the new supply of slaves, had ceased, and the available servile persons had to be treated with consideration. In the same direction of elevating the dependent classes worked the political situation of the lords. The lord was not a farmer, but rather a professional soldier, and was not in a position to conduct agriculture effectively. He could not budget his affairs on the basis of a fluctuating income and was disposed toward a traditional fixation of the dues of his dependents and hence toward meeting them on a contractual footing.

Thus the medieval peasantry became strongly differentiated within and held together through the power of the lords and the manorial law. Alongside the dependent classes, there were free peasants outside the community circle of the lord's estate, on freehold land subject only to quit-rents, and hence essentially private owners. Over such persons the lord had no judicial authority. These free-holders never disappeared entirely, but were found in considerable numbers in only a few places. One of these is Norway, where feudalism never developed; they were called ''odal'' peasants, in contrast with the landless, unfree classes dependent upon them. Another such locality is the marsh lands of the North Sea,—Frisia and Ditmarsh; similarly in parts of the Alps, Tyrol, and Switzerland, and in England. Finally there are the "mailed peasantry" of many parts of Russia, who were individual proprietors; to them were added later the Cossacks as a plebeian soldier class with the social position of small farmers.

As a consequence of the development of feudalism, when the landed nobility began to collect the taxes, there arose exemption from taxation of the nobility itself, with liability to taxation on the part of the unarmed peasantry. To increase the military power of the territory, the French feudal law set up the principle of *nulle terre sans seigneur,* intended originally to increase the number of benefices as a guarantee of military strength; on the same principle rested the compulsory reinfeudations imposed by the German king in connection with every grant of land. This differentiation as regards liability to taxation formed the basis of the policy of the princes in maintaining the peasant holdings. They could not consent to having the hide land alienated from the peasant, as the area subject to taxation was thereby decreased. Thus the territorial princes adopted the system of protecting the peasantry and forbade the nobility to confiscate the peasant holdings.

Several economic results also followed: 1. The large household of the lord and small household of the peasant subsisted side by side. The dues of the peasants originally served only to satisfy the requirements of the lord and were readily fixed by tradition. The peasants had no interest in making the soil yield more than was necessary for their own maintenance and for covering their obligatory payments, and the lord had as little interest in increasing the payments, as long as he did not produce for a market. The mode of life of the lord was but little different from that of the peasant. Thus "the walls of his stomach set the limits to his exploitation of the peasant," as Karl Marx observed. The traditionally fixed dues of the peasant class were protected by manorial law and by community of interest. 2. Since on account of the taxes involved, the state was interested in maintaining the peasantry, the jurists took a hand, especially in France. The Roman law did not generally, as commonly supposed, work toward the disintegration of the old Germanic peasant law, but on the contrary was applied in favor of the peasantry, against the nobility. 3. The attachment of the peasantry to the soil. This followed, in so far as personal fealty arose, or in consequence of the tax obligation, when the lord became answerable for their taxes; to an increasing degree also the nobility established it by usurpation. The peasant could withdraw from the community only by forfeiting his land and by securing another man to take his place.

4. The rights of the peasant in the land became extraordinarily diversified. In the case of unfree tenants the lord generally had the right to resume the holding at death. If he renounced the exercise of this right, having no tenants to spare, he at least assessed special dues, the heriot, etc. Free tenants either held leases terminable at any time or were copy-holders with permanent rights. In both cases the legal position was clear, but the state often interfered to forbid the termination of grants—the so-called tenant right. Among the dependents, who as freemen had originally commended themselves to a lord, arose an attachment to the lord and of the lord to them in return. The lord could not simply dismiss the villein, but as early as the time of the Sachsenspiegel was compelled to pay him a small capital in money.

5. The lords regularly appropriated to themselves the common mark and often the common pasture or almend as

well. Originally, the chieftain was head of the mark organization. Out of the lord's right of supervision evolved
in the course of the Middle Ages a feudal proprietorship
over the mark and the common pasture of the village. The
peasant wars of the 16th century in Germany were waged
primarily against this usurpation, and not against excessive
payments and dues. The peasants demanded free pasture
and free woodland, which could not be granted as the land
had become too scarce, and fatal deforestation would have
resulted, as in Sicily. 6. The lord had established in his
own favor numerous "socage rights" or *banalités* (*Bann-
rechte*) such as a compulsion on the part of the peasant to
grind grain at the lord's mill, to use his bakery, his
oven, etc. These monopolies arose, to begin with, without compulsion; for only the lord was in a position to
erect mills or other institutions. Later, oppressive force
was used to compel their utilization. Besides these the lord
possessed numerous *banalités* in connection with hunting
and the transportation of goods. They grew out of obligations to the chieftain, transferred to the later judicial overlord, and were exploited for economic ends.

The exploitation of the subjugated peasantry by the lords
was carried out, with two exceptions, not by means of
forced labor, but by making them into rent-payers. The
only two exceptions in the world will be treated later, in
connection with the development of capitalistic economy
within the manor (cf. Chapter VI). The grounds for this
method of exploitation were in the first place the traditionalism of the lords. They were too lacking in initiative to
build up a business enterprise on a large scale into which
the peasants would have fitted as labor force. In addition,
as long as the cavalry was the core of the army, the lords
were bound by their obligations as vassals and could not be
spared for agriculture, while the peasant could not be

spared for war. Moreover, the lord possessed no movable capital of his own, and preferred to transfer the risk of active operations to the peasant. Finally, there was in Europe the restriction of manorial law which bound the lords, while in Asia the latter could not rely on sufficient protection on going over to production for the market, since there was nothing corresponding to the Roman law at hand. Here there was no development at all of the demesne (*Fronhof*) or in-land, farmed by the lord.

The lords secured rentals, in numerous ways: 1. Through feudal dues, which the free peasant paid in goods, the servile one in labor. 2. Through fees on occasion of a change in tenant, enforced by the lord as a condition of the sale of the holding. 3. Fees in connection with inheritance and marriage, imposed as a condition of transmitting the land to heirs or for the privilege of letting the peasant's daughter marry outside the lord's jurisdiction. 4. Fees in connection with woodland and pasture, as for mast in the forest. 5. Indirect rents secured by imposing on the peasant transportation charges as well as the burden of building roads and bridges. The collection of all these fees and payments was carried out originally through the "villication" system which represents the type of manorial administration for south and west Germany as well as for France, and is everywhere the oldest form of feudal organization for the exploitation of land. This system presupposes the scattering of holdings. The lord sets over each of his widely separated holdings (*Hufen*) a *villicus* or bailiff, whose duty it is to collect the payments from his neighbors who are dependents of the lord, and to hold them to the performance of their obligations.

CHAPTER V[1]

THE POSITION OF THE PEASANTS IN VARIOUS WESTERN
COUNTRIES BEFORE THE ENTRANCE OF CAPITALISM

France.—Originally there were slaves (*serfs*) and half-free persons side by side. The slaves may be *serfs de corps,* subject to unlimited services, and over whom the lord has absolute authority short of life and death, or they may be *serfs de mainmorte* with limited service and the right of withdrawal; but the lord has the right of resuming disposal over the land on the death or removal of the tenant. The half-free peasants or villeins have the right of transferring their lands, and render fixed services or payments—the sign of an originally free status. These relations underwent extensive transformations as a result of two sets of circumstances. In the first place, the numbers of the servile population were notably reduced by wholesale emancipations as early as the 12th and 13th centuries. This took place contemporaneously and in connection with the introduction of money economy. It was in accord with the selfish interests of the lord, since free peasants could be made to bear much heavier burdens of dues.

A further cause was the origin of peasant unions. The village community organized itself as a corporation which assumed a joint obligation for the rents of the lord, in return for full autonomy in administration, which autonomy was also protected by the king. Both sides obtained an advantage from the arrangement: the lord because he

74

had only one debtor to deal with, and the peasants because their power was enormously increased. Temporarily, the unions were even summoned to the Estates General.

The nobility found the change the more convenient the more they evolved—in contrast with the Prussian Junkers of the time—into a courtier nobility, a class of *rentiers* living far from the land and no longer representing any organization for work, so that they were easily eliminated from the economic organization of the country in a single revolutionary night.

Italy.—The original agrarian organization was in this case changed at an early date through the buying up of the land by the townsmen, or expropriation of the occupiers in connection with political turmoil. The Italian towns early did away with personal servitude, limited the services and payments of the peasants and introduced cultivation on the shares, not originally with capitalistic designs but to cover the needs of the proprietors. The share tenants had to furnish the table supplies of the patricians, each being under obligation to supply a different sort of product. The movable capital was regularly furnished by the propertied townsman, who did not wish to employ his wealth in capitalistic agriculture. This system of share tenantry distinguished Italy and Southern France from other countries of Europe.

Germany.—Northwestern and southwestern Germany and the adjacent parts of northern France were the region especially characterized by the *villication* organization, with scattered holdings, referred to at the close of the preceding chapter. From this as a beginning the development of agricultural organization proceeded by very different courses in the southwest and the northwest. In southwest Germany the *villication* system disintegrated. The rights of the lord to the land, to personal fealty, and the justiciary right, became transformed into a simple right to receive a rental, while only relatively few compulsory services and dues in connection with the transfer of inheritance remained as relics. The Rhenish or southwest German peasant thus became in fact his own master, able to sell his holding or transmit it to heirs. This came about primarily because manorial law developed its greatest power here and because holdings were extremely scattered; several land holders often lived in one village. Land holding, judicial authority, and liege-lordship were in different hands, and the peasant was able to play off one against the other. The chief gain which the land holders were able to secure in west and southwest Germany was the appropriation of large portions of the common mark, and to a much smaller extent, of the common pasture.

In northwest Germany the *villication* system was dissolved by the landholders. As soon as they saw a possibility of marketing their products they became interested in an increase in the income from the land and in securing holdings suited to production for the market. Consequently, at the time of the Sachsenspiegel, and even a little earlier, there were wholesale emancipations of the serfs. The land thus liberated was leased for definite periods to free renters called "Meier" whose property became hereditary under strong pressure from the state, which protected them against unexpected increases in rental. If the proprietor wished to evict a tenant, the state compelled him to secure another peasant, so that the tax revenue would not be decreased. The interest of the lords in large holdings led to a law of single inheritance, the lord forcing the assumption of the holding by an heir. As a rule the rent was paid in kind, while money payments took the place of the compulsory feudal services. In certain parts of Westphalia, serfdom had persisted, but only to the extent that the lord could resume a part of the inheritance on the death of the tenant. In the southeast,—Bavaria, the upper Palatinate and southern Wurtemberg—the property rights of the peasant were often insecure. A distinction was made between hereditary tenure (*Erbstift*) and non-hereditary (*Leibgeding*) and also between protected leases and unrestricted leases (*Schutzlehen* and *Vollehen*). The latter were only for life and permitted the lord to increase the payments at the death of a holder or to grant the holding to someone else. The lord himself usually stood out for the law of compulsory inheritance. The payments consisted of tithes, and fees on occasion of change of tenant. Their amount depended on the hereditary or non-hereditary character of the property. The labor dues were very moderate. Personal bondage was the rule down to the 18th century, but signified nothing beyond a very small and modest and variously limited obligatory payment to the personal overlord who was often separated from the lord of the land.

Eastern Germany showed, down to the 16th century, the most ideal legal position of the peasantry. The cultivators usually held the land on terms of a quit-rent, rendered no labor services, and were personally free. Relatively large masses of land were in the hands of nobles who from the beginning were endowed with large-hides, often three or four or more in a single village. Judicial authority and land holding were identified to a considerable extent. This peculiarity made it easier later to subject the tenants to compulsory services and to convert into large scale farms the holdings which the nobles managed directly.

In *England*, there were *villains in gross* who were serfs and *villains regardant* who were technically in a higher position; they were strictly attached to the soil but were members of a popular court. Manorial law became very strong, making it difficult for the lords to oppress the peasants or increase their obligatory payments. The title to the land and the juridical authority were identified, and at the time of the Norman conquest unified districts were granted to vassals. But over the land holders stood a strong state, and the English kings possessed in their royal courts and trained jurists a power which put them in a position to protect the peasantry against the feudal landlords.

CHAPTER VI

The manorial system, which arose under the pressure of a strong military interest in connection with the economic, and was originally directed toward using dependent land and dependent labor force to support an upper class life, showed a strong tendency to develop in a capitalistic direction. This tendency manifested itself in the two forms of the plantation and estate economy.

(A) THE PLANTATION

A plantation is an establishment with compulsory labor, producing garden products especially for the market. The plantation economy universally arose wherever the conduct of agriculture by a class of overlords as a result of conquest coincided with the possibility of intensive cultivation, and, was especially characteristic of colonies. In modern times the plantation products have been sugar cane, tobacco, coffee, and cotton; in antiquity they were wine and oil. The course of development generally leads through a preliminary semi-plantation system. Here only the market is regulated and concentrated into one hand, while production is turned over to a servile class as compulsory labor, with joint liability of the community, attachment to the land, and payments to the owner of the semi-plantation, which is a colonizing corporation. This condition dominates in South America down to the revolution at the be-

79

ginning of the 19th century, and in the New England states down to the separation from the mother country.

Plantations proper are found scattered over the world at large. Twice did the system reach a classical development; first, in the ancient Carthago-Roman plantations, and second in the negro plantations in the southern states of the Union during the 19th century. The plantation proper operates with disciplined servile labor. We do not find, as in the case of the manorial economy, a large estate and individual small holdings of the peasants side by side, but the servile population are herded together in barracks. The main difficulty of the enterprise lies in the recruiting of laborers. The workers have no families and do not reproduce themselves. The permanence of such plantations is therefore dependent upon slave hunts, either through war or through periodical raids on a large slave hunting territory such as Africa was for the negro traffic. The plantation of antiquity [1] developed in Carthage, where it was scientifically described by Mago, as well as in the Latin literature by Cato, Varro, and Columella. A prerequisite for its existence is the possibility of obtaining slaves at all times in the market. The products of the Roman plantation are oil and wine. On the plantation we find side by side the *coloni* who are free small tenants, and the *servi* who are slaves. The *coloni* till the land in grain crops with stock and tools furnished them by the lord and hence constitute a labor force rather than a peasantry in the modern sense. The slaves are without families and without property and are herded together in barracks, combining dormitory, pesthouse, and cell for confinement against escape. Work goes forward under strict military routine, beginning with the answer to reveille in the morning, with march in closed ranks to and from work, and issue of clothing by a warehouse to which it must be returned.

The only exception is the *villicus* or inspector, who possesses a *peculium* and is *contubernalis,* meaning that he is permitted to marry a slave woman and has the right to keep a certain amount of livestock on the lord's pasture.

The hardest problem was that of keeping up the working population. As the natural increase through the promiscuous relations of the slaves was insufficient, an effort was made to stimulate the production of children by promising the slave women their freedom after the third birth. This measure proved vain because no life except prostitution awaited the freed women. The difficulties of the lord who maintained his dwelling in the town increased in view of the steady demand for slaves. Since the permanent supply of the slave market ceased to be possible with the termination of the great wars after the beginning of the imperial period, the slave barracks were doomed to disappear. The shrinkage of the slave market could have no other effect than that which the failure of coal mining would have on modern industry. The Roman plantation changed in character for the further reason that the center of gravity of the ancient culture shifted inland, while the slave barracks were bound to the neighborhood of the coast and the possibility of commerce. With this shifting of the center of gravity to the land, where traditional manorial economy dominated and corresponding conditions as to transportation obtained, and with the peace brought by the Empire, it was necessary to go over to another system. In the period of decline of the Empire, we therefore find the slaves, insofar as they are concerned with the agricultural work, provided with families and quartered in the *mansus serviles,* while on the other hand the colons are subjected to labor services and no longer merely to rent payments; that is, the two classes converge. The *possessor* class dominates the economic and political policy of the empire. Money economy and town life decline; the conditions approach the stage of barter economy.

Similar difficulties appeared in the southern states of the North American union. The plantation system arose here when the great inventions in the field of cotton utilization were made. In the last third of the 18th century were invented the cotton spinning machine (1768–69) and the loom (1785) in England, and in the United States the cotton gin for separating the fiber from the seed (1793); the latter first made possible effective utilization of the cotton crop. Thereupon developed the wholesale marketing of cotton which displaced linen and wool production. However, the mechanical utilization of the product led to entirely opposite effects in Europe and America. In the former, cotton gave the impulse to the organization of a free labor force, the first factories developing in Lancashire in England, while in America the result was slavery.

In the 16th and 17th centuries, efforts were made to use the Indians for mass production, but they soon proved themselves unserviceable, so recourse was had to the importation of negro slaves. But these, without families, did not reproduce themselves, and as the slave trade was forbidden by one after another of the New England states, great scarcity of negroes ensued after a single generation—by the end of the 18th century. The utilization of poor emigrants, who sought to pay the still very considerable costs of the ocean passage by plantation labor, proved insufficient. The next expedient was that of breeding negroes, which was carried on so systematically in many southern states that negro-breeding and negro-consuming states could be distinguished. At the same time there broke out a struggle for land for the application of negro labor. The system required cheap land and the possibility of constantly bringing new land under tillage. If the

labor force was dear the land had to be cheap, and negro
culture was exploitative (*Raubbau*) because the negroes
could not be trusted with modern implements and used
only the most primitive tools. Thus began the struggle
between the states with free and those with unfree labor.
The peculiar phenomenon was presented that the complementary productive factor "slave" alone yielded a rent,
while the land yielded none at all. Politically, this situation meant a struggle between the capitalistic classes of the
north and the plantation aristocracy of the south. On
the side of the former stood the free farmers, and on that of
the planters, the non-slave owning whites of the south, the
"poor white trash"; the latter dreaded the freeing of the
negroes on grounds of class prestige and economic competition.[2]

Slavery is profitable only when it is handled with the
most rigid discipline associated with ruthless exploitation.
Further requisites are the possibility of cheap provision
and feeding of the slaves and extensive mining-out cultivation, which again presupposes an unlimited supply of land.
When slaves became costly and celibacy could no longer
be maintained for them, the ancient plantation system fell,
and with it slavery. Christianity did not exert in this
case the influence commonly ascribed to it; it was rather
the Stoic emperors who began to protect the family and
introduced marriage among the slaves. In North America,
the Quakers were especially active in the abolition of
slavery. Its doom was sealed, however, from the moment
when (1787) Congress [*sic*] prohibited the importation of
slaves beginning with the year 1808, and when the available land threatened to become inadequate. The transformation of the slave economy into a share tenant system
which actually resulted, would apparently have come to
pass without the war of secession which was unleashed

through the withdrawal of the southern states from the Union. The mismanagement of the northern victors, who even gave the negroes a privileged position, resulted, after the withdrawal of the troops, in a universal exclusion of the negroes from the suffrage and the establishment of a strong caste distinction between whites and blacks. The negroes are share tenants bound by debt. Since the railroads are dependent upon the white land owners, the negroes can be excluded from commercial opportunities and their freedom of movement exists only on paper. Thus the emancipation brought about in a disorderly way the condition which must have become established spontaneously and gradually as soon as the factor "land" was exhausted.

(B) ESTATE ECONOMY

By an estate we understand a large-scale capitalistic establishment directed to production for the market, which may be either exclusively devoted to stock raising or exclusively to tillage, or may combine the two. If the central interest is extensive stock raising, the establishment may operate without capital as in the Roman Campagna. Here dominated the famous *latifundia* whose beginnings apparently go back to the baronial feuds of the theocratic state. The great Roman noble families were landed proprietors of the Campagna; complementary to them are renters who use their numerous herds primarily in the furnishing of milk to Rome. The cultivators, on the other hand were expropriated and removed.

Large scale stock raising, with little use of capital, dominates also in the Pampas of South America and in Scotland. In Scotland again the cultivators were expropriated. After the destruction of Scottish independence at the battle of Culloden in 1746, the English policy treated the old clan chieftains as "landlords" and the clansmen as their tenants. The result was that the landlords assumed the prerogative of owners in the course of the 18th and 19th centuries, drove off the tenants and converted the land into hunting grounds or sheep pastures.

Intensive capitalistic pastoral economy developed in England with the growth of the English woolen industry and its promotion by the English kings. After the 14th century, the kings, led by the possibility of levying taxes, granted favors first to exporters of raw wool and later to wool manufacturers producing for home consumption.[3] Thus began the transformation of the common pastures into sheep walks—the "enclosure" movement—by the landlords, who regarded themselves as proprietors of the common. The proprietors bought out the cultivators by wholesale or came to an agreement with them, on the strength of which they became large farmers and took up pastoral economy. The result of this process, which went on from the 15th to the 17th century and against which in the 18th century there was an agitation among the people as well as among the social writers, was the origin of a capitalistic class of large renters who leased land with a minimum of labor force and for the most part pursued the raising of sheep for the woolen industry.

Under another form of estate economy the interest centers in the production of grain. An example is England in the 150 years before the repeal of the corn laws under Robert Peel. Down to that time small farmers were displaced on an extensive scale to make way for a more effective cultivation by renters, under a system of protective duties and export bounties. Thus sheep farming and grain farming existed separately side by side, or were combined. This condition lasted until the protective duties on grain were abolished in consequence of the agitations of the Puritans and the English labor class. After this, grain culture was no longer profitable, and the labor force employed in it was released. The English low lands were extensively depopulated while in Ireland the small tenant agriculture persisted on the huge estates of the landlords of that time.

The complete opposite of England is afforded by Russia.[4] Here in the 16th century there were indeed slaves but the great mass of the peasantry consisted of free share tenants who gave half of their crop to the landlords. The latter possessed the right of terminating the lease at the end of any year, but seldom exercised it. Since, however, the landlords preferred a fixed money rent to the fluctuating payments in kind, they placed the peasantry on the basis of a fixed money rental (*obrok*). At the same time they attempted to extend the compulsory labor services, to which originally the slaves alone were subject, to the free tenants also; in this, the monastic holdings, which in general were the most economically farmed, took the lead. The growth of money economy resulted in throwing the peasants heavily into debt. Only a single crop failure was necessary for this result, and the freedom of movement of the peasant was lost. From the end of the 16th century, the Czars placed their power and that of the whole administrative organization of the empire at the service of the nobility. The latter, however, was threatened in its very existence because the great landlords were able to give the cultivators more favorable terms of lease, so that the lower nobility faced a scarcity of tenants. The czaristic policy sought to protect them against the great nobles. This purpose was served by the ukase of the Czar Boris Godunov in the year 1597; the leases were declared non-terminable, the peasants being in effect attached to the soil; they were also registered in a tax roll, which again led to a policy of protection of the peasantry on the part of the lords. With the change to a poll tax system under Peter the Great, the distinction between free peasantry and serfs disappeared. Both were attached to the soil and over both the landlord had unlimited power. The peasant had no more rights than a Roman slave. In 1713, the right of knouting was expressly granted to the lords; the inspector of the estate joined the young persons in marriage according to fiat, and the amount of the payments was fixed at the will of the proprietors, as was the levying of recruits. They had the authority to banish an obstreperous peasant to Siberia and could resume the holding of any peasant at any time, although many of the latter succeeded in concealing their possessions and achieving great wealth. There was no court in which the peasant could seek justice. He was exploited by the lord as a source of rent or of labor power, the former in central Russia and the latter in the west, where exportation was possible. These were the conditions under which the Russian peasantry entered the 19th century.

In Germany, there is a sharp distinction between the west, where leasing of land persisted, and the east and Austria, where demesne economy predominated.[5] Originally, the state of the peasants was much the same in the two regions, or even more favorable in the east. In the east there was originally no personal servitude and it had the best land law of Germany. The peasants were settled on large-hides (*Grosshufen*), of the extent of the old royal hide; eviction was forbidden by the state from the time of Frederick William I of Prussia and Maria Theresa, because the peasant was a tax payer and a recruit. In Hanover and Westphalia also, eviction was forbidden, but on the Rhine and in Southwest Germany it was permitted. None the less, the eviction of peasants took on large proportions in the east and did not in the west and south. The reasons are various. After the Thirty Years' War, which fearfully decimated the peasant population, the holdings were reassigned in the west, while in the east they were consolidated into estates. In the west [6] and south, intermingled holdings predominated, while in the east were the unified large farms of the nobles. But in the west and south, even where large, unified holdings of the nobility were the rule, no large estates developed. For here land-holding, personal suzerainty, and judicial authority were separate and the peasant could play one against the other, while in the east they were identified as an indivisible fief. This circumstance made it easy to evict the tenant or subject him to compulsory services, although originally only the magistrate and not the landlord had a right to these. Finally, there was less church land in the east than in the west, and the church traditionally showed more consideration to the peasant than did the lay proprietor. Even where in the east large holdings were in the hands of the church, as they were in Austria in the hands of the monasteries, the ecclesiastics managed more economically than the lay holders, but did not have the same interest in going over to export agriculture.

Thus the market relations played a decisive part in this contrast between the east and the west. Large estates arose where the local market could not absorb the available mass of grain production and it was exported abroad. But since a merchant in Hamburg was not in a position to negotiate with the individual peasant in the Mark or in Silesia, the transition to estate farming was inevitable. The peasant in the south and west, on the contrary, had a town in the vicinity, where he could market his products. Hence the landlord could use him as a source of rent, while in the east he could only be treated as labor power. With the decrease in the frequency of towns on the map, there is an increase in the frequency of estates. Finally, an additional force favoring the survival of the old time cultivators in the south and west was the power of manorial law, and the greater degree of traditionalism associated with it. It is even asserted that the Peasant War in west and south Germany had a part in this development. The war ended with the defeat of the peasantry, but operated as a lost general strike and meant the handwriting on the wall for the proprietors. But England had its peasant war in the 14th century and in spite of it the expropriation of the peasantry took place; and if Poland and east Germany had no peasant insurrections the fact is that these, like all revolutions, did not break out where the condition of the oppressed class was worst, that is in our case where the conditions of the peasant class were worst, but rather where the revolutionaries have attained a certain degree of self-consciousness.

The technical expression for the relation of the peasant to the landlord is, in the east, not servility (*Leibeigenschaft*) but hereditary dependency (*Erbuntertänigkeit*). The peasant is an appendage of the estate and is bought and sold with the latter. In Germany east of the Elbe, there existed alongside of the peasantry of the princely domains (which were very extensive, amounting in Mecklenburg to half the total land area), the peasantry of the private landlords. The proprietary rights varied widely. The German peasant originally lived under very favorable relations, holding his land subject to a quit-rent. In contrast, the rights of the Slavs were very insecure. This led to the result that conditions became worse for the Germans where the Slavs were in the majority. Thus it came about that in the east in the 18th century the mass of the peasantry lived under the law of serfdom (*lassitischem Recht*). The peasant had become an appurtenance of the estate. He possessed no secure hereditary title, nor even always a title for life, although he was already bound to the soil and could not leave the estate without the consent of the lord or without securing someone in his place. He was subject to *Gesindeszwangdienst*, similar to sergeanty in English feudal law; that is, he had not only to perform obligatory services but his children also had to go into the house of the lord as servants, even when the lord himself was only a renter of domain land. Any serf (*Lassit*) could be compelled by the lord to take up a holding. Finally, the lords assumed the right of increasing the labor dues and displacing peasants at will. Here, however, they came into sharp conflict with the princely power. The rulers of east Germany began to protect the peasantry; they feared, particularly in Austria and Prussia, the destruction of the existing peasant class, not out of love for the peasant as such, but to maintain his class, which was their source of taxes and recruits. It is true that the protection of the peasant was instituted only where a strong state was present; in Mecklenburg, in Swedish Hither-Pomerania and in the county of Holstein the large unified estate economy was able to develop.

About 1890 [7] an estate in the east Elbe country was a seasonal affair. The field work was unequally distributed throughout the year and in the winter the field hands took to auxiliary occupations, the disappearance of which later was a main source of labor difficulties. The estate had male and female servants for the regular farm labor throughout the year. In addition there was a second category of workers on the land, the "inst-folk." These were married persons living in their own homes, but in Silesia assembled in barracks. They worked on the basis of an annual contract terminable by either party. Their pay consisted either in a fixed allowance of products with the addition of some money, or in a variable share of the product, including the proceeds of the harvest and of the mill. Threshing was done by hand and lasted through the winter, and in general the sixth or tenth sheaf was given to the "instman." The instmen had a monopoly on this work; the estate owner could not transfer it to other persons. In addition, as long as the three-field rotation persisted, they had one strip in each of the three fields, which was tilled for them by the proprietor, and also had gardens in which they raised potatoes. They received little or no money wages, but fed swine for the market and also marketed any surplus from their share in the crops. Thus they were interested in high prices for hogs and grain, which gave them a common economic interest with the lord, whereas an agricultural labor proletariat paid in money would have desired low prices for these things. The stock and heavy implements were furnished by the lord, but the instmen had to provide flail and scythe.

The lord required additional laborers at harvest time and employed wandering laborers—the so-called "Landsberg harvesters"—or he hired men from the villages. In addition, the instman himself, unless he would see his wages reduced, had to furnish at least one additional hand during the summer and probably a second at harvest time, for which he had recourse to his wife and children, so that the family as a whole stood in a sort of labor partnership with the lord. Contractual freedom in the industrial sense obtained only with the migratory workers and the instmen of the dependent farmers, whose condition was found unamenable to "regulation" (cf. below). However, there had been for them a fundamental change since the time of hereditary serfdom, since at that period the estate proprietor had operated without capital of his own, with the aid of the hand and team work of the peasants; hence no separation of the worker from his tools had then taken place.

(C) The Dissolution of the Manorial System

The estate economy was similarly organized in Poland and White Russia, export countries which brought their grain to the world market through boat traffic on the Vistula and the Memel. In interior Russia, the lords preferred to lease the land to the peasants, who thus retained control of their own labor power.

The complicated mutual dependence of the proprietor and the peasant, the exploitation of the latter by the former as a source of rent or as labor force, and finally the tying up of the land through both, was the cause which brought about the disintegration of the manorial organization of agriculture. This change meant the personal emancipation of the peasant and agricultural laborer, with freedom of movement, the freeing of the soil from the communal organization of the peasants and from the rights of the overlord, and reciprocally the freeing of manorial land from the encumbrance of peasant rights where they existed, i. e., where the rulers followed a policy of protecting the peasantry. Liberation could take place in different ways. First, through expropriation of the peasants, who became free but landless, as in England, Mecklenburg, Hither-Pomerania, and parts of Silesia. Second, through expropriation of the overlord, who lost his land while the peasant became free with possession of the land. This occurred in France and southwest Germany, and in general in almost every region where the lords exploited the land by leasing, and also in Poland, as a result of Russian interference. Finally, it might come about through a combination of the two methods, the peasant becoming free with a part of the land. This was the course of events where an estate form of organization existed, which could not be easily displaced. Thus the Prussian state was compelled to lean upon its landed proprietors because it was too poor to replace them with salaried officials.

The breakdown of the manorial agricultural system made possible also the abolition of the hereditary judicial authority of the proprietors, the various socage rights or *banalités*, and finally all the political and religious restrictions upon the land in the way of obligatory infeudation or the so-called mortmain. Abolition of these incumbrances might take various forms: 1. Amortization laws relating to church lands, as in Bavaria. 2. Abolition or limitation of the fideicommissum, especially in England. 3. Finally, abolition of the fiscal privileges of the proprietory estates, such as freedom from taxation and similar political privileges, as was accomplished in Prussia by the tax legislation of the sixties of the 19th century. Such were the different possibilities. The result depended on the question who was to be expropriated, the landlord or the peasant, and if the latter whether with or without the land.

The motivating force in connection with the breakdown of the manorial system operated in the first place from within the manor and was primarily economic in character. The immediate cause was the development of market operations and market interests on the part of both lords and peasants, and the steady growth of the market for agricultural products in connection with money economy. However, these considerations either failed to bring about the dissolution of the manorial system, or if they did it was done in accordance with the interests of the lords who expropriated the tenants and used the land to establish large farming enterprises.

In general, it was necessary for other interests to come in from without. One such was the commercial interest of the newly established bourgeoisie of the towns, who promoted the weakening or dissolution of the manor because it limited their own market opportunities. The town and its economic policies on the one side and the manor on the other were antagonistic, not so much in the sense that one represented a barter economy and the other a purely money economy, for the manors produced to a large extent for the market, without the opportunities of which it would have been impossible for the landlord to raise large money payments from the peasants. Through the mere fact of the compulsory services and payments of the tenants, the manorial system set limits to the purchasing power of the rural population because it prevented the peasants from devoting their entire labor power to production for the market and from developing their purchasing power. Thus the interests of the bourgeoisie of the towns were opposed to those of the landed proprietors. In addition, there was the interest on the part of the developing capitalism in the creation of a free labor market, to which obstacles were opposed by the manorial system through the attachment of the peasants to the soil. The first capitalistic industries were thrown back upon the exploitation of the rural labor power in order to circumvent the guilds. The desire of the new capitalists to acquire land gave them a further interest antagonistic to the manorial system; the capitalistic classes wished to invest their newly acquired wealth in land in order to rise into the socially privileged landed class, and this required a liberation of the land from feudal ties. Finally, the fiscal interest of the state also took a hand, counting upon the dissolution of the manor to increase the taxpaying capacity of the farming country.

These are the various possibilities in connection with the dissolution of manorial economy. In detail, its development was extraordinarily complicated. In China,[8] the feudal system was abolished in the third century before our era, and private property in the land established. Shi-Huang-Ti, the first emperor of the Ching dynasty, rested his power on a patrimonial in contrast with a feudal army, relying for its support on taxation of the dependent classes. The Chinese humanists, the precursors of the later Confucians, took their stand on the side of the monarchy and played the same rationalizing role as the corresponding group in Europe. Since that time, fiscal policy in China has changed times without number.[9] The two poles between which it vibrated were those of a taxation state and a "managerial" (*leiturgisch*) state, i. e., between one paying its army and officials out of taxation and treating its subjects as a source of taxation and one utilizing them as a source of servile labor, supplying its needs by holding specified classes responsible for payments in kind. The latter policy is the one followed by the Roman Empire at the time of Diocletian, when compulsory communes were organized for the purpose. One system made the masses formally free, the other made them state slaves. The latter were utilized in China in the same way as they were in Europe in those cases where the lords exploited the dependent population as labor power and not through rent charges. In the latter case private property disappeared, and obligations to the land and attachment to the land, with periodical redistribution, came in. The final result of this development in China after the 18th century was the abandonment of the leiturgical principle in favor of the taxation principle; taxes were paid to the state, along with which unimportant remains of public labor services survived. The taxes flowed into the hands of the mandarins, whose payments to the court were rigidly fixed, while they pushed the taxes of the peasantry as high as possible. This, however, was notably more difficult because the power of the clans was so great that every official had to secure the consent of the Chinese peasantry. The result has been extensive liberation of the peasants. There are still a few tenants, but they are personally free and pay only a moderate rent.

In India, the manorial system still persists; indeed it first arose in a secondary manner out of the practice of tax farming by the fisc. English legislation protects the peasantry, who formerly had no rights, in the same way that Gladstone's laws protected the Irish in the possession of their holdings and against arbitrary increase in the traditional payments; but it has not in principle changed the established order.

In the near east, also, the feudal tenure exists, but only in a modified form, since the old feudal army has disappeared. Fundamental changes in Persia and other countries exist only on paper. In Turkey the institution of the *wakuf* (cf. below) has hitherto prevented a modernization of land holding relations.

In Japan, the medieval period comes down to 1861 when, with the downfall of the rule of the nobility, feudal land holding also fell away through the dissolution of the proprietary rights. The pillars of the feudal system, the Samurai, were impoverished, and turned to industrial life; out of this class the Japanese capitalists have developed.

In the Mediterranean region in antiquity,[10] feudal land holding was displaced only within the region immediately under the power of the great cities like Rome and Athens. The town bourgeoisie was in opposition to the landed nobility, with the further conflict between the townsmen as creditors and the country folk as debtors. This situation, in connection with the necessity of securing the great mass of peasants for military service, led in Greece to an endeavor to fit out the hoplites with land. This was the significance of the legislation of the so-called tyrants, as for example, the laws of Solon. The knightly families were compelled to enter the peasant organizations. The legislation of Cleisthenes of about 500 B. C. understood by democracy the condition that every Athenian, to enjoy the privileges of citizenship, must belong to a "demos," i. e., a village, just as in the Italian democracies of the middle ages the nobility were compelled to join the guilds. It was a blow against the land system with its scattered holdings, and against the power of the nobility, who up to that time had stood above and outside the villages. After this time the knights possessed only the same voting power and opportunity to hold office as any peasant. At the same time, the system of intermingled holdings was everywhere set aside.

The class struggles in Rome had similar results for the agricultural organization. Here the field division was in the form of squares of 200 acres and upward. Each holding was set off by a balk of turf which must not be plowed up; the *limites* were public roads, removal of which was also forbidden, in order to maintain accessibility. The land was transferable with extraordinary facility. This system of agrarian law must have been known in the time of the twelve tables and must have been established at a single stroke. It is a law in the interest of the town bourgeoisie, which treats the land holdings of the nobility after the fashion of territory used in towns for speculative building and systematically removes the distinction between land and movable property. Outside the immediate territory belonging to the town, however, the ancient land system was undisturbed. The civilization of antiquity—down to

Alexander the Great in the East and Augustus in the West —was riparian in character and the system of tenure remained unchanged in the interior; from here it later worked outward again, and finally conquered the entire Roman Empire, to remain the dominant institution through the first half of the middle ages. The merchant republics of the Italian towns, under the leadership of Florence, first took up the path toward liberation of the peasantry. To be sure, they deprived the peasants of political rights, to the advantage of the town rulers and councils, the crafts and the merchant guilds, until the nobility itself turned to the peasantry for support against the town population. In any case, the towns liberated the peasantry, in order to buy up the land and release themselves from the clutches of the ruling families (Cp. above, p. 75).

In England,[11] no legal emancipation of the peasants ever took place. The medieval system is still formally in force, except that under Charles II serfdom was abolished and infeudated land became private property, in "fee simple." The only explicit exception was the "copyhold" land, which was originally in the possession of unfree peasants, the occupier holding no formal grant, but only a copy of one recorded in the rolls of the manor. In England, the mere fact of the development of a market, as such and alone, destroyed the manorial system from within. In accordance with the principle fitting the situation, the peasants were expropriated in favor of the proprietors. The peasants became free but without land.

In France [12] the course of events is exactly the opposite. Here the revolution put an end to the feudal system at one blow in the night of August 4, 1789. However, the measure adopted at that time still required interpretation. This was given by the legislation of the Convention, which declared that all burdens against peasants' holdings in favor of overlords were presumed to be of feudal character and that they were abolished without compensation. In addition, the state confiscated the enormous estates of the émigrés and of the church, conferring them upon citizens and peasants. However, since equality of inheritance and distribution of holdings had arisen long before the abolition of the feudal burdens, the final result was that France, in contrast with England, became a land of small and medium sized farms. The process was one of creating property in the hands of the peasantry through the expropriation of the landlords. This was possible because the French landlord was a courtier-noble and not a farmer, seeking his living in the army or in civil service positions upon which he had in part a monopolistic claim. Thus no productive organization was destroyed but only a rent relation.

Similar in character but less revolutionary and rather by gradual steps was the course of development in south and west Germany. In Baden, the liberation of the peasants was begun as early as 1783 by the Margrave Charles Frederick, who was influenced by the Physiocrats. The crucial fact is that after the wars of liberation, the German states adopted the system of written constitutions, and no relationship in connection with which the name of bondage (*Leibeigenschaft*) could be used is compatible with a constitutional state. Hence the unlimited labor dues, taxes, and services which had anything of the character of personal servitude were everywhere abolished. In Bavaria, it was done under Montgelas and confirmed by the constitution of 1818; the peasants received freedom of movement and finally, favorable property rights. This happened in almost all of south and west Germany in the course of the 20's and 30's; only in Bavaria the substance of it was not achieved until 1848. In that year the last remains of the cultivators' burdens were removed by conversion into money obligations, in the handling of which state credit institutions lent aid. Specifically, in Bavaria personal dues were abolished without compensation; other dues were converted into money payments and made subject to extinction by purchase; at the same time, all feudal ties were unconditionally dissolved. Thus in south and west Germany, the landlord was expropriated and the land given to the peasant; the change was the same as in France except that it took place slowly and according to a more legal process.

Quite different was the course of events in the east—in Austria, and the eastern provinces of Prussia, in Russia, and in Poland. Here, if drastic measures had been taken as in France, a functioning agricultural organization would have been destroyed and only chaos would have resulted. It might have been possible to promote a disintegration of the manors into peasant holdings, as happened in Denmark, but it would not have been possible simply to declare feudal burdens abolished. The landed proprietors of the east possessed neither implements nor work animals. There was no rural labor force, but small holders subject to services of man and team, by whose labor the proprietor tilled his land; that is, it was an organization for working the land, which could not be summarily set aside. A further difficulty existed in the fact that there was no official class for the administration of the rural districts, and the government was dependent on the estate holding nobility to perform public functions on an honorary basis. Summary measures, such as the presence of an official staff of lawyers made possible in France, were therefore excluded here, as they were in England in view of the aristocratic justices of the peace.

If the protection and maintenance of the peasantry is regarded as the proper objective of an agrarian system, then the dissolution took place in an ideal manner in Austria. In any case, it was better than the Prussian methods, because the Austrian rulers, especially Charles VI and Maria Theresa, knew better what they were doing than did, for example, Frederick the Great, of whom his father said that he did not know how to terminate a lease and box the ears of the tenant.

In Austria,[13] with the exception of the Tyrol, where a free peasantry predominated, hereditary bondage and a landed nobility had existed side by side. The system of estates using the peasants as labor force was most common in Pomerania, Moravia, Silesia, Lower Austria, and Galicia; elsewhere, a renting system predominated. In Hungary, leasing and exploitation by servile labor were intermingled. The greatest degree of personal servitude obtained in Galicia and Hungary. Here were distinguished "rusticalists" who were subject to contributions according to a cadaster, and "dominicalists" who were settled on demesne land (*Salland*) and were not subject to contributions. The rusticalists were in part in the better position. They were divided again, as were also the dominicalists, into commuted and non-commuted. The holdings of the non-commuted were subject to retraction, while the commuted possessed hereditary rights.

After the second half of the 17th century, capitalistic tendencies began to intrude into this organization. Under Leopold I the state interfered, at first in a purely fiscal connection, under the form of a compulsory enrolment in cadasters. The policy was to determine from exactly what land the state could collect taxes. When this measure proved without effect, the authorities tried the system of "labor patents" (1680–1738). The object was legislative protection of the laborers; the maximum of work which might be demanded from every peasant was determined. The eviction of the peasants was not yet made impossible, however, and Maria Theresa adopted the system of tax "rectification," aiming to reduce the incentive to evict the peasantry by making the proprietor responsible for the taxes of any peasant displaced by him. But this measure also proved insufficient, and in 1750 the Empress interfered directly with peasant evictions, though again without accomplishing anything conclusive. Finally, in 1771, she promulgated the system of complete registration. The landed proprietors were compelled to draw up registers (*Urbarien*—a sort of Domesday Book) in which each peasant holding, with its obligations, was definitely fixed. At the same time, the peasants were given the right to commute the obligations and so to acquire hereditary possession. This expedient broke down in Hungary at once, while in Austria it met with notable success. It represented the attempt to maintain the existing number of peasants and to protect them against the advance of agrarian capitalism. It did not constitute a dissolution of the existing agricultural organization; the peasants were to be protected, but the nobility were also to maintain their position.

Under Joseph II the legislation first took on a revolutionary character. He began by dissolving personal bondage and granting what he understood by this dissolution, namely, freedom of movement, free choice of occupations, freedom in marriage, and freedom from sergeanty or obligatory domestic service. He gave the peasants, in principle, property in their holdings, and in the tax and registration law of 1789 struck out on a really new path. The former system of compulsory services and payments in kind on the feudal holdings was terminated, the dues and aids being converted into fixed money payments to the state.

This attempt to go over at one step to a taxation state broke down. The peasants were not in a position to realize from their products an income large enough to make the money payments, and the economic program of the proprietors was so violently disturbed that a great storm arose, forcing the emperor on his death bed to retract a large part of his reforms. Not until 1848, as a result of the revolution, were all the burdens of the peasantry removed, partly with and partly without compensation. Insofar as compensation was required, the Austrian state fixed a very moderate valuation of the services and set up credit institutions as a means of extinguishing them. This legislation represented the crowning of the efforts of Maria Theresa and Joseph II.

In Prussia,[14] there has been a pronounced and persistent distinction between the peasants on the crown lands and those on private holdings. For the former, Frederick the Great himself had been able to put through thoroughgoing protective measures. In the first place, he abolished the compulsory domestic service (*Gesindeszwangdienst*). Then, in 1777, he made the peasants' holdings hereditary. In 1779, Frederick William III proclaimed the abolition of compulsory services in principle, requiring every recipient of a lease on crown land to renounce them explicitly. Thus on the crown domains a modern agricultural system was gradually built up. In addition, the peasants were granted the right of purchasing full proprietory rights for a relatively moderate sum; the officialdom of the state concurred in these measures, not only on account of the income which the commutation money would bring to the treasury, but also because with acquisition of full proprietorship the claims of the crown peasantry against the state were extinguished and the labor of administration reduced.

With regard to the peasantry on private holdings, the

task was much more difficult. Frederick the Great wished to do away with servitude but encountered the formally effective objection that there was no servitude in Prussia, but only hereditary dependency. The crown was not in a position to effect anything against the nobility, and its own officialdom made up of the nobles. The catastrophe of Jena and Tilsit first brought about a change. In 1807, hereditary personal dependency was abolished. The question was what should become of the land which was held by the peasantry in unfree tenure. Prussian official opinion was divided. The alternative was whether to aim at the largest quantity of produce from a given piece of land, or to lay the emphasis on maintaining the maximum peasant population. In the first case the English agricultural system offered a model, as it then represented the highest degree of intensive cultivation; but this system involved sacrificing the population on the land. This course was favored by Over-President von Schoen and his circle. The other course meant turning away from the example of England and from intensive cultivation. After long negotiations appeared the Regulation Edict of 1816. It represented a compromise between administrative policy and the protection of the peasantry.

First, the peasants who owned teams were declared subject to "regulation," while the small cultivators were in effect excluded, since the state proprietors declared that they could not do without the hand labor. Even those with teams were only included if the occupied land was registered in the tax rolls and if they had occupied it since 1763. The selection of this year as the boundary point meant that a minimum of the peasant holdings were included in the scheme. The regulation became effective on application. The peasant received his holding as property and no longer furnished labor services or payments, but at the same time he lost his rights against the estate. That is, he renounced his right to receive from the proprietor help in emergencies, assistance in repairing buildings, to the use of the common pasture and woodland, and to advances from the estate to meet tax payments. Especially, however, the peasant had to turn over to the proprietor one-third of all hereditary possessions and half of non-hereditary possessions. This manner of regulation was extraordinarily favorable to the estate proprietor. He had indeed to provide himself with implements and stock, but he retained the hand labor of the *Kossäten,* while he was freed from the rights of pasture of the peasantry and could consolidate his holdings, since the prohibition of eviction was suspended at once. The peasant liable only for hand labor and not subject to the regulation could now be summarily evicted. In Silesia, the nobility, who were especially strong, secured still further exceptions in their own favor, while in Posen, where Polish proprietors were affected, the entire peasant class was made subject to the regulation.

Not until 1848 did the legislation take the final step in Prussia. In 1850, the dissolution of all burdens on the peasantry was proclaimed. Every peasant, with the exception of the day laborers, was now placed under the regulation and every obligation against peasant holdings was made subject to commutation, whether it resulted from the regulation or was independent of it. This included hereditary rents and other payments. It is true that in the meantime the holdings of the smaller peasants had long ago been appropriated by the estate proprietors.

The net result of the development in Prussia has been a decrease both in the numbers of the peasantry and the extent of peasant holdings. Since 1850 a progressive proletarizing of the working population has gone on. The decisive cause was the increase in the value of land. The earlier custom of granting land to the "instmen" was no longer profitable; their shares in the fruits of the threshing and grinding were also changed into money payments. Of especial importance was the introduction of sugar beet culture, which gave agriculture a highly seasonal character, requiring migratory labor; this was provided by the so-called "Sachsen-gänger," coming first from the Polish provinces of the east and later from Russian Poland and Galicia. For these people it was not necessary either to build dwellings or to allot land; they allowed themselves to be herded together in barracks and were satisfied with a style of living which any German laboring man would have rejected. Thus to an increasing extent a nomadic labor force took the place of the original land-bound peasantry and of the labor force of later times which was loyally attached to the land by a community of economic interest with the proprietor of the estate.

In Russia,[15] even Alexander I had talked about the emancipation of the peasants, but had done as little towards it as Nicholas I. The defeat of Russia in the Crimean war was required to set things in motion. Alexander II feared a revolution, and for that reason promulgated, in 1861, after endless consultations, the great manifesto liberating the peasants. The problem of dividing the land was solved in the following way. For each province of the empire was set a minimum and maximum holding for each person (nadyel); the amounts varied from three to seven hektares. The proprietor, however, could avoid the regulation altogether by giving the peasants outright a fourth part of the minimum share. In this way he acquired in effect a rural proletarian family completely dependent upon the opportunity to work on his estate. Otherwise the peasant received his share of land only for compensation. The latter was higher in proportion as the share was smaller, the law makers arguing from the better quality of the land and its greater yield. Moreover, during a certain transition period the obligatory services of the peasants were kept in force, and the commutation of dues by the peasant made dependent on the consent of the proprietor. The system resulted in the peasantry falling extensively in debt to the proprietors. The commutation payments were fixed relatively high, amounting to 6% for 48 years; they were still running when the revolution of 1905–07 broke out. More favorable terms were granted the peasants on the royal estates and crown lands, who were liberated with complete ownership of their land.

It is true that the Russian peasants were liberated only in one direction; they were freed from the proprietors, but not from the joint obligations of the commune. In regard to these, personal servitude was maintained. The peasant did not have freedom of movement, for the mir could recall anyone, no matter whom, who had grown up in the village. This right was kept intact because the Government saw in the so-called agrarian communism a conservative force and a support of czarism against the progress of liberalism (cf. above, p. 19).

Led by political considerations, the Russian government proceeded differently in the western provinces, especially in Poland,[16] where the Code Napoleon had abolished serfdom, although under the condition that on the removal of the peasant the land reverted to the overlord. This specification, which had led to wholesale expulsion of the peasants, was in its turn abolished in 1846. Then in 1864 the Russions carried out the liberation of the Polish peasants, as a measure directed against the Polish nobility, who had supported the revolution of 1863, and with the object of attaching the peasantry to Russian policy. In consequence, the relation of the peasant to the soil was determined on the basis of his own declaration. Thus the liberation took the form of an out-and-out dispossession of the Polish nobility. In particular, this fact explains the extensive woodland and pasture privileges of the peasants.

The dissolution of the feudal land system resulted in the agricultural system of today. In part, the peasantry are freed from the land and the land from the peasantry, as in England; in part the peasantry are freed from the proprietors, as in France; in part the system is a mixture, as in the rest of Europe, the east inclining more toward the English conditions.

The form of the final adjustment has been largely influenced by the laws of inheritance, in which regard there was the greatest contrast between England and France. In England, the feudal inheritance with primogeniture became universal for the land; the eldest son alone, whether of peasant or overlord, inherits all the land. In France, equal division of the land was the rule, even under the old regime; the civil code only made it obligatory. Within Germany we find the most extreme contrasts. Where individual inheritance persists it is not primogeniture in the English sense, but rather sets up a principal heir, (*anerbe*) who receives the land and is required to provide for other heirs. This law obtains in some · cases on purely technical grounds, as for example in connection with large estates, or a great farm in the Black Forest, where physical division is impossible; or it may be historically grounded, coming down from the period of feudal overlordship. The manorial lord was interested in the capacity of the land to support services, and hence in maintaining farms undivided. In Russia, we find agrarian communism down to the reforms of Stolypin in 1907; the peasant received his allotment of land not from his parents but from the village community,

Modern legislation has entirely abolished feudal ties. In some regions these have been replaced by a system of trusts or fideicommissa. These are first met with in the form of certain peculiar foundations in the Byzantine Empire, beginning with the 12th century. To protect the land against the emperors, it was given to the church and thus received a character of sanctity. The purpose for which the church could use it, however, was rigidly prescribed, as for example the maintenance of a number of monks. The remainder of the rent, to the amount of nine-tenths of the total, accrued permanently to the family establishing the foundation. Thus arose in the Moslem world the *wakuf,* a foundation apparently in favor of the monks or for some other pious purpose, but in reality designed to secure to a family a rent while preventing the Sultan from levying taxes on the land. This device of the fideicommissum was brought by the Arabs to Spain and then taken over by England and Germany. In England it aroused resistance, but the lawyers devised a substitute in the institution of "entails." The nature of the institution is this: the indivisibility and inalienability of holdings of land is secured by agreement on its transfer from one generation to the next, so that no change is possible during the lifetime of the holder. In this way the greater part of the land of England has been concentrated into the hands of a small number of families, while in Prussia a while ago one-sixteenth of the land was tied up in trusts. The result is that a latifundian ownership obtains in England, Scotland, and Ireland and also (before 1918) in parts of Silesia and the former Austro-Hungarian monarchy, and to a small extent in certain parts of Germany.

The manner in which the agrarian system developed and the feudal organization was displaced has had extraordinarily far-reaching consequences, not only for the progress of rural conditions but for political relations in general. Especially has it influenced the question whether a country was to have a landed aristocracy, and what form it would take. An aristocrat in the sociological sense is a man whose economic position sets him free for political activities and enables him to live for political functions without living by them; hence, he is a receiver of fixed income (*Rentner, rentier*). This requirement cannot be met by those classes who are bound to some occupation by the necessity of working to provide a living for themselves and their families, that is, by business men and laborers. In an agricultural nation, specifically, the complete aristocrat lives on ground rents. The only country which really possesses such an aristocracy in Europe is England—to a limited extent also the Austria of former times. In France, on the contrary, the expropriation of the landed classes led to an urbanization of political life, since only the plutocracy of the towns, and no longer the landed aristocracy, were economically free enough to make politics a profession. The economic development of Germany left only a thin stratum of landlords free for political life, chiefly in the eastern provinces of Prussia, where the expropriation of the peasants went farthest. The majority of the Prussian Junkers formed no such aristocratic stratum as the English landlords. They are rather a rural middle class with a feudal stamp, coming down from the past, whose members are occupied as agricultural entrepreneurs in the day-to-day economic struggle of business interests. With the fall in grain prices since the seventies and the rise in the demands of life, their fate was sealed, for the average knightly holding of 400 to 500 acres can no longer support a lordly aristocratic existence. This fact explains the extraordinarily sharp conflict of interests in which this class has stood, and still stands, and their position in political life.

With the dissolution of the manors and of the remains of the earlier agrarian communism through consolidation, separation, etc., private property in land has been completely established. In the meantime, in the course of the centuries, the organization of society has changed in the direction described above, the household community shrinking, until now the father with his wife and children functions as the unit in property relations. Formerly this was simply impossible for physical reasons. The household has at the same time undergone an extensive internal transformation, and this in two ways; its function has become restricted to the field of consumption, and its management placed on an accounting basis. To an increasing extent the development of inheritance law in place of the original complete communism has led to a separation between the property of the man and the woman, with a separate accounting. This two-fold transformation was bound up with the development of industry and trade.

PART TWO

INDUSTRY AND MINING DOWN TO THE BEGINNING OF
THE CAPITALISTIC DEVELOPMENT

CHAPTER VII

We understand by industry the transformation of raw
materials; thus the extractive operations and mining are
excluded from the concept. However, the latter will be
treated in connection with industry in what follows, so that
the designation "industry" embraces all those economic
activities which are not to be viewed as agricultural, trading, or transportation operations.

From the economic standpoint industry—in the sense of
transformation of raw materials—developed universally
in the form of work to provide for the requirements of a
house community. In this connection it is an auxiliary occupation; it first begins to be interesting to us when production is carried beyond household needs. This work may
be carried on for an outside household, especially for a
seigniorial household by the lord's dependents; here the
needs of the one household are covered by the products of
other (peasant) households. Auxiliary industrial work
may also be performed for a village, as in the case of
India. Here the hand workers are small farmers who
are not able to live from the product of their allotments
alone. They are attached to the village, subject to the disposal of anyone who has need of industrial service. They
are essentially village serfs, receiving a share in the products or money payments. This we call "demiurgical"
labor.

The second mode of transforming raw materials, for other than the needs of a household, is production for sale—that is, craft work. By craft work we understand the case in which skilled labor is carried on to any extent in specialized form, either through differentiation of occupations or technical specialization, and whether by free or unfree workers, and whether for a lord, or for a community, or on the worker's own account.

It will be seen that industrial work for the needs of the worker originally appears in the closed house community. In general the oldest form of specialization is a strict division of labor between the sexes. To the woman exclusively falls the cultivation of the fields; she is the first agriculturist. She is by no means given such a high position as Tacitus, who here waxes fanciful, represents in the case of the Germans. In ancient England the seduction of a wife was regarded as a mere property damage to be compensated by money. The woman was a field slave; upon her lay the entire work of tillage and all activity connected with the utilization of the plants grown upon the land, as well as the production of the vessels in which cooking was done, and finally the broad category of textile work—braiding of mats, spinning, and weaving. As to weaving there are indeed characteristic exceptions. In Egypt, Herodotus was rightly impressed by the fact that men (servile) worked at the looms, a development which took place generally where the loom was very heavy to manipulate or the men were demilitarized. To the man's share on the other hand fell everything connected with war, hunting, and livestock keeping, as also work in metals, dressing of leather, and preparation of meat. The last ranked as a ritualistic act; originally meat was eaten only in connection with orgies, to which in general the men alone were admitted, the women receiving what was left over.

Industrial work in communal form is found in occasional tasks, especially in house building. Here the work was so heavy that the single household and certainly the single man could not carry it out. Hence, it was performed by the village as invitation work on a mutual basis, enlivened by drinking, as is still done in Poland. Another example in very early time is work for the chieftain, and another is ship building, which was done by communal groups voluntarily formed for the purpose and which had a good chance of taking up piracy. Finally, it may happen that a number of free men join together for work in the production of metals, though the production of iron is a relatively late phenomenon. Originally houses were built without metal nails; the Alpine house has a flat roof in spite of the burden of snow, because there are no nails for a sloping roof.

As will be seen from the spread of invitation work, the earliest specialization by no means implies skilled trades. The latter are related in primitive lands to magical conceptions; the belief in things which can be achieved by the individual only by magical processes had to develop first. This was especially true of the medical calling; the "medicine man" is the earliest profession. In general every highly skilled occupation was originally regarded as influenced by magic. The smiths especially were everywhere viewed as characterized by supernatural qualities because a part of their art appears mysterious and they themselves make a mystery of it. The skilled occupations developed within the large household of a chieftain or landed proprietor, who was in a position to train dependent persons in a special direction, and who possessed the needs for which skilled work was requisite. The skilled occupation may also have evolved in connection with the opportunity for exchange. The decisive question in this connection is, has the industry access to a market? and also, who sells the final product after it has gone through the hands of the various producers? These questions are also vital for the struggles of the guilds and for their disintegration. A specialized skilled craftsman may produce freely for stock and for the market, selling his product as a small enterpriser. This extreme case we shall call "price work"; it presupposes command over raw materials and tools. One possibility is that the raw materials, and under some circumstances the tools, are provided by an association. Thus the medieval guild as a group bought and distributed certain raw materials, such as iron and wool, in order to safeguard the equality of the members.

The opposite extreme is that the craftsman is in the service of another as a wage worker. This appears when he is not in possession of raw material and tools but brings to the market his labor only, not its product. Between the two extremes stands the craftsman who works on order. He may be the owner of the raw materials and tools, giving rise to two possibilities. Either he sells to the consumer— who may be a merchant ordering from him; in which case we speak of free production for a clientele, or, he produces for an entrepreneur who possesses a monopoly of his labor power. The latter relation often results from indebtedness to the entrepreneur, or from the physical impossibility of access to the market, as for example in the export industries in the middle ages. This is called the "domestic" system, or more descriptively, the putting-out system or factor system; the craftsman is a price worker on another's account.

The second possibility is that raw material and tools—

one or the other or both—are provided by the one who orders the work, the consumer. Here we shall speak of wage work for a clientele. A final case is that in which the person ordering the work is an entrepreneur who has production carried on for gain; this is the case of domestic industry, the putting-out system. Here are associated on the one hand a merchant entrepreneur (*Verleger*) who commonly, though not always, purchases the raw materials, and under some circumstances also provides the tools, and on the other hand the wage worker on order in his home, who cannot bring his own product to the market because the requisite organization of craft work is absent.

With regard to the relation of the worker to the place of work, the following distinctions may be made. 1. The work is done in the worker's dwelling. In this case the craftsman may be a price worker who independently fixes the price of his product; or he may be a home worker for wages for a clientele, producing on the order of consumers; or finally, he may be a home worker for an entrepreneur. 2. On the other hand the work may take place outside the worker's dwelling. Here it may be itinerant work, work done in the house of the consumer, as is still common with seamstresses and dressmakers; such work was originally done by "wandering" laborers. On the other hand the work may be brought to the worker, but may be of such a nature that it cannot be carried on in his own house, as in the case of the whitewash industry. Finally, the work place may be an "ergasterion" or work shop, and as such separate from the dwelling of the worker. An ergasterion is not necessarily a factory; it may be a bazaar-shop where work place and place of sale are combined. Or, it may be leased in common by a number of workers; or finally, it may belong to a lord who puts his slaves to work in it, either selling the product himself or permitting the slaves to sell it on condition of a specified payment. The character of the ergasterion is most clearly seen in the modern shop enterprise where the conditions of work are prescribed by an entrepreneur who pays wages to the worker.

The appropriation of the fixed investment, under which the work place and means of work are included insofar as the latter do not come under the head of tools, may also be effected in various ways. There may be no need for a fixed investment, in which case we have to do with pure craft work, as in the medieval guild economy. The absence of fixed capital is characteristic of the latter to the extent that as soon as such capital appears the guild economy is in danger of dissolution. If there is a fixed investment it may be provided and maintained by an association,—village, town, or workers' organization. This case is common, and especially is met with repeatedly in the middle ages, the guild itself providing the capital. In addition we find seigniorial establishments which the workers are allowed to use for a payment; a monastery, for example, establishes a fulling mill, and grants free workers its use. Again it is possible that the seigniorial establishment may be not only placed at the disposal of free workers but used in production by workers under the *dominium* of the owner and whose product he himself sells. This we call *"oikos,"* or villa, craft work. Originated by the Pharaohs, it is found in the most varied forms in the establishments of the princes, landed proprietors, and monasteries of the middle ages. Under oikos craft work, however, there is no separation between the household and the enterprise, and the latter ranks only as an auxiliary interest of the entrepreneur.

All this is changed in the capitalistic establishment of an entrepreneur. Here work is carried on with means provided by the entrepreneur, and discipline is necessary.

The entrepreneur work shop counts as fixed capital, forming an item in the accounting of the entrepreneur; the existence of such capital in the hands of an individual is the fact which brought about the downfall of the guild system.

CHAPTER VIII

The starting point of the development is house industry, producing for the requirements of a small or large household. From this point the development may lead to tribal industry, which may arise in consequence of the possession by a tribe of a monopoly, either of certain raw materials or of certain products. Tribal industry is carried on originally as a welcome auxiliary source of income, but later to an increasing extent as a regular occupation. It signifies in the one as in the other of these stages that the products of household activity, prepared with the tools and raw materials of the house community, are brought to the market, so that a window is opened, as it were, in the self-contained household economy, looking out on the market. The monopoly of raw material may be conditioned by the exclusive occurrence of certain materials—stone, metals, or fibers, most commonly salt, metal, or clay deposits—within the territory of the tribe. The result of exploitation of a monopoly may be the appearance of wandering trade. It may be carried on by those who conduct the industry, as in the case of many Brazilian tribes or the Russian "kustar," who in one part of the year as a farmer produces products and in the other part peddles them. Again, it may be qualities of workmanship which are monopolized, as frequently in the case of wool products of artistic distinction, the worker being in the possession of a trade secret or special skill not readily transferred. This case involves

122

a special form of price-work in which the craft is monopolized through the possession of land and is attached to a tribe or clan by an hereditary charism. Specialization of production takes place between ethnical groups. It may be confined to the exchange of products between geographically adjacent regions, as in Africa, or there may be a wider development.

The one possibility leads to the establishment of castes, as in India.[1] Through the combination of individual tribal groups under an overlordship, tribal industries which originally lay side by side horizontally have here become arranged vertically in a stratification, and the ethnic division of labor is now found among persons subjected to a common master. The original relationship of the tribes as mutually foreign is expressed in a system of castes whose members do not eat together or intermarry and receive only specified services at each other's hands. The caste system has had tremendous consequences for the whole social organization of India, because it is anchored in ritualistic and hence religious institutions. It has stereotyped all craft work and thus made impossible the utilization of inventions or the introduction of any industry based on capital. The introduction of any technical improvement whatever at any time would have presupposed the founding of a new caste below all the old series previously existing. When the Communist Manifesto says of the proletarian that he has a world to win and nothing to lose but his chains, the expression would apply to the Indian[2] except that he can only get free of his chains in the after world, through the fulfillment to the last detail of his caste obligations in this. Every Indian caste had its production process traditionally fixed; one who abandoned the traditional process lost caste, and was not only expelled and made pariah but also lost his chance in the future world, the prospect of reincarnation in a higher caste. Hence, the system became the most conservative of possible social orders. Under the English influence it has gradually broken down, and even here capitalism is slowly making its way.

The second possibility which opens up in the stage of exchange between ethnic groups is evolution in the direction of market specialization. Regional division of occupations may be first "demiurgic"—that is, not yet related to a market though no longer inter-tribal, the village or a landed proprietor acquiring craft workers and compelling them to work for the village or the estate (oikos). Here is to be classified for example the village industry of India, and in Germany as late as the 14th century the lord of the land was considered under obligation to provide a corps of village craftsmen. Here we find local specialization for self-sufficient production, with which an hereditary proprietorship of work places is regularly associated.

Going beyond this is a sort of local specialization which in its end results leads to specialization for the market. Its prior stage is the specialization of village and manorial industry. In the village are found, on the one hand, peasants and, on the other, landed proprietors who bring about the settlement of craft workers to produce for the requirements of the lord, for payment in the form of a share in the harvest or otherwise. This contrasts with specialization for the market in that there is no exchange. Furthermore, it still carries the marks of specialization between ethnic groups, in that the craftsmen are foreigners; however, they include some peasants who have lost their status, because unable to maintain themselves, due to inadequacy of their holdings of land.

A different course is taken by the seigniorial form of exploitation of craft workers, that is, the large household or estate type of specialization carried out by princes or lords of the land for private or political purposes. Here also specialization takes place without exchange. The duty of furnishing particular services for the disposal of the lord is laid upon individual craftsmen or whole classes of such. In antiquity this arrangement was widespread. In addition to the *officia*—the officials of the great household, such as the office of treasurer, which was usually filled by a slave—appeared the *artificia*. These consisted chiefly of slaves and included certain categories of craft workers within the *familia rustica*, who produced for the needs of the large estates. Such were smiths, iron workers, building craftsmen, wheelwrights, textile workers—especially female in the gynecium or women's house—millers, bakers, cooks, etc. They are also found in the city households of the higher nobility, who have at their disposal large numbers of slaves. The list of the Empress Livia, the wife of Augustus, is known; it includes craft workers for the wardrobe and other personal requirements of the princess. A similar situation is found in the princely households of India and China, and again in the medieval manors, both of the lay lords and of the monasteries.

In addition to the craft workers for the personal needs of the lord, are those who serve his political requirements. An example on a large scale is the administration of the Pharoahs of the New Empire, after the expulsion of the Hyksos. Here we find a warehouse system replenished from the payments in kind of the dependent classes, and along with it extensive industrial specialization of hand work for the household and political needs of the king. The officials are paid in goods out of the storehouse, receiving a specified allotment, and the written claims to the goods circulate in commerce in the fashion of government notes today. The products are obtained in part from the work of peasants and in part from specialized estate industry.

In the large estates of the near east also, luxury crafts were developed and encouraged. The Egyptian and Mesopotamian kings caused the marvels of ancient oriental art to be developed by workers trained in their workshops and dependent upon them and thus gave the estate (oikos) a mission to fulfill in the history of culture.

In order that a transition be effected from this condition to production for a clientele and for the market, a circle of consumers with purchasing power to absorb the output was necessary; that is, an exchange economy of some extent had to develop. Here we have a situation similar to that found in the development of the peasantry. The prince, or lord, or slave holder, had his choice between utilizing the skill of the workers as labor power, himself producing for the market by means of them, and exploiting them as a source of rent. In the first case the lord became an entrepreneur utilizing the work of the unfree population; such a system is found both in antiquity and in the middle ages, the lord employing someone to look after the marketing. This person is the *negotiator,* the dealer, who is attached as an agent to the princely or other sort of household.

The way in which the lord may utilize his people as labor force in such a case may vary. He may employ them as unfree home workers; they remain in their own dwellings and are compelled to deliver certain quantities of goods, the raw materials for which may belong to them or may be furnished by the lord. In antiquity, this relation was widespread. Textiles and pottery products were brought to the market in this way, being produced mainly in the women's house (γυναικεῖον, gynecium). In the middle ages, the linen industry in Silesia and Pomerania arose in this manner; the lord is the merchant-capitalist-employer or "factor" (*Verleger*) of the craft worker.

Or, the lord could go over to shop industry. In antiquity we find among the auxiliary industries of the great landed proprietors terra cotta works, sand pits and stone quarries. We also find the large gynecium in which female slaves were used in spinning and weaving. Similarly in Carolingian times as to the gynecium. Shop industry developed to an especial extent in the monastic economy of the middle ages in the breweries, fulling mills, distilleries, and other industries of the Benedictines, Carthusians, etc.

In addition to auxiliary industries on the land, we find town industries with unfree labor. While in the rural industries the lord disposes of the products through the agency of his unfree labor force, in the towns it is generally the merchant who by means of his trading capital sets up establishments with unfree workers. This relation was common in antiquity. For example, tradition tells us that Demosthenes inherited from his father two ergasteria, a smithy shop, making weapons, and a work shop for the production of bedsteads—which at that time were objects of luxury and not necessities. The combination is explained by the fact that the father was an importer of ivory, which was used for inlaying both in the handles of swords and in the bedsteads, and had taken the shops with their slaves as a forfeit in consequence of the inability of his debtors to pay. Lysias also mentions a "factory" with a hundred slaves. In both cases we find production for a small upper class on the one hand and for war purposes on the other. In neither case, however, are we concerned with a "factory" in the modern sense, but only with an ergasterion.

Whether an ergasterion operates with unfree or with freely associated labor depends on the individual case. If it was a large establishment producing for the market with slave labor it was a case of labor accumulation, not of

specialization and co-ordination. Many persons worked together, each turning out independently a single class of
products. Over them all was set a foreman who paid the
lord double head dues and whose single interest lay in a
certain uniformity in the product. Under such relations
there could be no question of large scale production in the
sense of the modern factory, for the ergasterion had no
fixed capital, and did not usually belong to the lord, though
it might in some cases.

Furthermore, the special features of slave holding made
for the impossibility of the development of such an establishment into a modern factory. The human capital con-
sumes more in the very moment when the market fails,
and its upkeep was a very different matter from that of
a fixed capital in machines. Slaves were especially subject
to vicissitudes and exposed to risk. When a slave died it
meant a loss, in contrast with present conditions where the
risks of existence are shifted on to the free workers.
Slaves could also run away, especially in time of war, and
did so with especial frequency at a time of military mis-
fortune. When Athens collapsed in the Peloponnesian
War, the whole slave capital utilized in industry became a
loss. Furthermore, the price of slaves fluctuated in the
most astonishing way in consequence of the wars which were
the normal condition of antiquity. The Greek city-state
carried on war continuously; to contract a durable peace
was regarded as a crime; peace was concluded for a re-
spite, as commercial treaties are made today. In Rome
also, war was an every-day occurrence. Only in war time
were slaves cheap, in time of peace extraordinarily dear.
The lord had his choice in the treatment of this capital,
often obtained at high cost, either to keep the slave in a
barracks or to support his family along with him. In the
second case occupations of a different sort must be found

for the women; hence the lord could not specialize his establishment, but had to carry on several branches in combination in his oikos. If he did specialize, the death of a slave was very disastrous. An additional factor was the absence of all interest in the work on the part of the slave; only by means of quite barbaric discipline could be extracted from them the amount of work which free laborers give today under a system of contract. The large-scale establishments with slaves were therefore a rare exception; in all history they appear to a considerable extent only where there is an absolute monopoly of the branch of production concerned. The example of Russia shows that factories manned by servile workers were completely dependent on the maintenance of such a monopoly; the moment it was broken they collapsed in the face of competition with free labor.

It is true that the organization of antiquity often presents a somewhat different aspect. The lord does not appear as an entrepreneur but as an income receiver, utilizing the labor power of the slave as a source of rent. He had the slave taught some craft; then if he did not hire him out to a third party he allowed him to produce independently for the market, or himself to hire out for work, or finally, left him free to conduct his own business, imposing on him in each case a tax. Here we have economically free but personally unfree craftsmen. In this case the slave himself possessed a certain capital, or the lord lent him capital to carry on trade or small craft work (the *peculium*). The self-interest of the slave thus aroused had, according to Pliny, the result that the lord granted him even testamentary freedom. In this way the great mass of the slaves were utilized. A like condition is found in the middle ages, and also in Russia, and everywhere we find some technical designation for the tax as a proof that we are concerned not with an extraordinary but with a quite normal relation, ἀποφορά, *Leibzinz, obrok*.

Under this manner of utilizing the slaves, whether the lord operated on his own account depended on the presence of a local market, in contrast with a general one in which the slaves could sell their products or labor power. If the labor organization of antiquity and that of the middle ages start from the same point and are similar in the early stages and then later take quite different courses, the reason is found in the completely different character of the market in the two civilizations. In antiquity the slaves remained in the power of the lord, while in the middle ages they became free. In the latter there is a broad stratum of free craftsmen unknown to antiquity. The reasons are, several:

1. The difference in the consumptive requirements in the occident as compared to all other countries of the world. One must understand clearly what a Japanese or Greek household required. The Japanese lives in a house which is built of wood and paper; the mats and a wooden kettle-stand, which together yield a bed, together with dishes and crockery, form the whole establishment. We possess the auctioneer's list from the trial of a condemned Greek, possibly Alcibiades. The household exhibits an incredibly restricted equipment, works of art playing the leading role. In contrast, the household equipment of the medieval patrician is much more extensive and materialistic. The contrast rests on climatic differences. While in Italy heat is not indispensable, even today, and in antiquity the bed counted as a luxury—for sleeping one simply rolled up in one's mantle and lay down on the floor—in northern Europe stoves and beds were necessities. The oldest guild document which we possess is that of the bed ticking weavers of Cologne. It cannot be said that the Greeks

went naked; part of the body was covered, but their clothing requirement was not to be compared with that of the middle European. Finally, again in consequence of climatic relations, the German appetite was greater than that of the southerner. Dante somewhere speaks of the "German land of gluttons." As soon as it was possible to satisfy these needs, a much more extensive industrial production than that of antiquity necessarily developed among the Germans, in accordance with the law of diminishing utility. This development took place from the 10th to the 12th century.

2. The difference in the market as compared with antiquity, as regards extension. In the northern Europe of the 10th to the 12th centuries, purchasers in possession of buying power and industrial products were at hand to a much greater extent than in the countries of antiquity. The civilization of antiquity was coastal; no city of note lay more than a day's journey from the sea. The hinterland back of this thin coastal strip was, to be sure, included in the market area; but it possessed little purchasing power since it was in the product-economy stage of development. In addition, the culture of antiquity rested on slavery. As this civilization moved back from the coast and began to take on an inland character, the supply of slaves ceased. Hence the territorial lords endeavored to make themselves independent of the market by providing for their own needs with their own labor force. This autonomy of the *oikos* which Rodbertus [3] thought to be characteristic of the whole ancient world, is in reality a phenomenon of later antiquity and reaches its highest development in Carolingian times. Its first effect is a narrowing of the market, and later fiscal measures worked in the same direction. [4] The whole process signified an accelerated retrogression toward product economy. In the middle ages, on the

other hand, the market began in the 10th century to increase in extent through the growing purchasing power of the peasantry. Their dependency became less oppressive, the control of the lords losing in effectiveness because the intensivity of tillage was making progress, while the lord, who was tied to his military duties, could not profit by this progress but had to let the whole increase in rent go to the peasant. This fact made possible the first great development of the handicrafts. It began in the period of market concessions and of the founding of the towns, which in the 12th and 13th centuries moved eastward also. Viewed from the economic standpoint, the towns were speculative ventures of the princes; the latter wished to acquire taxable dependents and therefore founded towns and markets, as settlements of persons who bought and sold. These speculations did not always turn out happily. Those of the Polish nobility mostly failed when the growth of anti-semitism drove the Jews into the east and the nobles tried to exploit the movement in the founding of towns.

3. The third reason is the unprofitableness of slavery as a labor system. Slavery was profitable only when the slave could be cheaply fed. This was not the case in the north, where in consequence slaves were preferably exploited as rent payers.

4. The great fact of the instability of slave relations in the north. Runaway slaves were found everywhere in northern lands. There was no criminal news service, the lords were pitted against each other in regard to the slaves and one who escaped did not risk much, as he could find shelter with another lord or in a town.

5. The interference of the towns. The emperor especially granted privileges to the towns, giving rise to the principle "town air makes free." He decreed that anyone, no matter whence or from what class he came, be-

longed to the town if he settled there.   The citizenship of
the towns came in part from such acquisitions; in part it
was noble, in part made up of merchants, and in part of
dependent skilled craftsmen.

This development was favored by the increasing weakness of the imperial power and by the particularism of the
towns, which was promoted by this weakness; the towns
possessed the power, and were in a position to laugh in the
faces of the territorial lords.   The principle "town air
makes free" did not, however, go unopposed.   On the one
side the emperors were forced to promise the princes to op-
pose the seizing of new privileges by the towns; on the other
their poverty continually forced them to grant the privileges.   It was a contest of power in which finally the political power of the princes, who took an interest in the
towns, proved stronger than the economic power of the
territorial lords, whose interest lay in retaining their dependents.

The craftsmen who settled on the basis of these privileges
were of various origins and of divers legal status.   Only
exceptionally were they full citizens possessing land free
of obligations; in part they were persons subject to feudal
head dues, bound to make payments to some lord within or
without the town.   A third category consisted of the
"*Muntmannen*," in a sort of wardship status, who were
personally free but were commended to some free citizen
who represented them in court and to whom they owed
specific services in return for his protection.

In addition there would be manors within a town, possessing their own craftsmen and special craft regulations.
However, one must guard against the belief that the craft
system of the towns developed out of regulation of craft
work by the lords.   (See below, p. 144.)   In general the
craftsmen belonged to different personal overlords, and in

addition they were subject to the lord of the town territory. Hence only the town itself could originate a craft
ordinance, and it happened that the lord of the town excluded his own dependents from the legal rights which he
granted to the town, not wishing them to obtain the status
of the class of free craftsmen in the town itself. The
free craftsmen were without fixed capital; they owned
their own tools, but did not work on a basis of capital accounting. They were almost always wage workers who
carried to market their labor power and not their products. However, they produced for a clientele and originally on order; whether they remained wage workers or
became price workers depended on market conditions.

Wage work is always the rule where the work is done
for the wealthy classes, price work where it is done for
the mass of the people. The mass buys single, ready-made
articles; hence, the growth in the purchasing power of
the mass is the basis for the appearance of price work, as
later for that of capitalism. However, the distinction cannot be sharply drawn; wage workers and price workers
exist side by side, but in general wage workers predominate,
in the early middle ages as in antiquity, in India and
China, as in Germany. As such they may be either itinerant workers (workers in the house of the employer) or
home workers, depending largely on the costliness of the
material. Gold, silver, silk, and expensive fabrics were
not given the craftsman to work upon at his home but they
were made to come to the work, in order to guard against
theft and adulteration. On this account itinerant work
was especially common in the field of the consumption of
the upper social strata. On the contrary, those whose tools
were costly or heavy to transport were necessarily home
workers; such were the bakers, weavers, wine pressers and
millers; in these occupations we already find the beginnings

of a fixed capital.   Between the fields of wage work and price work there are intermediate cases where chance or tradition fixes the type.   In general, however, the terminology of wage work strongly predominates: ἐκδότης, μισθός, *merces;* all these expressions relate to wages, not to prices. The provisions of the edict of Diocletian also point in the direction of wage rather than price tariffs.

CHAPTER IX

A guild [1] is an organization of craft workers specialized in accordance with the type of occupation. It functions through undertaking two things, namely, internal regulation of work and monopolization against outsiders. It achieves its objective if everyone joins the guild who practices the craft in the location in question.

Guilds in the sense of unfree organizations were found in late antiquity and in Egypt, India, and China. These were organizations for taking care of compulsory contributions to the state. They arose in connection with the fact that the function of supplying the political needs of a prince or of a community was laid upon the various industrial groups and to this end production was organized on occupational lines. It has been assumed that the castes of India also arose out of such guilds, but in reality they grew out of relations between ethnic groups. Already existing castes were utilized by the state, which carried out its financing in kind by requiring that the industry supply products for its needs. In early antiquity the leiturgical guild is found, especially in connection with products important for military use. In the army of the Roman Republic a *centuria fabrum* or industrial craftsman existed alongside the knightly centurion. The later Roman state needed to bring in grain to keep the city population in a good humor. For this purpose it instituted the organization of the *navicularii*, upon whom was laid the task of

136

ship building. Fiscal considerations brought it about that in the last centuries of the Empire almost the whole of economic life was thus "leiturgically" organized.

Guilds are also met with as ritualistic associations. Not all the Indian castes are guilds, but very many are ritualistic guilds. Where castes existed, there were no guilds outside of them; and none were needed, for it is a feature of the caste system that every type of labor service is assigned to a special caste.

A third form of guild is the free association; this is characteristic for the middle ages. Its beginnings are possibly found in late antiquity; at least the Romanized late-Hellenism shows such tendencies toward organizations with guild characteristics. The wandering craftsman first appears at the beginning of our era. Without him the spread of Christianity would never have been possible; it was in the beginning the religion of the wandering craftsmen, to whom the Apostle Paul also belonged, and his proverb "he who does not work shall not eat" expresses their ethics. However, antiquity knew only the first impulses toward free guilds. In general, the craft work of antiquity has the character, as far as we can tell, of clan industry based on hereditary charism—when it was not attached to an oikos, or estate. The guild idea is entirely wanting in the classical democracy, which is the very opposite of guild democracy; on the columns of the erechtheion worked side by side Athenian citizens, free metics, and slaves. The reasons for its absence are of a partly political, but chiefly economic sort. Slaves and free persons could not participate in the same religious ritual. Moreover, the guild is absent where caste organization exists, because it is quite superfluous, and it has little significance where clan economy dominates, as in China. Here the individual craftsman of the town belongs to some village; there is no citizenship of Pekin, or any city whatever, and consequently no guild forming a part of the town organization.   In contrast, there are guilds in Islam. Guild revolutions even took place, although rarely, as in Bukhara.

The spirit of the medieval western guild is most simply expressed in the proposition, guild policy is livelihood policy.   It signifies the maintenance of a substantial burgherly prosperity for the members of the guild, in spite of increased competition in consequence of the narrowing of the opportunities of life; the individual guild member must obtain the traditional standard of life and be made secure in it.   This conception of the traditional standard of life is the analogue of the "living wage" of the present day.   The means which the guild adopted to reach this goal are of interest.

As to internal policy, the guild endeavored by every conceivable means to provide equality of opportunity for all guild members, which was also the objective in the case of the division of the fields into strips by the peasantry.   To realize this equality the development of capitalistic power must be opposed, especially by preventing the unequal growth of capital in the hands of individual masters and consequent differentiation among them; one master must not progress beyond another.   To this end, the processes of work were regulated; no master dared proceed in any other than the traditional manner.   The guild controlled the quality of the products.   It controlled and regulated the number of apprentices and laborers.   It regulated as far as possible the provision of raw material,—communally insofar as price work obtained at the time.   In addition the guild or the town did the purchasing of the raw material and disposed of it to the separate masters. As soon as the transition to price work had taken place and the craftsman as a petty capitalist possessed sufficient means to buy his own raw material, the guild demanded proof of the member's wealth.   This practice has held from the 14th century on.   Men without property could be employed by others as wage workers.   As soon as the field of action became restricted the guild was closed and the number of masters fixed, though this result was only reached in places.

Finally, the relation between the individual craftsmen was regulated. The guild maintained the position that the raw material must take the longest possible course in the individual shop, that the individual workman must keep the object worked upon in hand as long as possible. Hence it was required that the division of labor should be based on the final product and not on technical specialization of operations.   In the clothing industry, for example, the course of production from the flax to the finished garment was not cut transversely into separate individual processes of spinning, weaving, dying, finishing etc., but as far as possible the guilds insisted that specialization relate to final products; one worker must produce hose, another vests. Consequently, we find in the medieval lists two hundred guilds where, according to our way of thinking, counting on a technological basis, two or three thousand would have been required.   The guilds felt a very justifiable anxiety lest a cross-wise division of the process might place the worker nearest the market in a position to dominate the others and to depress them to the position of wage workers.

Thus far the guild follows a livelihood policy.   However, it also endeavored to secure and to maintain equality of opportunity for the members.   To this end free competition had to be limited, and the guilds established various regulations: 1. The technique of the industry. They fixed the number of workers, and especially of apprentices, a member might employ; more especially, where apprenticeship threatened to pass into the employment of cheap labor, the number of apprentices was limited to one or two for each master. 2. The form of the raw material. Especially in industries which had to mix metals, such as bell casting, a fairly strict control was exercised in order to maintain the quality of the result and also to exclude unfair competition. 3. The technique of the industry and the process of production, hence the manner of preparing malt, of working leather, of finishing cloth, of dyeing, etc. 4. They controlled the form of tools employed. The individual guild commonly assumed a monopoly over certain tools, which it alone was allowed to use; the type of the tool was traditionally prescribed. 5. The quality which the product must show before it could be offered on the market.

The guilds also regulated the economic relations of the industry: 1. They set up limitations on the amount of capital, so that no employing entrepreneur could develop within the guild, overshadowing other masters and pressing them into his service. To this end, all association with foreigners outside the guild was forbidden, although the prohibition was rarely enforced. 2. Those admitted to the guild were forbidden to work for other masters lest they might be reduced to the position of journeymen; similarly as to working for merchants, which was bound to lead immediately to a putting-out system. The finished product had to be delivered as wage work for a customer by the guild craftsman who worked for wages; for price workers, the free marketing of the product as price work was the ideal. 3. The guilds controlled the buying opportunities. They forbade forestalling, i. e., no guild member dared provide himself with raw materials ahead of his fellows. Not infrequently they established a right of equal sharing; if a shortage arose any guild member might demand that his brothers in the guild provide him with raw material at its cost to them. 4. The guilds also opposed individual selling ahead of other members. To achieve this they often proceeded to compulsory marketing and strengthened the regulation by forbidding price cutting and enticement of customers; thus the way was barred to price competition. 5. They forbade the sale of the products of outsiders; if a member violated this rule he was rated a merchant and expelled from the guild. 6. They regulated marketing, through price schedules, with a view to guaranteeing the traditional standard of life.

Externally, the policy of the guild was purely monopolistic. 1. The guilds strove towards and reached the objective that in very many cases the policing of the industry in matters affecting the craft was placed in their hands, and in such cases they maintained an industrial court. Otherwise they would not have been able to control the technique and procedure or to maintain equality of opportunity among members. 2. They strove towards and regularly achieved compulsory membership in the guild, at least literally, though it was often evaded in fact. 3. In many cases they succeeded in establishing a guild district; they everywhere strove for this, but fully achieved it only in Germany,—in England not at all, while in France and Italy they achieved partial success. A guild district means monopoly of a certain territory. Within this district, in which the guild established complete authority, no industry could be carried on except that of the guild. This measure was directed against migratory workers, who to a considerable extent were suppressed, and against rural industry. As soon as the guilds obtained power in the towns, their first thought was an endeavor to suppress competition from the country. 4. In case of a transfer of the product of one guild into the hands of another, the guilds set up price tariffs; internally, the price was a minimum price, against outsiders a monopoly price. 5. That the guild regulations might be effectively carried out, the division of labor must be as far as possible along occupational lines, not through transverse division of the process; that is, as already explained, a worker must produce a final product from beginning to end and keep it in his own hands. By all these measures the guilds opposed the development of large establishments within the guild-controlled industry. What they were not able to prevent was the development of putting out of work (*Verlag*), with its implication of dependence of the craftsmen upon the merchant.

As late products of guild history must be added some further regulations. These assumed that the guild had already arrived at the limit of its field of action, that only inter-local division of labor and capitalistic operation with extension of the market could create new industrial opportunities. In the first place, the guilds made the achievement of mastership increasingly difficult. This goal was reached in the first instance through the institution of the "masterpiece." A relatively late product of the development was that, from the 15th century on, strictly economic specifications were attached to the masterpiece. From the standpoint of value its production often had no significance or it even had nonsensical conditions attached; the requirement signified merely a compulsory period of work without remuneration to exclude persons without means. In addition to the requirement of the masterpiece, the masters who had achieved the position of price workers strove for a monopolistic position by prescribing a certain minimum capital for the prospective master.

At this point the organization of apprentices and journeymen appeared, being especially characteristic of continental Europe. First, the period of apprenticeship was fixed and progressively lengthened,—in England to seven years, elsewhere to five, and in Germany to three. After the apprentice finished his instruction he became a journeyman. For the latter also, a period of unremunerated work was prescribed. In Germany this condition led to the institution of the wander years. The journeyman must travel for a certain time before he was allowed to settle anywhere as a master, an arrangement which was never known in France, or in England. Finally, the guild frequently went on to limit the number of masters to an absolute maximum figure. This measure was not always taken in the interest of the guild as a monopoly, but was established by the city (its lord or its council), especially when the latter feared an insufficient productive capacity in products of military use or political importance as means of life, as a result of too large a number of masters.

With the closing of the guild was associated a tendency to hereditary appropriation of the position of master. The resulting preference of the sons of masters, and even their sons-in-law, for admission into the guild is a phenomenon common to all countries in the middle ages, although it never became a universal rule. With this development the character of certain parts of medieval craft work as small capitalism is determined, and corresponding to this character a permanent class of journeymen originates. This development took place not only where craft work was carried on as price work and a certain capital was necessary for the purchase of raw material and for carrying on the industry, but most commonly where the limitation of the number of masters was established.

CHAPTER X

In the large household of the feudal lords and princes as we have seen, the *artificia* existed alongside the *officia,* providing for the economic and political needs. Did the guilds develop out of these organizations on the landed estates as the so-called manorial law theory [1] had affirmed? This theory started from the assertion that as a demonstrable fact the manor included workers for its own needs, a seigniorial organization which was an integral part of the system of manorial law. The era of money economy begins in the granting of market concessions. The landed proprietors find it to their advantage to have markets on their land because they can collect duties from the merchants. Thus arises a market opportunity for the craftsman, who previously provided only the compulsory contribution to the needs of the lord. The next stage in the development is the town. It was regularly founded on the basis of an imperial grant to a prince or lord who used it to employ as a source of rent the craftsmen bound to him by the manorial law. On this account, the theory contends, he forced the guild organization upon the craftsman in view of his political designs of a military character or for his household purposes. Hence the guilds are originally official organizations of the lord of the town (*magisteria*). Now begins the third stage, the epoch of guild fusion. The craftsmen associated in this manorial law organization combine and become economically independent after they have gotten money in their hands through production for the market. Then begins the struggle for the market and for autonomy, in which the guilds are increasingly successful, and the lord is finally expropriated as a result of the introduction of money economy.

On the whole this theory is untenable. It does not take sufficient account of the fact that the lord of the town, —that is, the judicial lord—is a different functionary from the lord of the land and that the founding of the town is regularly connected in some way with the transfer of the judicial authority to the person to whom the town privilege is granted. The judicial lord is in a position, by virtue of his power as public judge, to lay upon those within his jurisdiction burdens similar to those which the lord of the land or personal liege lord laid upon his dependents. The judicial lord is indeed subject to certain limitations, in so far as he must strive to attract settlers by making the burdens as light as possible. In consequence of the judicial power we frequently find its holder in possession of compulsory services of dependents, such as were formerly met with only in connection with the personal liege lord. Heriot and the share of the lord in inheritance are thus not always a sure indication of personal bondage; the town lords also took such acknowledgments from persons free from bondage or compulsory land services. Consequently the craftsmen who were subject to such burdens do not necessarily have to trace their development back to the personal suzerainty of the judicial lords in question.

Still less positively valid is the assumption that the guild regularly developed out of manorial law. As a matter of fact we may find in one and the same town both separate manors and a tendency toward an exclusive unity which later develops into a guild. There is no possibility of asserting that the customary law of one of the manors was the basis of this unity. Often the territorial lords even strove to prevent their dependent craftsmen belonging to the *artificia* from joining the guilds. For it is not demonstrable that the associations which we find previous to the appearance of the guilds—the *fraternitates,* for example—developed into guilds. The *fraternitates* were religious societies, while the guilds were secular in origin. It is true that we know numerous instances in which religious associations later became the germs of those of a profane character, but it can be shown that the guilds were originally non-religious and laid claims to religious functions only in the later middle ages, especially after the appearance of the Corpus-Christi Day processions. Finally, the manorial law theory overestimates the power of the territorial lords in general. Where their authority was not combined with the judicial authority, it was relatively small.

The actual contributions of territorial dominion in the development of industry and the origin of the guilds lie in another field than that assumed by the manorial law theory. In connection with the market concession and the ancient tradition of skilled craftsmen separated from household and clan, it contributed to the production of the individual skilled artisan outside of household and clan groupings. Thus it is one of the elements which obstructed in the west the development toward household, clan, and tribal industry, such as took place in China and India. The result was achieved through the fact that the culture of antiquity moved inland from the coast. Inland towns arose which became the seats of craft groups locally specialized and producing for a local market, exchange between ethnic groups being displaced. The oikos-economy developed trained craftsmen; as a result of the fact that these began to produce for the market, the workers subject to head dues streamed into the towns and developed production for the market as a type. The guilds promoted this tendency and helped it to become dominant. Where the guilds were not victorious or did not originate at all, house industry and tribal industry persisted, as in the case of Russia.

The question whether the free or unfree craftsman is prior in the west cannot be answered in general terms. It is certain that the unfree are mentioned in the records earlier than the free. Moreover, to begin with, only a few sorts of craftsmen existed; in the *Lex Salica* only the *faber* occurs, who may be a smith or a wood worker or any other sort of artisan. In southern Europe free craftsmen are mentioned as early as the sixth century, in the north in the eighth, and from the Carolingian period they became more common.

But in contrast, the guilds first appear in the towns. To picture their origin clearly we must visualize the fact that the population of the medieval town was of mixed composition and that its privileges were not only for that class which was of free extraction. The majority of the inhabitants were unfree. On the other hand, compulsory services rendered to the town lord showing similarity to territorial or personal overlordship do not prove servility. In any case it is certain that a considerable fraction of the town craftsmen, perhaps a majority, did come from the unfree classes, and that only those who produced products for the market, and as price workers marketed them, were admitted to the status of *mercator*—a work technically equivalent to citizen (burgher). It is certain also that the mass of the craftsmen stood originally in a relation of wardship (*Muntmannentum*), and finally that the craftsman in so far and for so long as he remained unfree was subject to the judicial power of the lord, although only in matters requiring the consent of the baronial court. Hence, he was thus subject only in so far and for so long as he still possessed a land holding within a manor and was obligated to feudal land services; affairs of the market did not come before the baronial court but belonged to the jurisdiction of the mayor or the municipal court, to which the craftsman again was subject not because he was free or unfree but insofar as he was *mercator* and as such had a share in the affairs of the town.

In Italy, the guilds seem to have existed continuously from late Roman times. In contrast, no guild is to be thought of in the north whose laws did not rest on a grant from a judicial lord, for only he was in a position to exercise the compulsion necessary for maintaining guild life. Apparently, private associations of various sorts preceded the guilds; and in fact we know no more about the matter of origins.

Originally, the town lords reserved certain rights as against the guilds; especially, since they demanded certain services of a military and economic character as taxes from the guilds for the purposes of the town, they insisted on naming the head of the guild, and on grounds of subsistence policy and of police and military considerations they often carried control deep into the guilds' economic affairs. All these prerogatives of the town lords were later acquired by the guilds, either by way of revolution or for compensation through buying out the possessor. In general they were engaged in a struggle from the beginning. They contended first for the right to choose their own leaders and make their own laws; otherwise they would not have been in a position to carry out their monopolistic policies. In regard to compulsory membership in the guild they usually secured their end without difficulty, because it was in the interest of the town lord himself. They also struggled to free themselves from the burdens laid upon them,—compulsory services, due to town lord or town council, quit-rents both personal and connected with land, general taxes, and rents demanded of them. Often the contest ended in the guild converting the burden into a fixed money payment, the obligation of which it assumed as a group. As early as 1099 the struggle of the weavers of Mayence for freedom from the feudal dues were decided in their favor. Finally, the guilds struggled against wardship (*Muntmannentum*), especially the representation of the ward before the court by the patron, and in general for political equality with the upper class families.

After victory was won in these struggles the specific subsistence policy of the guilds begins with the tendency to establish the guild monopoly. Opposed to it were in the first place the consumers. They were unorganized, as today and always, but the town or the prince might become their champion. Both of these set up a vigorous resistance to the guild monopoly. In the interest of a better provision for the consumers the town often retained the right to name free masters without regard to the decision of the guild. Furthermore, the towns subjected the food industries to an extensive control through the establishment of municipal slaughter houses, meat markets, mills, and ovens, often imposing upon the craftsmen themselves the obligation to make use of these institutions. This regulation was the more easily put through since the guilds in their early days operated entirely without fixed capital. Moreover, the town struggled for power over the guild through the agency of price fixing, setting maximum wages or prices in opposition to the minimum wages and prices of the guilds.

Furthermore, the guild had competition to contend against. Under this head are included the craft workers of the landed estates, especially those of the monasteries, in the country and also in the towns themselves. In contrast with the lay lords, who were hindered by military considerations, the monasteries, thanks to their rational economic procedure, were in a position to set up the most varied industrial establishments and to accumulate considerable wealth. In so far as they produced for the market, they furnished notable competition for the guilds and were fought bitterly by the latter. Even in the Reformation period, the competition of monastic industrial work was one of the considerations which drove the burgher element to the side of Luther. In addition, the struggle was directed against the craftsmen in the country at large, both the free and the unfree, the settled and the itinerant workers. In this struggle the merchants regularly stood side by side with the rural craftsmen against the guilds. None the less the result was an extensive destruction of house industry and tribal industry.

A third struggle of the guilds was directed against the laborers, against those who were not yet masters, which set in as soon as the guild undertook limitation of numbers in any form or the closing of the guild or the raising of difficulties in the way of entry into mastership. In this connection are mentioned the prohibition against working on one's own account instead of that of a master, the prohibition against working in one's own dwelling—because the journeyman could not be controlled or subjected to house discipline—and finally the prohibition against marriage by the journeyman before he became a master; this prohibition could not be enforced and a married journeyman class became the rule.

The guilds struggled with the merchants, especially the

retailers, who met the needs of the town market and would draw their products from wherever they could obtain them most cheaply. Retail trade involved little risk in comparison with trade with remote regions and allowed a more secure profit. The retailers, of whom the merchant tailors formed a typical stratum, were the friends of the rural craftsmen and enemies of those of the town, and the struggles between them and the guilds are among the most intense known to the middle ages.

Parallel with the struggle against the retailers went wars within individual guilds and between various guilds. These arose first in cases where workers possessed of capital and others without it were present in the same guild, which presented an opportunity for the propertyless to become home workers for the wealthy members. A similar situation existed as between wealthy guilds and others possessing little capital, within the same production process. These struggles led in Germany, Flanders, and Italy to sanguinary guild revolutions, while in France only one guild outbreak occurred and in England the transition to the capitalistic domestic system was completed practically without revolutionary acts of violence. The field of such struggles is to be sought in situations where the process of production was divided transversely rather than on the basis of products. This was especially the case in the textile industry, where the weavers, walkers, dyers, tailors, etc. existed side by side, and the question arose as to which of these different units or stages in the single production process would force the others to leave it in control of the market, renounce to it the chance of large profits and become home workers on account of its members. The walkers were often victors, forcing the other divisions of the industry to be content with allowing them to purchase the raw materials and prepare them and market the finished product. In other cases it was the finishers, or weavers, and in London the tailors, who forced the previous stages of the process into their employ. In England the result was that wealthy masters in the guilds came no longer to have anything to do with craft work. The struggle often ended in a compromise, to be resumed later and go on to the winning of the market by one of the production stages. The course of events in Solingen is typical. The smiths, sword furbishers, and polishers, after a long struggle, concluded a treaty in 1487, according to which all three of the guilds were to retain free access to the market. Finally, however, the guild of furbishers obtained control. Most frequently the final stage of production secured the market as a result of the conflict, because knowledge of demand was most easily obtained from that vantage point. This was regularly the case where a certain end product enjoyed an especially favorable market. Thus in wartime the saddlers had an excellent opportunity for bringing the leather dressers under their power. Or, the stage which possessed the most capital might be victorious, those who employed the most valuable productive equipment succeeding in the effort to force the others into their service.

CHAPTER XI

The disintegration of the guilds, which took place after
the close of the Middle Ages, proceeded along several lines.
1. Certain craftsmen within the guilds rose to the
position of merchant and capitalist-employer of home
workers, i. e. of "factor" (*Verleger*). Masters with a
considerable invested capital purchased the raw material,
turned over the work to their fellow guildsmen who carried
on the process of production for them, and sold the finished
product. The guild organization struggled against this
tendency, but none the less it is the typical course of the
English guild development, especially in London. In spite
of the desperate resistance of the guild democracies against
the "older men," the guilds were transformed into "livery
companies," guilds of dealers in which the only full members were those who produced for the market, while those
who had sunk to the level of wage workers and home
workers for others lost the vote in the guild and hence
their share in its control. This revolution first made
possible progress in technique, whereas the dominance of
the guild democracies would have meant its stagnation.
In Germany we do not meet with this course of development; here if a craftsman became an employer or factor
he changed his guild, joining that of the shopkeepers, or
merchant-tailors or constablers, a guild of upper class importing and exporting merchants.

2. One guild might rise at the expense of another. Just as we find trading masters in many guilds, others changed entirely into mercantile guilds, forcing the members of other guilds into their employ. This was possible where the production process was transversely divided. Examples are found in England—the merchant tailors—and elsewhere. The 14th century especially is filled with struggles of the guilds for independence of other guilds. Frequently both processes run along together; within the individual guild, certain masters rise to the position of traders and at the same time many guilds become organizations of traders. The symptom of this eventuality is regularly the fusion of guilds, which took place in England and France but not in Germany. Its opposite is represented by the splitting of the guilds and the union of the traders, especially common in the 15th and 16th centuries. The dealers within the guilds of walkers, weavers, dyers, etc. form an organization and in common regulate the whole industry. Production processes of diverse character are united on the level of small shop industry.

3. Where the raw material was very costly and its importation demanded considerable capital, the guilds became dependent upon the importers. In Italy, silk gave occasion to this development, in Perugia, for example, and similarly for amber in the north. New raw materials might also provide the impetus. Cotton worked in this way; as soon as it became an article in general demand, putting-out enterprises arose alongside the guilds or through their transformation as in Germany, where the Fuggers took a notable part in the development.

4. The guilds might become dependent upon the exporters. Only in the beginnings of the industry could the household or tribal unit peddle its own products. As soon, on the other hand, as an industry became entirely or

strongly based on exportation, the factor-entrepreneur was indispensable; the individual craftsman failed in the face of the requirements of exportation. The merchant, however, possessed not only the necessary capital but also the requisite knowledge of market operations—and treated them as trade secrets.

The textile industry became the main seat of the domestic system; here, its beginnings go back into the early middle ages. From the 11th century on there was a struggle between wool and linen, and in the 17th and 18th centuries between wool and cotton, with the victory of the second in each case. Charlemagne wore nothing but linen, but later, with increasing demilitarization, the demand for wool increased and at the same time with the clearing of forests the fur industry disappeared and furs became constantly dearer. Woolen goods were the principal commodity in the markets of the Middle Ages; they play the leading role everywhere, in France, England and Italy. Wool was always partly worked up in the country, but became the foundation of the greatness and the economic prosperity of the medieval city; at the head of the revolutionary movements in the city of Florence, marched the guilds of the wool workers. Here again we find early traces of the putting-out system. As early as the 13th century independent wool factors worked in Paris for the permanent market of the Champagne fairs. In general we find the system earliest in Flanders, and later in England, where the Flanders woolen industry called forth mass production of wool.

In fact, wool determined the course of English industrial history, in the form of raw wool, partial products and finished goods. As early as the 13th and 14th centuries England exported wool and partial manufactures of wool. Under the initiative of the dyers and made-up clothing interests, the English woolen industry finally became transformed to the basis of exportation of finished products. The peculiar feature of this development is that it resulted in the rise of domestic industry through the rural weavers and the town merchants. The English guilds became predominantly trading guilds, and in the final period of the middle ages attached to themselves rural craftsmen. At this time the garment makers and the dyers were settled in the towns, the weavers in the country. Within the city trading guilds broke out finally the struggle between the dyers and garment makers on the one hand and the exporters on the other. Export capital and merchant-employer capital became separated and fought out their conflicts of interest within the woolen industry under Elizabeth and in the 17th century, while on the other side employer capital had also to contend with the craft guilds; this was the first conflict between industrial and trading capital. This situation, which became characteristic of all the large industries of England, led to the complete exclusion of the English guilds from influence on the development of production.

The further course of events followed different lines in England and France as compared with Germany, in consequence of the difference in the relation between capital and the craft guilds. In England, and especially in France, the transition to the domestic system is the universal phenomenon. Resistance to it ceased automatically without calling forth interference from above. As a result, in England after the 14th century, a small master class took the place of the working class. Precisely the opposite happened in Germany. In England, the development just described signified the dissolution of the guild spirit. Where we find amalgamation and fusion of various guilds, the initiative proceeds from the trading class, which was not to be restrained by guild limitations. They united within the guilds and excluded the masters without capital. Thus formally the guilds maintained themselves for a long time; the suffrage of the city of London, which was nothing but an organization of wealthy dignitaries, was a guild survival.

In Germany, the development proceeds in reverse order. Here the guilds more and more became closed groups in consequence of the narrowing of the field of subsistence policy, and political considerations also played a part. In England there was wanting the particularism of the towns, which dominates the whole of German economic history. The German town pursued an independent guild policy as long as it could, even after it was included in the territorial state of a prince. By contrast, the independent economic policy of the towns ceased early in England and France, as their autonomy was cut off. The English towns found the path to progress open because they were represented in Parliament, and in the 14th and 15th centuries— in contrast with later times—the overwhelming majority of the representatives came from urban circles. In the period of the Hundred Years War with France, the Parliament determined English policy and the interests brought together there pursued a rational, unitary industrial policy. In the 16th century a uniform wage was fixed, the adjustment of wages being taken out of the hands of the justices of the peace and given to the central authority; this facilitated entry into the guilds, the symptom of the fact that the capitalistic trading class, who predominated in the guilds and sent their representatives to parliament, were in control of the situation. In Germany, on the other hand, the towns, incorporated in the territorial principalities, controlled the guild policy. It is true that the princes regulated the guilds in the interests of peace and order,

but in the large their regulative measures were conservative and carried out in line with the older policy of the
guilds. In consequence the guilds maintained their existence in the critical period of the 16th and 17th centuries;
they were able to close their organization, and the stream
of the unchained forces of capitalism flowed through England and the Netherlands, less strongly even through
France, while Germany remained in the background.
Germany was as far from the position of leadership in
the early capitalistic movement at the close of the middle
ages and the beginning of the modern era as it had been
centuries before in the development of feudalism.

A further characteristic divergence is the difference
in regard to social stresses. In Germany, from the close
of the middle ages on, we find unions, strikes and revolutions among the journeymen. In England and France,
these became more and more rare since in those countries
the apparent independence of the home-working small
masters beckoned to them and they could work immediately
for the factor. In Germany, on the contrary, this apparent independence was not available as there was no
domestic industry, and the closing of the guilds established
a relation of hostility between the masters and the journeymen.

The pre-capitalistic domestic industry of the west did
not develop uniformly, or even as a rule, out of the craft
organization; this occurred to the smallest extent in
Germany and to a much greater extent in England.
Rather it quite commonly existed side by side with craft
work, in consequence of the substitution of rural craft
workers for urban, or of the fact that new branches of
industry arose through the introduction of new raw materials, especially cotton. The crafts struggled against the

putting-out system as long as they could, and longer in Germany than in England and France.

Typically, the stages in the growth of the domestic system are the following: 1. A purely factual buying monopoly of the factor in relation to the craft worker. This was regularly established through indebtedness; the factor compels the worker to turn over his product to him exclusively, on the ground of his knowledge of the market as merchant. Thus the buying monopoly is connected with a selling monopoly and taking possession of the market by the factor; he alone knowing where the products were finally to stop. 2. Delivery of the raw material to the worker by the factor. This appears frequently, but is not connected with the buying monopoly of the factor from the beginning. The stage was general in Europe but was seldom reached elsewhere. 3. Control of the production process. The factor has an interest in the process because he is responsible for uniformity in the quality of the product. Consequently, the delivery of raw material to the worker is often associated with a delivery of partial products, as in the 19th century the Westphalian linen weavers had to work up a prescribed quantity of warp and yarn. 4. With this was connected not infrequently, but also not quite commonly, the provision of the tools by the factor; this practice obtained in England from the 16th century on, while on the continent it spread more slowly. In general the relation was confined to the textile industry; there were orders on a large scale for looms for the clothiers who turned them over to the weavers for a rental. Thus the worker was entirely separated from the means of production, and at the same time the entrepreneur strove to monopolize for himself the disposal of the product. 5. Sometimes the factor took the step of combining several stages in the production process; this also was not very common, and was most likely to occur in the textile industry. He bought the raw material and put it out to the individual workman, in whose hands the product remained until it was finished. When this stage was reached the craft worker again had a master, in quite the same sense as the craftsman on an estate, except that in contrast with the latter he received a money wage and an entrepreneur producing for the market took the place of the aristocratic household.

The ability of the putting out system to maintain itself so long rested on the unimportance of fixed capital. In weaving, this consisted only of the loom; in spinning, prior to the invention of mechanical spinning machines, it was still more insignificant. The capital remained in the possession of the independent worker, and its constituent parts were decentralized, not concentrated as in a modern factory, and hence without special importance. Although the domestic system was spread widely over the earth, yet this last stage, the provision of the tools and the detailed direction of production in its various stages by the factor, was reached comparatively seldom outside the western world. As far as can be learned, no trace whatever of the system survived from antiquity, but in China and India it was present. Where it dominated, craftsmen might none the less in form continue to exist. Even the guild with journeymen and apprentices might remain, though divested of its original significance. It became either a guild of home workers,—not a modern labor organization but at most a forerunner of such,—or within the guild there might be a differentiation between wage workers and masters.

In the form of capitalistic control of unfree labor power, we find house industry spread over the world, as manorial, monastic and temple industry. As a free system it is found in connection with the industrial work of peasants; the cultivator gradually becomes a home worker producing for the market. In Russia especially, industrial development took this course. The "kustar" originally brought only the surplus production of the peasant household to market, or peddled it through third parties. Here we have a rural industry which does not take its course toward tribal industry but goes over into the domestic system. Quite the same thing is found in the east and in Asia,—in the east, it is true, strongly modified by the bazaar system, in which the work place of the craftsman is separate from his dwelling and closely connected with a general centralized market place in order, as far as possible, to guard against dependence on the merchant; to a certain extent this represents an intensification of the medieval guild system.

Dependence of urban as well as rural craft workers upon an employer (factor or "putter out") is met with. China especially affords an example, though the clan retails the products of its members and the connection with clan industry obstructed the development of domestic industry. In India the castes stood in the way of the complete subjugation of the craftsman by the merchant. Down to recent times the merchant was unable to obtain possession of the means of production to the extent we find true elsewhere, because these were hereditary in the caste. None the less, the domestic system in a primitive form developed here. The last and essential reason for its retarded development in these countries as compared with Europe is found in the presence of unfree workers and the magical traditionalism of China and India.

CHAPTER XII

SHOP PRODUCTION. THE FACTORY AND ITS FORE-RUNNERS [1]

Shop production, which implies separation between household and industry, in contrast with home work, appears in the most varied forms in the course of history. The forms are as follows: 1. Isolated small shops. These are found everywhere and always; the bazaar system especially, with its grouping together of a number of work shops to facilitate working together, rests on this separation. 2. The ergasterion. This also is universal; its medieval designation was *fabrica,* a term which is very ambiguous and may designate the cellar den leased by a group of workers and used as a shop, or a manorial institution for wage work with a *banalité* requiring its utilization by the workers. 3. Unfree shop industry on a large scale. This is a frequent occurrence in economic history generally, and seems to have been especially developed in later Egypt. It undoubtedly sprang from the gigantic estate of the Pharaoh; out of this seem to have developed separate shops with wage labor. Certain cotton working shops in upper Egypt in the late Hellenistic period were perhaps the first establishments of the kind, but this can not be finally asserted until the Byzantine and Islamic sources are made available. Probably such shops existed in India and China also, and they are typical for Russia, though here they appear as imitations of the west European factory.

Among earlier scholars, including Karl Marx, a distinction was current between factory and manufactory. The manufactory was described as shop industry, with free labor, without the use of any mechanical power but with the workers grouped and disciplined. This distinction is casuistical and of doubtful value. A factory is a shop industry with free labor and fixed capital. The composition of the fixed capital is indifferent; it may consist of a very expensive horse-power, or water-mill. The crucial fact is that the entrepreneur operates with fixed capital, in which connection capital accounting is indispensable. Hence a factory in this sense signifies a capitalistic organization of the process of production, i. e., an organization of specialized and co-ordinated work within a work shop, with utilization of fixed capital and capitalistic accounting.

An economic prerequisite for the appearance and existence of a factory in this sense is mass demand, and also steady demand,—that is, a certain organization of the market. An irregular market is fatal to the entrepreneur because the conjuncture risk rests on his shoulders. For example, if the loom belongs to him he must take it into account before he can discharge the weaver when conditions are unfavorable. The market on which he reckons must be both sufficiently large and also relatively constant; hence a certain mass of pecuniary purchasing power is necessary, and the development of money economy must have reached the corresponding stage, so that a certain demand can be depended upon. A further requisite is a relatively inexpensive technical production process. This requirement is implied in the fact of a fixed capital which requires the entrepreneur to keep his establishment going even when conditions are unfavorable; if he utilizes hired labor only, the danger is shifted to the worker, if the loom, for example, is left idle. In order to find a steady market,

again, he must produce more cheaply than under the traditional technique of house industry and the putting-out
system.

Finally, the development of the factory is conditioned
by a special social prerequisite in the presence of a sufficient supply of free laborers; it is impossible on a basis
of slave labor. The free labor force necessary for con-
ducting a modern factory is available only in the west in
the necessary quantity, so that here only could the factory
system develop. This mass of labor was created in England, the classical land of the later factory capitalism, by
the eviction of the peasants. Thanks to its insular position England was not dependent on a great national army,
but could rely upon a small highly trained professional
army and emergency forces. Hence the policy of peasant
protection was unknown in England and it became the
classical land of peasant eviction. The labor force thus
thrown on the market made possible the development first
of the domestic small master system and later of the industrial or factory system. As early as the 16th century
there was such an army of unemployed that England had
to deal with the problem of poor relief.

Thus, while in England shop industry arose, so to speak,
of itself, on the continent it had to be deliberately cultivated by the state,—a fact which partly explains the relative meagreness of information regarding the beginnings
of workshops in English records as compared with continental. With the end of the 15th century the monopolization of industrial opportunities in Germany caused a
narrowing of the field of livelihood policy and the problem
of the poor became urgent. As a result the first factories
arose as institutions for poor relief and for providing work.
Thus the rise of shop industry was a function of the
capacity of the economic order of the time to support

population.   When the guild was no longer able to provide the people with the necessary opportunity to earn a living, the possibility of transition to shop industry was at hand.

The fore-runners of factory system in the west.—The industry of the craft guilds was carried on without fixed capital and hence required no large initial cost.   But even in the middle ages there were branches of production which required an investment; industries were organized either through the provision of capital by the guild communally, or by the town, or feudally by an overlord. Before the middle ages, and outside of Europe, they were auxiliary to estate economy.   Among establishments of the work shop type which existed alongside craft work organized in the guilds, were included the following:

1.   The various kinds of mills.   Flour mills were originally built by the lords, either lords of the land or judicial lords; this applies especially to water mills, control of which fell to the lord by virtue of his right to the water. They were typically a subject of *banalités* or legally compulsory utilization (*Mühlenbann*), without which they could not have existed.   The majority of them were in the possession of territorial rulers; the Margraves of Brandenburg possessed no less than 56 mills in Neumark in 1337. The mills were small, but their construction was none the less beyond the financial capacity of the individual miller. In part they were acquired by the towns.   Regularly they were leased by the prince or town, the lease often being hereditary; the operation was always on a retail basis. All this applies to saw mills, oil presses, fulling mills, etc., as well as grain mills.   It sometimes happened that the territorial lord or the town leased the mill to urban families, giving rise to a mill-patriciate.   Toward the end of the 13th century, the partician families of Cologne who held 13 mills organized an association distributing the

profit in fixed shares; the organization was distinguished from a joint stock company by the fact that the mills were hired out for use, that is, exploited as a source of rent.

2. Ovens. In this connection again only those belonging to feudal landlords, monasteries, towns or princes, could produce revenue sufficient to perfect them technically. Originally they were built for the household requirements of the owners, but later their use was let for a fee and a *banalité* (*Backofenbann*) again arose.

3. Breweries. A great majority of breweries were originally built by feudal landlords and made subject to a *banalité* (*Braubann*) though destined particularly to supply the needs of the estate itself. Later the princes established breweries as fiefs and in general they made the conduct of such establishments a subject for concession. This development followed as soon as the sale of beer on a large scale began and there came to be a danger that too large a number of breweries in close proximity would fail to yield tax revenue. In the towns arose a municipal *Braubann*—aside from the preparation of the drink for a household—contemplating from the beginning an hereditary industry; thus the brewery was established on the basis of production for the market. Compulsory utilization of the brewery was an important right of the patricians. With the technical progress in the manufacture of beer, the addition of hops and the preparation of "thick beer" by stronger brewing, the brewery right became specialized, different types falling to different individual patrician burghers. Thus the right to brew attached only to individual patrician houses which had developed the most perfect technical methods. On the other hand there existed a right of free brewing, every citizen who possessed this right being entitled to brew at will in the established

brewery. Thus in the brewing industry also we find enterprise possessing no fixed capital but operating on a communal basis.

4. Iron foundries. These became of great importance after the introduction of cannon. Italy preceded other occidental countries with its *bombardieri*. To begin with the foundries were municipal establishments, since the towns were the first to use artillery, Florence, as we know heading the procession. From them the armies of the territorial princes took over the use of artillery, and state foundries arose. However, neither municipal nor state foundries were capitalistic establishments but produced directly for the military-political requirements of the owner, without fixed capital.

5. Hammer Mills. These arose with the rationalization of the working of iron. But far the most important of all such establishments worked in the field of mining, smelting, and salt production.

All the industries thus far considered are communally and not capitalistically operated. Establishments of a private economic character corresponding to the first stage of capitalism,—that is the possession of the work place, tools, and raw materials by a single owner, so that for the picture of a modern factory, only large machinery and mechanical power are wanting,—are found occasionally in the 16th century, perhaps even in the 15th century, but apparently none existed in the 14th. First arose establishments with the concentration of the workers in a single room, either without specialization of work or with limited specialization. Such industries, which are quite like the ergasterion, have existed at all times. Those in question here are distinguished from the ergasterion through working with "free" labor, although the compulsion of poverty is never absent. The workers who bound themselves to such establishments had no other choice in view of the absolute impossibility of finding for themselves work and tools, and later, in connection with poor relief, the measure was adopted of pressing people into them by force.

The organization of such a workshop, specifically one in the textile industry, is described for us by an English poem of the 16th century. Two hundred looms are collected in the work room; they belong to the enterpriser owning the establishment, who also furnishes the raw material and to whom the product belongs. The weavers work for wages, children being also employed as workers and helpers. This is the first appearance of combined labor. For feeding the workers, the entrepreneur maintained a complete staff of provision workers, butchers, bakers, etc. People marveled at the industry as a world wonder, and even the king visited it. But in 1555 at the urgent behest of the guilds, the king forbade such concentration. That such a prohibition should issue was characteristic of the economic conditions of the time. As early as the 18th century the possibility of suppressing a large industrial establishment was no longer to be thought of, on grounds of industrial policy and fiscal conditions alone. But in this earlier time it was still possible, for externally the whole distinction between the industry described and the domestic system was that the looms were brought together in the house of the owner. This fact represented a considerable advantage to the entrepreneur; for the first time disciplined work appeared, making possible control over the uniformity of the product and the quantity of output. For the worker there was the disadvantage—which still constitutes the odious feature of factory work—that he worked under the compulsion of external conditions. To the advantage for the entrepreneur of control of the work, was opposed the increased risk. If he put the looms out,

as a clothier, the chance of their being all destroyed at
a single stroke through some natural catastrophe or human
violence was much less than with their concentration in
one room; moreover, sabotage and labor revolt could not
easily be employed against him. In sum, the arrangement
as a whole represented only an accumulation of small industrial units within a single shop; wherefore it was so
easy, in England in 1543, to issue a prohibition against
maintaining more than two looms; for at most ergasteria
were destroyed, not organizations of specialized and co-
shop and free worker.

New evolutionary tendencies first appeared with the
technical specialization and organization of work and the
simultaneous utilization of non-human sources of power.
Establishments which internally represented specialization
and co-ordination were still an exception in the 16th century; in the 17th and 18th, the effort toward founding such
establishments is already typical. As non-human sources
of power, the first to be considered is animal power, the
capstan horse-power; natural forces came later, first water
and then air; the Dutch windmills were first used to pump
out the polders. Where labor discipline within the shop
is combined with technical specialization and co-ordination and the application of non-human sources of power,
we are face to face with the modern factory. The impetus
to this development came from mining, which first used
water as a source of power; it was mining which set the
process of capitalistic development in motion.

As we have already seen, a prerequisite for the transition from work shop industry to specialization and co-
ordination of labor with the application of fixed capital,
was, along with other conditions, the presence of a secure
market of minimum extent. Thus is explained the fact
that we first meet with such specialized industry, with

internal division of labor and fixed capital, working for
political requirements. Its earliest forerunners were the
minting works of the medieval princes; in the interests
of control these had to be operated as closed establishments. The coiners, called "house associates" (*Hausge-
nossen*) worked with very simple implements but the arrangement was one of workshop industry with intensive
internal specialization of labor. Thus we find here isolated
examples of the later factories. With the increase in
technical and organizational scope, such establishments
were set up to a large extent in the manufacture of
weapons, including the making of uniforms, as soon as it
became gradually established that the political ruler provided the clothing for the army. Introduction of the uniform presupposes a mass demand for military clothing, as
conversely, factory industry can only arise for this purpose after war has created the market. In the same category, finally, and in the first rank sometimes, belong still
other industries producing for war requirements, especially powder factories.

Alongside the requirements for the army in furnishing a secure market, was the luxury demand. This required factories for gobelins and tapestries, which began
to be common in princely courts after the crusades, as
decorations for the originally bare walls and floors, in
imitation of oriental usage. There were also goldsmith
goods and porcelain,—the factories of western princes being
patterned after the ergasterion of the Chinese emperors;
window glass and mirrors, silk, and velvet and fine cloth
generally; soap—which is of relatively recent origin, antiquity using oils for the purpose—and sugar, all for the
use of the highest strata of society.

A second class of such industries works for the democratization of luxury and the satisfaction of the luxury

requirements of broader masses through imitation of the produce destined for the rich. Those who could not have gobelins or buy works of art had a wall covering of paper, and thus wall-paper factories arose in the early days. Here belong also the manufacture of bluing, starch for stiffening, and chicory. The masses obtain in substitutes something to take the place of the luxuries of the upper strata. For all these products, with the exception of the last named, the market was at first very limited, being restricted to the nobility who were in possession of castles or castle-like establishments. Consequently none of these industries was capable of survival on any other basis than that of monopoly and governmental concession.

The legal position of the new industries in relation to the guilds was very insecure. They were antagonistic to the guild spirit and consequently suspect to the guilds. Insofar as they were not maintained or subsidized by the state, they at least sought to secure express privileges and concessions from the latter. The state granted these on various grounds—to guarantee provision for the requirements of noble households, to provide for the existence of the population which could no longer find support within the guilds, and finally for fiscal ends, to increase the tax paying power of the country.

Thus in France, Francis I founded the arms factory of St. Étienne and the tapestry works of Fontainebleau. With these begins a series of privileged *manufactures royales* for public requirements and for the luxury demand of the upper strata. The industrial development of France thus given a start takes on another form in the time of Colbert. The procedure of the state was simplified here as in England, through the granting of exemptions from the guilds in view of the fact that the privilege of a guild did not always extend over the whole town in which it was settled; for example, a considerable part of Paris lay outside the guild jurisdiction, and the fore-runners of the modern factories could be established in this *"milieu privilégié"* without arousing opposition.

In England the guilds were purely municipal corporations; guild law had no validity outside a town. Hence the factory industry could be established, in harmony with the procedure under the domestic system and workshop industry, in places which were not towns—with the result that down to the reform bill of 1832 the new industry could not send representatives to Parliament. In general, we have almost no record of such factories down to the end of the 17th century, but it is impossible that they were entirely absent. The reason is rather that in England manufacturing could get along without the support of the state because the guild power had so far disintegrated that it no longer held any privilege which was a bar to such industry. In addition, it may undoubtedly be assumed that the development in the direction of shop production would have gone on more rapidly if conditions such as those of Germany had existed and the possibility had not been present of producing under a small master system.

In the Netherlands likewise we hear almost nothing of governmental grants of privileges. None the less, many factories were founded by Huguenots at a relatively early date in Amsterdam, Haarlem, and Utrecht, for the making of mirrors, silks, and velvet.

In Austria in the 17th century the state endeavored to attract factories into the country by granting privileges which would be a protection against the guilds. On the other hand, we also meet with the founding of factories by the great feudal lords; of these the first is perhaps the silk weaving works of the Counts of Sinzendorff in Bohemia,

In Germany the first manufactories were founded on
municipal soil, and specifically in Zürich in the 16th
century, when Huguenot exiles founded the silk and brocade
industry here. They then spread rapidly among the German cities. In 1573 we find the manufacture of sugar and
in 1592 that of brocade in Augsburg, that of soap in Nuremburg in 1593; dye works in Annaberg in 1649, manufacture
of fine cloth in Saxony in 1676, cloth manufacture in Halle
and Magdeburg in 1686, the gold wire industry in Augsburg in 1698, and finally at the end of the 18th century,
widely scattered porcelain manufacture, partly conducted
and partly subsidized by the princes.

To sum up, it must be held at present, first, that the
factory did not develop out of hand work or at the
expense of the latter but to begin with alongside of and in
addition to it. It seized upon new forms of production
or new products, as for example cotton, porcelain, colored
brocade, substitute goods, or products which were not made
by the craft guilds, and with which the factories could
compete with the latter. The extensive inroads by the
factories in the sphere of guild work really belongs to the
19th century at the earliest, just as in the 18th century,
especially in the English textile industry, progress was
made at the expense of the domestic system. None the
less the guilds combated the factories and closed workshops growing out of them, especially on grounds of principle; they felt themselves threatened by the new method
of production.

As little as out of craft work did the factories develop
out of the domestic system, rather they grew up alongside the latter. As between the domestic system and the
factory the volume of fixed capital was decisive. Where
fixed capital was not necessary the domestic system has
endured down to the present; where it was necessary,

factories arose, though not out of the domestic system; an originally feudal or communal establishment would be taken over by an entrepreneur and used for the production of goods for the market under private initiative.

Finally, it is to be observed that the modern factory was not in the first instance called into being by machines but rather there is a correlation between the two. Machine industry made use originally of animal power; even Arkwright's first spinning machines in 1768 were driven by horses. The specialization of work and labor discipline within the workshop, however, formed a predisposing condition, even an impetus toward the increased application and improvement of machines. Premiums were offered for the construction of the new engines. Their principle—the lifting of water by fire—arose in the mining industry and rested upon the application of steam as a motive force. Economically, the significance of the machines lay in the introduction of systematic calculation.

The consequences which accompanied the introduction of the modern factory are extraordinarily far reaching, both for the entrepreneur and for the worker. Even before the application of machinery, workshop industry meant the employment of the worker in a place which was separate both from the dwelling of the consumer and from his own. There has always been concentration of work in some form or other. In antiquity it was the Pharaoh or the territorial lord who had products made to supply his political or large-household needs. Now, however, the proprietor of the workshop became the master of the workman, an entrepreneur producing for the market. The concentration of workers within the shop was at the beginning of the modern era partly compulsory; the poor and homeless and criminals were pressed into factories, and in the mines of Newcastle the laborers wore iron collars down

into the 18th century. But in the 18th century itself the
labor contract everywhere took the place of unfree work.
It meant a saving in capital, since the capital requirement
for purchasing the slaves disappeared; also a shifting of the
capital risk onto the worker, since his death had previously
meant a capital loss for the master. Again, it removed
responsibility for the reproduction of the working class,
whereas slave manned industry was wrecked on the question of the family life and reproduction of the slaves. It
made possible the rational division of labor on the basis
of technical efficiency alone, and although precedents existed, still freedom of contract first made concentration of
labor in the shop the general rule. Finally, it created
the possibility of exact calculation, which again could only
be carried out in connection with a combination of workshop and free worker.

In spite of all these conditions favoring its development,
the workshop industry was and remained in the early
period insecure; in various places it disappeared again,
as in Italy, and especially in Spain, where a famous paint-
ing of Velasquez portrays it to us although later it is
absent. Down into the first half of the 18th century it
did not form an unreplaceable, necessary, or indispensable part of the provision for the general needs. One
thing is always certain; before the age of machinery, workshop industry with free labor was nowhere else developed
to the extent that it was in the western world at the beginning of the modern era. The reasons for the fact that
elsewhere the development did not take the same course will
be explained in what follows.

India once possessed a highly developed industrial technique, but here the caste stood in the way of development
of the occidental workshop, the castes being "impure" to
one another. It is true that the caste ritual of India did

not go to the extent of forbidding members of different castes to work together in the same shop; there was a saying—"the workshop is pure." However, if the workshop system could not here develop into the factory, the exclusiveness of the caste is certainly in part responsible. Such a workshop must have appeared extraordinarily anomalous. Down into the 19th century, all attempts to introduce factory organization even in the jute industry, encountered great difficulties. Even after the rigor of caste law had decayed, the lack of labor discipline in the people stood in the way. Every caste had a different ritual and different rest pauses, and demanded different holidays.

In China, the cohesion of the clans in villages was extraordinarily strong. Workshop industry is there communal clan economy. Beyond this, China developed only the domestic system. Centralized establishments were founded only by the emperor and great feudal lords, especially in the manufacture of porcelain by servile hand workers for the requirements of the maker and only to a limited extent for the market, and generally on an unvarying scale of operation.

For antiquity, the political uncertainty of slave capital is characteristic. The slave ergasterion was known, but it was a difficult and risky enterprise. The lord preferred to utilize the slave as a source of rent rather than as labor power. On scrutinizing the slave property of antiquity, one observes that slaves of the most diverse types were intermingled to such a degree that a modern shop industry could produce nothing by their use. However, this is not so incomprehensible; today one invests his wealth in assorted securities, and in antiquity the owner of men was compelled to acquire the most diverse sorts of hand workers in order to distribute his risk. The final result, however, was that the possession of slaves militated against the establishment of large scale industry.

In the early middle ages, unfree labor was lacking or became notably more scarce; new supplies did indeed come on the market, but not in considerable volume. In addition there was an extraordinary dearth of capital, and money wealth could not be converted into capital. Finally, there were extensive independent opportunities for peasants and industrially trained free workers, on grounds opposite to the condition of antiquity; that is, the free worker had a chance, thanks to the continual colonization in the east of Europe, of securing a position and finding protection against his erstwhile master. Consequently, it was hardly possible in the early middle ages to establish large workshop industries. A further influence was the increasing strength of social bonds due to industrial law, especially guild law. But even if these obstacles had not existed, a sufficiently extended market for the product would not have been at hand. Even where large establishments had originally existed, we find them in a state of retrogression, like the rural large industries in the Carolingian period. There were also beginnings of industrial shop labor within the royal *fisci* and the monasteries, but these also decayed. Everywhere work shop industry remained still more sporadic than at the beginning of the modern era, when at best it could reach its full development only as a royal establishment or on the basis of royal privileges. In every case a specific workshop technique was wanting; this first arose gradually in the 16th and 17th centuries and first definitely with the mechanization of the production process. The impulse to this mechanization came, however, from mining.

CHAPTER XIII

In the beginning mining was a matter of surface operations. Turf and bog iron ore, as in interior Africa, and
alluvial gold as in Egypt, are probably the most important
mining products of primitive times. As soon as underground work was undertaken, and shafts and galleries had
to be driven, considerable expenditures of labor and material goods were necessary. These were exposed to extraordinary hazards, for one could never tell to what distance a vein would be productive or would return the
important operating expenses which the mine required. If
these were not kept up, the mine went to ruin and the
shaft was in danger of "drowning." The result was that
underground mining was undertaken co-operatively.
Where this happened there developed an obligation to the
industry, as well as a right, on the part of the associates;
the individual could not withdraw from the establishment
without endangering the group. The unit of operation
was small to begin with. In the early middle ages, not
more than two to five men worked in the same shaft.

Among the legal problems which developed in connection with mining, the first in order is the question, who has
the right to carry on mining at a given place. This may
receive an answer in various ways. First, it is possible
that the mark association may dispose of the right, though
positive examples of this are not found in the sources.

178

Again, it is conceivable that, in contrast with tribal operation, the right to these exceptional finds may inhere in the
tribal chieftain; but this also is uncertain, in Europe at
least.

In the periods for which we possess more than mere
guesses the legal situation is covered by two possibilities.
Either the right to quarry is treated as *pars fundi,* the
owner of the surface being also owner of what lies beneath
it (though this relates to the overlord's title to the
land and not that of the peasant) or, all hidden treasures
are "regalia"; the political ruler, that is the judicial lord, a
royal vassal or the king himself, disposes of them and no
one, not even the holder of the land himself, can carry on
mining without a concession from the political authority.
This regale on the part of the political ruler was founded
in the first place on the interest in the possession of precious
metals in connection with coinage. Other possibilities
arose in case the finder was taken into account either by
the landholder or the lord of the regale. Today the dominant principle is freedom of mining; anyone has a right
to prospect for minerals under specific formal requirements, and the finder who has secured a license and discovered a vein may exploit it even without consent of the
landholder, on condition only of payment for damage
inflicted. The modern system of free mining could be built
up more easily on the basis of the regale than on that of
feudal land law. If the landholder possessed the right, he
excluded everyone from the possibility of seeking for
minerals, while the lord of the regale, under some conditions might have an interest in attracting labor into the exploitation. In detail, the history of the development of
mining law and the mining industry took the following
course.

We have very little information regarding the earliest

industry outside the occident,—in India, and Egypt, for example, as to the mining works on Mount Sinai operated by the earliest Pharaohs. The mining organization of Greco-Roman antiquity is better known. The silver mines of Laurion belonged to the Athenian state, which leased the operation and distributed the yield to its citizens. The Athenian fleet which won the victory of Salamis was built through the renunciation of the silver by the citizens for a period of years. How the mines were operated we do not know. Some indication might be drawn from the fact that some very wealthy individuals owned mining slaves; Nicias, the commander in the Peloponnesian War, is supposed to have owned thousands, which he hired out to the lessee of the mines.

The sources for Roman conditions are not unambiguous. On the one hand the Pandects mention condemnation to mine labor, from which it would seem that the use of convict slaves or purchased slaves was normal. On the other hand, a selection of some sort must have taken place; at least the indications are that slaves who had committed any offense in the mine were whipped and expelled from mine work. In any case it is certain that the *lex metalli Vipascensis,* from Hadrian's time, discovered in Portugal, indicates that free labor was already employed. Mining was an imperial prerogative, but the existence of a mining regale is not to be inferred; the emperors had a free hand in the provinces and seizing the mines was a favorite exercise of their power. The technique which the *lex metalli Vipascensis* indicates is in contradiction with information from other ancient sources. In Pliny for example we find a row of slaves set to work hoisting water from the bottom of the mine to the surface by passing buckets. In Vipasca on the contrary, galleries for the same purpose are established beside the outer shaft. Medieval gallery building

goes back traditionally to antiquity, but in other ways much
of the *lex metalli Vipascensis* seems to echo later medieval
relations. Mining is placed under an imperial Procurator,
to whom corresponds the mine master of the political overlord in the middle ages. There is also the obligation to
work. The individual receives the right of driving five
putei into the ground, as in the middle ages five was the
maximum number of shafts. We must assume that he was
obliged to keep all five in operation. If he did not utilize
his right during a specified short period—shorter than in
the middle ages—it was taken from him and the privilege
might be taken up by anyone who was in a position to carry
on the work. We find also that in the beginning there
were certain compulsory payments, and if these were not
forthcoming the right to the mine was again thrown open.
A part of the mining fields was reserved for the fisc,
exactly as later in the early middle ages, and to it also a
part of the raw product had to be delivered; this was first
set at half, while in the middle ages it gradually sank to a
seventh or even less. The operations were carried on by
associated workers with whom any participant might come
to his own agreement. The association imposed obligatory
payments for the *socii,* to raise the cost of driving galleries
and shafts; if these payments failed the mining right again
became free.

In the middle ages Germany took the lead over all other
countries in the precious metals, while tin was mined in
England. In the first instance royal mines are found
here, though not on the basis of the regale but because the
land belonged to the king; an example is the Rammelsberg
near Goslar in the 10th century. Placer gold mining was
also carried on in the royal streams, the right being granted
by the king for a fee, again not on the basis of the regale
but on that of control over navigable waters. Leasing of

mining rights by the king is first met with under Henry II; here also the basis was not the regale but the lease of land to monasteries. In general, what was leased to the monasteries was only that to which the king had a legal right, by virtue of the control of the empire over the land. Originally the king possessed a tithing right in all mining products, which right was generally leased to private persons; but in the case of the monasteries this right is leased in the 11th century as imperial property.

Under the Hohenstaufens the relation of the political authority to mining advances a step farther. The conception of the regale which underlies the measures even of Conrad III was definitely formulated by Frederick Barbarossa; he declared that no one might obtain the *licentia fodiendi* without a concession from the king, for which a payment was to be made; even the feudal landlords had to get such a concession. The arrangement soon became an accepted fact, for the Sachenspiegel recognized the royal mining regale as an institution. However, the theoretical right of the king led at once to conflicts with the princes, whose right to the regale was first recognized in the Golden Bull.

The struggle over the mines between the crown and the feudal landholders is also met with in other countries. In Hungary, the king succumbed to the magnates, and if he wished to operate a mine was forced to buy the tract in question outright. In Sicily, where Roger I still recognized underground treasure as the property of the landholder, the kingdom established its claim to the regale in the second half of the 12th century. In France, the barons claimed the mining right as *pars fundi* down to about 1400. Then the crown obtained the victory and remained in absolute possession of the regale down to the revolution, which made the mines national property. In England, King John

claimed a universal regale, especially over the important
tin mines, but in 1305 the crown was forced to recognize
that the king did not have the right to make mining dependent upon a concession from him.   In the 16th century,
under Elizabeth, the regale was restricted in fact to the
precious metals, all other mines being treated as *pars
fundi;* thus the new industry of coal mining was free from
royal claims.   Under Charles I, the situation again wav-
ered, but finally the crown surrendered completely and
all underground treasures became the property of the
owners of the land or "landlords."

In Germany freedom of mining, that is, freedom of pros-
pecting, derived not from the mark community, but from
the "freed mountains" (*gefreiten Bergen*).   A "freed
mountain" is a region containing minerals in which a
landed proprietor may grant to anyone the privilege of
operating.   The Rammelsberg was still a royal establishment in the 10th century, but in the 11th century the king
leased it to the city of Goslar and the monastery of Walken-
ried.   The monastery in turn granted the mining right to
all comers on condition of payments on a free competitive
basis.   In a similar way the Bishop of Trent in 1185
granted to every member of a mining community made up
of free workers the concession for exploiting his silver
mines.   This step, which suggests both the granting of
markets and that of town privileges, is based on the position of extraordinary power which was obtained by the
free laborers from the 11th to the 14th century.   Skilled
mine workers were scarce and possessed a monopoly value,
and various particularistic political authorities competed
among themselves in promising them advantages.   These
included even freedom of mining, the right to excavate to
a certain prescribed extent.

On the basis of this development, the following epochs

may be distinguished in medieval Germany. First, the development seems to have proceeded out of a condition of concentrated exploitation by the strongest political authority, although feudal dues paid by peasants in connection with mines are occasionally mentioned. The next and most important epoch is that in which the mine workers occupy a position of great power. This resulted in an increasing transfer of mining works to the miners with expropriation of the lords, who became reduced to the position of mere tax receivers, utilizing underground treasures as a source of rent only. The mine owner is now the co-operative association of the workers. They divide the income in the same way in which peasants divided their holdings, that is, with the strictest maintenance of equality. The "mining community" arises, including all the mining interests, that is all those who work in the mine,—later those who have work done in them—yet with exclusion of the overlords. This association represents its members in external matters and guarantees the payments to the overlord. The result was responsibility of the individual members of the mining community (*Gewerken*) for the costs of mineral production. Operations were strictly small scale; seven shafts constituted the maximum which might be acquired by a single miner and the shafts themselves were nothing but primitive holes. As long as the miner operated the shafts he remained possessor; if he stopped operations for even the shortest period, he lost his holding. Since the mining community jointly guaranteed the payments, the overlord entirely gave up operations on his own account. His rental right, that is his share, steadily and rapidly declined from originally half the product to a seventh and finally to a ninth.

The next epoch is that of incipient differentiation among the workers. There arises a stratum of miners who do not take part in the actual work, alongside another of those who work but are dependent upon those who do not; hence, a development similar to that of the domestic system in industry. This condition was reached in many places as early as the 13th century although not yet predominant. Limitations on the shares were maintained however; large scale capitalism could not develop, but only a small *rentier* possession, although for short periods considerable profits were possible.

The third epoch is one of increasing capital requirements, resulting especially from the ever greater extent of the galleries. As it was necessary for ventilation and pumping to dig constantly deeper tunnels, which would pay for themselves only in the more remote future, considerable advances were required. Hence the capitalist enters the mining group.

The fourth stage was one of concentration in the mineral trade. Originally, each miner received his share of the product in kind, to do with as he pleased. In the face of this arrangement the mineral dealer was in a position to secure actual control over the output. His influence increased, and the typical aspect of the development is the appearance of wholesale dealers in minerals, especially in the 16th century.

Under the pressure of this situation the handling of minerals passed increasingly into the hands of the miners' general organization (*Gewerkschaft*) as a group, as in this way the miners sought to secure protection from the power of the dealers. This had the further consequence that the general union became director of operations, while originally the individual miner operated independently. A still further consequence was that the union became organized as a capitalistic association, with capital accounting, and that the share of the miners in the product came to them only through the treasury of the union. There came to be a periodical accounting, every individual worker receiving debits and credits according to his performance.

In detail, the development of the organization prior to the appearance of modern capitalism proceeded in the following way. The lord was forced by the union of the mine workers to renounce interference in operations; the miners (*Gewerken*) forbade his officials to enter the shafts and only the members of the association had rights of control over each other. The obligation to operate was maintained, though no longer in the interests of the lord, but rather in that of the miners' association (*Genossenschaft*), which was responsible for the quit-rents. The parallelism with the Russian village, where the individual remains attached to the soil, in spite of the abolition of serfdom, is apparent. A further step was definite appropriation in shares by the miners. It is a matter of controversy how the shares were arranged, whether they were originally physical shares out of which later *Kuxe* or abstract shares developed. All the wage workers belonged to the mining community, but the miners' organization included only owners of shares. How early the union (*Gewerkschaft*) appeared is doubtful, but it is certain that the membership of the mining community and of the miners' organization ceased to be identical.

After the mine workers had come into possession not only of the means of production but also of the raw material, there began a process of differentiation within the working class in the mining industry, and the disintegration which called forth capitalism. The increasing demand for mine workers resulted in increasing accessions to the class. The older workers, however, refused to accept the new arrivals into the community (*Gewerkschaft*). They became "*Ungenossen*," non-members, wage-earners in the position of apprentices in the service of an individual master who paid them on his own account. Thus arose associate or dependent miners, and an inner differentiation began, corresponding to the external one. Out of the distinction in position among individual workers in the production process arose a distinction in regard to the right to work in the mines. The increased need for specialization led, for example, to an increasing demand for mining smiths. These early became wage workers who in addition to a money wage received also a fixed share in the product. The difference in yield among different shafts also worked in the direction of differentiation. Originally the guild principle applied, in that the workers' organization possessed the right of sharing as a whole in any especially productive shaft and of distributing the benefit of its yield among all the mine workers. But this came to an end and to an increasing extent distinctions arose in the opportunities of individual mine workers with regard to risks. Sometimes enormous profits were made, and sometimes the miners went hungry. Increase in the freedom of transfer of shares likewise increasingly worked for differentiation, since the members who did not participate in the work took advantage of the marketability of their shares.

Thus a purely capitalistic interest was able to make its way into the human group of the mining community. The whole process was brought to completion through the increasing capital requirement resulting from increasing depth of the works. The construction of shafts for water supply, and various demands for expensive equipment, became constantly more imperative. The increased capital requirement led to the result, first, that only the propertied associates remained miners with full mining privileges, and second, that new grants were made more and more exclusively to persons who could show command over capital. In addition, the union on its part began to accumulate property. Originally it had none: the individual mine worker had to provide for his shaft and to advance the costs, and the union intervened only when he did not fulfill his obligation to operate. Now, however, the union was compelled to assist in relation to the capital requirement because to an increasing degree the building of shafts for clearing of water in addition to those for the working of the seams became the rule; at first the construction of galleries and shafts was divided between different associations, each being assured a share in the yield of the mine. These shares in the product were a thorn in the flesh of the miners. Increasingly they sought to get the excavations into their own hands. Now the union became a possessor of capital, but the former condition remained, the individual miner being responsible for the cost of his shaft. He had to advance the costs and this was considered his most important function after he no longer shared in the actual work. As before, again, he had to provide the individual workers, to make contracts with them and pay them, a condition which became progressively rationalized. The costs which the various shafts involved varied widely. The actual workers were in a position to maintain unity against the individual "miner." Thus finally the union itself took in hand the hiring and paying of the workers as well as meeting of the advances and costs for the shafts, and set up an accounting for the group as a whole, to begin with in small matters, on a weekly basis, and later year by year. The individual miner had only to make his advance and received the right to a share in the product, in kind to begin with. Finally the development ended in a condition in which the union as a whole sold the product and disbursed the proceeds to the individual members on a share basis.

With this development fell into disuse the measures by which in earlier times the miners had striven to limit the development of inequality among themselves. One of these was the prohibition against the accumulation of mining shares, of which originally not more than three could be united in the same hand. This and all similar restrictions had to disappear, the more certainly as the union itself took in hand the entire conduct of the industry, to an increasing extent as the fields were systematically extended, and as more frequently the enlarged fields were leased to individual shareholders. The new arrangements contrasted with previous conditions, under which the unselective admission of free workers into mining had led to an irrational technique and to irrational sinking of shafts. Furthermore the amalgamation of the unions (*Gewerkschaften*) progressed, to the end of systematizing operations and of suppressing unproductive shafts, a phenomenon met with in the mining of Freiberg as early as the end of the 15th century.

Such phenomena are suggestive in many ways of the history of the guilds. The development having reached this stage, the lords of the regale began to interfere, from the 16th century on, joining hands for the purpose with the mine laborers. The latter, who were dependent upon the small-capitalist "miners," suffered under the lack of planning and the hazardous character of the industry, as did the individual miners themselves, while at the same time the income of the holder of the regale was decreased. Through interference of the lords of the regale, in the interest of the profitableness of the lease as well as in the interest of the workers, unitary mining rights were established, out of which commerce in minerals developed. These rights are the immediate forerunner of the great capitalistic development; they rest on the basis of a rational technical and economic conduct of the industry in general. As a rudiment of the early development there remained the peculiar position of the mining community in the guild-like organization of the workers. On the other hand, the rational union was created by the lords of the regale, as a capitalistic organ of operation, with abstract shares, regulating the obligation of making advances and the right of exploitation. (Originally the number of *Kuxe* was 128.) The union as a whole employed the workers and dealt with the purchasers of the mineral.

Alongside the mines but independent of them were the smelteries. In common with the mines they belonged to the class of industries which took on relatively early the large scale character. For their operation charcoal was necessary; hence the large forest owners, that is the feudal lords and monasteries, were also typical smeltery owners of early times. Occasionally, though not in the majority of cases, the ownership of a smeltery was combined with mining. Small scale operations dominated down into the 14th century, so that for example a single English monastery might own no less than forty small furnaces. But it was also in connection with the monasteries that the first large furnaces were established. Where smelting and mining were in different hands, the ore buyers came in between, forming from the beginning a guild constantly at war with the miners' unions (*Gewerkschaften*). In their policies they are distinguished by the most unscrupulous methods, but in any case we must recognize in their combinations the germ of the first gigantic monopolies which appear at the end of the 15th and the beginning of the 16th century.

Finally, some notice must be given to the most valuable

and most crucial of all products peculiar to the western
world, namely coal. Even in the middle ages it was increasing slowly in significance. We find that the monasteries started the first coal mines; the mines of Limburg
are mentioned in the 12th century, those of Newcastle began production for the market as early as the 14th, while
in the 15th the production of coal was begun in the Saar
district. But all these enterprises produced for the requirements of consumers, not those of producers. In London, in the 14th century, the burning of coal was forbidden because it polluted the air, but the prohibition was
futile; the English exportation of coal increased so rapidly
that special offices had to be established for gauging the
shipping.

Smelting of iron with coal instead of charcoal first begins to be typical in the 16th century, thus establishing the
fateful union of iron and coal. A necessary result was a
rapid deepening of the mine shafts, and the technology
was confronted with the new question, how can water be
lifted with fire? The idea of the modern steam engine
originated in the galleries of mines.

PART THREE

COMMERCE AND EXCHANGE IN THE PRE-CAPITALISTIC AGE[1]

CHAPTER XIV

In its beginnings commerce [1] is an affair between ethnic groups; it does not take place between members of the same tribe or of the same community but is in the oldest social communities an external phenomenon, being directed only toward foreign tribes. It may, however, begin as a consequence of specialization in production between groups. In this case there is either tribal trade of producers or peddling trade in products of a foreign tribe. In any case the oldest commerce is an exchange relation between alien tribes.

The trade of a tribe in its own products may appear in various forms. It usually develops to begin with as an auxiliary occupation of peasants and persons engaged in house industry, and in general as a seasonal occupation. Out of this stage grow peddling and huckstering as an independent occupation; tribal communities develop which soon engage in commerce exclusively. But it may also happen that the tribe engaged in some specialized industry is sought out by others. Another possibility is the establishment of a commercial caste, the classical form being found in India. There trade is a monopoly in the hands of certain castes, specifically the banya caste, with ritualistic exclusion of others. Alongside this trade conducted on ethnically restricted lines is found also trade ritualistically restricted to sects, the magical-ritualistic limitations of the members of the sect excluding it from all

195

other occupations. This is the case with the Indian sect of the dschaina. The dschaina is forbidden to kill any living thing, especially a weak animal. Consequently, he cannot become a soldier, or pursue a multitude of occupations—for example, those in which fire is utilized, because insects might be destroyed; he cannot make a journey in the rain because he might trample upon earthworms, etc. Thus no occupation is open to the dschaina except trade at a fixed location, and the honorable character of the occupation is as well established as that of the banya caste.

Not essentially different is the development of the Jews as an outcast commercial people. Down to the exile there were all sorts of classes within the Jewish people, knights, peasants, craftsmen, and to a limited extent traders as well. Prophecy and the after effects of the exile transformed the Jews from a people with a fixed territory to an alien people and their ritual thenceforward prohibited fixed settlement on the land. A strict adherent to the Jewish ritual could not become an agriculturalist. Thus the Jews became pariah people of the cities and the contrast between the pharisaical "saint" and the home population outside the law is still discernible in the Gospels.[2] In this turning to trade, dealing in money was preferred because it alone permitted complete devotion to the study of the Law. Thus there are ritualistic grounds which have impelled the Jews to trade and especially to dealing in money, and have made of their dealings a ritualistically restricted tribal commerce or folk-commerce.

The second possibility open in the development of trade was the establishment of seigniorial trade, a stratum of lords appearing as its supporters. First the idea might occur to territorial lords—and did in fact everywhere occur—to market the surplus products of their estates. For this purpose they attached professional merchants to them-

selves as officials. To this category belongs the *actor* in
antiquity, who conducted his affairs in the name of the
lord, and similarly the *negotiator* in the middle ages;
the latter held as a fief, in consideration of a payment,
the marketing of the products of his monastic overlord; his
existence is not clearly demonstrable in Germany but
his kind occur everywhere else. *Actor* and *negotiator*
are not traders in the present sense of the word, but agents
of others. Another sort of seigniorial trade originated
in consequence of the position outside the law of foreign
traders, who everywhere required protection; this was to
be secured only through the political power, the noble
granting his protection as a concession and for a consideration. Even the medieval princes granted concessions to
traders and accepted payments from them in return. Out
of this protective arrangement trade on his own account by
the lord or prince frequently developed, as especially on all
the coasts of Africa, where the chieftains monopolized the
transit trade and themselves traded. On this trade monopoly rested their power; as soon as it was broken their position was gone.

Another form of trade which was taken up by princes
is gift trade. In the ancient east the political authorities
maintained themselves, when they were not at war with
each other, by mutual voluntary gifts. The tables of Tell-
el-Amarna, especially, from the period after 1400 B. C.,
show a lively gift trade between the Pharaohs and the
Levantine rulers. The common objects of exchange were
gold and war chariots against horses and slaves. Here
originally the free gift was the custom. Numerous
breaches of faith and trust which occurred in this connection gradually led to the imposition of mutual considerations so that a genuine trade on an accurate quantitative
basis grew out of the gift trade.

Finally, in many places, economic history reveals trade by princes on their own account.[3]   Very old examples on the most extensive scale are furnished by the Egyptian Pharaohs, who as ship-owners carried on exportation and importation.   Later examples are the doges of Venice, in the earliest period of their city, and finally, the princes of numerous patrimonial states of Asia and Europe, including the Hapsburgs to well along in the 18th century.   This trade could be carried on either under the direction of the prince himself, or he could exploit his monopoly by granting a concession or leasing the privilege.   In adopting the latter measures he gave the impulse to the development of an independent professional trading class.

CHAPTER XV

For the existence of commerce as an independent occupation, specific technological conditions are prerequisite. In
the first place there must be regular and reasonably reliable transport opportunities. One must, to be sure, think
of these in the most primitive possible terms through long
ages. Not only in the Assyrian and Babylonian times were
inflated goat skins used for the diagonal crossing of rivers,
but even in the Mohammedan period, skin-bag boats long
dominated the river traffic.

On land the trader had recourse far into the middle ages
to primitive transport media. The first was his own back,
on which he carried his goods down to the 13th century;
then pack animals or a two wheeled cart drawn by one or
at the most two horses, the merchant being restricted to
commercial routes as roads in our sense are not to be
thought of. Only in the east and in the interior of Africa
does caravan trade with slaves as porters appear to occur
fairly early. In general even there, the pack animal is the
rule. The typical animal of the south is the ass or the
mule; the camel does not appear until late, in the Egyptian
monuments, and the horse still later; it was originally used
for war and found application in the transport of goods
only in more recent times.

Traffic by sea had to make use of equally primitive means
of transportation. In antiquity, and likewise in the early
middle ages, the boat propelled by oars was the rule. The

construction we must picture as very clumsy; we find mention of the cords with which the plank boats had to be held together or they would break apart. It is true that sailing goes back so far that its invention cannot be determined, but it was not sailing in the sense that the term now bears. Originally it served only for supplementing the oars when winds were favorable, while tacking against the wind seems to have been still unknown in the early middle ages. The Eddas contain only a doubtful reference to it and it is doubtful whether the first use of tacking is to be ascribed to Andrea Doria as medieval tradition had it. From Homer and still later sources we learn that the ships were not so large but that they could be pulled up on the beach when a landing was made each evening. The anchor evolved very slowly in antiquity, from a heavy stone to an instrument in the form customary today. Shipping was at first, of course, purely coastal traffic; deep-sea navigation is an innovation of the Alexandrian period and was based on the observation of the monsoon. The Arabs first ventured to try to reach India by allowing it to drive them across over the open sea. Nautical instruments for determining location are among the Greeks the most primitive imaginable. They consisted of the odometer, which in the manner of a sand glass allowed balls to fall whose number indicated the miles passed over, and the "bolis" for determining the depth. The astrolabe is an invention of the Alexandrian period and not until that time were the first lighthouses established.

Shipping in the middle ages, like that of the Arabs, remained technically far behind Chinese practice. The magnetic needle and mariner's compass which were applied as early as the third and fourth centuries in China, were not known in Europe until a thousand years later. After the introduction of the compass in the Mediterranean and

Baltic seas it is true that a rapid development began. However, a fixed steering rudder behind the ship was not universal until the 13th century. Rules of navigation were a trade secret. They were objects of bargaining down to the days of the Hansards who in this connection became champions of progress. The decisive forward steps were the advances in nautical astronomy, made by the Arabs and brought by the Jews to Spain, where in the 13th century Alfonso X had the tables prepared which are known by his name. Compass maps were first known from the 14th century. When at that time the western world took up ocean navigation, it was confronted by problems which for the time being it had to solve with very primitive means. For astronomical observations the pole star offered in the north a tolerably secure basing point while in the south the Cross long served for orientation. Amerigo Vespucci determined longitude by the position of the moon. At the beginning of the 16th century its determination by clocks was introduced, these having been so far perfected that it was possible to determine longitude approximately by measuring the difference between their time and that shown by the sun at midday. The quadrant by which latitude could readily be determined seems to have been first used in 1594. The speed of ships corresponded to all these conditions. There was an extraordinary change on the introduction of sailing in contrast with the row boat. Yet in antiquity the stretch of sea from Gibraltar to Ostia required from eight to ten days, and the stretch from Messina to Alexandria about as long. After the English developed effective sailing methods in the 16th and 17th centuries, there were sailing ships which were not so far behind moderately fast steamers, although their speed was always dependent upon the wind.

CHAPTER XVI

FORMS OF ORGANIZATION OF TRANSPORTATION AND OF COMMERCE

(A) THE ALIEN TRADER

Commerce by sea is everywhere originally conjoined with piracy; the warship, pirate ship, and merchant ship are to begin with not distinguished from each other. The differentiation came about through the warship developing away from the merchant ship and not conversely, the warship being brought to such a technical development by the increase in the number of banks of oars and other innovations, that, in view of the costs and limited usefulness of the room left available for cargo, it was no longer available as a merchant ship. In antiquity the Pharaohs and the Egyptian temples are the first ship owners, so that we find in Egypt no privately owned shipping whatever. On the other hand private shipping is characteristic of the Greeks in Homeric times, and of the Phenicians. Among the Greeks the city king originally held possession of the ships both for trade and for piracy. But he could not prevent the growth of great families which shared in ship owning and finally tolerated him only as a *primus inter pares.*

Among the Romans in the earliest times, overseas trade was one of the main sources of the significance of the city. We do not know certainly how great was the ownership of tonnage, or the export trade; apparently, however, the Romans did not come to equal the Carthaginians in this

202

field.   Later they went over to a purely import or debit commerce.   After the Punic Wars private shipping rose from a zero level in Rome.   But the Roman policy was so strongly continental in character that the possession of shipping was originally regarded as unbecoming for a senator; under the Republic and even in the imperial period he was forbidden to have more ships than were necessary to market his own surplus products.

We do not know how the operation of shipping in antiquity was organized from an economic point of view. The only certainty is the increasing use of slaves as a means of propulsion.   The officers of the ships were skilled craftsmen.   We find on Roman and Greek ships, the captain, helmsman, and a flutist who gives the rhythm to the rowers.   Again, we have no clear idea of the relation between ship owners and merchants.   Originally the former were merchants themselves, but a special class of traders by sea in connection with foreign commerce is soon met with, the ἔμποροι of the Greek cities.   This foreign trade must have been very slight in extent, for as regards goods for the masses, especially the grain requirements of the large cities of antiquity, provision must have been on a basis of communal self-sufficiency.   In Athens the ship owners were obliged to bring back grain to the city as return cargo, while in Rome the state took in hand the provision of ships and supply of grain and regulated both far down into the imperial period.   This arrangement did indeed assure peace and security to the sea traffic and was very favorable to the foreign commerce, but it was not permanent.   The financial needs of the emperors, arising out of the necessity for a standing army on the frontier, forced upon them a leiturgical or compulsory service organization of state functions.   To an increasing degree these were taken care of not through taxation but leiturgically, the fisc organizing the various occupations along guild lines and laying upon them the labor burdens of the state.   In consideration of this duty they received a monopoly of their respective branches of industry.   This system led to a leiturgical organization of shipping also and consequently to an early retrograde development.   In the third century the private marine disappeared, as did the navy at the same time, giving piracy a chance for a new and strong development.

For knowledge of the arrangements brought about in antiquity by the requirement of legal forms for trade, we are restricted to very few remains.   We possess for one thing the *lex Rhodia de iactu* concerning shipping hazards. It shows that a number of merchants were generally carried on a ship. If goods had to be thrown overboard in a time of distress, the loss was borne equally by the participants.   Another institution, the sea loan (*foenus nauticum*), which was taken over by the middle ages from antiquity, is a consequence of the fact that trade by sea was affected by extraordinarily high risks.   If a loan was made on goods to go overseas, neither the lender nor the borrower reckoned upon repayment in case of loss of the ship.   The danger which both incurred was shared in such a way that the creditor received exceptionally high interest,—probably 30%—in exchange for which he bore the entire risk, and in the case of a partial loss his payment was also reduced.   From the court pleas of the Attic orators, Demosthenes and others, we know that sea loans resulted in affording to the lenders the possibility of getting sea commerce in their power to a large extent.   They prescribed to the ship owner the course and duration of the voyage and where he should market the goods.   The extensive dependence of the sea merchants upon the capitalists which finds expression in this arrangement leads us to infer that the former were weak in capital. In order to distribute the risk a number of lenders usually participated in the loan upon a single ship. Furthermore, it often happened that a slave of the creditor accompanied the cargo overseas, another indication of the dependence in which his trade stood in relation to the money power. The sea loan dominated the whole period of antiquity until Justinian forbade it as usurious. This prohibition had no permanent effect, resulting mainly in a change in the form of shipping credit.

Conditions in the middle ages are obscure. In harmony with pre-capitalistic institutions the shipyards belonged to the cities and were leased to the ship building guilds. Sea trade bore a less capitalistic character than in antiquity. The common form under which it was carried on was that of the association of all those interested in the same trading enterprise. During the whole medieval period a ship almost never went out on the account of a single individual, because of the risk, but was always built for a number of share holders; that is, partnership possession dominated. On the other hand, the various partners would be concerned in the ownership of several vessels. Like ship building and ownership, the individual venture was usually the occasion for an association. This included the ship owner, the officers, the crew, and finally the merchants. They were all brought together in a company and took goods with them, although the merchants often sent a representative or factor, an employee, instead of going themselves. The danger was borne in common and gain or loss distributed according to a fixed rule.

Alongside this organized community of risk existed the sea loan of the capitalists. The latter was preferred by the traveling merchants of the middle ages because it was advantageous for them to buy goods by means of loans and shift the risk to the creditors. According to the *constituum usus* of the maritime law of Pisa, the rate of interest was 35%; it fluctuated around this level but varied according to a tariff of grades of risk. Originally, all the merchants included in the risk community themselves went on the voyage and took the goods with them; those involved were small merchants who peddled their wares. This custom declined gradually and in its place appeared the commenda, and apparently the *societas maris* was of contemporary growth. The commenda is found in Babylonian and Arabian as well as Italian law and in a modified form in the Hanseatic. The essence of it is that in the same organization two types of associates are included, one of which stays in the home port while the other takes the goods overseas. The relation originally represented only personal convenience, certain ones out of a number of merchants, chosen in rotation, marketing the goods of the others. Later it became an arrangement for the investment of capital. Those who furnished the money were in part professional traders but in part, especially in the south, money capitalists, such as nobles who wished to employ their surplus wealth for gain in commerce. The organization was carried out according to the plan that to the traveling *socius* was given money or goods estimated in money; this investment formed the trading capital and was called by the technical name *commenda*. The goods were sold overseas and others bought with the proceeds, which again on the return to the home port were appraised and sold. The mode of dividing the gain was as follows: if the *socius* who remained at home furnished all the capital he received three-fourths; if, however, the investment was provided by him and the traveling socius jointly—generally in the ratio of two-thirds to one-third—the sharing was by halves. The characteristic feature of this business was that capitalistic accounting was employed for the first time; the capital at the end of the operation was compared with that at the beginning, and the excess determined and distributed as gain. As to form, however, there was no permanent capitalistic enterprise but only an individual venture, the accounts being closed after each expedition. This arrangement dominated sea trade throughout the middle ages and after the transition to permanent capitalistic business had taken place it remained the accounting form for the individual venture.

The turnover of medieval commerce as measured by modern standards was extremely small. It was carried on by mere small dealers who worked with trifling quantities. In 1277 the English exports of wool amounted to 30,000 double cwt. In this quantity 250 merchants shared, so that 120 double cwt. fell to each in a single year. The average amount of a commenda in Genoa in the 12th century was about 250 American dollars or 50 pounds sterling in silver. In the 14th century in the domain of the Hanseatic League, it was forbidden to take up more than one commenda and the amount was not higher than that given above. The total trade between England and the Hanseatic League at the time of its highest development came to less than 4,000 dollars or 800 pounds. For Reval the conditions can be followed in the customs registers; in 1369 there were 178 merchants concerned in 12 ships leaving the port, each of whom was involved for some 400 dollars on the average. In Venice the typical cargo amounted to $1,500, in the Hanseatic League in the 14th century to $1,250. The number of ships annually entering the port of Reval in the 15th century was 32 and for Luebeck, the most important Hanseatic port, in 1368, it is 430—against which are 870 departures. It was a crew of petty capitalistic traders who traveled themselves or got others to travel for them, and this fact explains the organization into companies.

On account of the danger from pirates, a single ship was not in a position to determine independently its time of sailing. Ships formed themselves into caravans and were either convoyed by armed vessels or were themselves armed. The average duration of the voyage of a marine caravan in the Mediterranean varied from a half year to a year. In Genoa only one caravan a year went to the Orient, in Venice two. The voyage in caravans resulted in an extremely slow turnover of the capital.

In spite of these conditions the significance of the commerce as a source of income must not be underestimated. In 1368 the turnover in all the Baltic ports together amounted to nearly $4,000,000 measured in silver—three times as much as the king of England received as the total revenue of the state.

In land commerce the risk was less, as the only danger came from robbers and not from natural catastrophes in addition; but in compensation the expenses were incomparably higher. Corresponding to the limited risk the company organization was absent; likewise any land loan analogous to the sea loan. Attempts were made to establish such an institution, but the Curia interposed against it as a notoriously usurious business.

In land commerce also it was the rule for the merchant to accompany his goods. Not until the 13th century were transport conditions secure enough that the merchant was released from regularly accompanying his goods, making instead the *victuarius* responsible for them, a condition which presupposed established business relations between consignor and consignee. Land commerce suffered under technical difficulties as a result of the condition of the roads. The Roman roads have been a subject of much talk but conditions were far from ideal on these also. Cato and Varro warned against using them on account of the low persons who frequented them and also the vermin, and counseled against putting up in any tavern near the road on account of the excessive charges imposed on travelers. In the outer provinces the Roman roads may have served for commerce also, but they were not primarily intended for this purpose and their straight line courses had no regard for its needs. In addition, in the Roman period, protection was given only to those roads which were important for the provisioning of the capital or for military and political purposes. Their upkeep was imposed on peasants as a governmental function, on consideration of exemption from taxation.

In the middle ages the feudal lords were interested in the maintenance of commercial routes from a fiscal standpoint. They cared for the roads through their *scararii* —peasants upon whom the maintenance of roads and bridges was imposed as one of the most oppressive burdens which the feudal organization knows at all—and tolls were collected in return. There was no agreement among the lords establishing a rational layout of the roads; each located the road in a way to make sure of recouping its cost in duties and toll. A systematic planning of roads is first found in Lombardy in the days of the Lombard League.

In consequence of all these facts the volume of land trade in the middle ages was much smaller even than that of trade by sea. As late as the 16th century the factor of a large commercial house traveled from Augsburg to Venice to get 16 bags of cotton. It has been computed that the goods which went over the St. Gothard pass in one year at the end of the middle ages would have filled only from one to one and a half freight trains. Considering the smallness of the volume the profit must have been correspondingly high to cover the duties and the costs of subsistence during the journey. In view of the condition of the roads the duration of the journey was also long. Even on land the merchant could not choose at will the time of the trip. The insecurity of the roads made it necessary to secure an escort, and the latter would wait until a considerable number of travelers came together.

Thus land trade, like that by sea, was bound to a caravan system. This is a primitive phenomenon and is found in Babylon as well as in the middle ages. In antiquity and in the orient there were officially designated caravan leaders. In the middle ages these were provided by the towns. Not until the peaceful conditions of the 14th and 15th centuries had established tolerable security could one begin to travel as an individual. On the technical side this was made possible through an organization of land transport in the form of the so-called pack train (*Rottfuhr*). The train system developed out of feudal arrangements, in which again the monasteries took the lead. The lord of the land placed horses, pack animals, carts, etc., at the disposal of the public for hire. The carts were provided in rotation by the possessors of certain peasant holdings upon which this burden was imposed. The feudal organization gradually gave place to a professional class, but a systematized industry only developed after the towns took the business of the trains in hand. The train workers organized themselves into a guild within the town, placing themselves under the strict discipline of the elected "forwarder" (*Aufgeber*) who dealt with the merchants and distributed the vehicles among the various members of the guild. Responsibility of the train leader was a principle generally recognized.

For inland shipping various forms of organization came into existence. The use of feudal or monastic ships and rafts often rested on the compulsion of a *banalité,* so that the lords actually had a monopoly over the movement of goods. In general, however, they were not able to exploit it themselves but transferred it to the union (*Einung*) of transport workers. Then this union of highly specialized workers secured possession of the monopoly and the lord was expropriated. In addition there arose rather early, though in general after the development of towns, free shipping guilds who regularly practised a system of rotation of the work. They transported goods in their own small vessels, the opportunities for gain being distributed according to rigorous rule by the guild. It also happened that the urban community took in hand the organization of shipping. On the Iser the burghers of Mittenwald had a monopoly of the rafting, the right to transport cargoes rotating among them in serial order. From the agricultural establishments at higher elevations heavy goods were rafted down stream, while goods of high value were hauled back to the higher regions. Finally, closed associations arose which took the shipping in hand, developing out of the feudal or guild organization—out of the former, for example, on the Salzach and the Inn. Originally the archbishop of Salzburg held the shipping monopoly as a fief; then arose a union of the ship operators who constituted themselves an inland merchant marine. The organization owned the ships, hired the transport workers, and took over the monopoly from the archbishop. In the 15th century he repurchased the privilege and granted it as a fief. On the Murg also, shipping rested on an industrial association of the forest shipping men, which grew out of the monopoly of wood and hence pertained to the owners of forest land. The large supply of wood in the

Black Forest resulted in the Murg shipping organization extending its field of operations to the Rhine, and it became divided into a Forest organization and a Rhine organization. Finally, the company took up the transportation of foreign goods with a view to the freight earnings. The Danube shipping organization in Austria and the Upper Rhine shipping organization developed out of guilds; thus in a way analogous to the situation of the mining community, shipping came into the hands of associations of workers.

The requirements to which these relations gave rise among the merchants, looked first in the direction of personal protection. Occasionally this provision took on a sacerdotal character, the foreign merchant being placed under the protection of the gods or of the chieftain. Another form was the conclusion of safe conduct agreements with the political powers of the region, as in upper Italy during the middle ages. Here later the burghers, by capturing their fortified places, forced the knights who threatened the trade to move into the towns and in part themselves took over the protection of the merchants. The fees for conduct were at one time the leading source of income for those living along the roads, as for example in Switzerland.

The second great requirement of commerce was legal protection. The merchant was an alien and would not have the same legal opportunities as a member of the nation or tribe, and therefore required special legal arrangements. One institution which served the purpose is that of reprisal. If a debtor of Genoa or Pisa, for example, could not or would not pay a debt in Florence or in Frankfort, pressure was brought to bear on his compatriots. This was unfair and in the long run intolerable, and the oldest commercial treaties aim at preventing such reprisals. Beginning with this primitive rule of retaliation the need of the merchant for legal protection gave rise to various institutions. Since the merchant as a foreigner could not appear before the court, he had to provide a patron who represented him; hence arose in antiquity the phenomenon of the proxenia, which manifests a combination of hospitality and representation of an interest. To it corresponds the law of hostage in the middle ages; the foreign merchant was authorized and required to place himself under the protection of a citizen, with whom he had to store his goods, and the host in turn was obliged to guard them on behalf of the community.

In contrast with these arrangements it constituted a great step in progress when with the increase in number of the merchants a hanse was organized. This was ordinarily a guild of foreign merchants carrying on trade in a distant city, who organized for mutual protection. It goes without saying that the organization pre-supposed a permit from the ruler of the city. With this organization of the merchants in a foreign country was regularly associated the establishment of special merchant settlements, which relieved the merchants of the necessity of immediately selling their goods. This purpose was served the world over by the caravansaries of the land trade and factories for sea commerce of the middle ages—the *fondachi*, warehouses and sales rooms. In this connection there were two alternatives. First, the sales rooms might be set up by the foreign merchants in their own interests, as was possible when their activity made them indispensable to the place where they settled. In this case they became autonomous, choosing their own governor, as for example the merchants of the German hanse in London. On the other hand, the home merchants might set up institutions for the foreigners, to control their access to the market and hold them in leash.

An example is the *fondaco* of the German merchants in Venice.

Finally, it became necessary to establish fixed times for trading; the buyer and seller must be able to find one another. This requirement was met by the fixed markets and gave rise to the market concessions. Markets were everywhere established for the foreign traders by concession from the princes,—in Egypt, India, and European antiquity, and in the middle ages. The object of such a concession was on the one hand the provision for the needs of the authority granting the concession, and on the other the promotion of fiscal aims; the prince wished to profit by the trade in the market. As a result the regulation of transport, for a consideration, was regularly associated with the market concession, as was also the establishment of a market court, partly in the interest of the prince who drew from it the court fees, and partly in the interest of the foreign traders who could not come before the regular domestic courts. There were also regulations affecting measures, weights and coinage and the time and method of trading. As compensation for these services the prince collected the market dues.

Out of this original relation between the merchants visiting the market and the authority granting the concession, evolved still other institutions. The merchants needed large quarters for having their goods tested, weighed and stored. An early development was a *banalité* involving compulsory use of the crane belonging to the prince, imposed as a method of taxation. Primarily, however, the fiscal interest was promoted by compulsory brokerage. The merchants also had to be checked in regard to the amount of their dealings, as payments were to be made on the basis of these. Accordingly brokers were established, an institution taken over by the west from the orient (*sim-*

sarius, sensarius, hence Italian *sensal*). In addition to these requirements was that of compulsory routing. Since the prince had to guarantee the safety of the merchant the latter must utilize the roads belonging to the prince. Finally, there was the compulsion of the market, requiring that, with a view to control, the trade of the foreign merchants must take place publicly, in the market or the warehouse.

(B) The Resident Trader

The conditions pictured in the preceding section apply not only to the trade of the early middle ages but also to Arabia and the world in general, so long as the foreign trader predominates. Totally different conditions arose when the class of resident merchants developed.

Typically, the phenomenon of the resident trader is a product of the development of towns, although undoubtedly there were resident merchants previously, in the market settlements in the neighborhood of fortresses. The resident merchant was technically designated *mercator.* By this term the middle ages understood a trader who had acquired the privilege of settlement in the town, and primarily a retailer, whether he sold his own products or those of foreigners. In certain legal sources the term is used as equivalent to merchant in modern commercial law; a *mercator* is one who buys and sells, *lucri causa.* But this usage, which appears especially in Rhenish documents, cannot be taken as the common one for the middle ages. In the population structure of the medieval towns the *mercator* was not a wholesaler but rather anyone who brought something to market, the craftsman as well as the professional trader.

The professional trading class of the towns developed in

the following way. The resident merchant is to begin with an itinerant trader. He travels periodically in order to market products at a distance or to secure products from a distance and is a peddler who has acquired a fixed residence. The next stage is that in which he has the traveling done for him, either by an employee or servant or by a partner; the one arrangement goes over into the other. The third stage is formed by the system of factories. The trader has increased in capital power to a point where he founds independent settlements at distant points, or at least maintains employees there, and so establishes an interlocal system of relations. Finally, the resident trader becomes completely fixed in his location and deals with distant regions by correspondence only. This condition did not become possible until the late middle ages because there was not sufficient interterritorial legal security.

The center of gravity in medieval trade lies in retailing. Even the merchant who brought in goods from a distance, as from the orient, centered his interest in selling directly to the consumers. The risk was less, the gain more steady and secure, and in general higher than would have been the case with wholesale trade, and the business possessed in a degree a monopolistic character. Even the Hansards were not merchants in the present sense, but emphasized chiefly the control of retail trade in foreign lands, seeking to exclude foreign competition in retailing in Russia, Sweden, Norway, and England. Even in the 16th century the Merchant Adventurers in England, to whom Elizabeth granted privileges, pursued this policy. Wholesalers in the proper sense perhaps did not exist at all in the early middle ages, and toward the end of the period only in small and slowly increasing numbers, in the large commercial centers of southern Europe; in the north they were still exceptional.[1]

The resident traders as a class had to contend against

other groups.[2] One series of such struggles were external, such as the struggle to maintain the monopoly of the urban market. This was contested by the non-resident tribal and clan trade, especially in distant commerce connected with tribal industry, and the trade of non-resident foreign trading peoples. Out of the wish to suppress such competition grew the conflict with the Jews. In the early middle ages no hostility to them can be found in Germany. Even in the 11th century the bishop of Speyer invited Jews to the town in order, as he expressed it, to increase the glory of his city. It was in the time of the crusades that the first wave of anti-semitism broke over Europe, under the two-fold influence of the war between the faiths and the competition of the Jews, although we find anti-semitic movements even in antiquity. Tacitus condemned the Jews on the ground of "superstition," and as a Roman despised all oriental "extasis" as contemptible. This struggle against the Jews and other foreign peoples—Caursines, Lombards, and Syrians—is a symptom of the development of a national commercial class.

The resident trader also contended with the merchants settled in the country, on the land. This struggle ended in the 15th century with the complete victory of the urban merchants; Duke Louis the Rich of Bavaria for example, (1450–1479), prided himself especially on having in the interest of control forced the rural merchants in his territory into the towns. Again, there was a struggle against retailing by other merchants, a struggle which took various forms. In part, the urban merchants established the requirement that foreign merchants could offer their wares for sale only on certain days. Sale direct to consumers was forbidden to them, and likewise, in the interest of control, all trade with each other, and finally compulsory disposal was imposed upon them; that is, the requirement of selling at a given time and place whatever goods they had brought to that place at that time, whether to consumers or to local merchants.

The resident merchants succeeded in still further intensifying their control over the foreigners. They imposed the compulsion of hosting, the obligation of taking up residence with particular citizens who should watch over their activities (see above, page 213). Since this gave rise to the danger of forbidden dealings between guest and host, they devised public warehouses with compulsory occupation of these. Frequently, though not always, the two arrangements were combined, as in the case of the *fondaco dei tedeschi* in Venice. Every German merchant must live in this *fondaco* and store all his goods there. The *fondaco* had almost no power of self-government; its officers were imposed on the German merchants by the city, which itself controlled them through brokers. Compulsory brokerage, which was one of the most effective of all these measures, prevented trading between the foreigners and local persons. The rise of the brokerage system was due to the monopolistic tendencies of the resident trade and to the wish of the city to control every single transaction of the foreigners. The broker could not transact any business of his own or enter into any partnership relation; he was officially dependent upon the fees which came to him in connection with the business under his supervision.

The second great object of contention in the merchant class was in regard to internal equality of opportunity. One of the members protected by the group must not have better chances than another, and this applied especially to retailing. This purpose was served by the prohibition of pre-sale or "forestalling," and the right of sharing. The first of these rules prohibited dealers from selling goods before they had been brought into the town.

On the other hand, if one merchant, due to superior capital power, had bought more goods than another, the right of sharing became operative; it specified that any member of the association could demand that a part of the goods in question be given up to him on payment of their actual cost. This provision was endurable only in the case of retailers; wholesale trade, insofar as it affected goods from a distance, could not be subjected to such stipulations without being prevented from developing altogether. As a result a bitter struggle set in as the wholesale trade succeeded in winning greater freedom.

A third conflict which had to be fought out by the resident trading class was the conflict over the field of action as such. This related to the endeavor to exploit the opportunities of the town to the greatest possible extent. It gave rise to the struggle over the staple compulsion and restriction as to streets, that is, the right to compel all merchants to use a specified street at a specified place and to market goods at a specified point or port. This requirement was to begin with rather favorable for the development of the trade; without the monopoly which it created with reference to specific places and streets it would have been impossible in view of the small volume of the trade, to provide the technical requirements and meet the costs of the necessary port and street development. But this does not alter the fact that for those who secured the monopoly, especially the town lords and the princes, purely fiscal considerations ruled. Every territorial lord attempted by war to gain possession of staple and street rights. The conflicts which arose were very violent in Germany, especially during the 14th and 15th centuries. The staple and street rights formed both an objective and a resource in the struggle. If the right was once attached to a certain place the lord in control could inflict serious damage by obstructing and barricading the streets, and also by political means. The history of English-French relations in the later centuries of the middle ages is full of examples.

Finally, the resident merchant class was in conflict with the consumer's interests, and was divided internally according as it was interested in the local market or in distant trade. The consumers wished as far as possible to buy at first hand from the foreign traders, while the interest of the great majority of the local merchants was opposed, looking toward regulating the market from the point of view of the retailer, while keeping open the possibility of securing supplies. In the long run it proved impossible to secure both interests. With the recognition of this fact began the splitting off of a wholesale trading interest and an opposition of interest within the mercantile group, while the interests of the retailer and the consumer began to draw together.

(C) The Trade of the Fairs

The regular activities of both the foreign and the resident merchant looked toward the consumers. In contrast, the first form of trade between merchant and merchant is met with at the fairs. Since in the middle ages the retailer with purely local interest predominated, the fair developed as the most important form of interlocal trade organization. It is characterisic, in the first place, that the fair is visited not by local men but by traveling merchants who come for the purpose, and second, that the trade is concerned with goods in hand. The latter point distinguishes it from the exchange of the present day, on which goods not present and often not yet produced are dealt in.

The typical fair is exemplified by those of Champagne.

In the four principal cities of Champagne six fairs were held, each of which lasted for 50 days, including the business of arranging and opening the fair, the payment of exchange, etc., so that with exception of holidays the year was filled by the six fairs. They were organized from above; there was a court of the fair, the *custodes nundinarum,* composed of a *civis* and, in view of the question of safe conduct, a *miles.* The fairs are first mentioned in 1174 and reached their highest development in the 13th and 14th centuries. They had police and financial power over those who attended them and as the extreme penalty could impose exclusion. This measure was adopted by other powers, notably the church; not infrequently was excommunication threatened on political or fiscal grounds in order to exclude an offender from the fair, and entire communes have met this fate. Champagne derived its commercial significance from the fact that it lay between the English wool producing region and the wool manufacturing region of Flanders on the one side, and Italy, the great importer of oriental goods, on the other. Consequently, among the goods which were dealt in, the first place was taken by wool and wool manufactures, especially cheap cloth. In exchange for these the south brought articles of high value, fine tanned sheepskins, spices, alum, fine wood for the inlaying of furniture, dies for coloring cloth, wax, saffron, camphor, gum, lace—a mixture of the products of southern climes and of the east. The cloth fair was the most important of all the fairs of Champagne and had the largest turnover. All the coinages of the world met there. In consequence Champagne was the first home of the money changing business and the classical point for the settlement of debts, especially for the repayment of the debts of the Church. The man of power in the worldly sense who did not pay his debts was in fact invulnerable

to the merchant in his "Burg." Quite different the prelate who must expect to be excommunicated by his spiritual
superior if he broke his word. The special credit reliability of the high spiritual orders thus established came to
expression in the fact that a considerable portion of the
bills of exchange were drawn upon prelates and were payable, on pain of excommunication, at the latest four days
before the beginning of the general settlement. The purpose of this rule was to secure to the merchant hard cash
for the business of the fair; it was mitigated by the fact
that the obligation of the prelate enforceable by church
action corresponded to an increased security of remit-
tances to him, which were similarly guaranteed by ecclesiastical penalties.

No other fair of the period achieved so great significance.
In Germany there was an attempt to establish a fair at
Frankfort; it did develop gradually but never achieved
the rank of the Champagne fairs or even that of Lyons.
In Eastern Europe Novgorod, later Nijni-Novgorod, was a
point of exchange between the Hanseatic merchants and
the fur traders and peasant producers of Russia. In England,[3] there were numerous fair towns [4] but none was the
equal of the fairs of Champagne.

CHAPTER XVII

FORMS OF COMMERCIAL ENTERPRISE

Rational commerce is the field in which quantitative reckoning first appeared, to become dominant finally over the whole extent of economic life. The necessity of exact calculation first arose wherever business was done by companies. In the beginning commerce was concerned with a turnover so slow and a profit so large that exact computation was not necessary. Goods were bought at a price which was fixed traditionally, and the trader could confine his efforts to getting as much as he could in sale. When trade was carried on by groups it was necessary to proceed to exact bookkeeping in order to render an accounting.

The technical means of computation were crude, down almost to the beginning of the modern period. Our system of characters, with values depending on their position, was an invention of the Hindus, from whom the Arabs took it over and was perhaps brought to Europe by the Jews. But not until the time of the crusades was it really known generally enough to serve as a method of computation; yet without this system, rational planning was impossible. All peoples who used a literal system of notation like that of antiquity and of the Chinese, had to have in addition some mechanical aid to computation. In antiquity and down to the late middle ages, the counting frame or *abacus* served this purpose and was still employed after the Arabic position digits had long been known. For as the column system made its way into Europe it was at first viewed as a disreputable means of securing an immoral advantage in competition, since it worked in favor of the competitors of the virtuous merchant who disdained its use. Consequently it was first sought to exclude it by prohibitions, and even the highly developed Florentine cloth making guilds repudiated it for a time. But the abacus made dividing difficult, and it was ranked as an obscure mystery; the computations which have come down to us from the Florence of that time, which were carried through with literal notation, are wrong to the extent of three-fourths or four-fifths. On the grounds of this antipathy, the Roman numerals were still written for making the entries in the account books after the computations were actually carried out with Arabic figures. Down to the 15th or 16th century, the position system of notation struggled for official recognition.

The first books on computation usable by merchants come from the 15th century, the older literature, going back to the 13th, not being popular enough. Occidental bookkeeping was built up on the basis of familiarity with the position notation; the like of it had not been seen in the world and only foreshadowings are found in classical antiquity. The occidental world alone became the abode of money computation, while in the orient computation in kind has remained the rule; (the accounting in terms of grain certificates in Egypt will be recalled—above p. 58).

It is true that there was bookkeeping in antiquity, in the banking business—the Greek τραπεζίται and the Roman *argentarii*. The entries, however, were documentary in character; they were not designed as an instrument of control in connection with income. Genuine bookkeeping first arose in medieval Italy, and as late as the 16th century, a German clerk traveled to Venice to secure instruction in the art.

Bookkeeping grew up on the basis of the trading company.[1] The family is everywhere the oldest unit supporting a continuous trading activity, in China and Babylonia, in India, and in the early middle ages. The son of a trading family was the confidential clerk and later the partner of the father. So through generations one and the same family functioned as capitalists and lenders, as did the house of Igibi in Babylonia in the 6th century B. C. It is true that in this case the transactions concerned were not extensive and complicated like those of today, but were of a simple sort. It is characteristic that we hear nothing more of bookkeeping either from Babylonia or Indian trading houses, although at least in India the position numerals were known. The reason apparently is that there, as in general in the orient and in China, the trading association remained a closed family affair and accountability was therefore unnecessary. The trading association extending beyond the members of a family first became general in the west.

The first form of group organization was occasional in character, the *commenda*, already referred to. The continual participation in such ventures might gradually lead to a permanent enterprise. This evolution in fact took place, although with characteristic differences between southern and northern Europe. In the south the traveling merchant was regularly the entrepreneur, to whom the *commenda* was given, because in view of his year long absence in the orient he could not be controlled. He became the entrepreneur and received commendas from various parties, up to ten or twenty, accounting to each *commendator* separately. In the north, in contrast, the *socius* who remained at home was just as regularly the entrepreneur; he was the one who entered into relations with numerous traveling *socii* whom he provided with commendas. The traveling factor was regularly forbidden to undertake more than one commenda and this brought him into dependence upon the settled partner who thus evolved into a managerial functionary. The reason is found in the difference between the commerce of the south and the north. In the south the journeys involved notably greater risk since they led into the orient.

With the spread of the commenda organization, developed permanent industrial enterprise. First, accountability penetrated into the family circle due to business connections with *tractators* from outside the family, since an accounting had to be made for each separate venture even when the particular commenda pertained to a member of the family. In Italy this development went forward more rapidly than in Germany, the south again taking the lead over the north. As late as the 16th century the Fuggers would indeed admit foreign capital into their affairs, but very reluctantly. (The Welsers were more broadminded in this regard.) In contrast, the association of outsiders in family business spread in Italy with increasing rapidity. Originally there was no separation between the household and the business. Such a separation gradually became established on the basis of the medieval money accounting while, as we have seen, it remained unknown in India and China. In the great Florentine commercial families such as the Medici, household expenditures and capital transactions were entered in the books indiscriminately; closing of the accounts was carried out first with reference to the outside commenda business while internally everything remained in the "family kettle" of the household community.

The prime mover in the separation of household and

business accounting, and hence in the development of the early capitalistic institutions, was the need for credit. The separation remained in abeyance as long as dealings were in cash only; but as soon as transactions were suspended over a long interval, the question of guaranteeing credit intruded. To provide this guaranty, various means were used. The first was the maintenance of the wealth of the family in all its ramifications, through maintaining the house-community even to remote degrees of kinship, an objective to which for example the palaces of the great commercial families in Florence owe their origin. Associated with this was the institution of joint responsibility of those who lived together; every member of the house-community was answerable for a debt of any other member.

Apparently this joint responsibility grew out of a traditional criminal liability; in the case of high treason the house of the guilty person was razed and his family destroyed as suspect. This idea of joint responsibility no doubt passed over into the civil law. With the permeation of outside capital and outside persons into the family business for the purpose of trade, it was renewed at irregular intervals. Out of it arose the necessity for an agreed allocation of the resources at the disposal of the individual for personal use and of the power to represent the house in external matters. In the nature of the case, the house-father could everywhere bind the family, but this joint responsibility nowhere developed to such lengths as in occidental commercial law. In Italy its root was in the household community and the stages in its development are the common dwelling, the common workshop, and finally the common firm. It was otherwise in the north, where the large family community was unknown. Here the credit requirement was met by having all the participants in the trading venture sign together the document establishing the responsibility. Then each participant was responsible for the group, usually without limit, though in the reverse direction the whole was not responsible for the parts. Finally, the principle became established that each participant was responsible for every other, even if he had not signed the document. In England the same result was achieved by the common seal or the power of attorney. After the 13th century in Italy, and after the 14th in the north, joint responsibility of all the members of a company for the debts of the firm as such was fully established.

The final stage in the development established as the most effective means for securing credit standing, and the method which outlived all the rest, separation of the property of the trading company as such from the private wealth of the associates. This separation is found at the beginning of the 14th century in Florence and toward the end of the same century in the north also. The step was unavoidable since to an increasing extent persons not members of the family belonged to the trading units; in addition it could not be avoided within the family itself when the latter came repeatedly to employ outside capital. Expenses for the family on one hand and personal expenses on the other were separated from business disbursements, a specified money capital being allocated to the business. Out of the property of the firm, for which we find the designation *corpo della compagnia,* evolved the capital concept.

In detail the development took various courses. In the south the field of its development was the great family commercial houses, not only in Italy but in Germany as well, as illustrated by the Fuggers and Welsers. In the north the course of development was through small-families and associations of small traders. The crucial fact was that the center of large money dealings and political money power lay in the south, as did also the bulk of the mineral trade and oriental commerce, while the north remained the abode of small capitalism. In consequence the forms of organization which developed in the two regions were quite different. The type of the southern commercial company was the *commandite,* in which one partner carried on the business and was personally responsible, the other participating through his investment and sharing in the gain. This development arose from the fact that in the south the traveling merchant holding the commenda was the typical entrepreneur, and when he took up a fixed abode he became the center of the permanent enterprise which took on the form of the commenda. In the north the relation was reversed. The sources from the Hanseatic region at first give the impression that there was no permanent enterprise but that the trade was split up into purely occasional ventures and into a number of inextricably confused individual transactions. In reality these individual ventures were permanent enterprises and are accounted for individually because the Italian (double entry) bookkeeping was not introduced until later.

The forms of organization are the *Sendeve* and the *Wedderleginge.* Under the first the traveling partner was given goods on commission, receiving a share in the gain; the latter was designed to enlist his interest in the business by ascribing to him a share in the capital of the transactions from which he was excluded.

CHAPTER XVIII

MERCANTILE GUILDS [1]

The mercantile guild is not a specifically German institution; it is found spread over the entire world, except that there are no unquestionable records of it in antiquity and in any case it did not in antiquity play a political role. In form the guild is either an organization of foreign traders for the purpose of legal protection against those of the locality, or it is an organization of native merchants. In the latter case it develops out of tribal industry and trade, as in China. The two forms are also found in combination.

In the occident, for example, we find to begin with only guilds of foreigners in particular localities; for example, the German trading guild in London of the 14th century, which established a storehouse called the "Steel-yard." Of an interlocal character were the hanses, a designation met with in Germany, England, and France, whose development varied much in detail. Closely related to them technically is the institution of the *Hansgraf* or count of the hanse, found in a number of towns. The hansgraf is an official granted a concession by the political authority, if not constituted by it, who is responsible for the legal protection of the merchant population engaged in interlocal trade represented by him; he never interferes in the form of trade itself.

Of the second type of guild, made up of resident merchants with the object of monopolizing the trade of a dis-

trict, there is an example in China, in the tea traders'
guild of Shanghai. Another is the kohong guild in Canton, whose 13 firms dominated the whole of external commerce as a monopoly down to the Peace of Nanking in
1842. The Chinese guild practised price regulation and
guaranty of debts, and held the power of taxation over
its members. Its criminal power was draconic; a breach
of regulations led to lynch justice on the part of the guild
members and even in the 19th century there were execu-
tions for violation of the set maximum number of apprentices. In domestic commerce, bankers' guilds, and trading guilds existed in China, as for example the bankers'
guild in Niu-Chwang. The Chinese guilds possessed great
significance for the development of the monetary institutions of the country. Debasement of coinage by the Mon-
gol emperors resulted in the disintegration of the coinage
system. The ensuing paper money regime led to the use
of silver in bars in the wholesale trade, and the guilds took
in hand their preparation. Thus the guild became the
center of monetary policy, achieving control of the determination of weights and measures, and appropriating to itself
criminal jurisdiction.

In India, the guilds appear in the time of Buddhism,
from the sixth to the fourth century B. C., and reach their
greatest development from the third century on. They
were hereditary organizations of traders with hereditary
rulers. Their highest development was reached when they
became money lenders to the various princes who were in
competition with each other, and their decay was the result
of the revival of castes which had been partly pushed into
the background by Buddhism; after the Indian middle ages
the policies of the princes again became dominant. Thus
was formed the caste of the lamani or banjari which appeared in the 16th century in the pursuit of the corn and

salt trade and the provisioning of the army and was perhaps one of the roots of the present day banya or trading
caste. In India we also meet with the differentiation of
forms of trade according to various confessional sects.
The dschaina sect is restricted by ritualistic considerations
to trading at fixed points; the wholesale and distant trade
based on credit is a monopoly in the hands of the Parsees,
who are not restricted by ritualistic considerations and are
distinguished by responsibility and truthfulness. Finally,
the bhaniya caste carries on retail trade and is to be found
in every connection where gain which is off-color from an
ethical standpoint is to be made. Thus its members engage in tax farming, official money lending, etc.

In contrast with China, the regulation of the coinage,
weights, and measures has in the west remained in the possession of the political authority, which either itself exercised the power or turned it over to the political agencies,
but has never granted it to guilds. The great power of the
guilds in this part of the world rests entirely on political
privileges. The forms of guilds are various. First to be
noticed is the city guild. This is a group which dominates
the city and controls especially in the economic interests
of industrial and trading policy. It is met with in a two-
fold form. Either it is a military union, such as the
compania communis in Venice and Genoa, or it may be a
separate union of the traders within the town (*merca-
danza*), growing up with the craft guild. The second main
type is the guild as a taxation unit, which is a specifically
English institution. The English guilds derive their power
from the fact that they took over from the king the function of collecting taxes (*firma burgi*). Only those who
paid taxes were members and one who paid none was
excluded and possessed no right to trade. The English

guild owed to this fact its control over citizenship in the city.

In detail the evolution of the occidental guilds was highly various. The English guild merchant reached the peak of development of its power in the 13th century, after which began a series of internal economic revolutions. In the 14th century followed its separation from craft work; one who wished to remain in the guild must renounce craft activity. Immediately, however, the trading members began to come to the fore in the craft guilds and separated out as "livery companies," that is as members in full standing, being raised above the poorer craft workers by the cost of the livery or regalia, which the latter were unable to meet.

The separation of the wholesale traders from the retail was not yet complete in the 16th century, although at that time the first guild of foreign traders, the Merchant Adventurers, was founded by a concession. It is true that English legislation endeavored to restrict the guilds along craft lines, permitting their members to trade only in one type of goods. On the other hand, the power of a strong state always stood over the guilds in England, although their interests were also represented in Parliament. In consequence the cities never had the power over the country which they obtained in Germany, and rural traders and land holders were always admitted to the guilds.

In Italy the development went forward within the individual city states. The guilds kept their purely local character; after the separation-leagues (*Sonderbund*) obtained the victory over the consular constitution, there began a struggle within the guilds, between the craft guilds and trading guilds. In Germany we find at first traces of a development similar to that in Italy. A symptom is the appearance of the burgomaster, who to begin with was an illegitimate guild master and whose position suggests that of the Italian *capitano del popolo*. In addition we find in many cities of north Germany a development resembling the English, a guild merchant determining the economic policy of the city. In a number of old rich cities of middle Germany we find, on the other hand, a guild which manages the city unofficially, as in Cologne the *"Richerzeche,"* the guild of the rich merchants which financed the revolution against the archbishops, binding the citizens together under oath against the town lords and thenceforward ruling permanently in the city and controlling admission to citizenship. The rule in Germany, however, is the presence of trading guilds, among which the shop keepers and merchant tailors stand out. The shop keepers correspond to the retailers of today. The merchant tailors, who cut up imported cloth and sold it to consumers, became dominant in the smaller towns in the north; they always had to contest the market with the weavers, but generally obtained the victory, while in the large towns the patrician families stood over them in rank and dignity.

One cannot speak of a systematic trading policy on the part of the towns dominated by guilds, and especially of the town leagues, in the middle ages. The towns carried on no trade on their own account; this did not begin until the 16th century. The policy of the German Hanse may stand as an exception. It alone consciously pursued a consistent commercial policy, which shows the following characteristics.

1. Only the citizens of the Hanse had a right to share in the commercial privileges which the Hanse secured.
2. It aimed at direct retail trade in foreign countries and abstained from the forwarding or commission business, a policy on the basis of which it went to pieces as soon as

a local commercial class arose in England, Scandinavia, and Russia.   3. The Hansards made use in trade of their own ships only; they could not lease those of outsiders nor sell Hanse ships or shares in them to outsiders.[2]   4. The Hansards carried on trade in merchandise only, entering into neither money transmission nor the banking business as did the Florentines.   5. The Hanse everywhere secured concessions for settlements and warehouses in order to keep its own members under control.   All its business activities were subjected to strict regulation; weights and measures were prescribed; no credit business could be transacted with outsiders, the object being to prevent outside capital from becoming influential in the organization; even marriage with non-members was prohibited.   6. The Hanse made the first effort toward standardization, carrying on trade in fixed types of goods—wax, salt, metals, fabrics.

7. On the negative side, the Hanse had no customs policy; at most it collected duties for war purposes.   Its internal policy was directed toward the dominance of a market aristocracy, and especially in the sense of suppressing the craft guilds.   In the aggregate these measures represent a policy organized in the interest of a resident foreign trading class.

CHAPTER XIX

MONEY AND MONETARY HISTORY [1]

From the evolutionary standpoint, money is the father of private property; it possesses this character from the beginning, and conversely, there is no object with the character of money which does not have that of individual ownership. The oldest private property consists in objects of individual handiwork, the tools and weapons of the man, and articles of adornment of both men and women. They are subject to a special law of inheritance from person to person, and in the field of such objects the origin of money is primarily to be sought.

Today, money has two special functions, serving as a prescribed means of payment and a general medium of exchange. Historically, the function of a prescribed means of payment is the older of the two. In this stage money does not enter into exchange, a characteristic made possible by the fact that many transfers of value take place from one economic unit to another which do not involve exchange but yet require a means of payment. Such are tribal gifts between chieftains, the bride price, dowries, head money, damage payments, and fines—payments which must be made in a standard medium. On a secondary level there become included payments from the chieftain to his followers, in contrast with those from subject to chieftain —that is the wage which the lord gives to his vassals in the form of a gift—and still later payments of generals to their soldiers. Even in a city like Carthage, and exclusively in the Persian Empire, the coinage of money appears only for the purpose of providing a means for making military payments, not as a medium of exchange.

In this stage of development, money in the unitary sense of today is not to be thought of; rather in each economic zone different sorts of services rendered correspond to specific sorts of goods which mediate the payment function, so that different species of money exist side by side. For example, never and nowhere could a man buy a wife for shells, but only for cattle, while in small transactions the shells were accepted because they were available in small denominations. Money which develops in this way in connection with intra-group payments we call internal money.

A further function, which is less characteristic of money today but which it has performed through long periods of history, is that of a medium for accumulating treasure. The chieftain who wished to maintain himself in his position must be prepared to support his followers and to compensate them by gifts on special occasions. Hence the extraordinary value which was placed on the *thesaurus* such as was possessed by every Indian rajah and every Merovingian king. The Nibelungen hoard is nothing else than such a thesaurus. As means of accumulation, various typical objects were employed, such things as the prince was accustomed to give as presents to his followers and which at the same time constituted objects valued for the purpose of making payments. Here again money was not a means of exchange but merely an object of class possession; one who possessed it kept it only on grounds of prestige and for nourishing his social self-esteem. In this function money required one of the most important characteristics which is demanded of it today, namely, that of durability, in contrast with that of portability. Elephant tusks and huge stones of a certain quality, and later gold, silver, copper, and metals of all kinds, serve as money and as a medium for accumulation. This class character money finds expression in two facts. The first is that in the primitive stage of development it is differentiated according to the sexes, the woman not daring to possess the same type of money goods as the man; thus the possession of certain aragonite stones was reserved to men while pearl shells were women's money only and were used for the morning-gift of the husband to the bride. In addition, class differentiation involved distinguishing chieftain money from that of the subjects; shells of a certain size could only be acquired and possessed by the chieftain and were paid out by him only in case of war or as presents.

The function of money as a general medium of exchange originated in foreign trade. Its source is in some cases a regular commerce by gifts outside the group, such as that revealed for Egypt and the ancient east in the Tell-el-Amarna tablets.

A state of peace between two peoples presupposed continual gifts between their rulers; this is really a quasi-commercial exchange between the chieftains, out of which chieftain trade as such develops. To omit the gifts means war. A second source is a foreign product of wide spread use. The typical clan and tribal trade imparts to certain objects, not obtainable locally and therefore highly prized, the function of a medium of exchange. This external money took over the internal function where quasi-commercial payments were to be made, such as duties or road tolls. The chieftain provided the safe conduct but had to permit the merchants to pay with the medium which they carried with them. In this way the external money made its way into the internal economy.

At this stage of development money appears in numerous forms: 1. As objects of personal adornment. The type is the cowry shell in Africa and the regions of the Indian Ocean, extending into the interior of Asia. In addition there has been a great quantity of objects serving as means of payment or exchange in circles of varying extent—beads, amber, coral, elephant tusks, and certain kinds of scalps. Regularly and primarily decorative money was internal money; it became a general medium of exchange where the same means of payment was used in different tribes. 2. Utility money. This was primarily external money. As a means for carrying out obligatory payments or evaluating other goods, various objects of general use are met with; for example, grain, as in Java, also cattle and slaves. It is not generally, however, such articles of common use but rather means of enjoyment such as tobacco, brandy, salt, iron tools, and weapons. 3. Clothing money. This primarily performed the functions of internal as well as external money. As clothing money we meet with furs, skins, and fabrics, which are not produced in the locality. 4. Token money. Under conditions which have not the least relation to modern monetary conditions it happens that after people have become accustomed to certain objects on social grounds or accustomed to making certain payments in them, the monetary function becomes attached to them as mere symbols which have no value or significance in themselves. Thus in interior British India Chinese game counters are found as money. In Russia there has been fur money, consisting of bits of fur with no use value, and similarly in southern regions the use of quantities of cotton as money developed into the preparation of strips in a form which excluded real value but adapted them for service as token money.

Since in this stage not one means of payment alone but

many circulate side by side, some scale of relative values is necessary. They are generally brought together in a scale, not in the sense that a unit of one is made equivalent to so many units of another but that several objects together form a value unit. Thus in Java the value unit consists of a certain very valuable stone and 20 pearl shells. Of the Missouri River Indians it is reported that the purchase price for a wife consisted of two knives, a pair of trousers, a blanket, a flint-lock, a horse, and a leather tepee. The meaning is that a woman is of equal value with a complete equipment for an Indian warrior and is sold by her tribe for this amount. It follows that the basis of such value scales is not merely economic qualities but the customary worth of the goods, their traditionally imposed social significance, and also the requirement for round numbers easily handled. In this connection again the decimal figures play a special role. Thus there are tribes in which ten cocoanuts equal in value a certain quantity of tobacco, 300 dolphin teeth correspond to a woman, etc.

Head money and expiatory payments also, and other considerations expressed in money, have no relation to economic values but to social valuation exclusively. The head money (wergeld) of a free Frank amounted to 200 solidi. This amount was fixed because it had to be brought into a certain relation with the head money for a half-free or servile person. Only traditionally imposed evaluations find expression in these principles. As soon as economic exchange relations make headway, as was already the case in the early middle ages, head money is no longer determined in terms of a claim for restitution of damage but it becomes a typical phenomenon that a larger amount is insisted upon. Evaluation in terms of a given monetary good by no means always implies payment in the same good, but may be only a standard in which the payment

of the individual is measured. The latter may depend
upon the capacity to pay of the dispenser—*"in quo potu-
erit"*—not according to a tariff but signifying rather a traditionally fixed consideration for restitution.

Out of the conditions just described evolved the distinctive position of the "noble" metals as a nominal basis of
monetary organization. The determining conditions of
this evolution are purely technical. The precious metals
oxidize with difficulty and hence are not easily destroyed,
while in consequence of their relative scarcity they have a
high value for the specific use of objects of adornment;
finally, they are relatively easy to shape and to subdivide.
The decisive fact was that the scales could be applied to
them, and were applied at a very early date. The grain of
wheat seems to have served as the earliest comparative
weight. It goes without saying that the precious metals
have also been employed in the form of objects of utility,
but were specialized as a means of payment even long before they became media of exchange. In the former case
they appear first in the chieftain trade; the tablets of Tell-
el-Amarna show that the western Asiatic rulers expected
from the Pharaohs more than anything else shipments of
decorative gold. A preferred form for the gift of the
prince to his followers was the gold ring; in the skaldic
language the king is specifically called the ring spender.

In the form of coinage, money first appears in the 7th
century before Christ. The oldest mints were located in
Lydia, probably on the coast, and arose out of the co-
operation of the Lydian king and the Greek colonists. A
forerunner of coined money was precious metal in bars
privately stamped by merchants, which appear in Indian
commerce and later in Babylonia and in China. The
shekel is nothing but a piece of silver with the stamp of
a certain mercantile family, which was recognized for

conscientiousness in weighing. The Chinese tael is similarly a piece of bar silver stamped by the mercantile guilds. Not until later did the political power take over the coinage, and shortly afterwards assume a monopoly of the activity. The last seems however to have been the case in Lydia. The Great King of Persia stamped the darics as a means for paying his Greek mercenaries.

The Greeks introduced coins into commerce as a medium of exchange. On the other hand, Carthage did not attempt coinage until three centuries after its invention, and even then the purpose was not to secure a medium of exchange but merely a means for paying its mercenary armies. In general the Phenician commerce was carried on entirely without money, and it was especially the technical advantage of coins which helped to establish the superiority of Greek trading activity. Even Rome, which carried on an export trade in primitive times, went over to coinage very late and to begin with only to the coinage of copper. It tolerated the stamping of precious metal in Capua, while in Rome itself the most diverse sorts of coins circulated until 269 B. C. when the coinage of silver was taken up. In India coinage is first met with between 500 and 400 B. C. and was in fact taken over from the west; really usable coins in the technical sense are first found after the Alexandrian period. In eastern Asia the conditions are obscure; perhaps an independent origin of coinage is to be assumed. Today, it is limited to the coinage of copper, in consequence of the persistent debasement by the mandarins.

. The technology of manufacturing coins had little in common with that of today before the 17th century. In antiquity the coins were cast, in the middle ages "struck," that is stamped, but until the 13th century it was purely a handicraft operation. The coin had to pass through the hands of not less than ten to twelve different craftsmen who worked with hand tools only. The costs of the process were extremely high, amounting to a fourth of the value for the small coins and was still as much as 10 per cent in the 14th and 15th centuries, while today it may be placed at 10 per thousand. In consequence of the primitive technique the accuracy even of the best coins varied; even with the English gold crown, in spite of relative perfection of the process, the variation was still 10%. Commerce reacted to these errors by accepting the coins where possible only by weight. For fineness the stamp was a fairly secure guaranty. The first relatively exact coins which were also maintained constant were the famous Florentine gold gulden, after 1252. A really reliable coinage in the technical sense dates, however, only from the end of the 17th century, although the use of machinery in coining occurs somewhat earlier.

By a metallic standard we today understand in the first place the enforcement of certain coinage as a means of payments, either in all amounts (standard money) or up to a certain maximum amount (subsidiary coins); in the second place, connected with this is the principle of free coinage of the standard money which with the deduction of minimal costs of manufacture anyone at any time has the right to have made and with it to make payments to an unlimited extent. The standard may be mono-metallic or bi-metallic. In the latter case the only conception which seems possible to us is the so-called double standard, that is the several metals are set by law in a fixed relation to each other, as for example in the Latin Monetary Union gold stands to silver in the ratio of 1 to 15½. The second possibility, which was much more prevalent earlier, is that of parallel standards. Under this rule there was either actual unrestricted coinage of the metals, with in general no scheduled value relation or only a periodical adjustment of a varying value relation. In the choice of the metal for coinage the matter of the needs of trade were decisive. Internal and local trade could use only a metal with a value not too high, and here we find silver or copper or both. Distant commerce could and from necessity did for a time get along with silver, but after the commerce grew in importance it preferred gold. For the actual circulation of gold, however, the legal relation to silver was decisive; whenever one of the metals was given an unfavorable valuation in comparison with the available supply, the consequence was that the coins stamped from that metal would be melted up and used in commerce in this condition.

The history of the value relation between the different metals shows a sharp contrast as between eastern Asia on the one hand and the western Asiatic and European conditions on the other. Because the eastern Asiatic countries were cut off from the outer world an abnormal relation arose and it was possible to maintain a relative valuation which never existed in the west. Thus in Japan for a time gold was valued only 5 times as high as silver. In contrast, the continuity was never completely broken in the west. In Babylon values were reckoned in terms of silver, which however was not coined by state agencies, but circulated in the form of privately stamped silver bars or shekels. The value of silver in comparison with gold was set at $13\frac{1}{3}$ to 1 and this relation remained the standard for antiquity. The Egyptians took over the Babylonian silver bars in the form of deben but reckoned in terms of copper, silver, and finally gold, side by side, large amounts being paid in gold.

For later antiquity and the time down to the Merovingians, the monetary policy of Rome was definitive. Here originally parallel standards of copper and silver prevailed and the effort was made to fix the ratio at 112 to 1. The important measure was the manufacture of the silver *sestertium* equal to a pound of metal. Gold was coined merely as a commercial coin while copper progressively declined to the level of credit money for small transactions and came finally to have the character of token money. Coinage was in fact predominantly in the hands of military generals whose names the gold and silver coins almost always bore, even in the republican period; they were preferred as payment for spoils of war, and served the purposes not of commerce but of paying the army.

When Cæsar took over the imperial power the first real regulation of standards was instituted, Cæsar going over to the gold standard. His *aureus* was intended to be equal to a hundred silver *sestercis* on the basis of a ratio of 11.9 to 1. Hence silver had somewhat increased in value, a sign of the fact that trade experienced an increasing need for it. The aureus maintained itself down to the time of Constantine, while silver was variously experimented with. Nero decreed the *denarius,* increasing the prestige of the aureus. Caracalla pursued the debasement of coinage systematically as a business, and his successors, the barrack emperors, followed in his path. This coinage policy, and not the alleged outflow of the precious metals to India or a failure of mining, ruined the Roman monetary organization. It was restored by Constantine the Great. He replaced the aureus with the gold *solidus* of which he coined 72 from a pound (327.45g.) of metal. In commerce the *solidus* probably passed by weight.

The gold *solidus* outlived the Roman empire. In the Merovingian period, it possessed the highest prestige in Germany within the area of the former Roman economic penetration, while to the east of the Rhine the older Roman silver coins circulated in a way somewhat similar to the

Maria Theresa dollar later in Africa. The change to the Carolingian rulers meant politically a shifting of the center of gravity from the western to the eastern portion of the Frankish empire; but in coinage policy, although much gold was imported into the empire from the east, it meant a change from a gold to a silver standard. Charlemagne after many measures not clear as to their import, established a unit pound of 409 grams—though this assumption is not undisputed,—and out of this pound coined 20 silver solidi of 12 denarii each. Officially, the Carolingian coinage system, the last survival of which is the English units of pounds sterling, shillings, and pence, remained in force to the end of the middle ages and with it, over by far the greater part of the continent, the silver standard.

The central problem for the coinage policy of the middle ages, however, was not that of the standard, but was raised by questions of an economic and social character which affected the production of coins. Antiquity took seriously the coinage monopoly of the state. In the middle ages on the contrary, the rule was appropriation of the coinage function by numerous territorial coinage jurisdictions and their proprietors. As a result, after around the middle of the 11th century, the Carolingian coinage system everywhere had only a common-law significance. The coinage right, it is true, remained officially reserved to the king, or emperor; but the manufacture of coins was carried out by an association of handicraft producers and the revenue from the coinage business fell to the individual coinage lord. Infeudation of the coinage right to individual coinage lords involved an incentive to debasement which was practised on a wide scale throughout the middle ages. In Germany the solidus sank from the 13th to the 16th century to a sixth of its original content; likewise in England the *denarius* from the 12th to the 14th century; in France, was originated the *solidus grossus,* a thick coin stamped on both sides, which competed intensively with the thin denarius coined in Germany in the 12th and 13th centuries and stamped on only one side (*Brakteaten*); but the new coin sank from the 14th to the 16th century to a seventh of its value.

The coinage debasement which affected silver led to the result that in commerce, which has to compute in stable units, the prestige of gold was increased. In consequence it was an epoch-making event when in 1252 the city of Florence minted a gold solidus of 3½ grams weight (*florenus, florin*) and maintained it at a weight as nearly uniform as was technically possible. Everywhere the new coinage was accepted, and it became the general monetary unit of commerce. Nevertheless we observe a pronounced increase in the price of silver, which can only have been caused by the urgent demand of the growing money economy for silver for use in trade. Toward 1500 the ratio between silver and gold increased from 12½ to 1 to 10½ to 1. At the same time there was an irrational fluctuation of the currencies in relation to each other and a difference between bullion and "pagament" or metal in the form of coin. While in wholesale trade men computed in terms of bars or Florentine gold gulden, in retail transactions the various coins were evaluated by agreement.

It was not only the greed of the coinage lords which was responsible for the debasement; it was due largely to the automatic working of the variation between specimens of the same coinage, which amounted to as much as 10%. Only the worst of the coins struck would remain in circulation, while the best made would be melted up at once, or in any case sorted out. It is true that the greed of the monetary lords contributed; they employed their monopoly to put out new coins, cancelling and calling in the old. But the latter were to a large extent in circulation outside their home district. The monopoly which a coinage lord officially claimed, he never could fully put into effect in his territory; a change could only be brought about through an agreement between several princes. Thus, aside from the coinage and good faith of the Florentines, the middle ages remained a period of coinage irrationality. Precisely because of this irrational condition in the production of coins, unrestricted coinage went without saying; since the coinage lord by increasing the mintage could secure an advantage from his business he strove to secure all the precious metal for his own mint. The possessors of precious metal were subjected to pressure in this connection; prohibitions on export were of common occurrence, especially in districts containing mines, and miners and shareholders in the mines of precious metals seemingly had no choice as to whether they should bring the metal to the mint of the coinage lord or not. Yet all these measures remained without effect. Not only was an enormous amount of smuggling carried on, but the coinage lord had to arrange by agreement to concede a supply of metal to the mints of other lords who possessed no mines, and this metal constantly returned to his district in the form of foreign coins. An irrational trade in coins persisted throughout the middle ages; the demand for the various sorts of coins could not be determined and the extreme fluctuations in the seigniorage operated to prevent adjustment of supply to demand; only the competition among the coinage lords caused them to renounce seigniorage.

After the 16th century the increased inflow of precious metal to Europe provided the economic basis for the establishment of more stable relations in the field of coinage, and at least in western Europe the absolute states had already cleared out the multiplicity of coinage lords with their competition among themselves. Down to the date mentioned Europe had been a region of permanent exportation of the precious metals; only the period of the crusades, lasting for about 150 years, with their spoils in gold, and also the produce of the plantations, had formed an interruption to this condition. At this time the discovery of the sea route to the East Indies by Vasco de Gama and Albuquerque broke the monopoly of the Arabs over the transit trade. The exploitation of the Mexican and Peruvian silver mines brought great quantities of American metal to Europe, while the discovery of an effective process for extracting silver, by amalgamation with mercury, contributed to the result. The quantity of precious metal obtained from Mexico and South America has been estimated for the period from 1493 to 1800 at nearly 2½ million kilograms of gold and 90 to 100 million kilograms of silver.[2]

The increase in the production of the metal meant immediately a sharp increase in the supply of coined silver. The silver standard permeated to the farthest confines of trade in Europe and reached its expression in the money of account. In Germany, the Florentine gold gulden was even brought out in silver (the Joachimstaler). This condition obtained until the Brazilian deposits of gold were opened up. Although exploitation of these lasted only for a short time—from the beginning to the middle of the 18th century—it dominated the market and resulted in the change of England to the gold standard, against the will of the English law makers and the advice especially of Isaac Newton. After the middle of the 18th century, silver production again came to the fore and influenced the French legislature at the time of the revolution, calling into being the French double standard.

But the rationalization of coinage could not at once be carried out. The condition which obtained before it was completed may be described by saying that innumerable kinds of coins were in circulation, yet no money, in the present day sense of the word. Even the imperial coinage edict of Ferdinand I in 1859 was forced to recognize thirty types of foreign coin. The extraordinary range of variation in the content of the same type of coin, due to the imperfection of the technique of manufacturing, especially in the case of the smaller coins, in connection with the great volume of the mintage, led to a restriction in Germany in the 16th century of the legal tender power of the silver coins, but without the transformation of these into subsidiary coins; the definite rational establishment of subsidiary coinage was reserved for English monetary policy to introduce. The official monetary unit was the gold gulden coined in silver, the Joachimstaler, but in fact the following development took place in the commercial field.

After the 13th and 14th centuries, commerce emancipated itself from coinage and reckoned in bullion, accepting coins only by weight, specifying payment in a certain type of coin, which had to be recognized as customary by the empire. Finally, it went over to deposit banking. The prototype of the latter was provided by China. Here the debasement of the coins had led to the establishment of metallic deposit banks for the commerce of the merchants. With the fixation of a weight unit the silver payments were made either by checks or instruments similar to checks, drawn on a bank in which the individual merchant kept his deposit of bar silver, or else by means of silver in stamped bars—taels—which, however, played no considerable role in comparison with the payment by checks.   Thus was created a bank money based on the possession of bullion by the merchants concerned and which was the exclusive means of payment for the persons connected with the deposit system.

Imitations of this prototype are found in the west as early as the 16th century: in Venice the Rialto bank; in Amsterdam, the Wisselbank, 1609; in Nuremburg in 1621; in Hamburg in 1629.   These banks reckoned by weight and only coined pieces were accepted in payment.   The individual account was usually subject to a minimum, as were the payments; thus in Amsterdam the minimum size of the draft or order were 300 gulden.   On the other hand, no payment above 600 gulden could be made in any other way than through the medium of the bank.   In Hamburg this bank standard persisted down to 1873.

Modern monetary policy is distinguished from that of the past by the absence of the fiscal motif; only general economic interests resting on the need of commerce for a stable basis of capital computation determine its character.   In this connection England took the lead of all other countries.

Originally, silver was in England the effective means of payment for all internal commerce while international trade was based on a gold money of account.   After the Brazilian discoveries, increasing amounts of gold flowed to England and the English government was subject to increasing embarrassment by the parallel system.   After gold became cheap it flowed to the mints and at the same time the silver circulation was endangered by the melting up of the silver coins.   As all loans had to be repaid in silver, capitalistic enterprise was interested in preventing the outflow of the silver.   At first the government attempted to maintain the parallel coinage by arbitrary measures, until in 1717 it decided to carry out a new definitive valuation.

Under the guidance of Isaac Newton the typical English gold coin, the guinea, was fixed in value at 21 shillings even though gold was still over-valued. When in the course of the 18th century gold continued to flow in, silver flowed out and the government proceeded to radical preventive measures. Gold was made the standard metal and all silver degraded to the position of subsidiary coin. It lost its unlimited legal tender and was alloyed and coined at more than its bullion value so that the danger of its leaving the country was removed.

After much experimenting, the French government finally adopted during the revolution a double standard, the basis of which was silver; 1000 francs were coined from 9 pounds of silver (222% to the kilogram) and the ratio of silver to gold was fixed at the current relative value of 15½ to 1. The extraordinary domestic demand for coin in France, which was stronger than that of England, led in fact to a stabilization in the value relation between gold and silver over a long period.

In Germany, the silver system had to be left intact during the 19th century, the first part of which shows a period of decreasing metal production. There was no central authority in a position to effect a transition of gold. Gold was however minted as a commercial coin with a legalized value, especially in Prussia; but the attempt to give gold a different position in the monetary standard was unsuccessful. The war indemnity of 1871 first enabled Germany to go over to the gold standard, a step which was facilitated by the sharp increase in the world's stock of gold which followed the Californian discoveries, while on the other hand the value ratio of 15½ to 1 was gradually destroyed.

These conditions determined the creation of the German Reichsmark equal to one-third Taler; since 30 Taler equalled a pound of silver, the ratio of 15½ to 1 made the pound of gold equal to 1395 marks.

CHAPTER XX

Prior to the period of capitalism the activity of a bank consisted primarily, wherever a plurality of kinds of money were in circulation, in the business of exchanging money. To this was added the necessity of a money disbursing business, especially that of making payments at a distance. In antiquity as a whole, and especially in Greece, we find as the typical banking transaction the assumption of obligations to make payments and the issue of letters of credit to travelers as a means of making payments at a distance, and in addition, not indeed exchange operations in the modern sense, but the creation of means of payment which suggest the check of the present day. Furthermore, the function of providing for the safekeeping of money, or deposit business, belongs to the very oldest of banking operations. It was so in Egypt, where the bankers were to a large extent administrators of property, and also in Rome. Where there was no coinage of any kind, as in Babylonia, and also in China and India, the business of money changing was absent. In its place the bankers were the agencies which stamped the silver bars which circulated as money, as in the case of the tael, and hence carried on the business of providing money.

Thus in the pre-capitalistic age the banks transacted a deposit business with transfer or assignment of credits for

the elimination of cash payments. The arrangement presupposed that the depositor-customer permanently maintained a deposit in the bank in question; correspondingly
we find bank "notes" even in Babylon. Yet one must not
think in this connection of bank notes in our sense, for the
modern bank note circulates independently of any deposit
by a particular individual. In contrast, the Babylonian
bank notes or tickets were merely a means for the more
rapid and secure transmission of payments between
depositor-customers. The extent of this more ancient deposit business is unknown; in any case one must guard
against thinking of conditions in terms too modern. The
relations were generally restricted to strictly local transactions and to those taking place between merchants; consequently the bank tickets were not a medium for general
circulation.

Peculiar to Babylon was the development out of the deposit business of the role of the banker as a lender of
credit. The professional banker made loans on a small
scale against pledges or personal security. The credit
function of the Babylonian banker was based on the absence of coinage. Payments were reckoned in silver
shekels, but these were not used for payment, so that the
banker was necessary as an intermediary; and in this connection he arranged for postponement, since he was also
often in a position to provide the means for payment in
cash, and afforded certainty to the seller by substituting
himself for the future payer. Another peculiarity in
Babylonia was that the banker regularly furnished commenda credit, that is, capital for enterprise; a large number
of commenda contracts have come down to us in cuneiform
writing, while we have no other example of such credit
business in the ancient world. The reason is that where
coined money was in use the banking business developed

out of coinage, but in Babylon it developed out of money, that is to say, credit, dealings.

In Rome, the occupation of the banker exhibits two special features. The first, which is of no particular concern to economic history, is that the banker was the professional auctioneer. In the second place, we find here for the first time the transaction of an account-current deposit business in the modern sense, and its recognition as a specific means for the liquidation of debts with the aid of the banker. In Rome the purpose of this business was originally to provide a uniform and secure means of payment, in view of the fact that the coinage of silver was not introduced until late and that the amount of the coinage depended upon the booty secured by the generals. This backwardness of coinage relations in Rome affords the simplest explanation for the fact that the deposit (*receptum*), and the order or draft (*actio receptitia*) drawn only against the balance of the account current, possessed so much significance, and that the bookkeeping of the banker was there subject to a unified legal regulation. The books of the Roman *argentarii* speak of receipts and expenditures, though not in the sense of the modern bookkeeping. A special book was kept for each individual customer, in which he was credited and debited (*acceptum ferre, expensum ferre*). These entries served to prove that payment had been made. Beyond this too little has survived of the bookkeeping of the *argentarii* to permit of more exact statements.

In general, however, the banks of antiquity were only exceptionally private undertakings, and these were subject to an extensive competition by temple banks and state banks. The temple of antiquity first served as a depository. Insofar as they served as banks this was their primary function, and in this connection they were much more famous than the depositories of the private bankers. The deposits in the temple were sacred and could not be stolen without committing sacrilege. The temple at Delphi was a storehouse for numerous private persons, and especially for the savings of slaves. Numerous inscriptions tell how the liberty of slaves has been purchased by the god; in reality the purchase was made out of the savings of the slaves which were given over to the temple for safekeeping in order to protect them from the master. The same function as depositories was performed by numerous temples in Babylon, Egypt, and Greece, while in Rome they lost this character in early times. In consequence, the temples in antiquity also became important lending agencies, especially for the princes, who secured more favorable terms from them than from private money lenders. It is true that we find the large money lender, even in the code of Hammurabi, but in general the treasury of the state and its money lender was the temple. This function was fulfilled in Babylon by the temple of the sun god Sippar, and in Egypt by the temple of Ammon; the treasury of the Attic maritime league was the temple of Athena.

A second source of competition for the private banker grew up in the state banks. The making of banking into a public function resulted, where it happened, not in consequence of mismanagement and bankruptcy of the bankers as in the middle ages, but from fiscal considerations. Not only had the money changing business developed into a fruitful source of profit, but for political reasons also it seemed advantageous to be in possession of the largest possible quantity of private deposits. In almost all the Hellenistic states, especially in Ptolemaic Egypt, the result was a royal banking monopoly. It is true that these establishments had nothing to do with the tasks of the modern state bank, such as note issue, regulation of standards, and coinage policy; they were purely fiscal institutions. The extraordinary power of the capitalistic knights as a class in Rome rested essentially on the fact that they succeeded in preventing such a monopolization of the banking function by the state.

The beginnings of medieval banking are diverse in character. In the 11th century we meet with *campsores,* money changers, who secured a considerable profit from their work. At the end of the 12th century the business of making payments at a distance was in their hands; it was carried out by means of the *cambium* or exchange letter, a device taken over from the Arabs. In contrast with antiquity, the business of lending money was only assumed by the resident banker relatively late or not at all; as a rule they loaned only large sums and only to the political powers. The small scale business in money was in the hands of an alien class, the Jews, Lombards, the Caursines, the two latter designations being used to include southerners of every sort. This consumptive credit in the hands of aliens was originally emergency credit at a very high rate of interest, and based on a pledge or other security. Alongside it appears at an early date the business of commenda credit. In the granting of such credit the bankers also took part, but were subject—in contrast with Babylonian conditions—to the competition of merchants dealing in goods of the most various sorts, and also that of private money lenders. The deposit business was called into existence by the continual monetary debasement. Communal banks arose among the merchant class with deposits in metal or in various coins at their bullion value, on the basis of which payments were made by deposit transfers or checks, limited to a certain minimum. For a time, deposit banking business was in the hands of the money changers, but in the long run they did not enjoy sufficient confidence, and large company banks arose.

In the field of medieval banking is further included the collection of taxes, corresponding roughly to the tax farming of antiquity. From the beginning of the 13th to the end of the 14th century this was the main source of the large fortunes, especially those of the Florentine banking families, the Acciajuoli, the Peruzzi, and the Medici. As these maintained their factors in all large commercial places, they were the natural agency for gathering from all quarters the taxes of the Curia, which was the greatest taxing power of the age; also they kept the most accurate accounts and accepted only full value money in the sense of the Florentine gold gulden. This function brought the collectors, as in the case of the mandarins in China, very large opportunities for profit, as it lay in their hands to evaluate the money of the various regions in terms of the coin demanded by the Curia.

Finally, the business of financing is to be named among the functions of medieval banking. By this, however, is not to be understood the financing of large enterprises in the present sense. The need for financing operations existed only exceptionally, and generally in connection with military ventures. In this field it was undertaken in Genoa as early as the 12th century. In this way, for example, the great sea expeditions of the Genoese against Cyprus were financed through the formation of a "maona," a share commenda enterprise for the conquest and exploitation of the island. In the same way to a large extent the wars of the cities among themselves were financed by organizations of creditors. For roughly a hundred years together the total tax and harbor customs receipts of Genoa were administered exclusively in the interests of such a consortium. Far beyond these limits went the financing operations of the great Florentine bankers in the Franco-English wars of the 14th century.

To the extent to which these transactions remained in private hands arose the questions out of what source the funds came, where the money went, and by what means the banks were at all able to meet an effective obligation to pay, which in fact tended to collapse. That is, we are confronted by the problem of the "liquidity" of the medieval bank. The liquidity of the institutions we have described was very poor. The money which the Peruzzi or other great Florentine bankers advanced to the citizens of Florence for their wars did not come out of their own capital, which would not have been at all sufficient, but out of deposits which they received on the grounds of their prestige, out of every circle of the population down to the lowest strata, and for a low rate of interest. But these deposits were payable on short notice while the war loans ran for long periods. Consequently the financial operations ended in bankruptcy as soon as the military ventures in which they were employed resulted unfavorably. This applies even to the Fuggers, for the way in which they finally settled with the Spanish crown meant that not only did they suffer enormous losses but also that the remainder of their wealth was tied up in forms on which they could not realize.

The private means of the large banking houses being insufficient for the financing of large enterprises of the state, and their liquidity being easily lost, the pressure of events was in the direction of monopolistic banking. The political authority which required money for its purposes received it only in return for a grant of various monopolies, of trade, of the customs, and of the banking business also. The prince, or the city, made banking a public enterprise and granted the privilege as a monopoly, or farmed it out to private persons in return for a loan of money. The oldest example of such a banking monopoly is the Banca di San Giorgio in Genoa, and the latest the Bank of England. Even this latter did not arise out of a voluntary organization of merchants but was a purely political undertaking which financed the War of the Spanish Succession. The distinction between it and the medieval banks lies only in the manner in which it was able to establish its business, namely on the basis of bills of exchange.

The present day bill of exchange is a means of payment characterized by the fact that three persons are involved in it; besides the receiver there are the drawer and the drawee. Of these the drawer is always responsible, as is also the drawee or acceptor, from the moment of acceptance. In addition, when the bill is transferred to third parties by endorsement, every individual endorser becomes responsible, with no question raised regarding the transaction in connection with which the bill was drawn. In case of non-payment a special process of execution is available which in the middle ages involved imprisonment for debt. The significance of the bill of exchange for the bank of today lies in these characteristics; they impart to it the certainty that specific sums can be drawn at a specified time and hence give it liquidity. In the middle ages there was no such possibility. It is true that the bill of exchange was known, but it then signified only an instrument similar to our checks. It was a mere means of payment, ordinarily of payment at a distance, by means of which one paid debts with money to which one had a claim at some other place; difference in place between the one who promised payment and the point where payment was made was essential to the instrument, especially as the canon law condemned with all its power the use of local bills as a usurious business.

The typical medieval bill originally consisted of two

separate documents. One of these, the "open letter," (*litera aperta*), was what we should call a domiciled bill. The merchant A in Genoa promised to pay to B in Barcelona on a certain day a certain sum, through C, the debtor of A. If the bill was issued by a prince it was drawn upon his treasury which had to pay to the court a certain sum. The second document, the "closed letter" (*litera clausa*) or "draft" evolved into the present bill. It informed the debtor of the drawer that he was to pay the sum on account of his creditor the drawer. The *literae apertae* had to be drawn up and witnessed officially while the *literae clausae* were ordinary letters. Both documents were placed in the hands of the person in favor of whom the bill was drawn. The further development consisted in the gradual dropping of the *literae apertae* on account of the expense. The binding promise which they originally contained became included in the draft and recognized as a part of the latter, which thus increased in significance; but it was still distinguished from the modern bill in that it was not negotiable by endorsement, which character it did not achieve until the 17th century.

It is true that it contained the formula *promitto tibi vel tuo certo nuntio*, which made it possible to place it in the possession of a third party and to legalize his receipt of the payment in place of the named receiver; but this order clause disappeared later because a regular machinery for making payments developed in the large fairs. These afforded the possibility of liquidating bills without incurring the risk of transporting money, by turning it over to a clearing house for entry, with payment only of net balances. Actually the bills were only discount instruments in connection with which it was tacitly assumed that they would be liquidated through a deposit bank or a local merchants' association. This condition worked to the advantage of the merchants engaged in the exchange business, giving them an interest in securing a monopoly of the fees for effecting exchange transfers, and they opposed endorsement. Thus even in the 16th century when any exchange was transferred a new bill had to be drawn instead of endorsing the old one. It is true again that in the 16th century the law of exchange had reached its present development, and equivocation on legal grounds was excluded by the maxim "chi accetta paghi" (the acceptor must pay). This unconditional assurance of payment made it possible for the bill of exchange to become the bank paper of today.

The part of the medieval banker in payments consisted in accepting the bill; the banker of today discounts it, that is, he pays it, with the deduction of the discount with the view of cashing it later and thus invests his operating capital in bills. The institution which first consistently carried on such an exchange business is the Bank of England.

English banking history before the founding of the Bank of England shows that the goldsmiths, as dealers in the precious metals and owners of stocks of metal, were in a position to carry on a banking business and often had a monopoly of the testing of coins as to weight and fineness, but that they never played the role of bankers in the sense described above. They received deposits in the manner of the medieval banker, and financed political enterprises, those of the Stuarts as well as of Cromwell. They also transacted a deposit business and in connection therewith issued paper means of payment, to their customers first, but the circulation of these "goldsmith notes" did not remain confined to this circle. The state bankruptcy of 1672 put an end to all this. When, at that time, the English government declared that it could not repay its debts but would pay interest on them only, while the depositor-

customers of the goldsmiths were entitled to withdraw their
capital at any time, the result was inability of the goldsmiths to meet the demand for payment of deposits.   The
result was that in England at this time, as earlier in the
Italian cities, there was a clamor among the depositors for
a public monopoly bank.

The political authorities took advantage of this demand
to monopolize the banking business and secure a share in its
profits for the state.   The merchants hoped for loans at a
low interest through the fact that a state bank, in view of
the security which it offered, would be in a position to
attract to itself deposits in large volume, and also hoped for
release from their coinage difficulties—although we cannot
be sure how they argued.   On the other hand, we must not
assume as applicable to that time the modern view according to which a large bank of issue undertakes the task of
using its credit through a suitable discount policy to draw
gold into the country or to force an accumulated stock into
circulation.   Rather it was hoped that the bank would
function as a deposit bank, that is, circulate its notes on the
basis of a definite quantity of metal and so assist in reducing the fluctuations in the ratio between gold and silver.

The final establishment of the Bank of England in 1694
was based on purely political motives with a view of financing the war of William of Orange with Louis XIV.   In its
establishment the procedure customary to the country
was employed; certain payments, especially the salt tax,
were pledged to the money lenders, and the participating
creditors were organized as governors into a company with
legal privileges.

The new establishment was combated by many interests.
Opposed to the project were, in the first place, the Tories,
as opponents of William of Orange, and, on the other hand,
the Whigs who on general principles feared the strengthen-

ing of the position of the king.   Hence the bank could only be organized as an independent private corporation, not as a state bank, and it was necessary to include in the act the specification that money could be advanced to the state only on the basis of a special authorization by Parliament. Hence in the view of the Tories the bank was consistent only with a republic, not a monarchy; they contended that a bank with such an organization presupposed a kingdom under the control of the capitalist groups interested in the bank.   Finally the goldsmiths also opposed the bank because they were excluded from the business, and also because, in common with the nobility, they feared the political and economic power of the merchant class.

The bank came into existence with a share capital of £1,200,000, all of which disappeared into the pockets of the state.   In exchange it received the right to deal in bills of exchange.   The last named right was by far the most important, since it was connected with the issue of notes. The use which the bank would later make of this right through its discount policy was in fact foreseen by no one. In any case, however, it was the first institution to begin systematically to purchase exchange, thereby shortening for producers as well as merchants the interval before the product reached the final consumer, by discounting the bills before maturity.   With the Bank of England the acceleration of capital turnover is the clearly conceived purpose of exchange dealings; it pursued this business in a systematic way as no bank had done before.

Only in part does the development of banking outside of Europe offer a parallel to that in Europe itself.   In India and China, banking retained down to the last few decades the character which it had in antiquity and in the middle ages.   It is distinguished from occidental banking by its extraordinary power in connection with the regulation

of monetary standards.   In China the banker conducts the
stamping of the *taels;* he determines the conditions of
credit, fixes the rate of interest, and designates all the conditions of making payments, so that the standardization of
commercial settlements lies entirely in his hands.   But this
mechanism of settlement is a credit business insofar as
foreign trade is concerned, which in Canton for example,
is in the hands of a few large Chinese houses.   As long as
the independent Chinese states existed the banks also carried on war financing, as in Europe; with the establishment
of the unitary Chinese empire this opportunity was lost.

In India the banking business in its entirety is strictly
regulated by sects or castes.   Here also in the period of
the great independent states political credit was financed
by the banks, and here also the unitary state of the Grand
Mogul put an end to this; subsequently political monetary
dealings were involved only in connection with governmental budgeting and the anticipation of income through
loans.   The functions of the banks in India and China today still consist essentially of the business of making payments and small or occasional credit operations.   There is
no business credit in any way systematized, no business organization which could make any use of our discount policy; the native Asiatic commerce knows only checks and
payment assignments of the most various sorts, but not the
bill of exchange.   That in addition the Chinese bankers still
possess a monopolistic control over the regulation of standards is explained by the enormous misuse of paper money
in China.

CHAPTER XXI

INTERESTS IN THE PRE-CAPITALISTIC PERIOD

In its beginnings interest is a phenomenon either of international or feudal law. Within a tribal village, or clan community, there is neither interest nor lending, since transfers of value in consideration for a payment are unknown. Where outside resources are used in economic life it is done under the form of neighborly help, such as invitation work in connection with house building or assistance in case of emergency, which rests on the duty of helping the clan brother without compensation. Even the Roman *mutuum*, a loan without interest, is a survival of these primitive conditions. The obligation to help in case of need receives an extension when it is taken over by religious communities and imposed upon brothers in the faith; the best known example is that of the Israelites. It is not the fact that they took interest which is peculiar to the Jews, for interest has been received everywhere in the world, including the medieval monasteries themselves; rather it was exceptional and repugnant to the western peoples that the Jews took interest from Christians but not from each other.

The prohibition in the Torah against taking interest or usury from the brother rests partly on military and partly on religious grounds. In the first place, the clan brother must not be imprisoned for debt and thus lost to the army. For this reason the ancient Egyptian religious code ascribed to the curse of the poor, a special force with the divine

267

powers and this idea passed over into the book of Deuteronomy. The distinction thus set up between internal and external ethics survived the exile; and after the Israelites became the Jews, interest was still forbidden between compatriots while it might be taken from foreigners ("Gojim"). Thus Maimonides could ask the question whether the Jew was under obligation to take interest from them.[1]

The prohibition of interest taking from a brother is also characteristic of early Islam and of Brahminism. Interest everywhere arises in the field of lending to foreigners outside the tribe or that of loans between classes. In this connection the contrast between creditor and debtor was originally always a contrast between a town-dwelling patritiate and rural peasants; it was so in China, India, and Rome, and the same conception also dominates in the Old Testament. The possibility that a prohibition against interest should arise rested on the fact that all credit was originally emergency credit and purely for consumptive purposes, so that the idea of a brotherly obligation could arise in opposition to the demand for interest by the master class; a further consideration is that behind the warning against interest there was a strong military interest since the creditor ran the risk of being reduced to the condition of a landless proletarian who would not be in a position to equip himself for war.

The occasion for breaking through the prohibition against interest was provided by the loan of concrete property. The first case is the cattle loan. Among nomads, the contrast between propertied and non-propertied persons is fearfully sharp. The man who owns no cattle is forthwith outlawed and can only hope to rise again to full citizenship through a loan of stock and stock breeding. Of similar import is the seed loan, which in Babylonia especially, confronts us as a customary usage. In the one case as in the other the object of the loan replaces itself manifold and it did not appear an unjust conception if the creditor reserved for himself a part of the fruits of his cattle or grain. In addition, the prohibition against interest was broken wherever town life developed.

In the Christian occident the need for credit for industrial purposes originally found expression rarely in the form of a loan with a definite interest but rather in that of an association. It was not the prohibition of usury by the church which was behind this arrangement, so much as the risk connected with oversea business ventures. In view of this risk a definite interest rate was not so much at issue in such transactions; instead, the creditor participated in the gain as compensation for the risk to which the capital he provided was subject. Hence the Italian *commenda*, the *dare ad proficuum de mari,* with an interest rate depending in accordance with a scale, on the port of destination. These primitive trading credit transactions were not affected by the ecclesiastical prohibitions of usury. On the contrary, a fixed loan against fixed interest became customary in connection with land transportation because the risk here was less than in overseas trade. The formula *salvum in terra* signified that the capital loan must be without reference to the result of the enterprise.

At the same time, however, the opposition to usury on the part of the church increased in energy. Hence the prohibition of interest is not a product of an age of purely natural economy, but the movement reached its full development only as it was allowed to lapse in the face of a growing money economy. Pope Gregory IX even condemned sea loans as usury. Equally false is the assertion that the church pursued an opportunistic policy in connection with interest and favored the development of capitalism.   In fact it pursued the war against interest with increased determination and forced many a man to restore interest on his death bed just as today the confessional enforces restitution of goods stolen from a master.   But the more money economy developed, the oftener was the prohibition evaded, and the church had to meet the situation by general indulgences.   Finally, in the face of the power of the great Florentine bankers in the 15th century it was confronted by facts which made all opposition fruitless. Theology then attempted to interpret the prohibition as leniently as possible, but the tragedy was that the church itself as a temporal power was forced to have recourse to loans at interest.

At first, before the church itself undertook the establishment of lending institutions (the *montes pietatis*) a way out was found in the money lending of the Jews.   This was characterized by the fact that it afforded the political authorities the possibility of adopting a "sponge policy"; that is, the population was exploited through their payments of interest to the Jews and at irregular intervals the state confiscated the profit and the outstanding loans and simultaneously banished the Jewish creditors.   In this way the Jews were hounded from city to city and from country to country; formal pools for robbing them were established between the princes, as for example between the Bishop of Bamberg and the Hohenzollern Burgrave of Nuremberg to the effect that they shared in the booty when the Jews fled from the jurisdiction of one to that of the other.   Meanwhile the attitude of the church to the taking of interest became increasingly cautious.   It is true that a formal suspension of the prohibition was never decreed, but in the course of the 19th century ecclesiastic depositions repeatedly recognized as legal the taking of interest under specified conditions.

In northern Europe the prohibition against usury was broken up by Protestantism, although not immediately. In the Calvinistic synods we repeatedly meet with the conception that a lender and his wife must not be admitted to the Lord's Supper, but Calvin himself declared in the *Constitutio Christiana* that the purpose of the prohibition of interest was only the protection of the poor against destitution and not the protection of the rich who carried on business with borrowed money. Finally, it was the Calvinistic leader in the field of classical philology, Claudius Salmasius, who in his book *De Usuris* in 1638, and in a number of later tracts, undermined the theoretical foundations of the prohibition against interest.

PART FOUR

THE ORIGIN OF MODERN CAPITALISM[1]

CHAPTER XXII

THE MEANING AND PRESUPPOSITIONS OF MODERN CAPITALISM

Capitalism is present wherever the industrial provision for the needs of a human group is carried out by the method of enterprise, irrespective of what need is involved. More specifically, a rational capitalistic establishment is one with capital accounting, that is, an establishment which determines its income yielding power by calculation according to the methods of modern bookkeeping and the striking of a balance. The device of the balance was first insisted upon by the Dutch theorist Simon Stevin in the year 1698.

It goes without saying that an individual economy may be conducted along capitalistic lines to the most widely varying extent; parts of the economic provision may be organized capitalistically and other parts on the handicraft or the manorial pattern. Thus at a very early time the city of Genoa had a part of its political needs, namely those for the prosecution of war, provided in capitalistic fashion, through stock companies. In the Roman empire, the supply of the population of the capital city with grain was carried out by officials, who however for this purpose, besides control over their subalterns, had the right to command the services of transport organizations; thus the leiturgical or forced contribution type of organization was combined with administration of public resources. Today, in contrast with the greater part of the past, our everyday needs are supplied capitalistically, our political

275

needs however through compulsory contributions, that is, by the performance of political duties of citizenship such as the obligation to military service, jury duty, etc. A whole epoch can be designated as typically capitalistic only as the provision for wants is capitalistically organized to such a predominant degree that if we imagine this form of organization taken away the whole economic system must collapse.

While capitalism of various forms is met with in all periods of history, the provision of the everyday wants by capitalistic methods is characteristic of the occident alone and even here has been the inevitable method only since the middle of the 19th century. Such capitalistic beginnings as are found in earlier centuries were merely anticipatory, and even the somewhat capitalistic establishments of the 16th century may be removed in thought from the economic life of the time without introducing any overwhelming change.

The most general presupposition for the existence of this present-day capitalism is that of rational capital accounting as the norm for all large industrial undertakings which are concerned with provision for everyday wants. Such accounting involves, again, first, the appropriation of all physical means of production—land, apparatus, machinery, tools, etc. as disposable property of autonomous private industrial enterprises. This is a phenomenon known only to our time, when the army alone forms a universal exception to it. In the second place, it involves freedom of the market, that is, the absence of irrational limitations on trading in the market. Such limitations might be of a class character, if a certain mode of life were prescribed for a certain class or consumption were standardized along class lines, or if class monopoly existed, as for example if the townsman were not allowed to own an estate or the knight or peasant to carry on industry; in such cases neither a free labor market nor a commodity market exists. Third, capitalistic accounting presupposes rational technology, that is, one reduced to calculation to the largest possible degree, which implies mechanization. This applies to both production and commerce, the outlays for preparing as well as moving goods.

The fourth characteristic is that of calculable law. The capitalistic form of industrial organization, if it is to operate rationally, must be able to depend upon calculable adjudication and administration. Neither in the age of the Greek city-state (polis) nor in the patrimonial state of Asia nor in western countries down to the Stuarts was this condition fulfilled. The royal "cheap justice" with its remissions by royal grace introduced continual disturbances into the calculations of economic life. The proposition that the Bank of England was suited only to a republic, not to a monarchy, referred to above (page 265) was related in this way to the conditions of the time. The fifth feature is free labor. Persons must be present who are not only legally in the position, but are also economically compelled, to sell their labor on the market without restriction. It is in contradiction to the essence of capitalism, and the development of capitalism is impossible, if such a propertyless stratum is absent, a class compelled to sell its labor services to live; and it is likewise impossible if only unfree labor is at hand. Rational capitalistic calculation is possible only on the basis of free labor; only where in consequence of the existence of workers who in the formal sense voluntarily, but actually under the compulsion of the whip of hunger, offer themselves, the costs of products may be unambiguously determined by agreement in advance. The sixth and final condition is the commercialization of economic life. By this we mean the general use of commercial instruments to represent share rights in enterprise, and also in property ownership.

To sum up, it must be possible to conduct the provision for needs exclusively on the basis of market opportunities and the calculation of net income. The addition of this commercialization to the other characteristics of capitalism involves intensification of the significance of another factor not yet mentioned, namely speculation. Speculation reaches its full significance only from the moment when property takes on the form of negotiable paper.

CHAPTER XXIII

THE EXTERNAL FACTS IN THE EVOLUTION OF CAPITALISM [1]

Commercialization involves, in the first place, the appearance of paper representing shares in enterprise, and, in the second place, paper representing rights to income, especially in the form of state bonds and mortgage indebtedness. This development has taken place only in the modern western world. Forerunners are indeed found in antiquity in the share-commandite companies of the Roman *publicani,* who divided the gains with the public through such share paper. But this is an isolated phenomenon and without importance for the provision for needs in Roman life; if it had been wanting entirely, the picture presented by the economic life of Rome would not have been changed.

In modern economic life the issue of credit instruments is a means for the rational assembly of capital. Under this head belongs especially the stock company. This represents a culmination of two different lines of development. In the first place, share capital may be brought together for the purpose of anticipating revenues. The political authority wishes to secure command over a definite capital sum or to know upon what income it may reckon; hence it sells or leases its revenues to a stock company. The Bank of St. George in Genoa is the most outstanding example of such financial operations, and along the same line are the income certificates of the German cities and treasury notes (*Rentenmeisterbriefe*) especially in Flanders. The significance of this system is that in place of the original condition under which unusual state requirements were covered by compulsory law, usually without interest and frequently never repaid, loans come to be floated which appeal to the voluntary economic interests of the participants. The conduct of war by the state becomes a business operation of the possessing classes. War loans bearing a high interest rate were unknown in antiquity; if the subjects were not in a position to supply the necessary means the state must turn to a foreign financier whose advances were secured by a claim against the spoils of war. If the war terminated unfortunately his money was lost. The securing of money for state purposes, and especially for war purposes, by appeal to the universal economic interest, is a creation of the middle ages, especially of the cities.

Another and economically more important form of association is that for the purpose of financing commercial enterprise—although the evolution toward the form of association most familiar today in the industrial field, the stock company, went forward very gradually from this beginning. Two types of such organizations are to be distinguished; first, large enterprises of an inter-regional character which exceeded the resources of a single commercial house, and second, inter-regional colonial undertakings.

For inter-regional enterprises which could not be financed by individual entrepreneurs, finance by groups was typical, especially in the operations of the cities in the 15th and 16th centuries. In part the cities themselves carried on inter-regional trade, but for economic history the other case is more important, in which the city went before the public and invited share participation in the commercial enterprise which it organized. This was done on a considerable scale. When the city appealed to the public, compulsion was exercised on the company thus formed to admit any citizen; hence the amount of share capital was unlimited. Frequently the capital first collected was insufficient and an additional contribution was demanded, where today the liability of the share holder is limited to his share. The city frequently set a maximum limit to the individual contribution so that the entire citizenship might participate. This was often done by arranging the citizens in groups according to the taxes paid or their wealth and reserving a definite fraction of the capital for each class. In contrast with the modern stock company the investment was often rescindable, while the share of the individual was not freely transferable. Hence the whole enterprise represented a stock company only in an embryonic sense. Official supervision was exercised over the conduct of operations.

In this form the so-called "regulated" company was common, especially in the iron trade as in Steier, and it was occasionally used in the cloth trade, as in Iglau. A consequence of the structure of the organizations just described was the absence of fixed capital and, as in the case of the workers' association, the absence of capital accounting in the modern sense. Share holders included not only merchants, but princes, professors, courtiers, and in general the public in the strict sense, which participated gladly and to great profit. The distribution of the dividends was carried out in a completely irrational way, according to the gross income alone, without reserves of any kind. All that was necessary was the removal of the official control and the modern stock company was at hand.

The great colonization companies formed another preliminary stage in the development of the modern stock company. The most significant of these were the Dutch and English East India companies, which were not stock companies in the modern sense. On account of the jealousy of the citizens of the provinces of the country the Dutch East

India Company raised its capital by distributing the shares among them, not permitting all the stock to be bought up by any single city. The government, that is the federation, participated in the administration, especially because it reserved the right to use the ships and cannon of the company for its own needs. Modern capital accounting was absent as was free transferability of shares, although relatively extensive dealings in the latter soon took place. It was these great successful companies which made the device of share capital generally known and popular; from them it was taken over by all the continental states of Europe. Stock companies created by the state, and granted privileges for the purpose, came to regulate the conditions of participation in business enterprise in general, while the state itself in a supervisory capacity was involved in the most remote details of business activity. Not until the 18th century did the annual balance and inventory become established customs, and it required many terrible bankruptcies to force their acceptance.

Alongside the financing of state needs through stock companies stands direct financing by measures of the state itself. This begins with compulsory loans against a pledge of resources and the issue of certificates of indebtedness against anticipated revenues. The cities of the middle ages secured extraordinary income by bonds, pledging their fixed property and taxing power. These annuities may be regarded as the forerunners of the modern consols, yet only within limitations; for to a large extent the income ran for the life of the purchaser, and they were tied up with other considerations. In addition to these devices the necessity of raising money gave rise to various expedients down to the 17th century. The emperor Leopold I attempted to raise a "cavalier loan," sending mounted messengers around to the nobility to solicit subscriptions; but in general he received for answer the injunction to turn to those who had the money.

If one desires to understand the financial operations of a German city as late as the close of the middle ages, one must bear in mind that there was at that time no such thing as an orderly budget. The city, like the territorial lord, lived from week to week as is done today in a small household. Expenditures were readjusted momentarily as income fluctuated. The device of tax farming was of assistance in overcoming the difficulty of management without a budget. It gave the administration some security as to the sums which it might expect each year, and assisted it in planning its expenditures. Hence the tax farm operated as an outstanding instrument of financial rationalization, and was called into use by the European states occasionally at first and then permanently. It also made possible the discounting of public revenues for war purposes, and in this connection achieved especial significance. Rational administration of taxation was an accomplishment of the Italian cities in the period after the loss of their freedom. The Italian nobility is the first political power to order its finances in accordance with the principle of mercantile bookkeeping obtaining at the time, although this did not then include double entry. From the Italian cities the system spread abroad and came into German territory through Burgundy, France, and the Hapsburg states. It was especially the tax payers who clamored to have the finances put in order.

A second point of departure for rational forms of administration was the English exchequer system, of which the word "check" is a last survival and reminder. This was a sort of checker board device by means of which the payments due the state were computed, in the absence of the necessary facility in operating with figures. Regularly, however, the finances were not conducted through setting up a budget in which all receipts and disbursements were included, but a special-fund system was used. That is, certain receipts were designated and raised for the purpose of specified expenditures only. The reason for this procedure is found in the conflicts between the princely power and the citizens. The latter mistrusted the princes and thought this the only way to protect themselves against having the taxes squandered for the personal ends of the ruler.

In the 16th and 17th centuries an additional force working for the rationalization of the financial operations of rulers appeared in the monopoly policy of the princes. In part they assumed commercial monopolies themselves and in part they granted monopolistic concessions, involving of course the payment of notable sums to the political authority. An example is the exploitation of the quicksilver mines of Idria, in the Austrian province of Carniola, which were of great importance on account of the process of amalgamating silver. These mines were the subject of protracted bargaining between the two lines of the Hapsburgs and yielded notable revenues to both the German and the Spanish houses. The first example of this policy of monopoly concession was the attempt of the Emperor Frederick II to establish a grain monopoly for Sicily. The policy was most extensively employed in England and was developed in an especially systematic manner by the Stuarts, and there also it first broke down, under the protests of Parliament. Each new industry and establishment of the Stuart period was for this purpose bound up with a royal concession and granted a monopoly. The king secured important revenues from the privileges, which provided him with the resources for his struggle against Parliament. But these industrial monopolies established for fiscal purposes broke down almost without exception after the triumph of Parliament.   This in itself proves how incorrect it is to regard, as some writers have done, modern western capitalism as an outgrowth of the monopolistic policies of princes.[2]

CHAPTER XXIV

THE FIRST GREAT SPECULATIVE CRISES [1]

We have recognized as characteristics and pre-requisites of capitalistic enterprise the following: appropriation of the physical means of production by the entrepreneur, freedom of the market, rational technology, rational law, free labor, and finally the commercialization of economic life. A further motif is speculation, which becomes important from the moment when property can be represented by freely negotiable paper. Its early development is marked by the great economic crises which it called forth.

The great tulip craze of Holland in the 1630's is often numbered among the great speculative crises, but it should not be so included. Tulips had become an article of luxury among the patricians who had grown rich in colonial trade, and suddenly commanded fantastic prices. The public was misled by the wish to make easy profits until with equal suddenness the whole craze collapsed and many individuals were ruined. But all of that had no significance for the economic development of Holland; in all periods it has happened that objects connected with gaming have become subject to speculation and led to crises. It is quite otherwise with John Law and the great speculation in France and the contemporary South Sea speculation in England, in the second decade of the 18th century.

In the financial practice of the large states it had long been customary to anticipate revenues by the issue of certificates, to be redeemed later. In consequence of the War of the Spanish Succession, the financial requirements of

286

the government rose to an extraordinary height in England as well as in France. The founding of the Bank of England supplied the financial needs of that country, but in France the state was already hopelessly in debt, and on the death of Louis XIV no one knew how the excessive debt was to be taken care of. Under the regency came forward the Scotchman, John Law, who thought he had learned something from the founding of the Bank of England, and had a theory of his own regarding financial affairs, although he had had no luck with it in England. He saw in inflation, that is the utmost possible increase in the medium of circulation, a stimulus to production.

In 1716, Law received a concession for a private bank which at first presented no exceptional character. It was merely specified that the credit obligations of the state must be received in payment for the capital, while the notes of the bank were to be accepted in the payment of taxes. In contrast with the Bank of England there was no clear plan as to the manner in which the bank was to have a regular and secure income so as to maintain the liquid character of its issues. In connection with this bank Law founded the Mississippi Company. The Louisiana territory was to be financed to the extent of a hundred million livres; the company accepted the same amount of obligations of the state as payment for stock and received in exchange the monopoly of the trade in a territory to be determined. If one examines the Louisiana plan it will be observed that a century would have been required before Louisiana would have yielded sufficient revenue to make possible the repayment of the capital. To begin with, Law intended to carry out an undertaking similar to the East India Company, entirely overlooking the fact that Louisiana was not, like India, an ancient civilized country, but a forest waste inhabited by Indians.

When, in 1718, he saw himself threatened by the competition of a stock company which wished to lease the indirect taxes, he combined the Mississippi Company with the Compagnie des Indes. The new company was to carry on the trade with India and China, but the political power was not available to secure for France the share in the Asiatic trade which England already possessed. However, the regency was induced to give to Law the right of coinage and the lease on all the taxes, involving power of life and death over the state, in exchange for a loan at 3% by means of which the gigantic floating debt was to be taken care of. At this point the public embarked on an insane course of speculation. The first year a 200 % dividend was declared and the price of shares rose from 500 to 9,000. This phase of the development can be explained only by the fact that short selling was impracticable since there was as yet no systematic exchange mechanism.

In 1720 Law succeeded in getting himself appointed Comptroller General of Finances. But the whole enterprise quickly disintegrated. In vain the state decreed that only John-Law-notes should be legal money; in vain it sought to sustain them by drastic restriction on the trade in precious metals. Law's fall was inevitable simply because neither Louisiana nor the Chinese or East India trade had yielded sufficient profit to pay interest on even a fraction of his capital. It is true that the bank had received deposits, but it possessed no liquid external resources for repayment. The end was a complete bankruptcy and the declaration that the notes were of no value. A result was an enduring discouragement on the part of the French public, but at the same time freely transferable share certificates, made to bearer, had been popularized.

In the same years a parallel phenomenon was exhibited by England, except that the course of development was not so wild as that in France. Soon after founding of the Bank of England, the idea of a competing institution became current (1696). This was the land bank project resting on the same ideas later presented in the proposals of the German agrarians, namely, of using land credit instead of bills of exchange as a cover for bank notes. But this project was not carried out because in England it was well understood that the necessary liquidity would be absent. This, however, did not prevent the occurrence that in 1711, after the fall of the Whig government, the Tories adopted a course similar to that followed a few years later by John Law.

The English nobility wished to create a centralized power in opposition to the specifically Puritan basis of the Bank of England, and at the same time the gigantic public debt was to be paid off. For this purpose was founded the South Sea Company, which made considerable advances to the state and in return received a monopoly of the South Pacific trade. The Bank of England was not shrewd enough to keep aloof from the project; it even outbid the founders and it was due only to the Tories, who on the ground of political repugnance refused it participation, that its offer was not accepted.

The course of events was similar to that of John Law's institution. Here also bankruptcy was unavoidable because the South Sea trade was not sufficient to pay interest on the sums advanced. Yet prior to this eventuality, just as in France, speculation gave rise to transferable certificates. The result was that enormous property was dissipated while many adventurers came out of it smiling, and the state—in a way none too honorable—achieved a substantial lightening of its burden of interest. The Bank of England remained standing in all its former prestige, being the only financial institution based on the rational discounting of exchange and hence possessing the requisite current liquidity. The explanation is that exchange represents nothing but goods already sold, and such a regular and sufficient turnover of goods no place in the world except London at that time could provide.

Speculative crises of a similar sort have taken place from that time forward, but never since on the same scale. The first crises in rational speculation began a full hundred years later, after the conclusion of the Wars of Liberation, and since that time they have recurred almost regularly at intervals of about 10 years—1815, 1825, 1835, 1847 etc. It was these which Karl Marx had in view when in the Communist Manifesto he prophesied the downfall of capitalism. The first of these crises and their periodic recurrence were based on the possibility of speculation and the resultant participation of outside interests in large business undertakings.

The collapse has resulted from the fact that in consequence of over-speculation, means of production, though not production itself, grew faster than the need for consumption of goods. In 1815 the prospect of the lifting of the continental blockade had led to a regular rage for founding factories; but the war had destroyed the buying power of the continent and it could no longer take the English products. This crisis was barely overcome, and the continent had begun to develop buying power, when in 1825 a new crisis set in because means of production, though not goods, had been speculatively produced on a scale never known before and out of correspondence with the needs.

That it was possible to create means of production to such an extent is due to the fact that with the 19th century the age of iron had begun. The discovery of the coking process, the blast furnace, and the carrying of mining operations to unprecedented depths, introduced iron as the basis of creating means of production, where the machines of the 18th century were built only of wood. Thus production was freed from the organic limitations in which nature had held it confined. At the same time, however, crises became an imminent factor of the economic order. Crises in the broader sense of chronic unemployment, destitution, glutting of the market and political disturbances which destroy all industrial life, have existed always and everywhere. But there is great difference between the fact that a Chinese or Japanese peasant is hungry and knows the while that the Deity is unfavorable to him or the spirits are disturbed and consequently nature does not give rain or sunshine at the right time, and the fact that the social order itself may be held responsible for the crisis, even to the poorest laborer. In the first case, men turn to religion; in the second, the work of men is held at fault and the laboring man draws the conclusion that it must be changed. Rational socialism would never have originated in the absence of crises.

CHAPTER XXV

FREE WHOLESALE TRADE [1]

In the course of the 18th century the wholesaler becomes finally separated from the retailer and comes to constitute a definite branch of the merchant class, whereas the Hansards, for example, were not yet typically wholesalers. Wholesale trade is significant, first, because it evolved new commercial forms. One of these is the auction, which is the means by which the importing wholesaler turns over his goods as quickly as possible and secures the means for making his payment abroad. The typical form of export trade, which takes the place of the fair as an institution, is consignment trading. It consists in the sending of goods to be sold to a third party, the consignee, who must market them according to the directions of the consignor. Thus consignor and consignee do not meet as the earlier traders did, at the fair, but the goods are sent abroad on a speculation. A positive prerequisite for trading on consignment is the establishment of regular exchange quotations on the point of destination, since otherwise the risk in consignment would be unbearably high. A negative requirement is that trading on the basis of samples is not yet established and hence the goods must be seen by the purchaser himself. Consignment trading is ordinarily overseas trade; it prevails where the merchant has no connection with the retailer.

Further development consists in the appearance of a buying commission man alongside the one who sells, the former buying abroad without sight of the goods. The oldest form of such trade was based on samples. It is true that selling at a distance existed before this development, "merchantable goods" being bought and sold which must come up to the traditionally established quality; whether they did so was decided by mercantile courts of arbitration. Sale by sample, however, is a specifically modern form of trading at a distance. It played a fundamental role in commerce in the latter part of the 18th and the 19th centuries, being displaced by standardization and the specification of grades, which makes it possible to do away with the sending of samples. The new practice requires that grades be definitely established. It was on the basis of trading by grades that speculation and exchange dealings in connection with commodities became possible in the 18th century.

The fair is a prior stage of the exchange. The two have this in common, that trading takes place between merchants only; the difference consists in the physical presence of the goods in the case of the fair, and also in the periodical repetition of the fair itself. An intermediate type between the exchange and the fair is the so-called "permanent fair." In all the great commercial centers there arose in the 16th to the 18th centuries establishments which bore the name of exchange or "bourse." However, exchange dealings in the strict sense did not yet take place in them since the majority of those who frequented them were not local persons but non-resident merchants who resorted to the "exchange" because of its connection with the fair and because the goods were typically on the spot or represented by samples and were dealt in on this basis and not according to standard grades. Exchange dealing in the modern sense first developed in the field of negotiable paper and money, not in that of goods, the former being standardized by nature. Only in the course of the 19th century were those commodities added which could be graded with sufficient accuracy.

The innovation in developed exchange dealings is the system of rational dealing in futures or speculation for a rise, i. e., selling with a view to buying the goods at a lower figure before the date of delivery. The absence of such trading involved the possibility of such crises as those of the Tulip Craze and the Mississippi Company. It is true that agreements to deliver goods not in possession of the salesman were earlier met with, but they were generally prohibited because it was feared that they would facilitate the buying up of goods to the disadvantage of consumers. It could nowhere be systematically carried out as in a modern exchange, where speculation for a rise is always present in opposition to speculation for a fall. The first objects subject to futures trading were money, especially paper money and bank notes, state annuities, and colonial paper. Here there could be difference of opinion as to the effect of political occurrences or the yield of enterprise and hence these instruments were an appropriate object for the practice of speculation. In contrast, industrial paper is entirely absent from the earliest price current bulletins. Such speculation underwent an enormous expansion with the building of railroads; these provided the paper which first unchained the speculative urge. Under the head of goods, grains, and a few colonial products available in large volume, and then other goods, were drawn into the circle of exchange speculation during the 19th century.

For the development of a wholesale trade carried out in such fashion, and specifically for speculative trade, the indispensable prerequisite was the presence of an adequate news service and an adequate commercial organization. A public news service, such as forms the basis of exchange dealings today, developed quite late. In the 18th century, not only did the English Parliament keep its proceedings secret, but the exchanges, which regarded themselves as merchants' clubs, followed the same policy in regard to their news information. They feared that the publication of general prices would lead to ill feeling and might destroy their business. The newspaper as an institution came into the service of commerce at an astonishingly late date.

The newspaper, as an institution, is not a product of capitalism. It brought together in the first place political news and then mainly all sorts of curiosities from the world at large. The advertisement, however, made its way into the newspaper very late. It was never entirely absent but originally it related to family announcements, while the advertisement as a notice by the merchant, directed toward finding a market, first becomes an established phenomenon at the end of the 18th century—in the journal which for a century was the first in the world, the "Times." Official price bulletins did not become general until the 19th century; originally all the exchanges were closed clubs, as they have remained in America virtually down to the present. Hence in the 18th century, business depended on the organized exchange of letters. Rational trading between regions was impossible without secure transmission of letters. This was accomplished partly by the merchant guilds and in part by butchers, wheelwrights, etc. The final stage in the rationalization of transmission of letters was brought about by the post, which collected letters and in connection therewith made tariff agreements with commercial houses. In Germany, the family of Thurn and Taxis, who held the postal concession, made notable advances in the rationalization of communication by letter. Yet the volume of correspondence is in the beginning surprisingly small. In 1633, a million letters were posted in all England while today a place of 4,000 population will equal the number.

In the field of commercial organization nothing was changed, at least in principle, in the period before the introduction of the railroads. In the 18th century, ocean ships had reached very little greater displacement than those of Venice at the close of the middle ages. It is true that their number was greater, and the size of warships had increased. This provided a stimulus for the multiplication and enlargement of merchant ships also, but the impulse could not be followed out in the epoch of wood construction. Inland shipping had been facilitated by the construction of locks, but it retained its guild organization down into the 19th century and in consequence experienced no startling innovations. Land transport also remained as before. The post produced no change; it merely forwarded letters and small packages, but did not concern itself with large scale production, which was decisive for economic life.

Only the roads underwent an extraordinary improvement, through the construction of turnpikes. In this the French government under Sully took the lead, while England leased the roads to private enterprisers who collected tolls for their use. The building of the turnpikes wrought a revolution in commercial life comparable to no other before the appearance of the railways. There is no comparison between the present density of road traffic and that of this period. In 1793, 70,000 horses went through the little town of Lüneburg while as late as 1846 only 40,000 were used in freight transport in all Germany. The costs of land carriage amounted to ten or twenty times the freight on the railways at a later time, and were three to four times as high as the charges for inland shipping at the same period. A half billion ton-kilometers was the highest figure for transportation for the movement on land in Germany, while in 1913, 67 billions were carried on the railroads.

The railway is the most revolutionary instrumentality known to history, for economic life in general and not merely for commerce, but the railway was dependent on the age of iron; and it also like so many other things, was the plaything of princely and courtier interests.

CHAPTER XXVI

At this point it is pertinent to inquire into the significance which the acquisition and exploitation of the great non-European regions had for the development of modern capitalism, although only the most characteristic features of the older colonial policy can be mentioned here. The acquisition of colonies by the European states led to a gigantic acquisition of wealth in Europe for all of them. The means of this accumulation was the monopolizing of colonial products, and also of the markets of the colonies, that is the right to take goods into them, and, finally, the profits of transportation between mother land and colony; the last were ensured especially by the English Navigation Act of 1651. This accumulation was secured by force, without exception and by all countries. The operations might take various forms. Either the state drew a profit from the colonies directly, administering them by its own agencies, or it leased them, in return for a payment, to companies. Two main types of exploitation are met with: the feudal type in the Spanish and Portuguese colonies, the capitalistic in the Dutch and English.

Forerunners of the feudal colonization form are especially the Venetian and Genoese colonies in the Levant, and those of the Templars. In both cases the opportunity for securing a money income was afforded by the subdivision of

298

the region to be exploited into fiefs, "encomiendas" in the case of Spain.

The capitalistic colonies regularly developed into plantations. Labor power was furnished by the natives. The opportunities for application of this labor system, from which favorable results had been secured in Asia and Africa, seemed about to expand enormously when it was transferred to trans-oceanic lands. It was found however that the American Indians were entirely unsuitable for plantation labor,[2] and importation of black slaves to the West Indies took the place of their use and gradually grew into a regular commerce of enormous extent.[3] It was carried on on the basis of slave trading privileges (*"assiento"*) the first of which was granted by the emperor Charles V in 1517 to the Flemings. These slave trading privileges played a large role in international relations well into the 18th century. In the treaty of Utrecht, England secured the right to import slaves into the Spanish possessions in South America, to the exclusion of all other powers, and at the same time assumed the obligation of delivering a certain minimum number. The results of the slave trade were considerable. It may be estimated that at the beginning of the 19th century some seven million slaves were living in the territory of the European colonies. Their mortality was extraordinarily high, running in the 19th century to 25% and to a multiple of that figure earlier. From 1807 to 1848, a further five million slaves were imported from Africa, and the aggregate of slaves transported thence overseas can be set equal to the population of a first class European power in the 18th century.

In addition to the black slaves there were white half-slaves, the "indentured servants"; they were especially numerous in the English North American colonies where in the 17th century their number surpassed that of the negroes. In part they were deported criminals, in part poor wretches who attempted in this way to earn their passage money, a small fortune.

The profits of the slave labor were by no means small. In England in the 18th century they were estimated at fifteen to twenty pounds sterling per slave per year. The profitableness of slave labor depended upon strict plantation discipline, ruthless driving of the slave, and perpetual importation—since the slaves did not perpetuate themselves—and finally exploitative agriculture.

This accumulation of wealth brought about through colonial trade has been of little significance for the development of modern capitalism—a fact which must be emphasized in opposition to Werner Sombart. It is true that the colonial trade made possible the accumulation of wealth to an enormous extent, but this did not further the specifically occidental form of the organization of labor, since colonial trade itself rested on the principle of exploitation and not that of securing an income through market operations. Furthermore, we know that in Bengal for example, the English garrison cost five times as much as the money value of all the goods carried thither. It follows that the markets for domestic industry furnished by the colonies under the conditions of the time were relatively unimportant, and that the main profit was derived from the transport business.

The end of the capitalistic method of exploiting colonies coincides with the abolition of slavery. Only in part did this come about through ethical motives. The only Christian sect which persistently and uniformly combated slavery was the Quakers; neither the Calvinists nor the Catholics nor any other denomination consistently and constantly advocated its abolition. A decisive event was the loss of the North American colonies. Even during the

War for Independence, the northern colonies prohibited slavery, and in fact from purely democratic political principles, because the people wished to avoid the development of a plantation system and a planter aristocracy. A religious motive also played a part in the shape of the traditional repugnance of the Puritans to feudalism of any sort. In 1794 the French Convention declared for the abolition of slavery on political equalitarian grounds, which were dressed up in an appropriate ideology. In the meantime, in 1815, the Congress of Vienna prohibited the slave trade. The interest of England in slavery was much reduced through the loss of the principal slave consuming region, its North American colonies. The decrees of the Congress made it possible for the English to suppress the foreign slave trade and at the same time themselves to carry on a buoyant smuggling business. From 1807 to 1847, five million human beings were carried from Africa to the English colonial territories in this way, with the actual sufferance of the government. Only after the parliamentary reform in 1833, was slavery really prohibited in England and by England for all its colonies, and the prohibition was at once treated seriously.

In the period from the 16th to the 18th century, slavery signified as little for the economic organization of Europe as it did much for the accumulation of wealth in Europe. It produced a large number of annuitants, but contributed in very small degree toward bringing about the development of the capitalistic organization of industry and of economic life.

CHAPTER XXVII

It is not easy to define accurately the concept of the factory. We think at once of the steam engine and the mechanization of work, but the machine had its forerunner in what we call "apparatus"—labor appliances which had to be utilized in the same way as the machine but which as a rule were driven by water power. The distinction is that the apparatus works as the servant of the man while in modern machines the inverse relation holds. The real distinguishing characteristic of the modern factory is in general, however, not the implements of work applied, but the concentration of ownership of workplace, means of work, source of power and raw material in one and the same hand, that of the entrepreneur. This combination was only exceptionally met with before the 18th century.

Tracing the English development, which determined the character of the evolution of capitalism—although England followed the example of other countries such as Italy— we find the following stages. 1. The oldest real factory which can be identified (though it was still driven by water power) was a silk factory at Derwent, near Derby, in 1719. It was conducted on the basis of a patent, the owner of which had stolen the invention in Italy. In Italy there had long been silk manufacture with various property relations, but the product was destined for luxury requirements and belonged to an epoch which is not yet characteristic for modern capitalism, although it must be named here because the implements of work and all material and product belonged to an entrepreneur. 2. The establishment of wool manufacture (1738) on the basis of a patent after the invention of an apparatus for running a hundred bobbins at once by the aid of water power. 3. The development of half-linen production. 4. The systematic development of the pottery industry through experiments in Staffordshire. Earthen vessels were produced under a modern division of labor and the application of water power and with the ownership of work place and implements by an entrepreneur. 5. The manufacture of paper, beginning with the 18th century, its permanent basis being the development of the modern use of documents and of the newspaper.

The decisive factor, however, in the triumph of the mechanization and rationalization of work was the fate of cotton manufacture. This industry was transplanted from the continent to England in the 17th century and there immediately began a struggle against the old national industry established since the 15th century, namely, wool, a struggle as intense as that in which wool had previously been involved against linen. The power of the wool producers was so great that they secured restrictions and prohibitions on the production of half-linen, which was not restored until the Manchester Act of 1736. The factory production of cotton stuff was originally limited by the fact that, while the loom had been improved and enlarged, the spindle remained on the medieval level, so that the necessary quantity of spun material was not available. A succession of technical improvements in the spindle after 1769 reversed this relation and with the help of water power and mechanical aids great quantities of usable yarn could be provided while it was impossible to weave the same quantity with corresponding speed. The discrepancy was removed in 1785 through the construction of the power loom by Cartwright, one of the first inventors who combined technology with science and handled the problems of the former in terms of theoretical considerations.

But for all this revolution in the means of work the development might have stopped and modern capitalism in its most characteristic form never have appeared. Its victory was decided by coal and iron. We know that coal had been used in consumption, even in the middle ages, as in London, in Luttich and Zwickau (above p. 191). But until the 18th century the technique was determined by the fact that smelting and all preparation of iron was done with charcoal. The deforestation of England resulted, while Germany was saved from this fate by the circumstance that in the 17th and 18th centuries it was untouched by the capitalistic development. Everywhere the destruction of the forests brought the industrial development to a standstill at a certain point. Smelting was only released from its attachment to organic materials of the plant world by the application of coal. It must be noted that the first blast furnaces appear as early as the 15th century, but they were fed with wood and were used not for private consumption but for war purposes, and in part also in connection with ocean shipping. In the 15th century, furthermore, was invented the iron drill for the preparation of cannon barrels. At the same time appeared the large heavy trip hammer, up to a thousand pounds weight, driven by water power, so that in addition to the handling of cast iron with the drill, mechanical forging was also possible. Finally, in the 17th century the rolling process was also applied in the modern sense of the word.

In the face of the further development arose two difficult problems. These were set, on the one hand, by the danger of deforestation and, on the other, by the perpetual inroads of water in the mines. The first question was the more pressing because in contrast with the expansion of the textile industry the English iron industry had shrunk step by step until at the beginning of the 18th century it gave the impression of having reached its end. The solution of the problem was reached through the coking of coal, which was discovered in 1735, and the use of coke in blast furnace operation, which was undertaken in 1740. Another step in advance was made in 1784 when the puddling process was introduced as an innovation. The threat to mining was removed by the invention of the steam engine. Crude attempts first showed the possibility of lifting water with fire and between 1670 and 1770, and further toward the end of the 18th century, the steam engine arrived at the stage of serviceability which made it possible to produce the amount of coal necessary for modern industry.

The significance of the development just portrayed is to be found in three consequences. In the first place, coal and iron released technology and productive possibilities from the limitations of the qualities inherent in organic materials; from this time forward industry was no longer dependent upon animal power or plant growth. Through a process of exhaustive exploitation, fossil fuel, and by its aid iron ore, were brought up to the light of day, and by means of both men achieved the possibility of extending production to a degree which would have previously been beyond bounds of the conceivable. Thus iron became the most important factor in the development of capitalism; what would have happened to this system or to Europe in the absence of this development we do not know.[2]

The second point is that the mechanization of the production process through the steam engine liberated production from the organic limitations of human labor. Not altogether, it is true, for it goes without saying that labor was indispensable for the tending of machines. But the mechanizing process has always and everywhere been introduced to the definite end of releasing labor; every new invention signifies the extensive displacement of hand workers by a relatively small man power for machine supervision.

Finally, through the union with science, the production of goods was emancipated from all the bonds of inherited tradition, and came under the dominance of the freely roving intelligence. It is true that most of the inventions of the 18th century were not made in a scientific manner; when the coking process was discovered no one suspected what its chemical significance might be. The connection of industry with modern science, especially the systematic work of the laboratories, beginning with Justus von Liebig, enabled industry to become what it is today and so brought capitalism to its full development.

The recruiting of the labor force for the new form of production, as it developed in England in the 18th century, resting upon the concentration of all the means of production in the hands of the entrepreneur, was carried out by means of compulsion, though of an indirect sort. Under this head belong especially the Poor Law, and the Statute of Apprentices of Queen Elizabeth. These measures had become necessary in consequence of the large number of people wandering about the country who had been rendered destitute by the revolution in the agricultural system. Its displacement of the small dependent peasant by large renters and the transformation of arable land into sheep pastures—although the latter has occasionally been overestimated—worked together constantly to reduce the amount of labor force required on the land and to bring into being a surplus population, which was subjected to compulsory labor. Anyone who did not take a job voluntarily was thrust into the workhouse with its strict discipline; and anyone who left a position without a certificate from the master or entrepreneur was treated as a vagabond. No unemployed person was supported except under the compulsion of entering the workhouse.

In this way the first labor force for the factories was recruited. With difficulty the people adapted themselves to the discipline of the work. But the power of the possessing classes was too great; they secured the support of the political authority through the justices of the peace, who in the absence of binding law operated on the basis of a maze of instructions and largely according to their own dictates. Down into the second half of the 19th century they exercised an arbitrary control over the labor force and fed the workers into the newly arising industries. From the beginning of the 18th century, on the other hand, begins the regulation of relations between entrepreneur and laborer, presaging the modern control of labor conditions. The first anti-trucking laws were passed under Queen Anne and George I. While during the whole middle ages the worker had struggled for the right to bring the product of his own labor to market, from now on legislation had to protect him against being paid for his work in the products of others and to secure for him remuneration in money. Another source of labor power was in England the small master class, the great majority of whom were transformed into a proletariat of factory laborers.

In the market for the products of these newly established industries, two great sources of demand appeared, namely war and luxury, the military administration and court requirements. The military administration became a consumer of the products of industry to the extent that the great mercenary armies developed and the more so as army discipline and the rationalization of arms and all military technique progressed. In the textile industry the production of uniforms was fundamental, as these could by no means be the product of the army itself but were a means of discipline in the interest of unitary regimentation, and in order to keep the soldiers under control. The production of cannon and fire arms occupied the iron industry, and the provision of supplies did the same for trade. In addition to the land army there was the navy; the increasing size of the war ships was one of the factors which created a market for industry. While the size of merchant ships had changed little before the end of the 18th century and as late as 1750 the ships entering London were typically of about 140 tons burden, war ships had grown to a size of a thousand tons in the 16th century and in the 18th this became the normal burden. The demand of the navy, like that of the army, increased further with the growth in the number and extent of the voyages (and this also applies to merchant ships) especially after the 16th century. Down to that time the Levant cruise had normally occupied a year; at this time ships began to remain much longer at sea and at the same time the increasing magnitude of campaigns on land necessitated a more extensive provision with supplies, munitions, etc. Finally, the speed of ship building and of the construction of cannon increased with extraordinary rapidity after the 17th century.

Sombart has assumed that the standardized mass provision for war is among the decisive conditions affecting the development of modern capitalism. This theory must be reduced to its proper proportions. It is correct that annually enormous sums were spent for army and navy purposes; in Spain 70 % of the revenues of the state went for this purpose and in other countries two-thirds or more.

But we also find outside the western world, as in the Mogul Empire and in China, enormous armies equipped with artillery (although not yet with uniforms), yet no impulse toward a capitalistic development followed from the fact. Moreover, even in the west the army needs were met to an increasing extent, developing in parallelism with capitalism itself, by the military administration on its own account, in its own workshops and arms and munition factories; that is, it proceeded along non-capitalistic lines. Hence, it is a false conclusion to ascribe to war as such, through the army demands, the role of prime mover in the creation of modern capitalism. It is true that it was involved in capitalism, and not only in Europe; but this motive was not decisive for the development. Otherwise the increasing provision of army requirements by direct action of the state would again have forced capitalism into the background, a development which did not take place.

For the luxury demand of the court and the nobility, France became the typical country. For a time in the 16th century, the king spent 10 million livres a year directly or indirectly for luxury goods. This expenditure by the royal family and the highest social classes constituted a strong stimulus to quite a number of industries. The most important articles, aside from such means of enjoyment as chocolate and coffee, are embroidery (16th century), linen goods, for the treatment of which ironing develops (17th century), stockings (16th century), umbrellas (17th century), indigo dyeing (16th century), tapestry (17th century), and carpets (18th century). With regard to the volume of the demand the two last named were the most important of the luxury industries; they signified a democratization of luxury which is the crucial direction of capitalistic production.

Court luxury existed in China and India, on a scale unknown in Europe; and yet no significant stimulus to capitalism or capitalistic industry proceeded from the fact. The reason is that the provision for this demand was arranged leiturgically through compulsory contributions. This system maintained itself so tenaciously that down to our own time the peasants in the region of Peking have been obliged to furnish to the imperial court the same objects as 3000 years ago, although they did not know how to produce them and were compelled to buy them from producers. In India and China the army requirements were also met by forced labor and contributions in kind. In Europe itself the leiturgical contributions of the east are not unknown, although they appear in a different form. Here the princes transformed the workers in luxury industry into compulsory laborers by indirect means, binding them to their places of work by grants of land, long period contracts, and various privileges—although in France, the country which took the lead in luxury industries, this was not the case; here the handicraft form of establishment maintained itself, partly under a putting-out organization and partly under a workshop system, and neither the technology nor the economic organization of the industries was transformed in any revolutionary way.

The decisive impetus toward capitalism could come only from one source, namely a mass market demand, which again could arise only in a small proportion of the luxury industries through the democratization of the demand, especially along the line of production of substitutes for the luxury goods of the upper classes. This phenomenon is characterized by price competition, while the luxury industries working for the court follow the handicraft principle of competition in quality. The first example of the policy of a state organization entering upon price competition is afforded in England at the close of the 15th century, when the effort was made to undersell Flemish wool, an object which was promoted by numerous export prohibitions.

The great price revolution of the 16th and 17th centuries provided a powerful lever for the specifically capitalistic tendencies of seeking profit through cheapening production and lowering the price. This revolution is rightly ascribed to the continuous inflow of precious metals, in consequence of the great overseas discoveries. It lasted from the thirties of the 16th century down to the time of the Thirty Years' War, but affected different branches of economic life in quite different ways. In the case of agricultural products an almost universal rise in price set in, making it possible for them to go over to production for the market. It was quite otherwise with the course of prices for industrial products. By and large these remained stable or rose in price relatively little, thus really falling, in comparison with the agricultural products. This relative decline was made possible only through a shift in technology and economics, and exerted a pressure in the direction of increasing profit by repeated cheapening of production. Thus the development did not follow the order that capitalism set in first and the decline in prices followed, but the reverse; first the prices fell relatively and then came capitalism.

The tendency toward rationalizing technology and economic relations with a view to reducing prices in relation to costs, generated in the 17th century a feverish pursuit of invention. All the inventors of the period are dominated by the object of cheapening production; the notion of perpetual motion as a source of energy is only one of many objectives of this quite universal movement. The inventor as a type goes back much farther. But if one scrutinizes the devices of the greatest inventor of precapitalistic times, Leonardo da Vinci—(for experimenta-

tion originated in the field of art and not that of science)—
one observes that his urge was not that of cheapening production but the rational mastery of technical problems as
such. The inventors of the pre-capitalistic age worked
empirically; their inventions had more or less the character of accidents. An exception is mining, and in consequence it is the problems of mining in connection with
which deliberate technical progress took place.

A positive innovation in connection with invention is
the first rational patent law, the English law of 1623, which
contains all the essential provisions of a modern statute.
Down to that time the exploitation of inventions had been
arranged through a special grant in consideration of a payment; in contrast the law of 1623 limits the protection of
the invention to 14 years and makes its subsequent utilization by an entrepreneur conditional upon an adequate roy-
alty for the original inventor. Without the stimulus of this
patent law the inventions crucial for the development of
capitalism in the field of textile industry in the 18th
century would not have been possible.

Drawing together once more the distinguishing characteristics of western capitalism and its causes, we find the
following factors. First, this institution alone produced
a rational organization of labor, which nowhere previously
existed. Everywhere and always there has been trade;
it can be traced back into the stone age. Likewise we
find in the most varied epochs and cultures war finance,
state contributions, tax farming, farming of offices, etc.,
but not a rational organization of labor. Furthermore we
find everywhere else a primitive, strictly integrated internal economy such that there is no question of any freedom of economic action between members of the same
tribe or clan, associated with absolute freedom of trade externally. Internal and external ethics are distinguished,

and in connection with the latter there is complete ruthlessness in financial procedure; nothing can be more rigidly prescribed than the clan economy of China or the caste economy of India, and on the other hand nothing so unscrupulous as the conduct of the Hindu foreign trader. In contrast with this, the second characteristic of western capitalism is a lifting of the barrier between the internal economy and external economy, between internal and external ethics, and the entry of the commercial principle into the internal economy, with the organization of labor on this basis. Finally, the disintegration of primitive economic fixity is also met with elsewhere, as for example in Babylon; but nowhere else do we find the entrepreneur organization of labor as it is known in the western world.

If this development took place only in the occident the reason is to be found in the special features of its general cultural evolution which are peculiar to it. Only the occident knows the state in the modern sense, with a professional administration, specialized officialdom, and law based on the concept of citizenship. Beginnings of this institution in antiquity and in the orient were never able to develop. Only the occident knows rational law, made by jurists and rationally interpreted and applied, and only in the occident is found the concept of citizen (*civis Romanus, citoyen, bourgeois*) because only in the occident again are there cities in the specific sense. Furthermore, only the occident possesses science in the present-day sense of the word. Theology, philosophy, reflection on the ultimate problems of life, were known to the Chinese and the Hindu, perhaps even of a depth unreached by the European; but a rational science and in connection with it a rational technology remained unknown to those civilizations. Finally, western civilization is further distinguished from every other by the presence of men with a rational ethic for the

conduct of life.   Magic and religion are found everywhere;
but a religious basis for the ordering of life which consistently followed out must lead to explicit rationalism is
again peculiar to western civilization alone.

CHAPTER XXVIII

CITIZENSHIP [1]

In the concept of citizenship (*Bürgertum*) as it is used in social history are bound up three distinct significations. First, citizenship may include certain social categories or classes which have some specific communal or economic interest. As thus defined the class citizen is not unitary; there are greater citizens and lesser citizens; entrepreneurs and hand workers belong to the class. Second, in the political sense, citizenship signifies membership in the state, with its connotation as the holder of certain political rights. Finally, by citizens in the class sense, we understand those strata which are drawn together, in contrast with the bureaucracy or the proletariat and others outside their circle, as "persons of property and culture," entrepreneurs, recipients of funded incomes, and in general all persons of academic culture, a certain class standard of living, and a certain social prestige.

The first of these concepts is economic in character and is peculiar to western civilization. There are and have been everywhere hand laborers and entrepreneurs, but never and nowhere were they included in a unitary social class. The notion of the citizen of the state has its forerunners in antiquity and in the medieval city. Here there were citizens as holders of political rights, while outside of the occident only traces of this relation are met with, as in the Babylonian patriciate and the Josherim, the inhabitants of a city with full legal rights, in the Old Testament.

The farther east we go the fewer are these traces; the notion of citizens of the state is unknown to the world of Islam, and to India and China. Finally, the social class signification of citizen as the man of property and culture, or of one or the other, in contrast with the nobility, on the one hand, and the proletariat, on the other, is likewise a specifically modern and western concept, like that of the bourgeoisie. It is true that in antiquity and in the middle ages, citizen was a class concept; membership in specific class groups made the person a citizen. The difference is that in this case the citizen was privileged in a negative as well as a positive sense. In the positive sense in that he only—in the medieval city for example—might pursue certain occupations; negatively in that certain legal requirements were waived, such as the qualification for holding a fief, the qualification for the tourney, and that for membership in the religious community. The citizen in the quality of membership in a class is always a citizen of a particular city, and the city in this sense, has existed only in the western world, or elsewhere, as in the early period in Mesopotamia, only in an incipient stage.

The contributions of the city in the whole field of culture are extensive. The city created the party and the demagogue. It is true that we find all through history struggles between cliques, factions of nobles, and office-seekers, but nowhere outside the occidental cities are there parties in the present-day sense of the word, and as little are there demagogues in the sense of party leaders and seekers for ministerial posts. The city and it alone has brought forth the phenomena of the history of art. Hellenic and Gothic art, in contrast with Mycænean and Roman, are city art. So also the city produced science in the modern sense. In the city civilization of the Greeks the discipline out of which scientific thinking developed, namely mathematics, was given the form under which it continuously developed down to modern times. The city culture of the Babylonians stands in an analogous relation to the foundation of astronomy. Furthermore, the city is the basis of specific religious institutions. Not only was Judaism, in contrast with the religion of Israel, a thoroughly urban construction—a peasant could not conform with the ritual of the law—but early Christianity is also a city phenomenon; the larger the city the greater was the percentage of Christians, and the case of Puritanism and Pietism was also the same. That a peasant could function as a member of a religious group is a strictly modern phenomenon. In Christian antiquity the word *paganus* signified at the same time heathen and village dweller, just as in the post-exilic period the town-dwelling Pharisee looked with contempt on the Am-ha-aretz who was ignorant of the law. Even Thomas Aquinas, in discussing the different social classes and their relative worth, speaks with extreme contempt of the peasant. Finally, the city alone produced theological thought, and on the other hand again, it alone harbored thought untrammeled by priestcraft. The phenomenon of Plato, with his question of how to make men useful citizens as the dominant problem of his thought, is unthinkable outside the environment of a city.

The question whether a place is to be regarded as a city is not answered on the basis of its spatial extent.[2] From the economic standpoint, rather, both in the occident and elsewhere, the city is in the first place the seat of commerce and industry, and requires a continuous provision of the means of subsistence from without. From an economic standpoint, the various categories of large places are distinguished by the source from which supplies come and the means by which they are paid for. A large place which does not live on its own agricultural production may pay for its imports by its own products, that is industrial products, or through trade or rents, or finally by means of pensions. The "rents" represent salaries of officials or land rents; subsistence on pensions is illustrated by Wiesbaden, where the cost of imports is met by the pensions of political officials and army officers. Large places may be classified according to the dominance of these sources of income to pay for the imports of subsistence goods, but this is a condition common to the world at large; it belongs to large places and does not distinguish a city.

A further general characteristic of a city is the fact that in the past it was generally a fortress; throughout long periods a place was recognized as a city only if and so long as it was a fortified point. In this connection the city was regularly the seat of government, both political and ecclesiastical. In some cases in the occident a *civitas* was understood to mean a place which was the seat of a bishop. In China it is a decisive characteristic that the city is the seat of a mandarin,[3] and cities are classified on the basis of the rank of their mandarins. Even in the Italian Renaissance the cities were distinguished by the grade of their officials and upper class residents, and the rank of the resident nobility.

It is true that outside the western world there were cities in the sense of a fortified point and the seat of political and hierarchical administration. But outside the occident there have not been cities in the sense of a unitary community. In the middle ages, the distinguishing characteristic was the possession of its own law and court and an autonomous administration of whatever extent. The citizen of the middle ages was a citizen because and insofar as he came under this law and participated in the choice of administrative officials. That cities have not existed outside the occident in the sense of a political community is a fact calling for explanation. That the reason was economic in character is very doubtful. As little is it the specific "Germanic spirit" which produced the unity, for in China and India there were unitary groups much more cohesive than those of the occident, and yet the particular union in cities is not found there.

The inquiry must be carried back to certain ultimate fundamental facts. We cannot explain the phenomena on the basis of the feudal or political grants of the middle ages or in terms of the founding of cities by Alexander the Great on his march to India. The earliest references to cities as political units designate rather their revolutionary character. The occidental city arose through the establishment of a fraternity, the συνοικισμός in antiquity, the *coniuratio* in the middle ages. The juristic forms, always relating to externals, in which the resulting struggles and conflicts of the middle ages are clothed, and the facts which lie behind them, cannot be distinguished. The pronouncements of the Staufers against cities prohibit none of the specific presumptions of citizenship, but rather the *coniuratio*, the brotherhood in arms for mutual aid and protection, involving the usurpation of political power.

The first example in the middle ages is the revolutionary movement in 726 which led to the secession of Italy from the Byzantine rule and which centered in Venice. It was called forth especially by opposition to the attack on images carried out by the emperors under military pressure, and hence the religious element, although not the only factor, was the motive which precipitated the revolution. Previous to that time the *dux* (later *doge*) of Venice had been appointed by the emperor, although, on the other hand, there were certain families whose members were constantly to a predominant extent appointed military tribunes or district commandants. From then on the choice of the

tribunes and of the *dux* was in the hands of persons liable
to military service, that is, those who were in a position to
serve as knights.   Thus the movement was started.   It requires 400 years longer before in 1143 the name *Commune
Venetiarum* turns up.   Quite similar was the "synœcism"
of antiquity, as for example the procedure of Nehemiah in
Jerusalem.   This leader caused the leading families and a
selected portion of the people on the land to band themselves together under oath for the purpose of administration and defense of the city.   We must assume the same
background for the origin of every ancient city.   The *polis*
is always the product of such a confraternity or synœcism,
not always an actual settlement in proximity but a definite
oath of brotherhood which signified that a common ritualistic meal is established and a ritualistic union formed
and that only those had a part in this ritualistic group who
buried their dead on the acropolis and had their dwellings
in the city.

For the fact that this development took place only in
the occident there are two reasons.   The first is the peculiar
character of the organization for defense.   The occidental
city is in its beginnings first of all a defense group, an
organization of those economically competent to bear arms,
to equip and train themselves.   Whether the military organization is based on the principle of self-equipment or on
that of equipment by a military overlord who furnishes
horses, arms and provisions, is a distinction quite as fundamental for social history as is the question whether the
means of economic production are the property of the
worker or of a capitalistic entrepreneur.   Everywhere outside the west the development of the city was prevented by
the fact that the army of the prince is older than the city.
The earliest Chinese epics do not, like the Homeric, speak
of the hero who fares forth to battle in his own chariot, but

only of the officer as a leader of the men. Likewise in India an army led by officers marched out against Alexander the Great. In the west the army equipped by the war lord, and the separation of soldier from the paraphernalia of war, in a way analogous to the separation of the worker from the means of production, is a product of the modern era, while in Asia it stands at the apex of the historical development. There was no Egyptian or Babylonian-Assyrian army which would have presented a picture similar to that of the Homeric mass army, the feudal army of the west, the city army of the ancient *polis*, or the medieval guild army.

The distinction is based on the fact that in the cultural evolution of Egypt, western Asia, India, and China the question of irrigation was crucial. The water question conditioned the existence of the bureaucracy, the compulsory service of the dependent classes, and the dependence of the subject classes upon the functioning of the bureaucracy of the king. That the king also expressed his power in the form of a military monopoly is the basis of the distinction between the military organization of Asia and that of the west. In the first case the royal official and army officer is from the beginning the central figure of the process, while in the west both were originally absent. The forms of religious brotherhood and self equipment for war made possible the origin and existence of the city. It is true that the beginnings of an analogous development are found in the east. In India we meet with relations which verge upon the establishment of a city in the western sense, namely, the combination of self equipment and legal citizenship; one who could furnish an elephant for the army is in the free city of Vaiçali a full citizen. In ancient Mesopotamia, too, the knights carried on war with each other and established cities with autonomous administration.

But in the one case as in the other these beginnings later disappear as the great kingdom arises on the basis of water regulation. Hence only in the west did the development come to complete maturity.

The second obstacle which prevented the development of the city in the orient was formed by ideas and institutions connected with magic. In India the castes were not in a position to form ritualistic communities and hence a city, because they were ceremonially alien to one another. The same facts explained the peculiar position of the Jews in the middle ages. The cathedral and the eucharist were the symbols of the unity of the city, but the Jews were not permitted to pray in the cathedral or take part in the communion and hence were doomed to form diaspora-communes. On the contrary, the consideration which made it natural for cities to develop in the west was in antiquity the extensive freedom of the priesthood, the absence of any monopoly in the hands of the priests over communion with the gods, such as obtained in Asia. In western antiquity the officials of the city performed the rites, and the resultant proprietorship of the *polis* over the things belonging to the gods and the priestly treasures was carried to the point of filling the priestly offices by auction, since no magical limitations stood in the way as in India. For the later period in the west three great facts were crucial. The first was prophecy among the Jews, which destroyed magic within the confines of Judaism; magical procedure remained real but was devilish instead of divine. The second fact was the pentecostal miracle, the ceremonial adoption into the spirit of Christ which was a decisive factor in the extraordinary spread of the early Christian enthusiasm. The final factor was the day in Antioch (Gal. 2; 11 ff.) when Paul, in opposition to Peter, espoused fellowship with the uncircumcised. The magical barriers between clans, tribes, and peoples, which were still known in the ancient *polis* to a considerable degree, were thus set aside and the establishment of the occidental city was made possible.

Although the city in the strict sense is specifically a western institution, there are within the class two fundamental distinctions, first between antiquity and the middle ages and second between southern and northern Europe. In the first period of development of the city communities, the similarity between the ancient and medieval city is very great. In both cases it is those of knightly birth, the families leading an aristocratic existence, who alone are active members in the group, while all the remaining population is merely bound to obedience. That these knightly families became residents of the city is entirely the consequence of the possibility of sharing in trade opportunities. After the success of the Italian revolution against Byzantium, a portion of the Venetian upper class families collected in the Rialto because from that point commerce with the orient was carried on. It is to be remembered that in the sea trade and naval warfare Venice still formed a part of the Byzantine system although it was politically independent. Similarly in antiquity, the wealthy families did not carry on trade on their own account but in the capacity of ship owners or money lenders. It is characteristic that in antiquity there was no city of importance which lay more than a day's journey distant from the sea; only those places flourished which for political or geographical reasons possessed exceptional opportunities for trade. Consequently Sombart is essentially incorrect in asserting that ground rent is the mother of the city and of commerce. The facts stand in the reverse order; settlement in the city is occasioned by the possibility and the intention of employing the rents in trade, and the decisive influence of trade on the founding of cities stands out.

In the early middle ages the course of events in the rise
of a new individual in Venice was somewhat as follows.
He began as a trader, that is a retailer; then he proceeded
to travel overseas, securing from the upper class families
a credit of money or goods which he turned over in the
Levant, sharing his profit on his return with those who
provided the loan. If he was successful he got himself
into the Venetian circle either by way of land or ships.
As a ship owner or land owner the way was open for his
ascent into the nobility, down to the closing of the Grand
Council in 1297. The ordinary designation of the members
of the aristocracy living on the rent of land and of capital
—both resting on trading profit—is in Italy *scioperato*,
in Germany *ehrsamer Müssiggänger*—"honorable idler."
It is true that among the nobility in Venice there were always families which continued to carry on trade as a profession, just as in the period of the Reformation noble families who had lost their wealth turned to the quest of a
livelihood by way of industry. But normally the full citizen and member of an urban noble class is a man who possesses land as well as capital, and lives on an income but
does not himself take part in trade or industry.

Thus far the medieval development coincides with that
of antiquity; but their ways part with the establishment of
democracy. At the outset, to be sure, there are similarities
to be noted in this connection also: Δῆμος, *plebs*, *popolo*
and *Bürgerschaft* are indifferent words which refer in the
same way to the breaking in of democracy; they designate
the mass of citizens who do not pursue the knightly life.
The noble, the man of knightly station and feudal qualifica-
tions, is watched, deprived of the suffrage and outlawed, as
the Russian bourgeoisie were by Lenin.

The basis of democratization is everywhere purely military in character; it lies in the rise of disciplined infantry,

the *hoplites* of antiquity, the guild army in the middle ages. The decisive fact was that military discipline proved its superiority over the battle between heroes.[4] Military discipline meant the triumph of democracy because the community wished and was compelled to secure the co-operation of the non-aristocratic masses and hence put arms, and along with arms political power, into their hands. In addition, the money power plays its role, both in antiquity and in the middle ages.

Parallelism is also manifest in the mode in which democracy establishes itself. Like the state in the beginning, the *popolo* carries on its struggle as a separate group with its own officials. Examples are the Spartan ephors as representatives of the democracy against the kings, and the Roman tribunes of the people, while in the Italian cities of the middle ages the *capitano del popolo,* or *della merca-danzao,* are such officials. It is characteristic of them that they are the first concededly "illegitimate" officials. The consuls of the Italian cities still prefix the *dei gratia* to their titles but the *capitano del popolo* no longer does so. The source of the power of the tribune is illegitimate; he is *sacrocanctus* precisely because he is not a legitimate official and hence is protected only by divine interference, or popular vengeance.

The two courses of development are also equivalent in regard to their purpose. Social and not economic class interests are decisive; it is a question primarily of protection against the aristocratic families. The *popolani* know that they are rich and have fought and won the great wars of the city along with the nobility; they are armed, and hence feel themselves discriminated against and are no longer content with the subordinate class position which they have previously accepted. Similarity exists also, and finally, in the means available to the officials of the separate organi-

zation (*Sonderbund*). Everywhere they secure the right
of intervention in legal processes in which the plebeians are
opposed to the aristocrats. This purpose is served by the
right of intercession of the Roman tribune as well as the
Florentine *capitano del popolo,* a right which is carried out
through appeal or through lynch justice.[5] The *Sonderbund* sets up the claim that the statutes of the city shall be
valid only after they have been ratified by the plebeians,
and finally establishes the principle that only that is law
which they have determined. The Roman legal principle:
ut quod tributim plebs iussisset populum tenerit has its
counterpart in the Florentine *ordinamenti della giustizia,*
and in the exclusion of all non-workers from Lenin's labor
dictatorship.

The further instrumentality of democracy in establishing
its domination is compulsory entry into the *plebs.* In antiquity the nobles were forced to enroll in the *tribus* and in
the middle ages in the guilds, although the final significance
was not, in many cases, perceived. Finally, there is everywhere a sudden and quite enormous multiplication of offices, a plethora of officialdom called forth by the need of
the victorious party for remunerating its members with the
spoils of the contest.

Thus far there is coincidence between the democracy of
antiquity and that of the middle ages. But alongside the
points of agreement there are categorical differences. At
the outset there is an ultimate distinction as regards the divisions into which the city falls. In the middle ages these
consist of the guilds, while in antiquity they never possessed
the guild character. Scrutinizing the medieval guilds from
this point of view we notice that different guild strata suc-
cessively rise to power. In Florence, the classical guild
city, the earliest of these strata, became distinguished as
the aggregate of the *arti maggiori* from the *arti minori.*

The first group includes on the one hand merchants, dealers in exchange, jewelers, and in general entrepreneurs who require a considerable industrial capital; on the other hand it includes jurists, physicians, apothecaries, and in general the "persons of property and culture" in the sense of the modern bourgeoisie. In regard to the guilds made up of entrepreneurs one may assume that at least 50% of the members lived on income or soon came to do so. This category of persons of property and culture was known as the *popolo grasso*, the "fat" people. Exactly the same expression is found in the Psalms, which are specifically the poetry of resentment of the virtuous and pious against the superior class of annuitants and nobility, against the "fat," as they are repeatedly called in the psalms themselves.

In the *arti maggiori* are included the small capitalists, while to the *arti minori* belong the butchers, bakers, weavers, etc., who in Italy at least, were situated at the border of the working class although in Germany to some extent they became large entrepreneurs. The mere laborers, on the other hand, the *ciompi*, only very exceptionally achieved power, as a rule only when the nobility allied itself with the lowest strata against the middle class.

Under the domination of the guilds, the medieval city pursued a special type of policy, called town-economy. Its objective was in the first place to maintain the traditional access to occupation and livelihood, and, in the second place, to make the surrounding country subservient to the town interest to the utmost extent through *banalités* and compulsory use of the town market. It sought further to restrict competition and prevent the development toward large-scale industry. In spite of all, an opposition developed between trading capital and craft work organized in guilds, with a growth of domestic industry and of a permanent journeyman class as a forerunner of the modern

proletariat.   Nothing of all this is to be found in antiquity
under the rule of democracy.   It is true that in the early
period there are vestiges of such conditions.   Thus in
Rome, the *fabri* of the military organization of Severus,
hand-workers, army smiths etc., are perhaps such a survival.
But in the period of fully developed democracy, there is
no mention of anything of the sort, and not until the late
Roman period are traces again found.   Thus in antiquity
the guild, as the ruling power in the town, is absent, and with
it guild policy, and also the opposition between labor
and capital which is present even at the close of the middle
ages.

In place of this conflict we find in antiquity the opposition between the land owner and the landless.   *Proletarius*
is not, as Mommsen avers, a man who can only serve the
state by providing children, but rather the disinherited
descendant of a land owner and full citizen, that is of an
assiduus.   The entire policy of antiquity was directed toward the prevention of such *proletarii;* to this end servitude for debt was restricted and debtor law alleviated.
The ordinary contrast in antiquity was that between urban
creditor and peasant debtor.   In the city dwelt the money
lending patriciate; in the country, the small people to
whom it lent its money; and under the ancient law of debt
such a condition led readily to the loss of the land and
proletarization.

For all these reasons, the ancient city had no subsistence
policy like that of the middle ages, but only a policy directed to maintaining the κλῆρος, the *fundus,* on which a
man could live and fully equip himself as a soldier.   The
aim was to guard against weakening the military power
of the community.   Hence the great reforms of the Gracchi
must absolutely not be understood in the modern sense
as measures pertaining to a class struggle; their ob-

jective is purely military; they represent the last attempt to maintain the citizen army and avoid the substitution of mercenaries. The opponents of the aristocracy in the middle ages were, on the one hand, the entrepreneurs and, on the other, the craft workers, while in antiquity they were always the peasantry. Corresponding to the distinction between these conflicts, the city of antiquity is divided along different lines than the medieval. In the latter the noble families are compelled to join the guilds while in the ancient city they were forced into villages, (*demoi, tribus*), districts made up of rural landholders, in which they came under the same law as the peasant holder. In the middle ages they were made into craftsmen, in antiquity into peasants.

The development of ancient democracies is further characterized by the fact that different strata differentiate within the democracy itself. First, the *classis* rose to power, the stratum of the ὅπλα παρεχομενοι, who were able to equip themselves fully with the coat of mail and shield and who consequently could be employed in the front rank. Next, in consequence of the naval policy in a portion of antiquity, especially Athens, the non-possessing class rose to domination because the fleet could only be manned by including all strata of the population. The Athenian militarism led to the result that in the popular assembly the sailors finally secured the whip hand. In Rome the analogous course of events first took place with the invasion of the Cimbri and Teutones. However, it did not lead to the granting of citizenship to the soldiers, but to the development of a professional army with its Imperator at the head.

In addition to these distinctions between the ancient and the medieval development, there is a further distinction in class relations. The typical citizen of the medieval guild

city is a merchant or craftsman; he is a full citizen if he
is also a householder. In antiquity on the contrary, the
full citizen is the landholder. In the guild city, accordingly, class inequality obtains. The non-landholder requires the landholder as his *Salmann* ("truehander")
in order to acquire land; he is at a legal disadvantage and
this subordinate legal position is only gradually equalized
and not everywhere completely. In his personal relations,
however, the citizen of the medieval city is free. The principle "town air makes free" asserted that after a year and
a day the lord no longer had a right to recall his runaway
serf. Although the principle was not everywhere recognized and was subjected to limitations, especially by the
legislation of the Hohenstauffens, it corresponded to the
legal consciousness of the city citizenship which on the
basis of it pressed its military and taxation interests.
Hence the equalization of classes and removal of unfreedom
became a dominant tendency in the development of the
medieval city.

In contrast, antiquity in the early period emphasized
class distinctions similar to those of the middle ages; it
recognized the distinction between the patrician and the
client, who followed the knightly warrior as a squire; it
recognized relations of dependency and slavery as well.
But with the growth of the power of the city and its development toward democracy, the sharpness of class distinctions increases; slaves are purchased or shipped in in
large numbers and form a lower stratum constantly growing in numbers, while to them are added the freedmen.
Hence the city of antiquity, in contrast with that of the
middle ages, shows increasing class inequality. Finally,
no trace of the medieval guild monopoly is to be found in
antiquity. Under the dominance of the Athenian democracy we find in the sources relating to the placing of the

columns of the Erechtheion that free Athenians and slaves worked together in the same voluntary group and slaves are placed over free Athenian workers as foremen, a relation which would have been unthinkable in the middle ages, in view of the existence of a powerful free industrial class.

Taken in its entirety the foregoing argument leads to the conclusion that the city democracy of antiquity is a political guild. It is true that it had distinctive industrial interests and also that these were monopolized; but they were subordinate to military interests. Tribute, booty, the payments of confederate cities, were merely distributed among the citizens. Thus like the craft guild of the closing period of the middle ages, the democratic citizens' guild of antiquity was also interested in not admitting too many participants. The resulting limitation on the number of citizens was one of the causes of the downfall of the Greek city states. The monopoly of the political guild included cleruchy, the distributing of conquered land among the citizens, and the distribution of the spoils of war; and at the last the city paid out of the proceeds of its political activity theater admissions, allotments of grain, and payments for jury service and for participation in religious rites.

Chronic war was therefore the normal condition of the Greek full citizen, and a demagogue like Cleon was conscious of his reasons for inciting to war; war made the city rich, while a long period of peace meant ruin for the citizenship. Those who engaged in the pursuit of profit by peaceful means were excluded from these opportunities. These included the freedmen and metics; among them we first find something similar to the modern bourgeoisie, excluded from the ownership of land but still well-to-do.

Military reasons explain the fact that the city state of

antiquity, so long as it maintained its characteristic form, developed no craft guilds and nothing similar to them, that instead it erected a political military monopoly for the citizenship and evolved into a soldiers' guild. The ancient city represented the highest development of military technique in its time; no equivalent force could be sent against a hoplite army or a Roman legion. This explains the form and direction of industry in antiquity with relation to profit through war, and other advantages to be attained by purely political means. Over against the citizen stands the "low-bred"; anyone is low-bred who follows the peaceable quest of profit in the sense of today. In contrast with this the center of gravity of military technique in the early middle ages lay outside the cities, in the knighthood. Nothing else was equal to an armed feudal host. The result was that the guild army of burghers—with the single exception of the battle of Courtray in 1302—never ventured offensive operations but was only defensively employed. The burgher army of the middle ages could therefore never fulfill the acquisitive guild function of the ancient hoplite or legion army.

Within the western world we find during the middle ages a sharp contrast between the cities of the south and those of the north. In the south, the knighthood was generally settled in the city, while in the north the opposite is the case; from the beginning they had their dwellings outside or were even excluded. In the north the grant of privileges for a city included the specification that it might prohibit the residence of high political officials or knights; on the other hand the knighthood of the north closed its ranks against the urban patriciate and treated the latter as inferior by birth. The cause is found in the fact that the founding of the cities took place in different epochs in the two regions. In the time when the Italian communes began their rise the knightly military technique was at its height; hence the town was forced to take the knights into its pay or to ally itself with them. In their essence the Guelph-Ghibelline wars between the cities are struggles between different knightly groups. Hence the city insisted upon the knights taking up their residence or forced upon them the *inurbamento;* it did not wish them to operate from their castles to make the roads unsafe and it wished to secure for its citizens the task of providing for their needs.

The most extreme contrast with these conditions is found in the English city which, as distinguished from the German and Italian, never formed a city state and with rare exceptions never was able or never sought to dominate the surrounding country or extend its jurisdiction over it. For this achievement it had neither the military power nor the desire. The independence of the English city rested on the fact that it leased the taxing power from the king, and only those were citizens who shared in this lease, according to which the designated sum was furnished by the city as a unit. The special position of the English city is explained in the first place by the extraordinary concentration of political power in England after William the Conqueror, and further by the fact that after the 13th century the English communes were united in Parliament. If the barons wished to undertake anything against the crown, they were compelled to resort to the pecuniary aid of the towns, as on the other hand the latter were dependent upon them for military support. From the time of their representation in Parliament the impulse and the possibility of a political policy of isolation on the part of the towns were removed. The opposition between city and country disappeared early and the cities accepted numerous landed gentlemen into their citizenship. The town burghers finally secured the upper hand, although down to the most recent times the nobility retained formal leadership in affairs.

Turning to the question as to the consequences of these relations in connection with the evolution of capitalism, we must emphasize the heterogeneity of industry in antiquity and in the middle ages, and the different species of capitalism itself. In the first place, we are met in the most widely separated periods with a multiplicity of non-rational forms of capitalism. These include first capitalistic enterprises for the purpose of tax farming—in the occident as well as in China and western Asia—and for the purpose of financing war, in China and India, in the period of small separate states; second, capitalism in connection with trade speculation, the trader being entirely absent in almost no epoch of history; third, money-lending capitalism, exploiting the necessities of outsiders. All these forms of capitalism relate to spoils, taxes, the pickings of office or official usury, and finally to tribute and actual need. It is noteworthy that in former times officials were financed as Cæsar was by Crassus and endeavored to recoup the sums advanced through misuse of their official position. All this, however, relates to occasional economic activity of an irrational character, while no rational system of labor organization developed out of these arrangements.

Rational capitalism, on the contrary, is organized with a view to market opportunities, hence to economic objectives in the real sense of the word, and the more rational it is the more closely it relates to mass demand and the provision for mass needs. It was reserved to the modern western development after the close of the middle ages to elevate this capitalism into a system, while in all of antiquity there was but one capitalistic class whose rationalism might be compared with that of modern capitalism, namely, the

Roman knighthood. When a Greek city required credit or leased public land or let a contract for supplies, it was forced to incite competition among different interlocal capitalists. Rome, in contrast, was in possession of a rational capitalistic class which from the time of the Gracchi played a determining role in the state. The capitalism of this class was entirely relative to state and governmental opportunities, to the leasing of the *ager publicus* or conquered land, and of domain land, or to tax farming and the financing of political adventures and of wars. It influenced the public policy of Rome in a decisive way at times, although it had to reckon with the constant antagonism of the official nobility.

The capitalism of the late middle ages began to be directed toward market opportunities, and the contrast between it and the capitalism of antiquity appears in the development after the cities have lost their freedom. Here again we find a fundamental distinction in the lines of development as between antiquity and medieval and modern times. In antiquity the freedom of the cities was swept away by a bureaucratically organized world empire within which there was no longer a place for political capitalism. In the beginning the emperors were forced to resort to the financial power of the knighthood but we see them progressively emancipate themselves and exclude the knightly class from the farming of the taxes and hence from the most lucrative source of wealth—just as the Egyptian kings were able to make the provisions for political and military requirements in their realms independent of the capitalist powers and reduce the tax farmers to the position of tax officials. In the imperial period of Rome the leasing of domain land everywhere decreased in extent in favor of permanent hereditary appropriation. The provision for the economic needs of the state was taken care of through compulsory contributions and compulsory labor of servile persons instead of competitive contracts. The various classes of the population became stratified along occupational lines and the burden of state requirements was imposed on the newly created groups on the principle of joint liability.

This development means the throttling of ancient capitalism. A conscript army takes the place of the mercenaries and ships are provided by compulsory service. The entire harvest of grain, insofar as regions of surplus production are concerned, is distributed among the cities in accordance with their needs, with the exclusion of private trade. The building of roads and every other service which has to be provided for is laid on the shoulders of specific personal groups who become attached by inheritance to the soil and to their occupations. At the end the Roman urban communities, acting through their mayors in a way not very different from the village community through its common meeting, demand the return of the rich city councilmen on property grounds, because the population is jointly responsible for the payments and services due to the state. These services are subject to the principle of the *origo* which is erected on the pattern of the ἰδία of Ptolemaic Egypt; the compulsory dues of servile persons can only be rendered in their home commune. After this system became established the political opportunities for securing gain were closed to capitalism; in the late Roman state, based on compulsory contributions (*Leiturgiestaat*) there was as little place for capitalism as in the Egyptian state organized on the basis of compulsory labor service (*Fronstaat*).

Quite different was the fate of the city in the modern era. Here again its autonomy was progressively taken away. The English city of the 17th and 18th centuries had ceased to be anything but a clique of guilds which could lay claim only to financial and social class significance. The German cities of the same period, with the exception of the imperial cities, were merely geographical entities (*Landstadt*) in which everything was ordered from above. In the French cities this development appeared even earlier, while the Spanish cities were deprived of their power by Charles V, in the insurrection of the *communeros*. The Italian cities found themselves in the power of the "signory" and those of Russia never arrived at freedom in the western sense. Everywhere the military, judicial, and industrial authority was taken away from the cities. In form the old rights were as a rule unchanged, but in fact the modern city was deprived of its freedom as effectively as had happened in antiquity with the establishment of the Roman dominion, though in contrast with antiquity they came under the power of competing national states in a condition of perpetual struggle for power in peace or war. This competitive struggle created the largest opportunities for modern western capitalism. The separate states had to compete for mobile capital, which dictated to them the conditions under which it would assist them to power. Out of this alliance of the state with capital, dictated by necessity, arose the national citizen class, the bourgeoisie in the modern sense of the word. Hence it is the closed national state which afforded to capitalism its chance for development—and as long as the national state does not give place to a world empire capitalism also will endure.

CHAPTER XXIX

(A) THE STATE ITSELF; LAW AND OFFICIALDOM

The state in the sense of the rational state has existed only in the western world. Under the old regime in China [1] a thin stratum of so-called officials, the mandarins, existed above the unbroken power of the clans and commercial and industrial guilds. The mandarin is primarily a humanistically educated literatus in the possession of a benefice but not in the least degree trained for administration; he knows no jurisprudence but is a fine writer, can make verses, knows the age-old literature of the Chinese and can interpret it. In the way of political service no importance is attached to him. Such an official performs no administrative work himself; administration lies rather in the hands of the chancery officials. The mandarin is continually transferred from one place to another to prevent his obtaining a foothold in his administrative district, and he could never be assigned to his home province. As he does not understand the dialect of his province he cannot communicate with the public. A state with such officials is something different from the occidental state.

In reality everything is based on the magical theory that the virtue of the empress and the merits of the officials, meaning their perfection in literary culture, keep things in order in normal times. If a drought sets in or any untoward event takes place an edict is promulgated intensi-

338

fying the examinations in verse-making, or speeding up legal trials in order to quiet the spirits. The empire is an agrarian state; hence the power of the peasant clans who represent nine-tenths of the economic life—the other one-tenth belonging to commercial and trading guild organizations—is entirely unbroken. In essence things are left to take care of themselves. The officials do not rule but only interfere in the event of disturbances or untoward happenings.

Very different is the rational state in which alone modern capitalism can flourish. Its basis is an expert officialdom and rational law. The Chinese state changed over to administration through trained officials in the place of humanistically cultured persons as early as the 7th and 11th centuries but the change could be only temporarily maintained; then the usual eclipse of the moon arrived and arrangements were transformed in reverse order. It cannot be seriously asserted, however, that the spirit of the Chinese people could not tolerate an administration of specialists. Its development, and that of the rational state, was rather prevented by the persistence of reliance upon magic. In consequence of this fact the power of the clans could not be broken, as happened in the occident through the development of the cities and of Christianity.

The rational law of the modern occidental state, on the basis of which the trained official renders his decisions, arose on its formal side, though not as to its content, out of Roman law. The latter was to begin with a product of the Roman city state, which never witnessed the dominion of democracy and its justice in the same form as the Greek city. A Greek heliast court administered a petty justice; the contestants worked upon the judges through pathos, tears, and abusing their opponents. This procedure was also known in Rome in political trials, as the orations of

Cicero show, but not in civil trials where the prætor appointed an *iudex* to whom he gave strict instructions as to the conditions requiring a judgment against the accused or the throwing out of the case. Under Justinian the Byzantine bureaucracy brought order and system into this rational law, in consequence of the natural interest of the official in a law which would be systematic and fixed and hence easier to learn.

With the fall of the Roman empire in the west, law came into the hands of the Italian notaries. These, and secondarily the universities, have on their conscience the revival of Roman law. The notaries adhered to the old contractual forms of the Roman empire and re-interpreted them according to the needs of the time. At the same time a systematic legal doctrine was developed in the universities. The essential feature in the development, however, was the rationalization of procedure. As among all primitive peoples the ancient German legal trial was a rigidly formal affair. The party which pronounced wrongly a single word in the formula lost the case, because the formula possessed magical significance and supernatural evils were feared. This magical formalism of the German trial fitted in with the formalism of Roman law. At the same time the French kingdom played a part through the creation of the institution of the representative or advocate whose task it was especially to pronounce the legal formulas correctly, particularly in connection with the canon law. The magnificent administrative organization of the church required fixed forms for its disciplinary ends in relation to the laity and for its own internal discipline. No more than the bourgeoisie could it take up with the Germanic ordeal or judgment of God. The business man could not permit commercial claims to be decided by a competition in reciting formulas, and everywhere secured exemptions from this legalistic contest and from the ordeal. The church also, after hesitating at first, ended by adopting the view that such procedure was heathenish and not to be tolerated, and established the canonical procedure on lines as ra- tional as possible. This two-fold rationalization of pro- cedure from the profane and spiritual sides spread over the western world.

In the revival of the Roman law has been seen the basis for the downfall of the peasant class, as well as for the development of capitalism. It is true that there were cases in which the application of Roman law principles was dis- advantageous to the peasant. An example is the transfor- mation of the old mark community rights into feudal ob- ligations, the individual who stood at the head of the mark community (*Obermärker*) being recognized as a proprietor in the Roman sense and the holdings of the associates bur- dened with feudal dues. On the other hand, however, it was especially through the jurists trained in the Roman law that in France the kingdom was able to obstruct the eviction of peasants by the lords.

As little is the Roman law the basis without qualification for the development of capitalism. England, the home of capitalism, never accepted the Roman law, for the reason that in connection with the royal courts existed a class of advocates who guarded the national legal institutions against corruption. This class controlled the development of legal doctrine, for from its ranks were chosen, as they still are, the judges. It prevented Roman law from being taught in English universities, in order that persons from outside the class might not reach the judicial bench.

In fact all the characteristic institutions of modern cap- italism have other origins than Roman law. The annuity bond, whether arising out of a personal debt or a war loan, came from medieval law, in which Germanic legal ideas played their part. Similarly the stock certificate arose out of medieval and modern law and was unknown to the law of antiquity. Likewise the bill of exchange, to the development of which Arabic, Italian, German, and English law contributed. The commercial company is also a medieval product; only the commenda enterprise was current in antiquity. So also the mortgage, with the security of registration, and the deed of trust, as well as the power of attorney, are medieval in origin and do not go back to antiquity.

The reception of the Roman law was crucial only in the sense that it created formal juristic thinking. In its structure every legal system is based either on formal-legalistic or on material principles. By material principles are to be understood utilitarian and economic considerations, such for example as those according to which the Islamic cadi conducts his administration. In every theocracy and every absolutism justice is materially directed as by contrast in every bureaucracy it is formal-legalistic. Frederick the Great hated the jurists because they constantly applied in a formalistic sense his decrees which were based on material principles, and so turned them to ends with which he would have nothing to do. In this connection, as in general, the Roman law was the means of crushing the material legal system in favor of the formal.

This formalistic law, is however, calculable. In China it may happen that a man who has sold a house to another may later come to him and ask to be taken in because in the meantime he has been impoverished. If the purchaser refuses to heed the ancient Chinese command to help a brother, the spirits will be disturbed; hence the impoverished seller comes into the house as a renter who pays no rent. Capitalism cannot operate on the basis of a law so constituted. What it requires is law which can be counted upon, like a machine; ritualistic-religious and magical considerations must be excluded.

The creation of such a body of law was achieved through the alliance between the modern state and the jurists for the purpose of making good its claims to power. For a time in the 16th century it attempted to work with the humanists, and the first Greek gymnasia were established with the idea that men educated in them would be suitable for state officials; for political contests were carried out to a large extent through the exchange of state papers and only one schooled in Latin and Greek had the necessary equipment. This illusion was shortlived. It was soon found that the products of the gymnasia were not on that account alone equipped for political life, and the jurists were the final resort. In China, where the humanistically cultured mandarin ruled the field, the monarch had no jurists at his disposal, and the struggle among the different philosophical schools as to which of them formed the best statesmen waged to and fro until finally orthodox Confucianism was victorious. India also had writers but no trained jurists. In contrast the western world had at its disposal a formally organized legal system, the product of the Roman genius, and officials trained in this law were superior to all others as technical administrators. From the standpoint of economic history this fact is significant in that the alliance between the state and formal jurisprudence was indirectly favorable to capitalism.

(B) THE ECONOMIC POLICY OF THE RATIONAL STATE

For the state to have an economic policy worthy of the name, that is one which is continuous and consistent, is an institution of exclusively modern origin. The first system which it brought forth is mercantilism, so-called. Before the development of mercantilism there were two widespread commercial policies, namely, the dominance of fiscal interests and of welfare interests, the last in the sense of the customary standard of living.

In the east it was essentially ritualistic considerations, including caste and clan organizations, which prevented the development of a deliberate economic policy. In China, the political system had undergone extraordinary changes. The country had an epoch of highly developed foreign trade, extending as far as India. Later, however, the Chinese economic policy turned to external exclusiveness to the extent that the entire import and export business was in the hands of only 13 firms and was concentrated in the single port of Canton. Internally, the policy was dominated by religious considerations; only on occasion of natural catastrophes were abuses inquired into. At all times the question of co-operation of the provinces determined the viewpoint, and a leading problem was set by the question whether the needs of the state should be provided by taxation or through compulsory services.

In Japan, the feudal organization led to the same consequences and resulted in complete exclusiveness as regards the outer world. The object was here the stabilization of class relations; it was feared that foreign trade would disturb conditions as to the distribution of property. In Korea, ritualistic grounds determined the exclusive policy. If foreigners, that is profane persons, were to come into the country the wrath of the spirits was to be feared. In the Indian middle ages we find Greek and Roman merchants, as well as Roman soldiers, and also the immigration of Jews with grants of privileges to them; but these germs were unable to develop, for later everything was again stereotyped by the caste system, which made a planned economic policy impossible. An additional consideration was that Hinduism strongly condemned traveling abroad; one who went abroad had on his return to be re-admitted to his caste.

In the occident down to the 14th century a planned economic policy had a chance to develop only in connection with the towns. It is true that there were beginnings of an economic policy on the part of the princes; in the Carolingian period we find price fixing and public concern for welfare expressed in various directions. But most of this remained on paper only, and with the exception of the coinage reform and the system of weights and measures of Charlemagne, everything disappeared without leaving a trace in the succeeding period. A commercial policy which would have been gladly adopted in relation to the orient was rendered impossible by the absence of shipping.

When the state under its prince gave up the fight, the church interested itself in economic life, endeavoring to impose upon economic dealings a minimum of legal honesty and churchly ethics. One of its most important measures was the support of the public peace, which it attempted to enforce first on certain days and finally as a general principle. In addition, the great ecclesiastical property communities, especially the monasteries, supported a very rational economic life, which cannot be called capitalistic economy but which was the most rational in existence. Later these endeavors more and more fell into discredit as the church revived its old ascetic ideals and adapted them to the times. Among the emperors again are found a few beginnings of commercial policy under Frederick Barbarossa, including price fixing and a customs treaty with England designed to favor German merchants. Frederick II established the public peace but in general pursued a purely fiscal policy favoring merely the rich merchants; to them he granted privileges, especially customs exemptions.

The single measure of economic policy on the part of the German kings was the conflict over the Rhine tolls, which however was futile in the main, in view of the great number of petty lords along the river. Aside from this there was no planned economic policy. Measures which give the impression of such a policy, such as the embargo of the emperor Sigmund against Venice, or the occasional closing of the Rhine in the struggle with Cologne, are purely political in character. The customs policy was in the hands of the territorial princes, and even here with few exceptions a consistent effort to encourage industry is wanting. Their dominant objectives were, first, to favor local as against distant trade, especially to promote interchange of goods between the towns and the surrounding country; export duties were always to be maintained higher than import duties. Second, to favor local merchants in the customs. Road tolls were differentiated, the prince endeavoring to favor his own roads in order the more conveniently to exploit them as a source of revenue; to this end they even went to the length of requiring the use of certain roads, and systematized the law of the staple. Finally, the city merchants were given privileges; Louis the Rich of Bavaria prided himself on suppressing the rural merchants (above, p. 193).

Protective duties are unknown, with few exceptions, of which the Tirolese duties on wine, directed against the competition of imports from Italy, are an example. The customs policy as a whole is dominated by the fiscal point of view and that of maintaining the traditional standard of living. The same applies to the customs treaties, which go back to the 13th century. The technique of the customs fluctuated. The original custom was an ad-valorem duty of one-sixtieth the value; in the 14th century this was increased to a one-twelfth, in view of the fact that the duty was made to function also as an excise. The place of our modern measures of economic policy, such as protective tariffs, was taken by direct prohibitions against trade, which were very frequently suspended when the standard of living of domestic craftsmen, or later of employing factors, was to be protected. Sometimes wholesale trade was allowed and retail trade was prohibited. The first trace of a rational economic policy on the part of the prince appears in the 14th century in England. This was mercantilism, so-called since Adam Smith.

(C) Mercantilism

The essence of mercantilism[2] consists in carrying the point of view of capitalistic industry into politics; the state is handled as if it consisted exclusively of capitalistic entrepreneurs. External economic policy rests on the principle of taking every advantage of the opponent, importing at the lowest price and selling much higher. The purpose is to strengthen the hand of the government in its external relations. Hence mercantilism signifies the development of the state as a political power, which is to be done directly by increasing the tax paying power of the population.

A presupposition of the mercantilistic policy was the inclusion of as many sources of money income as possible within the country in question. It is, to be sure, an error to hold that the mercantilistic thinkers and statesmen confused ownership of the precious metals with national wealth. They knew well enough that the source of this wealth is the tax paying power, and all that they did in the way of retaining in the country the money which threat-

ened to disappear through the commerce was done exclusively with a view to increasing this taxable capacity. A
second point in the program of mercantilism, in obvious
immediate connection with the power-seeking policy characteristic of the system, was to promote the largest possible
increase in the population; in order to sustain the increased
numbers, the endeavor was to secure to the greatest extent
external markets; this applied especially to those products
in which a maximum quantity of domestic labor was em-
bodied, hence finished manufactures rather than raw materials. Finally, trade was to be carried on as far as possible
by the merchants of the country, in order that its earnings
should all accrue to the taxable capacity. On the side of
theory, the system was supported by the doctrine of the
balance of trade, which taught that the country would
be impoverished if the value of imports exceeded that of
exports; this theory was first developed in England in the
16th century.

England is distinctively the original home of Mercantilism. The first traces of the application of mercantilistic
principles are found there in the year 1381. Under the
weak king Richard II, a money stringency arose and Parliament appointed an investigating commission which for
the first time dealt with the balance of trade concept in all
its essential features. For the time being it produced only
emergency measures, including prohibitions of importation and stimulation of exportation, but without giving to
English policy a truly mercantilistic character. The real
turning point is generally dated from 1440. At that time,
in one of the numerous Statutes of Employment, which
were passed for the correction of alleged abuses, two propositions were laid down which indeed had been applied
before, but only in an incidental way. The first was that
foreign merchants who brought goods to England must

convert all the money which they received into English goods; the second that English merchants who had dealings abroad must bring back to England at least a part of their proceeds in cash. On the basis of these two propositions developed gradually the whole system of mercantilism down to the Navigation Act of 1651, with its elimination of the foreign shipping.

Mercantilism in the sense of a league between the state and the capitalistic interest had appeared under two aspects. One was that of class monopoly, which appears in its typical form in the policy of the Stuarts and the Anglican church,—especially that of Bishop Laud who was later beheaded. This system looked toward a class organization of the whole population in the Christian socialist sense, a stabilization of the classes with a view to establishing social relations based on Christian love. In the sharpest contrast with Puritanism, which saw every poor person as work-shy or as a criminal, its attitude toward the poor was friendly. In practice, the mercantilism of the Stuarts was primarily oriented along fiscal lines; new industries were allowed to import only on the basis of a royal monopoly concession and were to be kept under the permanent control of the king with a view to fiscal exploitation. Similar, although not so consistent, was the policy of Colbert in France. He aimed at an artificial promotion of industries, supported by monopolies; this view he shared with the Huguenots, on whose persecution he looked with disfavor. In England the royal and Anglican policy was broken down by the Puritans under the Long Parliament. Their struggle with the king was pursued for decades under the war cry "down with the monopolies" which were granted in part to foreigners and in part to courtiers, while the colonies were placed in the hands of royal favorites. The small entrepreneur class which in the meantime had grown up, especially within the guilds though in part outside of them, enlisted against the royal monopoly policy, and the Long Parliament deprived monopolists of the suffrage. The extraordinary obstinacy with which the economic spirit of the English people has striven against trusts and monopolies is expressed in these Puritan struggles.[3]

The second form of mercantilism may be called national; it limited itself to the protection of industries actually in existence, in contrast with the attempt to establish industries through monopolies. Hardly one of the industries created by mercantilism survived the mercantilistic period; the economic creations of the Stuarts disappeared along with those of the western continental states and those of Russia later. It follows that the capitalistic development was not an outgrowth of national mercantilism; rather capitalism developed at first in England alongside the fiscal monopoly policy. The course of events was that a stratum of entrepreneurs which had developed in independence of the political administration secured the systematic support of Parliament in the 18th century, after the collapse of the fiscal monopoly policy of the Stuarts. Here for the last time irrational and rational capitalism faced each other in conflict, that is, capitalism in the field of fiscal and colonial privileges and public monopolies, and capitalism oriented in relation to market opportunities which were developed from within by business interests themselves on the basis of saleable services.

The point of collision of the two types was at the Bank of England. The bank was founded by Paterson, a Scotchman, a capitalist adventurer of the type called forth by the Stuarts' policy of granting monopolies. But Puritan business men also belonged to the bank. The last time the bank turned aside in the direction of speculative capitalism was in connection with the South Sea Company.

Aside from this venture we can trace step by step the process by which the influence of Paterson and his kind lost ground in favor of the rationalistic type of bank members who were all directly or indirectly of Puritan origin or influenced by Puritanism.

Mercantilism also played the role familiar in economic history. In England it finally disappeared when free trade was established, an achievement of the Puritan dissenters Cobden and Bright and their league with the industrial interests, which were now in a position to dispense with mercantilistic support.

CHAPTER XXX

THE EVOLUTION OF THE CAPITALISTIC SPIRIT

It is a widespread error that the increase of population is to be included as a really crucial agent in the evolution of western capitalism. In opposition to this view, Karl Marx made the assertion that every economic epoch has its own law of population, and although this proposition is untenable in so general a form, it is justified in the present case. The growth of population in the west made most rapid progress from the beginning of the 18th century to the end of the 19th. In the same period China experienced a population growth of at least equal extent—from 60 or 70 to 400 millions, allowing for the inevitable exaggerations; this corresponds approximately with the increase in the west. In spite of this fact, capitalism went backward in China and not forward. The increase in the population took place there in different strata than with us. It made China the seat of a swarming mass of small peasants; the increase of a class corresponding to our proletariat was involved only to the extent that a foreign market made possible the employment of coolies ("coolie" is originally an Indian expression, and signifies neighbor or fellow member of a clan). The growth of population in Europe did indeed favor the development of capitalism, to the extent that in a small population the system would have been unable to secure the necessary labor force, but in itself it never called forth that development.

Nor can the inflow of precious metals be regarded, as

Sombart suggests, as the primary cause of the appearance of capitalism. It is certainly true that in a given situation an increase in the supply of precious metals may give rise to price revolutions, such as that which took place after 1530 in Europe, and when other favorable conditions are present, as when a certain form of labor organization is in process of development, the progress may be stimulated by the fact that large stocks of cash come into the hands of certain groups. But the case of India proves that such an importation of precious metal will not alone bring about capitalism. In India in the period of the Roman power, an enormous mass of precious metal—some twenty-five million *sestertii* annually—came in in exchange for domestic goods, but this inflow gave rise to commercial capitalism to only a slight extent. The greater part of the precious metal disappeared in the hoards of the rajahs instead of being converted into cash and applied in the establishment of enterprises of a rational capitalistic character. This fact proves that it depends entirely upon the nature of the labor system what tendency will result from an inflow of precious metal. The gold and silver from America, after the discovery, flowed in the first place to Spain; but in that country a recession of capitalistic development took place parallel with the importation. There followed, on the one hand, the suppression of the *communeros* and the destruction of the commercial interests of the Spanish grandees, and, on the other hand, the employment of the money for military ends. Consequently, the stream of precious metal flowed through Spain, scarcely touching it, and fertilized other countries, which in the 15th century were already undergoing a process of transformation in labor relations which was favorable to capitalism.

Hence neither the growth of population nor the importation of precious metal called forth western capitalism. The external conditions for the development of capitalism are rather, first, geographical in character. In China and India the enormous costs of transportation, connected with the decisively inland commerce of the regions, necessarily formed serious obstructions for the classes who were in a position to make profits through trade and to use trading capital in the construction of a capitalistic system, while in the west the position of the Mediterranean as an inland sea, and the abundant interconnections through the rivers, favored the opposite development of international commerce. But this factor in its turn must not be overestimated. The civilization of antiquity was distinctively coastal. Here the opportunities for commerce were very favorable, (thanks to the character of the Mediterranean Sea,) in contrast with the Chinese waters with their typhoons, and yet no capitalism arose in antiquity. Even in the modern period the capitalistic development was much more intense in Florence than in Genoa or in Venice. Capitalism in the west was born in the industrial cities of the interior, not in the cities which were centers of sea trade.

Military requirements were also favorable, though not as such but because of the special nature of the particular needs of the western armies. Favorable also was the luxury demand, though again not in itself. In many cases rather it led to the development of irrational forms, such as small work shops in France and compulsory settlements of workers in connection with the courts of many German princes. In the last resort the factor which produced capitalism is the rational permanent enterprise, rational accounting, rational technology and rational law, but again not these alone. Necessary complementary factors were the rational spirit, the rationalization of the conduct of life in general, and a rationalistic economic ethic.[1]

At the beginning of all ethics and the economic relations

which result, is traditionalism, the sanctity of tradition, the exclusive reliance upon such trade and industry as have come down from the fathers.   This traditionalism survives far down into the present; only a human lifetime in the past it was futile to double the wages of an agricultural laborer in Silesia who mowed a certain tract of land on a contract, in the hope of inducing him to increase his exertions.   He would simply have reduced by half the work expended because with this half he would have been able to earn twice as much as before (sic).   This general incapacity and indisposition to depart from the beaten paths is the motive for the maintenance of tradition.

Primitive traditionalism may, however, undergo essential intensification through two circumstances.   In the first place, material interests may be tied up with the maintenance of the tradition.   When for example in China, the attempt was made to change certain roads or to introduce more rational means or routes of transportation, the perquisites of certain officials were threatened; and the same was the case in the middle ages in the west, and in modern times when railroads were introduced.   Such special interests of officials, landholders and merchants assisted decisively in restricting a tendency toward rationalization. Stronger still is the effect of the stereotyping of trade on magical grounds, the deep repugnance to undertaking any change in the established conduct of life because supernatural evils are feared.   Generally some injury to economic privilege is concealed in this opposition, but its effectiveness depends on a general belief in the potency of the magical processes which are feared.

Traditional obstructions are not overcome by the economic impulse alone.   The notion that our rationalistic and capitalistic age is characterized by a stronger economic interest than other periods is childish; the moving spirits of modern capitalism are not possessed of a stronger economic impulse than, for example, an oriental trader. The unchaining of the economic interest merely as such has produced only irrational results; such men as Cortez and Pizarro, who were perhaps its strongest embodiment, were far from having an idea of a rationalistic economic life. If the economic impulse in itself is universal, it is an interesting question as to the relations under which it becomes rationalized and rationally tempered in such fashion as to produce rational institutions of the character of capitalistic enterprise.

Originally, two opposite attitudes toward the pursuit of gain exist in combination. Internally, there is attachment to tradition and to the pietistic relations of fellow members of tribe, clan, and house-community, with the exclusion of the unrestricted quest of gain within the circle of those bound together by religious ties; externally, there is absolutely unrestricted play of the gain spirit in economic relations, every foreigner being originally an enemy in relation to whom no ethical restrictions apply; that is, the ethics of internal and external relations are categorically distinct. The course of development involves on the one hand the bringing in of calculation into the traditional brotherhood, displacing the old religious relationship. As soon as accountability is established within the family community, and economic relations are no longer strictly communistic, there is an end of the naive piety and its repression of the economic impulse. This side of the development is especially characteristic in the west. At the same time there is a tempering of the unrestricted quest of gain with the adoption of the economic principle into the internal economy. The result is a regulated economic life with the economic impulse functioning within bounds.

In detail, the course of development has been varied. In

India, the restrictions upon gain-seeking apply only to the two uppermost strata, the Brahmins and the Rajputs. A member of these castes is forbidden to practice certain callings. A Brahmin may conduct an eating house, as he alone has clean hands; but he, like the Rajput, would be un-classed if he were to lend money for interest. The latter, however, is permitted to the mercantile castes, and within it we find a degree of unscrupulousness in trade which is unmatched anywhere in the world. Finally, antiquity had only legal limitations on interest, and the proposition *caveat emptor* characterizes Roman economic ethics. Nevertheless no modern capitalism developed there.

The final result is the peculiar fact that the germs of modern capitalism must be sought in a region where officially a theory was dominant which was distinct from that of the east and of classical antiquity and in principle strongly hostile to capitalism. The *ethos* of the classical economic morality is summed up in the old judgment passed on the merchant, which was probably taken from primitive Arianism: *homo mercator vix aut numquam potest Deo placere;* he may conduct himself without sin but cannot be pleasing to God. This proposition was valid down to the 15th century, and the first attempt to modify it slowly matured in Florence under pressure of the shift in economic relations.

The typical antipathy of Catholic ethics, and following that the Lutheran, to every capitalistic tendency, rests essentially on the repugnance of the impersonality of relations within a capitalist economy. It is this fact of impersonal relations which places certain human affairs outside the church and its influence, and prevents the latter from penetrating them and transforming them along ethical lines. The relations between master and slave could be subjected to immediate ethical regulation; but the relations between the mortgage creditor and the property which was pledged for the debt, or between an endorser and the bill of exchange, would at least be exceedingly difficult if not impossible to moralize.[2] The final consequence of the resulting position assumed by the church was that medieval economic ethics excluded higgling, overpricing and free competition, and were based on the principle of just price and the assurance to everyone of a chance to live.

For the breaking up of this circle of ideas the Jews cannot be made responsible as Sombart does.[3] The position of the Jews during the middle ages may be compared sociologically with that of an Indian caste in a world otherwise free from castes; they were an outcast people. However, there is the distinction that according to the promise of the Indian religion the caste system is valid for eternity. The individual may in the course of time reach heaven through a course of reincarnations, the time depending upon his deserts; but this is possible only within the caste system. The caste organization is eternal, and one who attempted to leave it would be accursed and condemned to pass in hell into the bowels of a dog. The Jewish promise, on the contrary, points toward a reversal of caste relations in the future world as compared with this. In the present world the Jews are stamped as an outcast people, either as punishment for the sins of their fathers, as Deutero-Isaiah holds, or for the salvation of the world, which is the presupposition of the mission of Jesus of Nazareth; from this position they are to be released by a social revolution. In the middle ages the Jews were a guest-people standing outside of political society; they could not be received into any town citizenship group because they could not participate in the communion of the Lord's Supper, and hence could not belong to the *coniuratio*.

The Jews were not the only guest people (see pages 196, 217); besides them the Caursines, for example, occupied a similar position. These were Christian merchants who dealt in money and in consequence were, like the Jews, under the protection of the princes and on consideration of a payment enjoyed the privilege of carrying on monetary dealings. What distinguished the Jews in a striking way from the Christian guest-peoples was the impossibility in their case of entering into *commercium* and *conubium* with the Christians. Originally the Christians did not hesitate to accept Jewish hospitality, in contrast with the Jews themselves who feared that their ritualistic prescriptions as to food would not be observed by their hosts. On the occasion of the first outbreak of medieval anti-semitism the faithful were warned by the synods not to conduct themselves unworthily and hence not to accept entertainment from the Jews who on their side despised the hospitality of the Christians. Marriage with Christians was strictly impossible, going back to Ezra and Nehemiah.

A further ground for the outcast position of the Jews arose from the fact that Jewish craftsmen existed; in Syria there had even been a Jewish knightly class, though only exceptionally Jewish peasants, for the conduct of agriculture was not to be reconciled with the requirements of the ritual. Ritualistic considerations were responsible for the concentration of Jewish economic life in monetary dealings (cf. above page 196). Jewish piety set a premium on the knowledge of the law and continuous study was very much easier to combine with exchange dealings than with other occupations. In addition, the prohibition against usury on the part of the church condemned exchange dealings, yet the trade was indispensable and the Jews were not subject to the ecclesiastical law.

Finally, Judaism had maintained the originally universal

dualism of internal and external moral attitudes, under which it was permissible to accept interest from foreigners who did not belong to the brotherhood or established association. Out of this dualism followed the sanctioning of other irrational economic affairs, especially tax farming and political financing of all sorts. In the course of the centuries the Jews acquired a special skill in these matters which made them useful and in demand. But all this was pariah capitalism, not rational capitalism such as originated in the west. In consequence, hardly a Jew is found among the creators of the modern economic situation, the large entrepreneurs; this type was Christian and only conceivable in the field of Christianity. The Jewish manufacturer, on the contrary, is a modern phenomenon. If for no other reason, it was impossible for the Jews to have a part in the establishment of rational capitalism because they were outside the craft organizations. But even alongside the guilds they could hardly maintain themselves, even where, as in Poland, they had command over a numerous proletariat which they might have organized in the capacity of entrepreneurs in domestic industry or as manufacturers. After all, the genuine Jewish ethic is specifically traditionalism, as the Talmud shows. The horror of the pious Jew in the face of any innovation is quite as great as that of an individual among any primitive people with institutions fixed by the belief in magic.

However, Judaism was none the less of notable significance for modern rational capitalism, insofar as it transmitted to Christianity the latter's hostility to magic. Apart from Judaism and Christianity, and two or three oriental sects (one of which is in Japan), there is no religion with the character of outspoken hostility to magic. Probably this hostility arose through the circumstance that what the Israelites found in Canaan was the magic of the agricultural god Baal, while Jahveh was a god of volcanoes, earthquakes, and pestilences. The hostility between the two priesthoods and the victory of the priests of Jahveh discredited the fertility magic of the priests of Baal and stigmatized it with a character of decadence and godlessness. Since Judaism made Christianity possible and gave it the character of a religion essentially free from magic, it rendered an important service from the point of view of economic history. For the dominance of magic outside the sphere in which Christianity has prevailed is one of the most serious obstructions to the rationalization of economic life. Magic involves a stereotyping of technology and economic relations. When attempts were made in China to inaugurate the building of railroads and factories a conflict with geomancy ensued. The latter demanded that in the location of structures on certain mountains, forests, rivers, and cemetery hills, foresight should be exercised in order not to disturb the rest of the spirits.[4]

Similar is the relation to capitalism of the castes in India. Every new technical process which an Indian employs signifies for him first of all that he leaves his caste and falls into another, necessarily lower. Since he believes in the transmigration of souls, the immediate significance of this is that his chance of purification is put off until another re-birth. He will hardly consent to such a change. An additional fact is that every caste makes every other impure. In consequence, workmen who dare not accept a vessel filled with water from each other's hands, cannot be employed together in the same factory room. Not until the present time, after the possession of the country by the English for almost a century, could this obstacle be overcome. Obviously, capitalism could not develop in an economic group thus bound hand and foot by magical beliefs.

In all times there has been but one means of breaking down the power of magic and establishing a rational conduct of life; this means is great rational prophecy. Not every prophecy by any means destroys the power of magic; but it is possible for a prophet who furnishes credentials in the shape of miracles and otherwise, to break down the traditional sacred rules. Prophecies have released the world from magic and in doing so have created the basis for our modern science and technology, and for capitalism. In China such prophecy has been wanting. What prophecy there was has come from the outside as in the case of Lao-Tse and Taoism. India, however, produced a religion of salvation; in contrast with China it has known great prophetic missions. But they were prophecies by example; that is, the typical Hindu prophet, such as Buddha, lives before the world the life which leads to salvation, but does not regard himself as one sent from God to insist upon the obligation to lead it; he takes the position that whoever wishes salvation, as an end freely chosen, should lead the life. However, one may reject salvation, as it is not the destiny of everyone to enter at death into Nirvana, and only philosophers in the strictest sense are prepared by hatred of this world to adopt the stoical resolution and withdraw from life.

The result was that Hindu prophecy was of immediate significance for the intellectual classes. These became forest dwellers and poor monks. For the masses, however, the significance of the founding of a Buddhistic sect was quite different, namely the opportunity of praying to the saints. There came to be holy men who were believed to work miracles, who must be well fed so that they would repay this good deed by guaranteeing a better reincarnation or through granting wealth, long life, and the like, that is, this world's goods. Hence Buddhism in its pure form was restricted to a thin stratum of monks. The laity found no ethical precepts according to which life should be molded; Buddhism indeed had its decalogue, but in distinction from that of the Jews it gave no binding commands but only recommendations. The most important act of service was and remained the physical maintenance of the monks. Such a religious spirit could never be in a position to displace magic but at best could only put another magic in its place.

In contrast with the ascetic religion of salvation of India and its defective action upon the masses, are Judaism and Christianity, which from the beginning have been plebeian religions and have deliberately remained such. The struggle of the ancient church against the Gnostics was nothing else than a struggle against the aristocracy of the intellectuals, such as is common to ascetic religions, with the object of preventing their seizing the leadership in the church. This struggle was crucial for the success of Christianity among the masses, and hence for the fact that magic was suppressed among the general population to the greatest possible extent. True, it has not been possible even down to today to overcome it entirely, but it was reduced to the character of something unholy, something diabolic.

The germ of this development as regards magic is found far back in ancient Jewish ethics, which is much concerned with views such as we also meet with in the proverbs and the so-called prophetic texts of the Egyptians. But the most important prescriptions of Egyptian ethics were futile when by laying a scarab on the region of the heart one could prepare the dead man to successfully conceal the sins committed, deceive the judge of the dead, and thus get into paradise. The Jewish ethics knows no such sophisticated subterfuges and as little does Christianity. In the Eucharist the latter has indeed sublimated magic into the form of a sacrament, but it gave its adherents no such means for evading the final judgment as were contained in Egyptian religion. If one wishes to study at all the influence of a religion on life one must distinguish between its official teachings and this sort of actual procedure upon which in reality, perhaps against its own will, it places a premium, in this world or the next.

It is also necessary to distinguish between the virtuoso religion of adepts and the religion of the masses. Virtuoso religion is significant for everyday life only as a pattern; its claims are of the highest, but they fail to determine everyday ethics. The relation between the two is different in different religions. In Catholicism, they are brought into harmonious union insofar as the claims of the religious virtuoso are held up alongside the duties of the laymen as *consilia evangelica*. The really complete Christian is the monk; but his mode of life is not required of everyone, although some of his virtues in a qualified form are held up as ideals. The advantage of this combination was that ethics was not split asunder as in Buddhism. After all the distinction between monk ethics and mass ethics meant that the most worthy individuals in the religious sense withdrew from the world and established a separate community.

Christianity was not alone in this phenomenon, which rather recurs frequently in the history of religions, as is shown by the powerful influence of asceticism, which signifies the carrying out of a definite, methodical conduct of life. Asceticism has always worked in this sense. The enormous achievements possible to such an ascetically determined methodical conduct of life are demonstrated by the example of Tibet. The country seems condemned by nature to be an eternal desert; but a community of celibate ascetics has carried out colossal construction works in

Lhassa and saturated the country with the religious doctrines of Buddhism.   An analogous phenomenon is present in the middle ages in the west.   In that epoch the monk is the first human being who lives rationally, who works methodically and by rational means toward a goal, namely the future life.   Only for him did the clock strike, only for him were the hours of the day divided—for prayer. The economic life of the monastic communities was also rational.   The monks in part furnished the officialdom for the early middle ages; the power of the doges of Venice collapsed when the investiture struggle deprived them of the possibility of employing churchmen for oversea enterprises.

But the rational mode of life remained restricted to the monastic circles.   The Franciscan movement indeed attempted through the institution of the tertiaries to extend it to the laity, but the institution of the confessional was a barrier to such an extension.   The church domesticated medieval Europe by means of its system of confession and penance, but for the men of the middle ages the possibility of unburdening themselves through the channel of the confessional, when they had rendered themselves liable to punishment, meant a release from the consciousness of sin which the teachings of the church had called into being.   The unity and strength of the methodical conduct of life were thus in fact broken up.   In its knowledge of human nature the church did not reckon with the fact that the individual is a closed unitary ethical personality, but steadfastly held to the view that in spite of the warnings of the confessional and of penances, however strong, he would again fall away morally; that is, it shed its grace on the just and the unjust.

The Reformation made a decisive break with this system. The dropping of the *concilia evangelica* by the Lutheran

Reformation meant the disappearance of the dualistic ethics, of the distinction between a universally binding morality and a specifically advantageous code for virtuosi. The other-worldly asceticism came to an end. The stern religious characters who had previously gone into monasteries had now to practice their religion in the life of the world. For such an asceticism within the world the ascetic dogmas of protestantism created an adequate ethics. Celibacy was not required, marriage being viewed simply as an institution for the rational bringing up of children. Poverty was not required, but the pursuit of riches must not lead one astray into reckless enjoyment. Thus Sebastian Franck was correct in summing up the spirit of the Reformation in the words, "you think you have escaped from the monastery, but everyone must now be a monk throughout his life."

The wide significance of this transformation of the ascetic ideal can be followed down to the present in the classical lands of protestant ascetic religiosity. It is especially discernible in the import of the religious denominations in America. Although state and church are separated, still, as late as fifteen or twenty years ago no banker or physician took up a residence or established connections without being asked to what religious community he belonged, and his prospects were good or bad according to the character of his answer. Acceptance into a sect was conditioned upon a strict inquiry into one's ethical conduct. Membership in a sect which did not recognize the Jewish distinction between internal and external moral codes guaranteed one's business honor and reliability and this in turn guaranteed success. Hence the principle "honesty is the best policy" and hence among Quakers, Baptists, and Methodists the ceaseless repetition of the proposition based on experience that God would take care of his own. "The Godless cannot trust each other across the road; they turn to us when they want to do business; piety is the surest road to wealth." This is by no means "cant," but a combination of religiosity with consequences which were originally unknown to it and which were never intended.

It is true that the acquisition of wealth, attributed to piety, led to a dilemma, in all respects similar to that into which the medieval monasteries constantly fell; the religious guild led to wealth, wealth to fall from grace, and this again to the necessity of re-constitution. Calvinism sought to avoid this difficulty through the idea that man was only an administrator of what God had given him; it condemned enjoyment, yet permitted no flight from the world but rather regarded working together, with its rational discipline, as the religious task of the individual. Out of this system of thought came our word "calling," which is known only to the languages influenced by the Protestant translations of the Bible.[5] It expresses the value placed upon rational activity carried on according to the rational capitalistic principle, as the fulfillment of a God-given task. Here lay also in the last analysis the basis of the contrast between the Puritans and the Stuarts. The ideas of both were capitalistically directed; but in a characteristic way the Jew was for the Puritan the embodiment of everything repugnant because he devoted himself to irrational and illegal occupations such as war loans, tax farming, and leasing of offices, in the fashion of the court favorite.[6]

This development of the concept of the calling quickly gave to the modern entrepreneur a fabulously clear conscience,—and also industrious workers; he gave to his employees as the wages of their ascetic devotion to the calling and of co-operation in his ruthless exploitation of them through capitalism the prospect of eternal salvation, which in an age when ecclesiastical discipline took control of the whole of life to an extent inconceivable to us now, represented a reality quite different from any it has today. The Catholic and Lutheran churches also recognized and practiced ecclesiastical discipline. But in the Protestant ascetic communities admission to the Lord's Supper was conditioned on ethical fitness, which again was identified with business honor, while into the content of one's faith no one inquired. Such a powerful, unconsciously refined organization for the production of capitalistic individuals has never existed in any other church or religion, and in comparison with it what the Renaissance did for capitalism shrinks into insignificance. Its practitioners occupied themselves with technical problems and were experimenters of the first rank. From art and mining experimentation was taken over into science.

The world-view of the Renaissance, however, determined the policy of rulers in a large measure, though it did not transform the soul of man as did the innovations of the Reformation. Almost all the great scientific discoveries of the 16th and even the beginning of the 17th century were made against the background of Catholicism. Copernicus was a Catholic, while Luther and Melanchthon repudiated his discoveries. Scientific progress and Protestantism must not at all be unquestioningly identified. The Catholic church has indeed occasionally obstructed scientific progress; but the ascetic sects of Protestantism have also been disposed to have nothing to do with science, except in a situation where material requirements of everyday life were involved. On the other hand it is its specific contribution to have placed science in the service of technology and economics.[7]

The religious root of modern economic humanity is dead; today the concept of the calling is a *caput mortuum* in the world.   Ascetic religiosity has been displaced by a pessimistic though by no means ascetic view of the world, such as that portrayed in Mandeville's Fable of the Bees, which teaches that private vices may under certain conditions be for the good of the public.   With the complete disappearance of all the remains of the original enormous religious pathos of the sects, the optimism of the Enlightenment which believed in the harmony of interests, appeared as the heir of Protestant asceticism in the field of economic ideas; it guided the hands of the princes, statesmen, and writers of the later 18th and early 19th century.   Economic ethics arose against the background of the ascetic ideal; now it has been stripped of its religious import.   It was possible for the working class to accept its lot as long as the promise of eternal happiness could be held out to it.   When this consolation fell away it was inevitable that those strains and stresses should appear in economic society which since then have grown so rapidly.   This point had been reached at the end of the early period of capitalism, at the beginning of the age of iron, in the 19th century.

NOTES

PART ONE

CHAPTER I

1. General References.—A. Meitzen, *Siedelung und Agrarwesen der West- und Ostgermanen, der Kelten, Römer, Finnen und Slawen.* 4 vols. Berlin, 1896; G. F. Knapp, *"Siedelung und Agrarwesen nach A. Meitzen,"* in his *Grundherrschaft und Rittergut,* 101 ff. (Criticism of Meitzen); Max Weber, Article, "Agrargeschichte, Altertum," in the *Handwörterbuch der Staatswissenschaften,* 3d ed., I, 52 ff. Jena, 1909.

2. See G. Hanssen, "Ansichten über das Agrarwesen der Vorzeit" in *Neues staatsbürgerliches Magazin,* vol. III (1835) and vol. VI (1837)— reprinted in his *Agrarhistorischen Abhandlungen,* 2 vols., Leipsic, 1880–1884; also, G. von Maurer, *Einleitung zur Mark- Hof- Dorf- und Stadtverfassung,* Munich, 1854; E. de Laveleye, *De la propriété et de ses formes primitives,* Paris, 1874 (English translation, *Primitive Property,* London, 1878).

For orientation as to the origin and course of the controversy, see G. von Below, "Das kurze Leben einer vielgenannten Theorie," in the volume, *Probleme der Wirtschaftsgeschichte,* Tuebingen, 1920; also, Max Weber, "Der Streit um den Character der altgermanischen Sozialverfassung," in *Jahrbb. f. National-ökonomie und Statistik,* vol. LXXXIII (1904).

3. The hide organization has recently been the subject of a controversy closely connected with that regarding the theory of primitive communism. The older view saw in it a result and expression of the communal field system, but later writers contend for a manorial origin. Rübel, again, maintains that it was an institution originally peculiar to the Salian Franks and was spread over all Germany by the Frankish kingdom.

4. Cp. in general, Max Weber, *Gesammelte Aufsätze zur Religionssoziologie,* Tuebingen, 1920, I, 350, and references there cited.

5. But it is not these arrangements which explain the stability

371

of Indian conditions, as Karl Marx affirmed, but rather the caste system, just as in China it is the clan economy.

6. The principal contrast in agrarian economy between Europe and specifically Asiatic regions goes back to the fact that neither the Chinese nor Javanese peoples knew the use of milk from animals, while on European soil milking is met with as far back as Homer. On the other hand, in India since the middle ages, cattle cannot be slaughtered, and even today the upper castes condemn the eating of meat. Hence milk animals and meat animals are both absent in Asia over wide areas.

CHAPTER II

1. Cp. the right to bear arms, which existed to the time of the Peasants' War. It will be seen that there is a right corresponding to the duty of the freeman to participate in the juridical community.

2. This investigation goes back to J. J. Bachofen, *Das Mutterrecht*, Stuttgart, 1861. The "matriarchal" (*mutterrechtliche*) origin of the family asserted by Bachofen was taken over into the works of L. H. Morgan (especially *Ancient Society*, New York, 1871), and of H. S. Maine (*Ancient Law*, London, 1861), and became the foundation of the socialistic theory. Cp. the works of Bebel, Engels, and Cunow. E. Grosse (*Die Formen der Familie und die Formen der Wirtschaft*, Freiburg and Leipsic, 1896) represents the reaction against a one-sided mother-right theory. Indicating the present state of knowledge, and in general free from bias, is Marianne Weber, *Ehefrau und Mutter in der Rechtsentwicklung*, Tuebingen, 1907.

3. Cp. J. G. Frazer, *Totemism and Exogamy*, London, 1910.

4. Cp. Genesis, 34, 8 ff.

CHAPTER III

1. The fate of the Israelites in Egypt is thus explained.

2. Cp. Max Weber, *Gesammelte Aufsätze zur Religionssoziologie*, II, 69 ff.

3. Cp. A. Helps, *The Spanish Conquest in America*. 4 vols. London, 1855–1861. The *encomienda* presupposes the system of *repartimientos*, or distribution of the Indians among the lords on a basis of number of individuals.

4. Cp. Max Weber, *Wirtschaft und Gesellschaft* (*Grundriss der Sozialökonomik* III Abt.), Tuebingen, 1922, 724 ff.

5. Cp. the summarizing sketches of P. Vinogradoff, "Origins of Feudalism," in the *Cambridge Mediæval History*, II, 631 ff., and "Feudalism," Ibid., III, 458 ff.

CHAPTER IV

1. Cp. A. Dopsch, *Die Wirtschaftsentwicklung der Karolingerzeit*, 2d ed., 2 vols., Weimar, 1921–22; also P. Vinogradoff, reference in Note 5 of Chap. III; H. Sée, *Les classes rurales et le régime domaniale en France*, Paris, 1901; F. Seebohm, *The English Village Community*, 4th ed., London, 1890; P. Vinogradoff, *Villainage in England*, Oxford, 1892, and *The Growth of the Manor*, 2d ed., London, 1911; F. W. Maitland, *Domesday Book and Beyond*, Cambridge, 1897; F. Pollock and F. W. Maitland, *The History of English Law before the Time of Edward I*, 2d ed., 2 vols., Cambridge, 1898; R. Kötschke, *Wirtschaftsgeschichte*, 80 ff.

2. Against the attempt of Dopsch to interpret the Capitulare de Villis as a special dispensation for Aquitania, see G. Baist, *Vierteljahrschrift f. Sozial- und Wirtschaftsgeschichte* VII (1914), 22 ff. and J. Jud and L. Spitzer, *Wörter und Sachen*, VI (1914/15), 116 ff.

CHAPTER V

1. General References.—E. Bonnemère, *Histoire des paysans depuis la fin du moyen âge jusqu'à nos jours*, 4th ed., 3 vols., Paris 1886; G. Vicomte d'Avenel, *Histoire économique de la propriété, des salaires, des denrées et de tous les prix en générale 1200–1800*, 6 vols., Paris, 1886–1920; References below, on Chapter VI.

CHAPTER VI

1. Cp. M. Weber, *Die römische Agrargeschichte in ihrer Bedeutung für das Staats- und Privatrecht*, Stuttgart, 1891; articles, "Agrargeschichte" (by M. Weber) and "Kolonat" (by M. Rostowzew) in the *Handwörterbuch*, 3d ed. (with extensive references).

2. Cp. J. E. Cairnes, *The Slave Power, its character, career and probable designs*, New York, 1862; H. J. Nieboer, *Slavery as an industrial system*, The Hague, 1900; B. DuBois, *The suppression of the African slave trade*, New York, 1904; G. Knapp, *Die Landarbeiter in Knechtschaft und Freiheit*, 2d ed., Leipsic, 1909, 1 ff.

3. See references in Note 5 of Chap. III and Note 1 of Chap IV; also the histories by Ashley, Rogers, and Cunningham.

GENERAL ECONOMIC HISTORY

4. Cp. E. v. Stern, *Die russische Agrarfrage und die russische Revolution*, Halle, 1918.

5. Cp. G. von Below, *Territorium und Stadt*, Munich and Leipsic, 1900, 1–94; Th. Knapp, *Gesammelte Beiträge zur Rechts- und Wirtschaftsgeschichte*, etc., Tuebingen, 1902; W. Wittich, in *Grundriss der Sozialökonomik*, VII (1914) 1 ff., and in the *Handwörterbuch*, V–3 (1911) 208 ff. (Article, "Gutsherrschaft").

6. Cp. L. Brentano, *Erbrechtspolitik. Alte und neue Feodalität*, Stuttgart, 1899.

7. Cp. M. Weber, *Die Verhältnisse der Landarbeiter im ostelbischen Deutschland*, Leipsic, 1892.

8. Cp. articles, "Bauernbefreiung" (by G. Knapp et al.) in the *Handwörterbuch* II–3, 541 ff, and (by J. C. Fuchs) in the *Wörterbuch der Volkswirtschaft*, I–2, 365 ff.

9. Cp. survey in M. Weber, *Gesammelte Aufsätze zur Religionssoziologie*, I, 350 ff.

10. For references see M. Weber's article in the *Handwörterbuch*, 3d ed., I, 182 ff.

11. See references in Note 5 of Chap. II and Note 1 of Chap. IV.

12. Cp. M. Kowalewsky, *La France économique et sociale à la veille de la révolution*, vol. I, Paris, 1909; E. Bonnemère, *Histoire des paysans depuis la fin du moyen âge jusqu'à nos jours*, 4th ed., Paris, 1886; H. Sée, *Les classes rurales et le régime domaniale en France*, Paris, 1901.

13. Cp. K. Grünberg, *Die Bauernbefreiung und die Auflösung des gutsherrlich-bäuerlichen Verhältnisses in Böhmen, Mähren und Schlesien*, 2 Pts., Leipsic, 1894; Ibid., *Studien zur österr. Agrargeschichte*, Leipsic, 1901; Emil Kun, *Sozialhistorische Berträge zur Landarbeiterfrage in Ungarn*, Jena, 1903.

14. Cp. G. F. Knapp, *Die Bauernbefreiung und der Ursprung der Landarbeiter in den älteren Teilen Preussens*, 2 Pts., Leipsic, 1897; and Ibid., *Die Landarbeiter in Knechtschaft und Freiheit*, 2d ed., Leipsic, 1909.

15. Cp. W. G. Simkhovitsch, "Bauernbefreiung (Russland)," in the *Handwörterbuch der Staatswissenschaften*, 3d ed., II, 604 ff., and references there cited.

16. Cp. Count Rostworowski, *Die Entwicklung der bäuerlichen Verhältnisse im Königreich Polen*, Jena, 1896; K. v. Gaszczynski, *Die Entwickelung der bäuerlichen Selbständigkeit im Königreich Polen*, Munich, 1905.

PART TWO

CHAPTER VII

1. By way of introduction to industrial history, see the works of W. J. Ashley, H. Boos, H. deB. Gibbins, G. Schmoller (Volkswirtschaftslehre, Vol. I), Karl Bücher, N. S. B. Gras, A. P. Usher.

CHAPTER VIII

1. Cp. B. H. Baden-Powell, *The Land Systems of British India*, 3 vols., Oxford, 1892, and *The Indian Empire*, 4 vols., Oxford, 1908–09; also Max Weber, *Ges. Aufsätze zur Religionssoziologie*, II, 1 ff., 91 ff., and passim.

2. Max Weber, *Ges. Aufsätze zur Religionssoziologie*, II, 121.

3. Max Weber, *Die römische Agrargeschichte in ihrer Bedeutung für das Staats- und Privatrecht*, Stuttgart, 1891.

CHAPTER IX

1. On guild history see M. Chwostoff, *Sketches on the Organization of Industry and Trade in Greek and Roman Egypt*, Kazan, 1914; I. P. Waltzing, *Études historiques sur les corporations professionelles chez les Romains*, Brussels, 1895–1900; G. von Schönberg, "Zur wirtschaftlichen Bedeutung des deutschen Zunftgewerbes im Mittelalter," in *Jahrbücher für Nationalökonomie und Statistik*, IX (1868); K. Th. von Inama-Sternegg, *Deutsche Wirtschaftsgeschichte*, 3. Teil, Leipsic, 1901; also works on English industrial history.

CHAPTER X

1. Schmoller was one of the leading advocates of this theory; see his *Die Strassburger Tücher- und Weberzunft*, Strassburg, 1879–81.

CHAPTER XI

1. General References.—Schmoller, reference in Note on Chap. X; A. Abram, *Social England in the 15th Century*, London, 1909, 1–21, 117–130; G. Unwin, *Industrial Organization in the 16th and 17th Centuries*, London, 1904; É. Martin-Saint-Léon, *Histoire des corporations de métiers*, 2d ed., Paris, 1909; H. Hauser, *Ouvriers du temps passé*, 2d ed., Paris, 1906.

CHAPTER XII

1. General References.—E. Levasseur, *Histoire des classes ouvrières en France*, 2d ed., 2 vols., Paris, 1900–1901 (Summary in English, Agnes Bergeland, *History of the Working Class in France*, Chicago, 1918.); R. W. C. Taylor, *Introduction to a History of the Factory System*, London, 1886; J. E. Thorold Rogers, *Six Centuries of Work and Wages*, 2d ed., London, 1912; W. Sombart, *Der moderne Kapitalismus*, 4th ed., 2. Bd., 2 Hlbbd., Munich and Leipsic, 1921.

CHAPTER XIII

1. General References.—I. B. Mispoulet, *Le régime des mines à l'époque romaine et au moyen-âge*, Paris, 1908; O. Hué, *Die Bergarbeiter*, Stuttgart, 1910.

PART THREE

CHAPTER XIV

1. General References.—Ch. Letourneau, *L'évolution du commerce dans les diverses races humaines*, Paris, 1897; E. Levasseur, *Histoire du commerce de la France*, 2 parts, Paris, 1911–12; H. Pirenne, "Villes, marchés et marchands au moyen-âge," in *Revue historique* LXVII (1898); *History of Domestic and Foreign Commerce of the United States*, 2 vols., Washington, 1915 (with an exhaustive bibliography of American economic history).

CHAPTER XV

1. General References.—Articles "Verkehrsmittle und -wege," and "Verkehrswesen im deutschen Mittelalter," in *Handwörterbuch der Staatswissenschaften;* O. T. Mason, *Primitive Travel and Transportation*, New York, 1897; W. L. Lindsay, *History of Merchant Shipping and of Ancient Commerce*, 4 vols., London, 1874–1876.

2. M. Weber, *Ges. Aufsätze zur Religionssoziologie*, III, 351 ff., 403.

CHAPTER XVI

1. See the papers of G. von Below: "Grosshändler und Kleinhändler im deutschen Mittelalter"; Über Theorien der wirtschaftlichen Entwieklung der Völker"; and, "Der Untergang der mittel-

NOTES 377

alterlichen Stadtwirtschaft,"—all in the volume, *Probleme der Wirtschaftsgeschichte*, Tuebingen, 1917.

2. Concerning the organization of commerce in medieval England, see E. Lipson, *An Introduction to the Economic History of England*, vol. I, London, 1915; also, N. S. B. Gras, *Evolution of the English Corn Market from the 12th to the 18th Century*, Cambridge, (Mass.), 1915; and references in these works.

CHAPTER XVII

1. Max Weber, *Zur Geschichte der Handelsgesellschaften im Mittelalter*, Stuttgart, 1889.

CHAPTER XVIII

1. General References.—Chas. Gross, *The Gild Merchant*, 2 vols., Oxford, 1890; Lipson, see Note 2 of Chap. XVI; H. B. Morse, *The Guilds of China*, London, 1909.—On India, see M. Weber, *Gesammelte Aufsätze zur Religionssoziologie*, II, 84 ff., and the works of W. Hopkins there referred to.—W. E. Lingelbach, *The Merchant Adventurers of England*, Philadelphia, 1902.

2. Through this requirement the Hanse aroused the persistent antagonism of Danzig, which did not wish to have its shipbuilding industry placed at a disadvantage.

CHAPTER XIX

1. General References.—W. Ridgeway, *The Origin of Metallic Currency and Weight Standards*, Cambridge, (Eng.), 1892; W. A. Shaw, *The History of Currency, 1252–1894*, London, 1895; Articles by W. Lexis, in the *Handwörterbuch*, on "Gold," "Währungsfrage," "Silberwährung," etc.; (Cp. Report of Director of the U. S. Mint, 1896, pp. 266–80 and ff.—Tr.) J. L. Laughlin, *Principles of Money*, New York and London, 1903; W. W. Carlile, *Evolution of Modern Money*, London, 1901.

2. See the estimates, which are in fair agreement, by Soetbeer (in Petermann's *Geographischen Mitteilungen*, Ergänzungsband, 1879, p. 54) and W. Lexis (in *Jahrbücher für Nationalökonomie und Statistik* XXXIV (1880), pp. 361 ff.). The estimates of F. De Laiglesias, however (in *Los caudales de India en la primera metad del siglo XVII*, Madrid, 1904), lead to a result almost fifty-fold different, in the downward direction.

CHAPTER XX

1. General References.—*History of the Banking of All Nations*, London, 1896; R. Ehrenberg, *Das Zeitalter der Fugger*, 2 vols., Jena, 1896; A. Andreades, *History of the Bank of England* (Trans. H. S. Foxwell, London, 1909); References in the *Handwörterbuch der Staatswissenschaften*, 3d ed., II, 359 f., 368 f.

CHAPTER XXI

1. Moreover, this view is not unknown to the unworldly love doctrine of the earliest Christians. The later prohibition of interest by the Church rested on Luke 6, 35; but according to A. Merx there was a misreading of the text. (*Die vier kanonischen Evangelien nach ihrem ältesten bekannten Texte*, II 2, I, 223 ff.) This misreading, he says, passed into the Vulgate on the authority of Clement of Alexandria, and became the basis of the Church's later position.

PART FOUR

1. General References on Part Four.—J. A. Hobson, *Evolution of Modern Capitalism*, 2d ed., London, 1906; L. Brentano, *Die Anfänge des modernen Kapitalismus*, 4th ed., 2 vols., Munich and Leipsic, 1922; G. Schmoller, "Die geschichtliche Entwicklung der Unternehmung," *Jahrbuch für Gesetzgebung, Verwaltung und Volkswirtschaft*, XIV–XVII (1890–1893); A. Toynbee, *Lectures on the Industrial Revolution of the 18th Century in England*, London, 1884; W. Sombart, *Die deutsche Volkswirtschaft im 19. Jahrhundert*, 3d ed., Berlin, 1913.

CHAPTER XXIII

1. General References.—W. Sombart, *Der Moderne Kapitalismus*, Munich and Leipsic, 1916; J. Strieder, *Studien zur kapitalistischen Organisationsform, Kartelle, Monopole und Aktiengesellschaften im Mittelalter und zu Beginn der Neuzeit*, Munich and Leipsic, 1914; Julius Klein, *The Mesta. A Study in Spanish Economic History, 1273–1836*, Cambridge (Mass.), 1920; J. and S. Davis, *Essays in the earlier history of American corporations*, 2 vols., Cambridge (Mass.), 1917; G. Cawston and A. H. Keane, *Early Chartered Companies*, London, 1896; R. Muir, *The Making of British India, 1756*

to 1858, Manchester, 1915; P. Bonnassieux, *Les grandes compagnies de commerce*, Paris, 1892.

2. Cp. H. Levy, *Economic Liberalism* (Eng. Trans., London, 1913.)

CHAPTER XXIV

1. General References.—W. R. Scott, *The Constitution and Finance of English, Scottish and Irish Joint Stock Companies to 1720*, 3 vols., Cambridge (Eng.) 1910–1912; A. Aftalion, *Les crises périodiques de surproduction et leur retour périodique en France, en Angleterre et aux États-Unis*, Paris, 1913; M. Bouniatian, *Geschichte der Handelskrisen in England*, Munich, 1908; N. A. Brisco, *The Economic Policy of Robert Walpole*, New York, 1907.

CHAPTER XXV

1. General References.—Sombart, *Der moderne Kapitalismus*, II, 429 ff.; Articles "Börsenwesen" (by R. Ehrenberg) and "Märkte und Messen" (by K. Rathgen) in the *Handwörterbuch*, 3d ed., vols. III and IV; Article "Post," (by P. D. Fischer and M. Aschenborn), Ibid., VI–3; J. C. Hemmeon, *History of the British Post Office*, Cambridge (Mass.), 1912; Article "Zeitungen," by L. Salomon, *Handwörterbuch*, 3d ed., vol. VIII.

CHAPTER XXVI

1. General References.—H. Merivale, *Lectures on Colonisation and Colonies*, 2d ed., London, 1861; H. E. Morris, *History of Colonisation from Earliest Times to the Present Day*, 2 vols., London, 1904; G. L. Beer, *The Old Colonial System*, 1600–1754, 2 vols., New York, 1912; A. Sartorius von Waltershausen, *Die Arbeitsverfassung der englischen Kolonien in Nordamerika*, Strassburg, 1894; St. B. Weeks, *The Southern Quakers and Slavery*, Baltimore, 1898.

2. A parallel is found in the fact that the negroes long ago showed themselves unsuitable for factory work and the operation of machines; they have not seldom sunk into a cataleptic sleep. Here is one case in economic history where tangible racial distinctions are present.

3. The principal supporters of the slave trade were originally the Arabs, who have maintained their position to the present in Africa. In the middle ages the Jews and the Genoese divided the business; they were followed by the Portuguese, the French, and finally the English.

CHAPTER XXVII

1. General References.—A. Riedler, *Über die geschichtliche und Zukünftige Bedeutung der Technik*, Berlin, 1900; L. Beck, *Geschichte des Eisens*, 5 vols., Brunswick, 1884–1903; Chas. Babbage, *On the Economy of Machinery and Manufactures*, London, 1832; G. von Schulze-Gaevernitz, *Der Grossbetrieb, ein Wirtschaftlicher und sozialer Fortschritt*, Leipsic, 1892; Survey in Sombart, *Der moderne Kapitalismus*, I, 481 ff. and II, 609 ff.; L. Darmstaedter, *Handbuch zur Geschichte der Naturwissenschaften und Technik*, Berlin, 1908.

2. On the other hand the exploitative mining out of the underground wealth must have a limit in time; the age of iron cannot last over a thousand years at most.

CHAPTER XXVIII

1. General References.—M. Weber, *Wirtschaft und Gesellschaft*, Tuebingen, 1922, pp. 513 ff.; N. D. Fustel de Coulanges, *La cité antique*, Paris, 1864.

2. Otherwise Peking would have to be regarded as a "city" from the beginning, and at a time when nothing of the nature of a city existed in Europe. Officially, however, it is called "the five places," and is administratively handled in parts as five large villages; hence there are no "citizens" of Peking.

3. In contrast, the officials and princes in Japan resided in castles down to the modernization; places were distinguished according to size.

4. The Indian armies, even in the oldest Greek reports from the time of Alexander the Great, had tactical divisions and organization, but also exemplified the combat between heroes. In the armies of the Grand Mogul, the knights who equipped themselves retained their place alongside the warriors enlisted and equipped by the war-lord, and enjoyed a higher social esteem.

5. The parallelism with the German revolution of 1918 stands out; the soldiers' councils demanded power to nullify judicial decisions.

CHAPTER XXIX

1. Cp. M. Weber, *Gesammelte Aufsätze zur Religionssoziologie*, Tuebingen, 1920, I, 276 ff., and works there referred to.

2. On Mercantilism, see Article, "Merkantilsystem" in the *Handwörterbuch*, 3d ed., VI, 650 ff., and the illuminating article, "Bal-

ance of Trade" etc. in Palgrave, *Dictionary of Political Economy*, 3 vols., London, 1895; also, Adam Smith, *Wealth of Nations*, Book IV; G. Schmoller, *The Mercantile System* (Eng. Trans. in Ashley's Economic Classics); W. Sombart, *Der Bourgeois*, Munich and Leipsic, 1913; P. Clément, *Histoire du système protecteur en France*, Paris, 1854; A. P. Usher, *History of the Grain Trade in France*, 1400–1710, Cambridge (Mass.), 1913.

CHAPTER XXX

1. Cp. M. Weber, *Gesammelte Aufsätze zur Religionssoziologie*, I, 30 ff.

2. Ibid., I, 544.

3. W. Sombart, *The Jews and Modern Capitalism* (Trans. by M. Epstein) London, 1913.

4. As soon as the Mandarins realized the chances for gain open to them, these difficulties suddenly ceased to be insuperable; today they are the leading stockholders in the railways. In the long run, no religious-ethical conviction is capable of barring the way to the entry of capitalism, when it stands in full armor before the gate; but the fact that it is able to leap over magical barriers does not prove that genuine capitalism could have originated in circumstances where magic played such a role.

5. M. Weber, *Gesammelte Aufsätze zur Religionssoziologie*, I, 63 ff., 163 ff., 207 ff.

6. In a general way, though with necessary reservations, the contrast may be formulated by saying that Jewish capitalism was speculative pariah-capitalism, while Puritan capitalism consisted in the organization of citizen labor. Cp. M. Weber, *Gesammelte Aufsätze zur Religionssoziologie*, I, 181 ff., Note 2.

7. Cp. also E. Troeltsch, *Die Soziallehren der Christlichen Kirchen und Gruppen*, 2 vols., Tuebingen, 1913 (reprinted 1919). Among the opponents of the above conceptions of Max Weber regarding the significance of Calvinism should be mentioned L. Brentano (*Die Anfänge des modernen Kapitalismus*, Munich, 1916, 117 ff.) and G. Brodnitz (*Englische Wirtschaftsgeschichte*, I, 282 ff.). (Another exposition in English of Weber's theories in this field may be found in two articles by P. T. Forsyth, Calvinism and Capitalism," *Contemporary Review*, 1910. Cp. also R. H. Tawney, *Religion and the Rise of Capitalism*, London and New York, 1926.—Tr.

INDEX OF NAMES

SUBJECT INDEX

Accounting (Bookkeeping) 224 f.;
prerequisite of capitalism, 275.
Actor, trader of antiquity, 197.
Administration (see State, Law),
338 ff.
Agrarian organization, primitive,
3 ff. See Contents, Part I, also
under various countries. Agr.
Communism, theory, 3 ff., 24,
secondary, in orient, 60.
Almende, Chapter I. See Common pasture.
Alpine hubandry, 11.
Ancestor worship (China), 48.
ανδρειον, 40.
Animals, use of, 24, 38. See Horse.
Antiquity (Europe) Coastal
character of civilization, 55 f.,
81, 97 f., 146, 354; feudal relations disappear near large
cities, 96 f.; easy collapse of
money economy, 60, 131; oikos
or estate craft work, 126-30;
living standards, 130 f.; guilds,
136 f.; slavery obstacle to factory industry, 176 f.; shipping
organization, 203-5; money,
244 ff.; banking, 254 f., 256;
growth of cities comp. w. middle ages, 323 f.; war the normal condition, 331. See Greece,
Rome.
Anti-semitism, 217.
Apparatus, and machine, 302.
Apprenticeship, regulation by
guilds, 143; apprentices organize, 143; Statute of Apprentices, 306.
Appropriation, forms, 26 ff. See
Property.
Arabic notation, 223 f.
Argentarii (Roman bankers),
256.

Art, a city product, 316.
Arti maggiori and *minori*, 327.
Asceticism and economic life,
364 ff.
Association, forms of in develop-
ment of capitalism, 280 ff.
Assyria, irrigation culture, 57.
Astronomy and navigation in
late middle ages, 201.
Austria, dissolution of feudalism
with protection of peasantry,
100-03; early factories, relation
to guilds and state, 172.
Avunculate, 29, 40.

Babylon, Babylonia, sacerdotal
prostitution, 32; irrigation culture, 57; monetary history,
244; banking, 257; traces of
citizenship idea, 315.
Balance, in capitalistic accounting, 275, 282.
Banalité (*Bannrecht*, socage
right), 68, 72; shipping, 211;
Banat, see South Slavs.
Banjari, Indian trading caste,
231 f.
Bank of England, 261, 264 ff.,
287, 289 ff., 350 f.
Bank money, 250 f.
Banking, in the pre-capitalistic
age, 254-66 (Chap. XX). Original functions, exchange and
safe deposit, 254 f.; banker as
lender peculiar to Babylon,
255; in Rome, account-current
business, 256; temple and state
banks typical of antiquity,
256 ff.; medieval banking, 258
ff.; state finance operations,
259 ff.; liquidity, 260 f.; bill of
exchange, evolution of, 261 ff.;

385

tile industry, 155 ff.; growth alongside guild industry, 158 f.; stages, 159 f.; basis of permanence the unimportance of fixed capital, 160; later stages confined to west, 160; limited development with free workers outside Europe, 160 f.; not displaced by early factories, 173.

Dschaina, Indian trading sect, 196, 232.

Duc-duc, 40.

Dues and fees, feudal, 73.

Dutch East India Company, agrarian system, 21 f.; organization, 281 f.

Egypt, disintegration of clan by political forces, 46; chieftain trade, 55; irrigation culture, 56 f.; officialdom of state, 57; ἴδια, 57; grain banks, 58; craft work for the state, 125; early shipping, 202; monetary history, 244; banking, 254, 257; law prohibiting interest, 267 f.

ἐκδότης, 135.

ἔμποροι, 203.

Enclosure of land, in Germany, 14; in England, see Estate Economy.

Encomienda, 61.

Endogamy, 29, 35; a phenomenon of retrogression, 36.

England, Germanic land settlement form, 10; condition of peasantry prior to capitalism, 77 f.; effect of strong state of Normans on feudalism, 78; pastoral and cereal estates, 85 f.; no formal abolition of feudalism, 98; guild masters separate from craft work, 152, 153; guild development, contrast w. Germany, 153 f., 156-8; significance of representation of towns in Parliament, 157; guilds and early factories, 172; struggle over mining rights, 182 f.; mercantile guilds (Guild Merchant), 232 f.;

separation of wholesale and retail trade, 233; monetary history, 249, 251 f.; banking history, 263-5 (see Bank of England); policy towar's slavery, 300 f.; type of N. European city, 333 f.; mercantilism in, 348 f.; Church of E., economic policy, 349.

Enterprise, and capitalism, 275; forms of commercial, 223 ff. (Chap. XVIII). See Commerce.

Erbex (free-holding farmer) in Westphalia, 11; in India, 23.

Ergasterion, 119 f.; (*fabrica*), 162.

Estate economy, 84-92; definition, forms, 84; for stock raising, 84 f.; in England, 85 f.; in Russia, 86 f.; in Germany, 87-92; Poland and White Russia, 92. See Oikos-Economy.

Estates General (France), 75.

Ethics, internal and external, 312; rational E. peculiar to west, 312 f.; attitude of classical E. antagonistic to capitalism, 357, based on impersonality of relations, 357 f.; Roman E. characterized by *caveat emptor*, 357; internal vs. external E., 356; breakdown of dualism, 313, 356 ff.; dualism maintained by Jews, 359 f.

Exchange, the, as an institution, 293 f.; exch. quotations requisite for consignment trading, 293.

Exchequer, English, 283.

Exogamy, basis of, 36.

Faber (*fabri*), 147, 328.

Fabrica (*ergasterion*), workshop, universally found, 162.

Factor (*Verieger*) and factor system. See Domestic System, Putting-Out System. F. under slavery, 126; rise of, 153 ff.

Factory, meaning, prerequisites and development, 162-77 (Chap. XII). See also technology

the fall of the Roman Empire, rationalization of procedure, 340 ff.; formalistic vs. material law, 342; development of law and administration, 343.

Leiturgical vs. taxation principle of state organization, China, 95, Rome, 95, 130 f.; L. guilds (Rome), 136 f., 203 f., 336.

Letters, postal service, 295 f.

Levirate, 29, 42.

Lex Rhodia de iactu, 204.

Lex Salica, 147.

Licentia fodiendi, 182.

Litera aperta, and *litera clausa*, 262.

Livery companies, 153.

Living standards, ancient vs. modern, 130 f.

Lombards, in medieval finance and banking, 217, 258.

Lords, See Seigniorial proprietorship, Manor, etc. Powers in medieval towns, 147-8.

Luxury demand, relation to early capitalism, 170 f., 309 ff.

Machines, not the cause of early factories, 174; character and role, 302 ff. See Factory, Inventions, Technology.

Magic, as basis of totemic clan, 27; copulation a form of, 31; as source of seigniorial property, 54; in relation to early skilled work, 117; traditionalism, obstacle to growth of domestic system in India, China, 161; in relation to growth of cities in east vs. west, 322 ff.; intensifies primitive traditionalism, 355; role of rational prophecy in destroying, preparation of capitalism, significance of Judaism and Christianity, 360 ff.

Manor, the, 65 ff. (Chap. IV); three elements in the lord's power, 65; "immunity," 65;

free and unfree persons, effacement of differences, 66; status and tenure, 66 f.; effects of consolidation of holdings, 68; policy of princes, 70, its economic effects, 70 ff.; dominance of rent method of exploitation in the west, 72 f.; capitalistic development, 79 ff. (Chap. VI); two forms of development, 79; plantation, 79-84 (see Plantation); estate, 84-92 (see Estate); dissolution of manorial system, 92-111; possible processes of liberation, 92 f.; motives operating, internal, 93, external, town interests, 93 f.; course of events, China, 95 f., India, 96, Near East, 96, Japan, 96, Mediterranean region, Greece, 95 f., Rome, 97 f., England, 98, France, 98 f., Germany, west, 98 f., east, 99 ff., Austria, 101-3, Prussia, 103-6, Russia, 106 f., Poland, 107; influence of inheritance laws, 108; modern land tenure, in Moslem world, 108 f., in England, 109; results, landed aristocracy, England, E. Germany, 110 f.

Manorial law, manorial court, 68; M. L. theory of guild origin, 144 f., criticized, 145 ff.

Mansi ingenuiles, 67, *mansi serviles*, 67.

Mark, common, 8; mark association, 8, 27; appropriation of mark by lords, 71.

Market, concessions, 55, 132, 214; production for, 122 ff., development of, 126-34; extension of in antiquity vs. middle ages, 131; regular mass demand prerequisite to factory, 163 f., 169 ff., 307 ff.; freedom of, aspect of capitalism, 276; character of precapitalistic limitations, 276 f.; war demand, 307 f.; luxury demand,

308 f.; these two demands outside Europe, 308 ff.

Marriage, socialistic theory of
evolution of M. and family,
28 ff.; group M. 29; by capture, 30, 36, 39; contractual,
30; M. and property, 30; temporary, 33; legitimate, 36 ff.,
39; polyandry and polygamy,
42; M. by exchange of sisters,
42; with dowry and without,
50. See also Clan, Endogamy,
Exogamy, Family.

Masterpiece, guild, 142.

Matriarchate, 30, 37, 39.

Meat, use of, 38.

Medicine man, first profession,
117. See Magic.

Mediterranean Sea, in economic
development, 354.

Men's house, 39 ff.

Mercator (equivalent to citizen),
147; as resident merchant, 215.

Mercantilism, 347-51; first rational economic policy of the
state, 343; nature of policy,
347 f.; M. in England, 348 f.;
two aspects, class monopoly,
349 f., nationalistic, 350 f.; disappearance in England, 351.

Merces, 135.

Merchant, dominance of production by, 154, 156; in export
trade, 155. See Commerce,
Guilds, mercantile.

Merchant Adventurers, the, 216,
233.

Metals, as money, 241 ff.; precious, not primary cause of
capitalism, 352 f. See Mining,
Money.

Middle Ages, oikos craft work,
125; obstacles to development
of factory industry, 177; mining, 181 ff.; shipping, 204 ff.;
roads, 209; monetary problems
and policies, 246 ff.; banking,
258 ff.; interest on money and
ideas regarding, 269-71; compared with antiquity as to

growth of cities, 323 ff. See
topics and countries.

Miles, in Champagne fairs, 221.

Military demand, and capitalism, 354. See Factory.

Military organization, relation
to growth of cities, east vs.
west, 320 f., 324 f., 328 f., 331 f.
See also Interest, Agrarian organization, Peasant protection,
Seigniorial proprietorship.

Milking, 24 (Chap. I, note 6),
38.

Mills, mill-compulsīon, 165 f.

Mining, source of impulse to
mechanization, 177, 312. History of prior to capitalism,
162-191 (Chap. XIII); methods, primitive and early, 178;
legal relations, 178 f.; *pars
fundi* vs. regale, 179; Greco-
Roman conditions, 179 f.; middle ages, 180 ff.; struggle of
crown and lords, Germany,
Hungary, France, England,
181 ff.; organization, epochs,
183 ff.; differentiation in personnel, 187 ff.; role of capital,
187 ff.; analogy to guild history, 189 f.; smelteries and
ore dealers, 190; coal in the
middle ages, 190 f.; union of
coal and iron, 191.

Mir (Russia), 17 ff.; origin, 19;
destruction, 18.

μισθός, 135.

Mississippi Company, 287 ff.

Mohammedanism, and prostitution, 30; and sexual freedom,
33.

Money, and Chinese guilds, 231;
nature and history, 236-53
(Chap. XIX); father of private property, 236; origin,
236; functions and order of
their appearance, 236 ff.; early
forms, 238 f.; relation and
value of forms, 239 ff.; metals
and coinage, 241 f.; technique
of coinage 242 f.; standards,

Peons (*nexi*), 54.
Persia, persistence of feudalism, 96.
Persian Empire, money in, 237, 242.
Phenicians, primitive shipping, 202; commerce non-monetary, 242.
Piracy, 199, 208.
Plantation economy, 79-84; definition, 79; semi-plantation, 79, in S. Am. and New Eng., 79 f.; two classical developments of P. E., Carthage-Rome and U. S. A., 80; problem of slave labor, 80, of slave supply, 81 f., of land supply, 82 f.; abolition of slavery, 83 f.
Plow, primitive, in general vs. in Germany, 5 f.
Plow association (Scotland), 15 f.
Poland, estate economy, 92; dissolution of feudalism, 107 f.
Polyandry, and polygamy, 42.
Popolo grasso, 327.
Population growth in west and in China, not the cause of capitalism, 352.
Poor law, English, 306. Poor as source of labor for factory industry, 167, England, 306, Germany, 164.
Postal service, 295 f.
Power, relation to early factories, 169. See Technology.
Precaria, 67.
Price revolution of 16th and 17th centuries, 311. See also Money.
Price work, 118, 134 f.
Proletarius, proletariate, 328.
Promiscuity, in socialistic theory of marriage history, 29 f.
Property systems and social groups, 26-50 (Chap. II); forms of appropriation, 26 ff.; forms of groupings, 26 f.; house community and clan, socialistic theory of marriage and property, 28-37; evolution of the family, survey of primitive economic life and institutions, forms of family and of property, 37-43; the clan and its property relationships, 43-46; the house-community and its property relationships, 46-50; property in land, established by dissolution of feudalism, 111; in position of guild master, 143; money the father of P., 263; P. in means of production, aspect of capitalism, 276. See Communism, Investment.
Prophecy, and disruption of the clan, 45; relation to capitalism, 362 ff.
Prostitution, 30 ff.; sacerdotal, 31 ff.; status of contractual, 31; struggle of religious against, 32 f.; P. in middle ages, 33.
Protestantism, and interest taking, 271; relation to growth of capitalism, 365 ff.
Proxenia, in medieval trade, 213.
Prussia, dissolution of feudalism with compromise of peasant interests, 103-6.
Puritans, and corn-law repeal, 86; attitude toward labor and economic policy, 349, 351. See also Bank of England, Protestantism.
Putting out system (domestic system), 118, 153 ff.

Quadrant, nautical, 201.
Quakers, and slavery, 83, 300.

Railways, 295 ff.
Rationality and capitalism, 275; R. organization of labor peculiar to capitalism, 312; rational state, 338 ff. (see Law, State); rational ethic, 312 f.; commerce first field of R., 223; R. in technology and science, 313 ff.; in ethics and conduct of life, 354 ff.; process of development, 356 ff. See Capitalism.

Shipping (see Commerce) Relation to war and piracy, 202; inland S. in middle ages, 211 f.; growth of to 18th century, 308.

Shop industry, in antiquity, 127 ff., in medieval monasteries, 127. Shop production, 162 ff. (Chap. XII). Forms, 162; shop and factory, 162 f.; in China, 176. See Factory, forerunners.

Silver, see Coinage, Mining, Money.

Simsarius, sensarius, sensal, 215.

Slavery, in middle ages, 66 ff., 69; in plantation economy, 80 ff., Rome, 81, southern states of U. S. A., 82, 83 f.; problem of supply, 81, 82; of management, 83; in ergasterion, 120; slaves as craft workers in antiquity, 125-30; problems of the system, 128 ff.; slaves exploited by rent charges, 129 ff.; reasons for progress of liberation in medieval manors and towns, 130-34; slavery an obstacle to development of factory in antiquity, 176 f.; mine slaves in antiquity, 180; slavery in colonies, 299 ff., abolition of slavery, role of Christian sects and of various nations, 300 f. See Christianity, Quakers.

Smelteries, in middle ages, 190.

Socage district (*Bannbezirk*), 68. S. rights (*banalités, Bann rechte*), 72.

Social groupings in relation to economic technique, 38 (and Chap. II *passim*).

Socialism, theory of marriage and family evolution, 28 ff., criticism, 34 ff.; S. and crises, 290 f.

Societas maris, 205.

Sonderbund, 233.

South America, stock-raising estates on pampas of, 84.

South Sea Company, 288 ff.

South Slavs, economic system of, 11 ff. See Zadruga.

Spain, decay of early factories, 175.

Sparta, communal exploitation of subject population, 52.

Spear land, 26, 42.

Specialization, between ethnic groups, 123; geographical, 123, 124; in village and manor, 124 f. See Stages in development of industry.

Speculation, and capitalism, 278; development of, 294 f.; S. and early crises, 294; speculative trade and news service, 294 f. See Crises.

Stages, in economic evolution, 37 f.; in development of industry, 122 ff. (Chap. VIII); primitive tribal and house industry, 122 f.; caste, 123 f.; local specialization, 123, 124; specialization on the manor, 124, on an estate (antiquity), 124 f., in a political unit (Egypt), 125 f.; production for a market, with unfree labor, 126 ff.; by slaves subject to rent charges, 129 f.; development of free craft work in medieval Europe, 130-4.

Staple compulsion, 219.

State, the, absorbs the city in modern west, 336 f.; alliance with capital, 337. The rational state, meaning and development, 338-51 (Chap. XXIX); peculiar to the west, 338; contrast with China, 338 f.; rational law and Roman law, 339 ff.; economic policy of S., 343-47; a modern phenomenon, 343; why absent in the east, in antiquity and the middle ages, 344 f.; germs of protectionism, 346 f.; mercantilism (q.v.) 347-51.

Steam engine, 302, 305 ff.

Steel-yard, Hanseatic branch in London, 230.

ants, 199; Californian gold discoveries, 252; religious denominations and economic life, 366.

Vassal vs. freeman, 67.
Vengeance, duty of clan, 27.
Venice, trading nobility, 55; form of guild, 232; Rialto bank, 251; prototype of occidental city, 319 ff.
Victuarius, 208.
Village, primitive agricultural, sketch of Germanic, 4; description, 5 ff. See Agrarian organization, India, Russia.
Villains, See England, Peasants.
Villicus, villication system, 73, 75.

Wage work vs. price work, 118, 119, 134 f.
Wander years, in guild system, peculiar to Germany, 143.

Wandering trade, 122.
War, demand for military goods, relation to early capitalism, 170, 307 ff.
War loans, a modern phenomenon, 280.
Wardship, status of early medieval craftsmen, 147 f.; guild struggles against, 149.
Wedderleginge, 229.
Wesphalia, settlement form, 11.
White Russia, land system, 17; estate economy, 92.
Wild field grass husbandry, 16.
Woman, position of, in primitive society, 38 ff.; in antiquity, 116 f. See Sexes, Family, Marriage, Matriarchate.
Woolen industry in development of capitalism, 303.

Zadruga, of South Slavs, 12, 47.